CHINESE NETIZENS' OPINIONS
ON DEATH SENTENCES

CHINA UNDERSTANDINGS TODAY

Series Editors: Mary Gallagher and Xiaobing Tang

China Understandings Today is dedicated to the study of contemporary China and seeks to present the latest and most innovative scholarship in social sciences and the humanities to the academic community as well as the general public. The series is sponsored by the Lieberthal-Rogel Center for Chinese Studies at the University of Michigan.

Resisting Spirits: Drama Reform and Cultural Transformation in the People's Republic of China
    Maggie Greene

Going to the Countryside: The Rural in the Modern Chinese Cultural Imagination, 1915–1965
    Yu Zhang

Power over Property: The Political Economy of Communist Land Reform in China
    Matthew Noellert

The Global White Snake
    Liang Luo

Governing and Ruling: The Political Logic of Taxation in China
    Changdong Zhang

Chinese Netizens' Opinions on Death Sentences: An Empirical Examination
    Bin Liang and Jianhong Liu

CHINESE NETIZENS' OPINIONS ON DEATH SENTENCES

An Empirical Examination

Bin Liang and Jianhong Liu

UNIVERSITY OF MICHIGAN PRESS
Ann Arbor

Copyright © 2021 by Bin Liang and Jianhong Liu
All rights reserved

For questions or permissions, please contact um.press.perms@umich.edu

Published in the United States of America by the
University of Michigan Press
Manufactured in the United States of America
Printed on acid-free paper
First published November 2021

A CIP catalog record for this book is available from the British Library.

Library of Congress Cataloging-in-Publication Data

Names: Liang, Bin, 1972– author. | Liu, Jianhong, 1954– author.
Title: Chinese netizens' opinions on death sentences : an empirical
   examination / Bin Liang, Jianhong Liu.
Description: Ann Arbor : University of Michigan Press, 2021. |
   Series: China understandings today | Includes bibliographical
   references and index. |
Identifiers: LCCN 2021028042 (print) | LCCN 2021028043 (ebook) |
   ISBN 9780472132690 (hardcover) | ISBN 9780472038732
   (paperback) | ISBN 9780472129287 (ebook)
Subjects: LCSH: Capital punishment—China—Public opinion—21st
   century. | Criminal justice, Administration of—China—
   Case studies. | Online social networks—Political aspects—China.
Classification: LCC HV8699.C6 L53 2021 (print) | LCC HV8699.C6
   (ebook) | DDC 364.660951—dc23
LC record available at https://lccn.loc.gov/2021028042
LC ebook record available at https://lccn.loc.gov/2021028043

In memory of Dr. Roger Hood
A true pioneer in this field whose work and research tremendously impacted the studies of the death penalty worldwide (including in China)

Acknowledgments

As usual, we would like to express our gratitude to a number of people. First, during this project, we have received great assistance from three graduate students from University of Macao, including Qingge Liu, Shan Cui, and Honglan Shuai. Their diligent work with data collection and help with background research made this project possible in the first place.

Second, we would like to acknowledge feedback by anonymous external reviewers at different stages of this project (i.e., reviews of the book proposal and the final draft), whose comments, suggestions, and critiques helped us with our revisions and improved the quality of this manuscript.

Third, we would like to thank both Christopher Dreyer and Kevin Rennells from the University of Michigan Press for their timely support throughout this project, despite challenges during the pandemic.

Lastly, we are indebted to the love and support from our family members, including Ying, Gloria, Li, John, and Vivian. In their love and support, we find inspiration and motivation to continue our research in and beyond this project.

Contents

ONE. Study of Chinese Public Opinion on Capital Punishment
in a New Environment ... 1

TWO. Diversity of Netizens' Opinions: The Breadth and the Depth ... 26

THREE. Rationales of Netizens' Decisions:
Why Do They Support or Reject Death Sentences? ... 58

FOUR. Interactions: How Do Netizens Respond to Each Other? ... 91

FIVE. Variances of Netizens' Opinions: Crime Types,
Defendants and Victims, Legal Procedures,
and Media Reporting ... 116

SIX. Criminal Justice System and Its Professionals in the
Eyes of Netizens ... 140

SEVEN. Social, Systemic, and Structural Problems:
How Are Netizens' Opinions Embedded within
the Framework of Contemporary Chinese Society? ... 169

EIGHT. Netizens' Discussion of Death Sentences:
Rationality or Irrationality? ... 198

NINE. The Lin Senhao Case: A Live Debate of Life or Death ... 230

TEN. Public Opinion in a Unique Form ... 260

Appendix 1. Summaries of All Cases ... 281

*Appendix 2. Officially Charged Crimes and Number of
Offenders Being Charged* ... 299

*Appendix 3. Total Numbers of Netizens' Comments,
       Reply Comments, and Use of Foul Language*   301

Appendix 4. Basic Reporting Statistics by Cases   303

Appendix 5. Select List of Foul Words   307

References   309

Index   323

Digital materials related to this title can be found on the Fulcrum platform via the following citable URL: https://doi.org/10.3998/mpub.11481664

CHAPTER 1

Study of Chinese Public Opinion on Capital Punishment in a New Environment

> "In this case, who represents public opinion?
> Which side represents justice?"
> —"Life is not a child's play (生活岂可儿戏)"
> (Guangzhou, Guangdong)

On December 11, 2015, when the Lin Senhao case (#1, see chapter 9) finally came to a conclusion after his execution, a netizen (i.e., an internet user) with the user ID "Life is not a child's play" raised the questions above to reflect on the heated discussions that lasted almost a full year between netizens who supported Lin's death sentence and those who pleaded mercy on Lin's behalf. This is just one example of Chinese netizens' online comments on a high-profile case. As simple as they appear, both questions by this netizen go directly to the core issues of public opinion—namely, how to measure and evaluate public opinion, especially when someone's life is at stake.

Based on a qualitative study of Chinese netizens' comments on 63 capital cases in which death sentences were meted out in 2015, this study is an effort to examine Chinese public opinion on China's use of capital punishment. Chapter 1 provides the general background of this study. We first discuss why the often-claimed "overwhelming public support" by the Chinese government is problematic. Second, we review past studies of Chinese public opinion on China's use of the death penalty. Next we explain the methodology of our study, introduce data collected, and discuss both strengths and limitations of our data. Fourth, we briefly review China's death penalty practice with an emphasis on policy changes over time and the existing system in order to lay out the context of our discussions. Lastly, we introduce and summarize the content of the remaining chapters.

Problems of the "Overwhelming Public Support" Claim

With the largest population in the world, China is one of the nations with the oldest continuous history. Its use of capital punishment dates back thousands of years (H. Lu and Miethe 2007). Though there were brief moments of limited use of capital punishment in China's history (e.g., the Tang dynasty witnessed a halt of execution from 747 to 759; cited in Johnson and Zimring 2009, 246), China had never officially abolished the practice (Qiu 2002a; Y. Wang 2016). The use of capital punishment has been "inherited" and continued after the establishment of the People's Republic of China (PRC) as both a political weapon against enemies of the state (N. Zhang 2016) and a legal weapon against criminals. The PRC government carefully guards its data on capital punishment as "state secrets," but it is a well-known fact that China is the leading user of the death penalty in the world, with the largest numbers of annual death sentences and executions (Liang and Lu 2016).

The Chinese government often claims "overwhelming public support" to buttress its use of capital punishment, though China has never conducted a national poll on citizens' opinions on the death penalty (not to mention a referendum) (J. Lu 2005). While some scholars have downgraded the significance of public opinion on death penalty policy changes worldwide (e.g., Johnson and Zimring 2009) and in China (e.g., Johnson and Miao 2016), there is little doubt that the "overwhelming public support" has been utilized as a justification for China's continued use of capital punishment (B. Zhao 2015, 14).

We argue that the "overwhelming public support" claim is problematic for several important reasons. First, there is no clear definition of what should be properly considered "public opinion." Often it seems to be confined, by both the Chinese government and some scholars (e.g., Kong 2017; C. Yang 2011), to the mathematical majority support of the polled people in a survey. For instance, W. Li claimed that "China has the highest public support rate for the death penalty in the world" (2007, 58) and cited two surveys specifically: one conducted in 2002, in which 88% of the Chinese respondents opposed abolition of capital punishment, and the other conducted online by Sina.com.cn (新浪网, one of the biggest commercial websites in China) in 2003, in which 75.8% of the respondents supported retention of the death penalty (compared to 13.6% who supported abolition). Similarly, C. Yang (2011, 18) cited the results of an online survey conducted by the *Information Times* (信息时报, a commercial newspaper, http://www.xxsb.com/) and Sina.com.cn in 2008 to show the majority support: among 28,670 respondents, 67.2% (19,256) supported China's death penalty, while 11.1% (3,177) opposed it and 21.8% (6,237) reported a neutral opinion.

Such a majority of support based on survey results could be misleading, however, as the results depend on what question is asked and how it is asked (Durham, Elrod, and Kinkade 1996; Jones 1994). In the case of China, since no effort has been made to cover a nationwide representative sample, the results also depend on the targeted subjects of a survey. For example, legal scholars in China (especially criminal law scholars) have seemingly reached a consensus since the mid-2000s to restrict and limit the use of the death penalty in China and set a long-term goal to eventually abolish it (e.g., J. Lu and Li 2006; M. Zhang 2005b). Another interesting contrast can be made between the general public opinion and the opinion of criminal justice professionals. One survey of the latter (e.g., judges, prosecutors, police, lawmakers, and lawyers) (n = 455) conducted in Beijing and Hubei in 2007 and 2008 showed a very high overall death penalty support rate of 91.2%; the lowest among all professional groups came from lawyers, among whom an 81.3% support rate was recorded (Oberwittler et al. 2010). Such rates were significantly higher than the 57.8% support rate of the general public recorded in the same survey, though no satisfactory explanation has been offered regarding the higher support rate among professionals in China to date. Without proper foundation and careful examination, the overreliance on the numerical majority support would fail to consider a series of important questions such as whose opinion should be counted, how to count public opinion, and if equal weight should be assigned to people's opinions in policy making (B. Zhao 2015, 19).

Second, the oversimplified term "overwhelming public support" seriously overlooks variations based on key relevant factors such as crime type (e.g., what is the capital crime?), information on offenders and victims, and other circumstances (e.g., mitigating and aggravating circumstances). For example, given the fact that China's laws allow a great number of capital offenses (see review below) and that criminals could be death-sentenced for nonviolent and nonlethal crimes (e.g., corruption offenses, drug offenses), Chinese public opinion is subject to significant changes dependent on the nature of crimes. J. Zhao's study (2015), based on a survey (n = 1,010) conducted in one midsize city in 2013, examined respondents' opinions on the crime of organizing prostitution (a nonviolent, nonlethal capital crime). The results showed that merely 4.1% of the respondents chose capital punishment as their preferred choice of punishment based on information provided in a vignette mimicking a real case. Based on surveys of eight countries (China included), Roger Hood (2018), a world-renowned death penalty expert, pointed out that opinions on the death penalty were far more nuanced and moderate than what governments apparently believed or were prepared to accept. Misinterpreting the majority support in survey results, the death penalty is often advocated as the *only* appropriate punishment instead of *a* punishment. This is an easy pitfall in China.

Third, two other issues about public opinion on the death penalty have *not* yet been properly addressed in the context of China. One is the rationality of people's comments, and the other is whether Chinese people's attitudes are subject to change given new knowledge or information. For the former, a number of Chinese scholars have pointed out that Chinese public opinion on this issue is emotional, subject to change, and thus *irrational* (W. Li 2007; J. Lu 2005; Tang and Wang 2007; Z. Wang 2017; C. Yang 2011; Yuan 2009b). Nevertheless, none of these studies provide a clear definition of rationality and none provide empirical support of irrationality beyond mere observations of emotionally charged "calls for kill" by netizens in high-profile cases. A detailed analysis of the rationality of people's opinions is thus warranted. For the latter, American Supreme Court Justice Thurgood Marshall opined his famous Marshall hypotheses in the *Furman v. Georgia* case (408 U.S. 238) in 1972. Justice Marshall suggested that American citizens do not know much about America's death penalty practice but believed that they would be subject to reasoned persuasion and that the majority of them would oppose the use of capital punishment once they become informed about the flawed American death penalty system. The Marshall hypotheses have been subsequently tested in the United States, but its equivalents in non-US nations such as China have lagged behind. A public opinion survey ($n = 4,472$) based on face-to-face interviews conducted in Beijing, Hubei, and Guangdong provinces between November 1, 2007, and January 20, 2008, showed that 69.2% of the respondents admitted they had little or no knowledge (or "don't know") about China's capital punishment, compared to 30.8% who claimed they had some or much knowledge (Oberwittler et al. 2010; Qi and Oberwittler 2009). Further, 74.1% of the respondents expressed that they were *not* very interested in death penalty issues (or chose "don't know"), compared to 25.9% who expressed interest. The results suggest that the Chinese general public likely does not know much about China's death penalty system and practice. Liang, Liu, and Lu's study (2019) is the only known attempt to examine whether Chinese people are subject to reasoned persuasion. Based on a nonrandom college student sample, the results showed promising signs of opinion change after students were better informed, but the effect of student learning depends on what knowledge is conveyed and how it is conveyed. In any event, the oversimplified "overwhelming majority support" argument fails to address the rationality of people's opinions and the capability and likelihood of people's opinion changes after reasoned persuasion.

In short, we argue that the "overwhelming public support" claim by the Chinese government is problematic, as it fails to uncover the diversity and complexity of public opinions. Instead, we need a new way to enrich our understanding of Chinese public opinion on capital punishment.

Studies of China's Public Opinion on Capital Punishment

There have been extensive studies on public opinion on the death penalty in Western nations (especially in the United States). Based on survey and poll data, these studies have covered a wide range of topics, such as the extent of public support (Harris 1986), the rationales for people's support (Bohm 1987, 1992; Warr and Stafford 1984), potential factors that influence people's support (Britt 1998; Fan, Keltner, and Wyatt 2002; Niven 2002; Tyler and Weber 1982), whether people's attitudes may change given new knowledge or information (e.g., the famous Marshall hypotheses) (Bohm, Clark, and Aveni 1990; Bohm, Vogel, and Maistro 1993; Lambert and Clarke 2001), and the potential impact of public opinion on death penalty practice (Brace and Boyea 2008; Cullen, Fisher, and Applegate 2000; Jacobs and Kent 2007; Kelley and Braithwaite 1990).

Over time, scholars have come to a consensus that the oversimplified abstract question used in polls (e.g., "Do you favor or oppose the death penalty for persons convicted of murder?") is problematic and misleading and fails to uncover the complexities of public opinion (Ellsworth and Ross 1983; Jones 1994; Murray 2003). For instance, Bowers, Vandiver, and Dugan (1994) argued that the general abstract survey question merely reflects people's *acceptance* of but not their *preference* for the death penalty. When presented with other alternatives, such as life imprisonment without possibility of parole, people's support for the death penalty declines significantly (see also McGarrell and Sandays 1996). In recent years, scholars have turned to the use of vignettes (sometimes based on real cases) and more qualitative studies (e.g., focus groups) to explore how respondents may favor punishment other than the death penalty, given different factual scenarios (Burgason and Pazzani 2014; Durham et al. 1996; Falco and Freiburger 2011; Mills and Zamble 1998).

Compared to the Western literature, empirical research on this subject is extremely limited in China, though the Chinese government often cites the "overwhelming public support" to buttress its use of the death penalty. As discussed above, such an oversimplified claim fails to uncover tremendous variations across different groups of respondents and different types of crimes. In particular, the avant-garde group of the Chinese academia has started promoting reduction and restriction of China's capital punishment since the 2000s, and some scholars have openly called for abolition (e.g., J. Lu 2015b; Qiu 2004b). Many leading Chinese legal scholars have written actively and progressively on topics such as the impact of human rights on capital punishment (e.g., J. Lu 2015a; Qiu 2001, 2002a), potential problems with traditional concepts of retribution and deterrence (Qiu 2002b, 2003; Q. Zhang 2012), and lack of sufficient due process protections of China's death penalty practice (J. Lu 2015c; Qiu 2004a). Further, scholars have made constructive suggestions on what legal experts and judges should endeavor in order to reduce the use of capital punishment (Lao 2015; M. Zhang 2005a, 2005b, 2013) and outlined reform blueprints that aim at eventual abolition (J. Lu 2004, 2015b; J. Lu and Li 2006; J. Lu and Liu 2011; J. Lu and Liu 2014). It is thus not a coincidence that this collective effort by the academia has accompanied a series of reform measures by the criminal justice system to reduce China's use of capital punishment in the new century (see review below).

It is within this context that Chinese scholars have paid increasing attention to the role of public opinion (*minyi*, 民意 or *yulun*, 舆论), and realized that minyi, particularly measured by the numerical majority support for the death penalty, has become a major obstacle to China's further restriction and potential abolition of the death penalty (W. Li 2007; Liu, Yi, and Zhang 2013). The study of China's public opinion on the death penalty is still at its infancy compared to the country's Western counterparts, and studies based on empirical data are scarce. The bulk of existing studies in this field can be divided into three groups. First, a number of scholars have turned to survey data and examined the quantitative numerical support of Chinese citizens (for Chinese domestic studies, see, e.g., Yuan 2009a; Zeng 2015; H. Zhang and He 2011; J. Zhao 2015; for studies conducted by overseas scholars, see a summary by S. Jiang 2016). One major common problem with these studies is the quality of research design or nonrepresentative and nonrandom sampling. Studies conducted by Chinese domestic scholars often do *not* elaborate on methodology, but problems of their data and sampling have been widely acknowledged within the academia (Yuan 2009a; Zeng 2015). Though with more rigor, similar problems have persisted among studies by overseas scholars. Jiang (2016), for example, examined thirteen studies derived from ten surveys, 11 of which were conducted by overseas scholars. Eight of these surveys turned to convenient college student samples, and only one study managed to use a random sample (which covered only three regions, including Hubei, Guangdong, and Beijing).

Collectively, existing survey studies have confirmed the overall numerical majority support for the death penalty in China, though the support rates (in percentages) have varied greatly from the 50s (e.g., 57%) (Z. He 2009; Qi and Oberwittler 2009) to the 90s (e.g., 97%) (Kuang et al. 2010). Some of these studies managed to cover a variety of capital crimes, including nonviolent and nonlethal crimes (e.g., drug offenses, corruption), and the results showed that the support rates for specific crimes generally declined when the perceived severity of the crime lessened (Kuang et al. 2010; Oberwittler et al. 2010; Qi and Oberwittler 2009; Zeng 2017). Further, some of these studies tested statistical correlations between one's support for capital punishment and other relevant factors. For instance, a number of them showed that consistent with Western research, Chinese death penalty supporters tend to embrace major justifications of punishment, such as deterrence, retribution, and incapacitation (Jiang, Lambert, and Nathan 2009; Jiang, Lambert, and Wang 2007; Liang, Lu, Miethe, and Zhang 2006; Oberwittler and Qi 2009; Wu, Sun, and Wu 2011). Besides demographics, several variables, such as one's fear of crime, victimization experience, and belief in punitive penal ideology, were found to correlate with one's support for capital punishment (Oberwittler and Qi 2009; Wu, Sun, and Wu 2011). In a few comparative studies (Cao and Cullen 2001; Jiang, Lambert, Wang, Saito, and Pilot 2010; Qi and Oberwittler 2009; Wu, Sun, and Wu 2011), Chinese respondents reported higher levels of support for capital punishment than their counterparts in other countries.

Second, looking beyond the statistical and abstract form of minyi, some scholars have paid more attention to another form of minyi—that is, people's spontaneous reactions to controversial cases (J. Lu 2005; Y. Wang 2015; Xiao 2009; N. Zhang 2010). Fu (2016), for instance, called this form of minyi "penal populism" and contrasted Chinese penal populism with that of the United States. As Fu argued, Chinese penal populism often targets individual cases and tries to influence judicial sentencing instead of legislation or governmental policies. Facing pressure from this form of minyi, Chinese courts find themselves in a difficult position to uphold the law, respond to minyi, and maintain a "harmonious society" all at the same time (Miao 2013). Moreover, the impact of this minyi on individual cases is very unpredictable, as it is influenced by factors such as the media, judicial rulings, and actions by administrations (Tang and Wang 2007; J. Zuo 2009). For example, J. Zuo (2009) argued that the impact of this form of minyi is rather limited and that the real determinative external factors are the media and the top-down political decisions, the so-called will of the officials (官意). Nevertheless, there is little denial that this individual case–based minyi has already affected judicial decision making in practice (E. Li 2016; B. Zhao 2015). Belkin (2017), for instance, paid special attention to judicial policies that have pressured Chinese judges to consider "people's feelings" as exemplified by online minyi with the growing use of the internet. Citing a number of high-profile cases in recent decades, Belkin showed how judicial decisions had been swayed by the demands of fervent netizens. Belkin expressed serious concerns about such "judicial populism" and believed that it would not help judges regain public trust and enhance social stability but could weaken the legitimacy of the Chinese judiciary.

Based on a sample of 217 death penalty cases (from 1997 to 2014), Yuan et al. (2015) further categorized individual case–based minyi into two groups: minyi of the victims and their family members, and minyi of the general public. Yuan et al.'s statistics showed that the death penalty support rate was higher for the general public (56.7%) than for the victims and their family members (45.2%) (though they did not explain exactly how the support rates were measured). Moreover, they found that death sentencing was statistically correlated with the general public support rate—that is, the higher the public support for a death sentence, the more likely a defendant received a death sentence. But no significant correlation was found between death sentencing and the support rate of the victims and their family members. The support rate of the victims and their family members, however, was correlated with consequences of crimes, means of crimes, and defendants' repentance. Thus, Yuan et al. suggested that Chinese judges' consideration of minyi from both groups could be reasonable despite instances in which minyi improperly influenced case outcomes.

Third, seeing potential problems of minyi in both the statistical form and the form of spontaneous challenge to individual cases, a number of scholars tried to pinpoint root causes for China's minyi and proposed ways to better guide minyi in order to carry out further death penalty reforms (E. Li 2016; W. Li 2007; G. Liu et al. 2013; G. Sun 2009; Tang and Wang 2007; X. Xiao 2009; Zeng 2016; W. Zhang 2015b; B. Zhao and Zhang 2013). It is evident that scholars hold different opinions and propose different solutions. For instance, G. Liu et al. (2013) attributed minyi to both historical reasons (e.g., the impact of traditional Chinese culture such as people's belief in harsh punishment) and modern reasons (e.g., emerging social problems in transitional Chinese society, lack of transparency about China's death penalty practice). Y. Wang (2015), in contrast, argued that the rise of minyi was due to the increasing confrontation between substantive justice and procedural justice. While the masses emphasize the result (its legitimacy) based on their belief in substantive justice, criminal justice reform measures in the new century have shifted to more protections of procedural justice. When the gap between these two widens, the masses turn to minyi to pressure the judiciary and "seek justice" in individual cases. Scholars also disagreed on the proper roles that minyi should play in both legislation and criminal justice practice. While most scholars argued that the Chinese minyi is emotional, unpredictable, and irrational (W. Li 2007; J. Lu 2005; Tang and Wang 2007; Z. Wang 2017; C. Yang 2011; Yuan 2009b), others suggested that the use of the death penalty satisfies the retributive needs of the public, provides a foundation for public trust, and helps maintain a stable social order (Jia 2016; W. Zhang 2015b).

As discussed earlier, scholars noticed variations of minyi across different types of crimes. While reduced use of capital punishment against criminals of economic crimes is more acceptable to the public (e.g., Zeng 2017), such reduction against violent offenders and corrupt officials would present a greater challenge. W. Zhang (2015a), for example, tied the strong anticorruption sentiment of the Chinese public to their resentment of social inequality and privileges enjoyed by government officials. As Zhang argued, the belief in capital punishment by the public reflects their distrust of the criminal justice system. Dissatisfied with the lack of an effective system to counter rampant corruption, Chinese citizens view capital punishment as their last hope for equity and fairness. Given such variations of minyi, scholars suggested that different strategies be taken in dealing with different capital crimes (e.g., He 2009). What those strategies would be, however, is subject to debate. While some emphasized the importance of insulating Chinese courts from the influence of minyi in individual cases (Tang 2006; B. Zhao 2015), others argued that further death penalty reforms (including abolition) should gain the majority approval of the public and that it is thus important to carry out an active dialogue with the masses and educate them (Kong 2017; Sun 2009; C. Yang 2011).

In sum, studies of Chinese public opinion on capital punishment have been growing in the last two decades and have focused on both the statistical form of minyi and the spontaneously erupted minyi in individual cases. Given the limitations of samples and sampling, past quantitative studies failed to reach the general population on a broad base. In addition, the general abstract questions asked in surveys often failed to uncover great variations of people's opinions, which are often subject to changes given different circumstances. In contrast, studies of minyi in individual cases, though situated in a specific context, were *not* systematically designed and covered only a few high-profile cases. The focus of these studies was often on how public indignation influenced judicial decision making instead of the actual content of public opinions. Collectively, past studies failed to systematically examine the complexities and nuances of Chinese public opinion. Besides the numerical majority support and unpredictable minyi in individual cases, we know very little about the contents of Chinese public opinion on capital punishment, their rationales, and their variations. In this study, we aim to fill that gap by turning to Chinese netizens and examining their opinions on a number of capital cases.

Methodology: A Qualitative Study of Chinese Netizens' Opinions on Death Sentences

Data employed in this study are designed to explore and examine Chinese netizens' opinions on the death penalty. Given the impracticability of conducting a national representative survey in China and other weaknesses associated with survey studies (e.g., lack of specific contexts), we turned to a forum of public comments from which we collected netizens' comments on news about China's death sentences. Specifically, data were collected in spring 2016 in two steps. First, we conducted an extensive news search via the search engine of Sina.com.cn. All stories that reported death penalty cases in 2015 (from January 1 to December 31) were included in our sample. In cases with multiple defendants, as long as one of them was sentenced to death (including suspended death sentences), the case was included. Second, once we identified all such cases, we collected all case reports and netizens' comments that followed the reports and stored them separately as documents for analysis. Sina.com.cn creates a special section for netizens' comments (网友评论区) for each piece of news, which serves exactly our purpose. Given our focus on netizens' comments, we made a judicious decision to omit cases that received very few comments; we followed a rule of thumb to eliminate cases with fewer than three comments. As a result, 62 cases with a total 122 offenders were omitted from the final sample. Though the numbers of *cases* (i.e., 62) and *offenders* (i.e., 122) in the unused sample seem significant compared to the final sample (see below), it is the number of *comments* that mattered in our analyses. Indeed, a close examination of the unused sample produced merely nine comments in eight cases. Specifically, 54 cases of the unused sample produced zero comments, seven cases produced one comment, and one case produced two comments. These nine unused comments are essentially negligible compared to the 38,512 comments included in our final sample. Further, an examination of the content of these nine comments adds nothing new to results of our analyses. In terms of offenses, capital offenses covered in the unused sample were all represented in our final sample, except one case of counterfeiting currency.[1] This case of counterfeiting currency nevertheless produced no comment from the netizens.

A total of 63 cases with 123 defendants were collected in our final sample. Appendix 1 lists all 63 cases by order, including the date(s) that each case was reported, basic facts of the case, and a brief review of relevant legal history and legal ruling(s). In several cases, partial characters of defendants' names were deliberately unreported and replaced by a Chinese character "某" (which can be translated as "so and so" or "unknown"). We used "x" to replace the unreported character(s). In December, for example, there are two defendants with the same family name ("Li"), and their first names were unreported. To distinguish them, we labeled one case "Li 'x' (#58)" and the other "Li 'x' #2 (#61)." Appendix 2 lists officially charged crimes by months and the number of offenders being charged in each crime. The capital crimes covered in our sample involved 11 different types of offenses, led by homicide, drug trafficking, and sexual offenses. Appendix 3 lists the total numbers of comments by cases. As shown, our cases generated a total of 38,512 comments. Thirty-four cases (54% of all cases)

---

1. Counterfeiting currency was a capital offense in the 2015 Criminal Law (Article 170) but is no longer death-eligible with the Amendment of the Criminal Law in 2017.

had fewer than 100 comments, 18 cases (28.6%) had comments falling between 100 and 500, 5 cases (8%) had more than 500 but less than 1,000 comments, and 6 cases (9.5%) generated more than 1,000 comments. The Lin Senhao case (#1) generated the most comments (n = 17,611). Appendix 4 summarizes basic reporting statistics of cases, including the number of words and the number of videos and pictures (if any) that accompanied the story (or stories). As shown, the average length for all reported stories is about 1,000 (1,023 to be exact) words, and the range goes from 89 words (the Gu Junshan case, #26) to 4,924 words (the Wang Jianghua and Wang Jinpeng case, #35). Short videos were utilized in 12 cases. While the Lin Senhao case (#1) generated the most videos (21 videos) among all cases, the longest video coverage (measured by length) occurred in the Liu Han et al. case (#5), with coverage of almost 20 minutes in two videos. Photographs were used in 27 cases to accompany the stories, and the Lin Senhao case (#1) had 38 pictures, the most of all cases. We also documented some special information in our cases, such as interviews with family members and lawyers and attachment of judicial judgments.

Our methodology is innovative and unique in several respects. First, unlike quantitative survey research, our approach is largely qualitative in nature (i.e., content analysis of netizens' comments), which allows us to examine the content of Chinese netizens' opinions in depth. Unlike general abstract questions posed in surveys, comments by netizens were made based on information reported in a specific case, thus within a specific context. Compared to vignettes used in survey studies, cases in our sample are all real, so concern about artificial manipulation in vignettes is no longer an issue. Further, our data collection was systematically designed, representing a significant improvement compared to studies of individual case-based minyi in a few high-profile cases.

Second, though they are not a national representative sample, Chinese netizens serve as a better representation than samples in previous studies in terms of geographic coverage. The China Internet Network Information Center (CNNIC 2019) reported that the total number of Chinese internet users (defined as "Chinese citizens who used the internet in the last six months") had reached 829 million (59.6 % of China's total population) by December 2018 and that 98.6% of them (i.e., 817 million) access the internet via mobile phones. The growth of Chinese netizens over the years is tremendous compared to a start of 620,000 netizens in 1997 (a mere 0.03% of the national population). This high level of internet usage enabled us to tap into opinions of interested netizens in our study. While geographical restrictions were often a major limitation in past studies, data in our cases covered all 31 provinces in mainland China and Taiwan, Hong Kong and Macau. Nevertheless, it must be pointed out that regional (i.e., provincial) coverage in our sample was uneven: seven regions (Beijing, Guangdong, Shandong, Jiangsu, Henan, Shanghai, and Zhejiang) had more than 1,000 comments, while Taiwan, Macau, Qinghai, Tibet, and Ningxia had fewer than 50 comments throughout the whole year.[2] On the one hand, the number of comments originating from a region could be correlated with the overall internet usage of that particular region. For instance, out of the seven regions with the highest number of comments, six are ranked among the top 15 regions with the highest internet usage rates (CNNIC 2017, table 6, 36–37), with Henan as the only exception. With 1,197 comments, Henan generated the sixth-largest number of comments in our sample, but it is ranked only 28th among 31 provinces (not counting Taiwan, Macau, and Hong Kong), with the fourth-lowest internet usage rate (43.4%) by 2016 (CNNIC 2017, table 6). Qinghai, Ningxia, and Tibet, though generating the smallest numbers of comments in our sample, do not belong to the group with the lowest internet usage rate in the nation (ranked 11th, 20th, and 22nd, respectively). On the other hand, the active participation by netizens from a particular region might have something to do with the nature of reported cases. For example, two cases in our sample (Liu Danao, #47; Yang Xueqi, #62) occurred in Henan, drew more netizens from Henan, and generated 221 and 174 comments, respectively (33% of all comments from Henan). In other words, the uneven regional participation might be due to the influence of a combination of factors. Despite such unevenness, the coverage of the whole nation geographically is unprecedented compared to that found in past studies.

Third, another advantage of our sample is the voluntary participation by netizens who showed vested interest in death penalty issues. Studies in the past indicated that the death penalty is *not* a salient issue to average citizens. As the only randomly sampled survey, Oberwittler et al.'s study (2010) found that 74.1% of respondents expressed no interest or indifference on death penalty–related issues. If uninterested respondents are forced to share their opinions in a survey, serious concerns could be raised about the usefulness of their answers besides issues such as validity and reliability. In comparison, our naturalistic approach provides an opportunity to draw people who have true interest in the subject to

---

2. Data on regional variations are not reported but available upon request.

participate. Netizens in our study shared their opinions voluntarily, thus reducing potential problems of social desirability bias and other methodological issues.

Fourth, related to the issue of rationality, past Western studies have explored the likelihood that the death penalty opinions of average citizens could be subject to reasoned persuasion (e.g., the famous Marshall hypotheses). Often such testing primarily utilized a one-direction intervention model in which information (intervention) is instilled from the researcher to the subjects (see a summary in Liang et al. 2019). In her study of Japanese people's opinions on capital punishment, M. Sato (2014) turned to discussions among focus group participants and explored how *public deliberation* (two-way discussion) may change Japanese people's support for capital punishment. In our design, the online discussion (i.e., exchanges of netizens' comments) to some extent resembles the public deliberation employed by Sato. Such self-initiated interactions, missing from survey studies, allow us to examine the content, form, and effect of these interactions and to study the potential effect of rational deliberation among Chinese netizens, thus adding significantly to past studies.

While we argue that our design is unique and opens up opportunities to examine Chinese netizens' opinions on death sentences in new ways, there are limitations to our sampling and sample. To start off, it should be noted that Chinese netizens are *not* a full and accurate representation of the whole nation because of the issue of digital divide (that is, the divide between internet users and nonusers, primarily due to lack of access). One particular concern is that people without a "voice" (access to the internet in this case) often represent the less-privileged groups in China, and their opinions could be less punitive and thus less favorable to capital punishment (as witnessed in other nations, such as the lower death penalty support rate by blacks in the United States; see, e.g., Cochran and Chamlin 2006). We turned to several demographic measures to explore potential differences between Chinese netizens and the Chinese population in general. First, CNNIC data (2019) showed that the total number of Chinese netizens living in rural areas reached 222 million by the end of 2018, representing 26.7% of all internet users. Compared to its national population percentage (41.2% by 2017; China Statistical Yearbook 2018), rural residents are still *underrepresented* among internet users, despite their continued growth over the years. Second, the percentages of male and female internet users were 52.7% and 47.3%, respectively, by 2018 (CNNIC 2019), very close to their national statistics (51.2% and 48%, respectively, in 2017).

Third, by age breakdown, 67.8% of Chinese netizens are between 10 and 39 years of age, 15.6% between 40 and 49, and 12.5% above 50 (CNNIC 2019). Their corresponding statistics of the national population by 2017 were 40.6%, 16.9%, and 31%, respectively (calculated based on data from the China Population and Employment Statistics Yearbook 2018). It is thus evident (and not surprising) that the younger generations (below 40) are overrepresented among internet users while the older generations are underrepresented. Fourth, by education levels, 38.7% of internet users are middle school students, 24.5% are high school or equivalent-level students, and 18.6% have a college education or higher (CNNIC 2019). Compared to corresponding national statistics (38.1% with middle school education, 17.6% with high school education or equivalent, and 13.9% with college education or higher [China Statistical Yearbook 2018]), Chinese internet users with high school education are underrepresented, and users with college or higher education are slightly overrepresented.

In addition to the problem of digital divide, we cannot guarantee that netizens in our sample are accurately representative of all Chinese internet users. First, netizens in our sample "consumed" legal materials (i.e., death penalty cases) and, as a group, could be different from netizens who do not consume legal materials but perhaps other kinds of online materials. This is highly likely under the assumption that netizens look for information and materials that feed into their interests. The fact that the death penalty is not a salient issue to most citizens based on survey results confirms that our sample could be very different from netizens who show little interest in capital punishment. Second, by extension of the same logic, even among netizens who consume legal materials, we cannot guarantee that they all think alike. In particular, netizens who choose to express their opinions online could be different from those who peruse legal cases but choose to remain silent (J. Zhao 2015). Aside from selection bias, lack of individual and personal background information on netizens is another major weakness due to the nature of our data. Besides the user ID and the origin place, we could not ascertain other information such as gender, age, education, or profession of a particular netizen. Therefore, our analyses focus on the content of comments, not the commentators. The reliability and validity of the comments are more important.

With regard to reliability and validity of netizens' comments, two concerns need to be addressed. First is the concern about China's internet censorship, which is well known and has evolved along with the growth of China's internet use (see, e.g., a summary in Liang and Lu 2010). Besides the "Great Firewall of China" (which blocks certain websites from operating in China) and "keyword blocking" (which prevents users from posting texts that contain banned words or phrases), the most extensive and aggressive censorship is "content filtering," tasked to and completed by hundreds of thousands of internet police, monitors, and the so-called 50-cent party members (see chapter 4) hired by governments at all levels to "supervise" the internet. As King, Pan, and Roberts (2013) showed, however, China's internet censorship appears to be rather selective and strategically targets comments that entice social mobilization, particularly collective actions. As a result, individual-level (sometimes intense) criticisms of the government, officials, and policies are tolerated. Content-wise, the majority of cases in our sample deal with individual wrongs and therefore do not trigger the filtering warnings as suggested by King, Pan, and Roberts. In a number of cases, netizens' comments did turn into a critique of governmental policies (see chapter 7), but it is difficult to gauge the risk level of their discussions (e.g., discussions about the "one-child" policy and corruption are judged medium-risk items by King, Pan, and Roberts). Unlike King, Pan, and Roberts's study, which traced netizens' posts over time to measure the filtering effect, we collected our data at one point in time and cannot gauge changes in netizens' posts. In a few places, we did find examples that seemed to suggest some filtering effects. For example, in the Liu Danao case (#47), one netizen wrote, "I'm here for the 300,000 comments!!!!!!!! I'd like to find out who deserves to die!!!!!!!!!!" Nevertheless, we recorded only 3,221 comments in this case (see appendix 3), and we are not sure how to explain this huge gap (e.g., possibly due to this netizen's overcounting of people's "likes" or the unlikely 90% filtering effort). In a few other instances, netizens commented that they could not find their old posts, which might suggest a filtering effect (i.e., deletion). By all likelihood, in our judgment, the filtering effect should not affect the quality of our data and analysis, as we witnessed plenty of sensitive criticisms from netizens in our sample (similar to examples shared by King, Pan, and Roberts), and our data exhibit a high degree of saturation as major themes and topics are repeated across different cases.

Compared to censorship and filtering, the second concern might be more real based on our observation—that is, deliberate manipulation by *shuijun* (water armies, 水军). "Shuijun" refers to someone who is hired to post comments deliberately to serve specific purposes; one well-known example is the "50-cent party members" hired by the governments to do cheerleading (King, Pan, and Roberts 2017). Shuijun often flood the comments section with aggressive postings to draw the attention of others and achieve their desired effect. For instance, in the Lin "x"ping and Ye "x"tian case (#16), one netizen (ID "5269727374") repeated seven times in six minutes (from 7:43 to 7:49) the same message that attacked another netizen. In the Yuan Junkai et al. case (#12), a netizen (ID "1ald0at91b") left seven almost identical posts to call for harsh punishment (i.e., torture in prison) in 16 minutes (from 13:22 to 13:38). Both are examples of blatant aggressive postings. In comparison, there are possible cases of more subtle and hidden manipulations. For instance, in the Lin Senhao case (#1), one netizen (ID "Wings of water and fire (水炎之翼)" from Nanjing, Jiangsu) left a message that disputed leniency arguments from Lin's supporters at 10:59 on August 3, 2015. About 13 minutes later (at 11:12), another netizen repeated the exact same message but with a different ID ("A piggy would like to clime the tree (猪猪要爬树)" from Guangzhou, Guangdong). Also in Lin's case, from 15:59 to 20:03 on November 16, four netizens with four different IDs from the same region (Jinan city, Shandong province) repeated the same or nearly identical message that attacked Lin's defense lawyer(s). Granted, these examples are *not* direct proof that shuijun manipulated the comments section, but they did look very suspicious. On the other hand, such manipulations, even if true, did *not* appear to be efforts initiated by the government and represented a very tiny, almost negligible fraction of the comments in our sample. More importantly, they often aimed to manipulate the total numbers of comments of a certain nature but did *not* affect the type and content of netizens' comments, which are the primary focus of our qualitative study.

In sum, compared to the national population, Chinese netizens as a collective group are younger and better educated and tend to come from an urban living background. Further, our sample may not accurately represent the whole Chinese netizen population. Nevertheless, given that a nationwide representative sample is not reachable in the existing social and political context of China, we turned to a unique source: the Chinese netizens in this study. With acknowledged limitations, our netizen sample represents significant improvement in its geographical coverage and avoids some potential problems of survey studies (e.g., respondents' social desirability bias in providing appealing answers, researchers' manipulation of vignettes to "feed" factual information) due to the authenticity of cases in our sample and netizens' voluntary participation. Moreover, our study is qualitative in nature, and netizens' exchanges of opinions online allow us to examine their interactions. Our overall goal is *not* to make inferential statistical analyses. Rather, we aim to uncover the diversity of netizens' comments (including the breadth, depth, and variation of their opinions) and the content of their opinions. As argued, "Online behavior has become such a large and important part of human life that the expression observed in social media is now important in its own right, regardless of whether it is a good measure of non-internet freedoms and behaviors" (King, Pan, and Roberts 2013, 331). In the case of China, given the lack of meaningful participation channels offline, the internet has become an important platform for Chinese people to voice their opinions (Yang 2009; Zheng 2008; Zhou 2006). In recent years, Chinese scholars have increasingly recognized the importance of studying minyi online and its impact on China's legal reforms (Liang 2014), particularly the use of the death penalty (Xiao 2009; C. Yang 2011). Our design, to our best knowledge, represents the first attempt to empirically study netizens' opinions on capital punishment systematically.

A Brief Review of China's Death Penalty Practice

China's death penalty laws, policies, and practices have gone through tremendous changes in the last four decades (Liang and Lu 2016). While a comprehensive review is not appropriate in this book, it is useful to lay out the context and explain the existing system to facilitate the audience's understanding of issues to be discussed in the coming chapters. Our review below focuses on policy changes over time and the current system and practice.

Policy Changes over Time

After ten years of turmoil due to the infamous Cultural Revolution (1966-76), 1979 witnessed the formalization of the PRC's legal system. Both the Criminal Law (CL) and the Criminal Procedural Law (CPL) were enacted for the first time. A total of 28 death-eligible offenses (also known as "capital offenses"—that is, offenses that could potentially subject offenders to capital punishment based on laws) were stipulated in the CL. Articles 144–147 of the 1979 CPL gave the Supreme People's Court (SPC) the final review and approval authority for death penalty cases.

Such formalization of the legal system, however, failed to wrestle with policy changes in the 1980s and 1990s. Facing worsening public security (e.g., rising crime rates), the central government turned to "get tough" policies typified by nationwide "strike hard" campaigns against crimes and criminals.[3] As a result, the 1980s and 1990s witnessed expanded use of capital punishment. New capital offenses were added through new decrees adopted by the Standing Committee of the National People's Congress in the early 1980s (see Liang 2016). By the time the CL was revised in 1997, the total number of capital offenses had reached 68. Important safeguards designed to prevent potential mistakes and limit death sentences were abandoned. For instance, to assist the "strike hard" campaigns, the SPC's final review and approval authority was delegated to provincial high courts in the 1980s. Such a delegation in essence made defunct the final review and approval procedure, as the provincial high courts exercised both the appellate review power as the courts of second instance and the final review and approval power on behalf of the SPC.

A change of course was finally set in place in the new twenty-first century. The SPC in particular led a series of reform measures to formalize the procedure of the death penalty review with a goal to prevent errors and limit the use of the death penalty. For instance, in 2005 the SPC issued the "Notice on Further Improving Appellate Trials [i.e., Trials of Second Instance] in Death Penalty Cases" and mandated an open-court appellate trial. In 2007 the SPC took back its final review and approval power for all death penalty cases and jointly issued the "Opinion on Further Strictly Enforcing the Law to Ensure the Quality of Death Penalty Cases" with three other ministries. In 2010 the SPC issued the "Opinion on Certain Issues Concerning Implementation of the Criminal Justice Policy of Balancing Leniency and Severity," and this new "balancing leniency and severity" (*kuanyan xiangji*, 宽严相济) policy replaced the "strike hard" policy as the dominant criminal justice policy of the new century. In the same year, joined by four other ministries, the SPC issued the "Rules on Certain Issues Concerning Examination and Judgment of Evidence in Death Penalty Cases" and the "Rules on Certain Issues Concerning Exclusion of Illegal Evidence in Criminal Cases," both of which aim to deal with evidentiary issues in criminal cases and raise the bar of evidentiary quality

---

3. The famous "strike hard" campaigns were short-term, concentrated crime campaigns initiated by the Chinese government from time to time that aimed to quash the number of crimes in a short period of time. Though its crime-control effect is rather limited, the policy serves other important political and social functions (see, e.g., Liang 2005; Tanner 2010; Trevaskes 2002, 2003, 2004, 2010).

control. In 2011 and 2015, the 8th and 9th Amendments of the CL made 21 (13 and 9, respectively) previous capital offenses death-ineligible. As a result, the total number of death-eligible offenses contained in the current 2020 CL has been cut down to 46.

Existing System and Practice

The current 46 capital offenses still cover a wide range of crimes, including violent crimes (e.g., murder and robbery) and nonviolent and nonlethal crimes (e.g., drug offenses and bribe taking). Three groups of defendants are exempted from capital punishment under the current CL, including minors under 18 years of age at the time of crime commission, criminal defendants 75 years of age or older (unless the offender used especially cruel crime methods), and female defendants who are pregnant at the time of the sentence (Article 49). To date, China still guards statistics of annual death sentences and executions as state secrets. Past studies that estimated such numbers based on various sources indicate that at least thousands of people would be death-sentenced and executed each year in China, and in "get tough" years (e.g., years when "strike hard" campaigns were in operation), the numbers could have reached tens of thousands (e.g., H. Lu, Li, and Hu 2016).

Three dominant players of China's criminal justice system are the public security organs (the police), the people's procuratorates, and the people's courts, thus corresponding to the Chinese term *gong-jian-fa* (公检法). Though they are supposed to function independently, the coalition among them, often nicknamed the "assembly line," could pose serious problems in practice (e.g., lack of effective checks and balances among three branches; see, e.g., R. Chen 2000).

The Chinese court system has three provincial levels: basic people's court, intermediate people's court, and high people's court. At the national level, there is the SPC. The Chinese judiciary follows a two-tiered trial system, and the ruling of the court of second instance is typically final. Due to the grave nature of death penalty cases, it is the intermediate people's courts that are charged with jurisdiction over the first instance trial (Article 21 of the current 2018 CPL), whereas the provincial high courts have jurisdiction over the second instance trial. For cases resulting in a death sentence with immediate execution, the final review and approval authority rests with the SPC (Articles 246–251 of the CPL).

With regard to the trial of first instance, though a significant number of rights (e.g., right to cross-examination, right to assistance of legal counsel) have been conferred to defendants and defense, some issues persist. Compared to prosecution, criminal defense is still very weak (S. Liu and Halliday 2016). For example, a Chinese defendant does not have the right to remain silent, and both the procuratorate and the judge may question the defendant during a trial. Defendants are expected to cooperate with law enforcement agencies and the procuratorate and their "good attitude" can be legally considered for granting more-lenient sentences by judges. Defendants' right for cross-examination is also weakened in practice, as witnesses often do not testify in court, and documents and written testimonies are routinely permitted and admitted as evidence. Moreover, the adjudicative body that hears the case may *not* be the one that decides the final sentence, especially when a case is of "significant importance." Sentencing decisions instead can be made by an adjudicative committee of a people's court behind closed doors, to which the defense has no formal access.

The current CPL demands that the trial of second instance (that is, appellate review for death penalty cases) shall be conducted openly (Article 234), and the scope of the review shall *not* be limited to contested issues but to cover all facts and evidence and to determine if the law is applied appropriately (Article 233). Though the law aims to conduct a comprehensive review de novo by the court of second instance, there are questions whether this is actually implemented. Often, when the appellate courts find errors in a case, they send the case back to the lower courts for a retrial instead of directly amending the sentence, and little details are provided to the lower courts about the appellate courts' decisions (Liebman 2015).

As mentioned above, to tackle the issue of local protectionism and to standardize the practice of death penalty review nationwide, the SPC finally took back its power to review and approve death-sentenced cases in 2007, thus functioning as the last gatekeeper. Articles 246–251 of the current CPL lay out specific requirements for the SPC's final review. For example, Article 249 stipulates that the review shall be done by a three-person collegial panel, and Article 251 stipulates that the SPC shall interrogate the defendant and listen to the opinion of a defense lawyer if the defense lawyer so requests. Nevertheless, because the SPC review is *not* an open procedure, the whole process is operated rather opaquely. In addition, due to a lack of judicial independence, the SPC's decisions are likely to be affected by both internal and external factors. Internally, new policies (e.g., the "balancing lenience with severity" policy) may affect how the

SPC functions and how it guides and instructs lower court judges at different levels; externally, top-down policies from the Chinese Communist Party (CCP), referred to as the Party-state (e.g., maintaining stability and building a harmonious society), may put pressure on the SPC to appease strong feelings of the public. It is within this context that minyi (e.g., public indignation in particular as a commonly cited justification for judicial rulings) may have significant influence over judiciary decisions in China.

If a death sentence with immediate execution is affirmed by the SPC, the decision is final. An execution must be carried out within seven days (Articles 261–262 of the CPL). During this small window, however, an execution can be stopped through the adjudication supervision procedure (审判监督程序, Articles 252–258) or when errors of a ruling are detected or a defendant performs meritorious services during this window or a defendant is pregnant (Article 262). In practice, such post-SPC review challenges rarely occur (H. Lu, Li, and Hu 2016).

Organization of the Book

The major goal of this book is to examine Chinese public opinion on the death penalty in depth. To achieve this goal, as explained in the "Methodology" section above, we turn to Chinese netizens and study their opinions on death sentences meted out to 123 capital offenders in 2015. Chapter 1 has provided the general background of this study. We first described the purpose of the study and discussed problems of the "overwhelming public support" claim by the Chinese government. Second, we reviewed previous studies of Chinese public opinion on the use of the death penalty. Third, we explained the methodology of our study, introduced the data collected, and discussed both strengths and limitations of our data. Next, we briefly reviewed China's death penalty practice to set up the context of our discussions. Now we introduce the remaining chapters.

In chapter 2 we focus on the content of netizens' comments and pay particular attention to the ***diversity*** of the comments. The diversity of netizens' opinions, we argue, is reflected in three important aspects: First, the opinions of the Chinese netizens in our study covered a broad range of topics (the breadth), ranging from their positions about a particular death sentence and parties involved in a particular case; to their critical evaluation of China's criminal justice system and its professionals; to their critique of the government and governmental officials; to their reflections on related social, systemic, and structural issues; to their questioning of media reporting; and to many others. Second, the diversity of netizens' opinions is also reflected in diverse views on each topic, many times with netizens holding opposing views (the depth). Such depth makes up an important component of the diversity of netizens' opinions. Third, diversity is further reflected in the variances of netizens' opinions given different circumstances. (The variances of netizens' opinions are discussed in chapter 5.) In chapter 2 we focus on the first two components of the diversity and survey the most important topics and views as explicitly reported by Chinese netizens in our cases.

In chapter 3 we focus on the *rationales* explicitly expressed by Chinese netizens in their support of or opposition to death sentences (and China's use of the death penalty in general). For death penalty supporters, a number of important rationales were reported, including but not limited to retribution, deterrence, justice/law requirement, just desert, payback, public order/safety, and social impact/indignation. In contrast, opponents of death sentences questioned retribution, deterrence, and indignation and expressed concerns about fairness of law and the legal system and wrongful convictions; some even called for outright abolition of capital punishment.

In chapter 4 we focus on netizens' *interactions*—that is, exchanges of comments by netizens. Netizens' interactions displayed three general forms, including counterarguments, concurring arguments, and personal attacks. While counterarguments focused on the substance of arguments, personal attacks focused on individual netizens and often utilized foul language and personal threat. In addition to these three general forms, three specific netizen exchanges are examined as well, including the argument of "thinking in others' shoes," the practice of questioning others' motivations and identifications, and netizens' reactions to "online violence." Though online interactions and exchanges could be potentially developed into a platform where netizens engage in civil dialogues and deliberations, Chinese netizens' heated (and sometimes intimidating and violent) debates seemingly cast doubt about the viability of such potentials.

In chapter 5 we focus on the *variances* of netizens' opinions, which is another important component of the diversity. Consistent with results from other nations, Chinese netizens' opinions on death sentences are *not* immutable. Rather, their opinions often change given different circumstances. Specifically, we focus on four key factors that may have influenced netizens' opinions (as evident from our data). First, we examine how different crime types (e.g., violent crimes, corruption, narcotics offenses) may have influenced netizens' opinions. Second, we examine how different defendants and victims may have generated different responses from the netizens. Third, we examine the impact of different legal procedures and explore potential different netizen responses accordingly. Lastly, we focus on media reporting and examine how it may have affected netizens' comments and how Chinese netizens sometimes openly challenged and questioned media reporting.

In chapter 6 we focus on Chinese netizens' explicit comments about China's *criminal justice system and its professionals*. Because death penalty cases involve the most difficult decisions of the criminal justice system, how the system functions and how professional players within the system perform make up significant portions of netizens' discussions online. Specifically, we examine, in sequence, netizens' challenges and questions to the judicial system (i.e., courts and judges), the police (and policing), the correctional system, criminal defense lawyers, and other peripheral players (e.g., legal experts and public intellectuals). Our examination covers both positive and negative comments made by netizens in specific cases.

In chapter 7 we turn to the bigger picture and examine China's *social, systemic, and structural problems*. Often, netizens' comments and discussions related to a particular case were embedded in bigger social, systemic, and structural problems. As a matter of fact, cases in our data that generated the most heated discussions were often cases that reflected acute social, systemic, and structural problems of contemporary Chinese society. Specifically, we examine, in sequence, the influence of commercialization and power of money; official corruption; social unrest; the one-child birth control policy; challenges to China's health-care system; and challenges to China's "demolition and relocation" policy and practice. Specific cases are discussed as examples of these social, systemic, and structural problems.

In chapter 8 we focus on the issue of *rationality* and examine whether the Chinese netizens' comments and discussions online in our study were rational or irrational. We argue that Habermas's communicative rationality (1984/1987) provides the most insight to our analysis in this context. Accordingly, examples of irrationality we found include personal attacks (e.g., use of foul language, personal threats, cursing), netizens' calls to punish innocent people and forgo proper legal procedures, and various discriminations (e.g., based on one's geographic origin, race/ethnicity, gender, or nationality). In comparison, examples of rationality include netizens' case comparisons and suggestions. Both domestic and international case comparisons are common methods adopted by Chinese netizens to question (or support) death sentences and seek "justice and fairness." Suggestions made by netizens are tailored toward specific issues in cases, and the internal logic of making suggestions (especially constructive ones) indicates strong elements of rational deliberation.

Having examined all major topics in previous chapters, chapter 9 hones in on one particular case, the famous **Lin Senhao poisoning case**, which generated the most comments ($n = 17{,}611$) in our sample. We first provide an overview of the case (facts and legal history), and then we examine the most critical issues of Lin's case, including netizens' debate on Lin's legal defense, their debate on Lin's death sentence (e.g., whether sympathy is warranted and a second chance should be given), their attitudes toward both Lin's family and the victim's family, and how netizens both supporting and opposing Lin tried to argue minyi and influence *yulun* online. In a way, Lin's story showcased many major issues discussed in previous chapters.

In chapter 10 we argue that short of other effective means as alternatives, Chinese netizens' online comments and discussions have become a unique form of Chinese public opinion. Though it includes many problems, this form of public opinion provides a platform that allows Chinese netizens to express their independent opinions, to exchange information, and to conduct and engage conversations with others. Specifically, in cases of death sentences, it has become an important means for netizens to seek "justice and fairness" based on their own standards and judgments, condemn the evils (e.g., criminals, official corruption), and sometimes criticize the government, its officials, and unpopular policies. To look to the future, we make some modest suggestions to media reporting, the government, and Chinese netizens. Lastly, we conclude the chapter with overall lessons that we have drawn from this empirical study.

CHAPTER 2

Diversity of Netizens' Opinions
The Breadth and the Depth

In chapter 2 we focus on the content of netizens' comments in our study, paying particular attention to the *diversity* of the comments. The diversity of netizens' opinions is reflected in three important aspects: First, Chinese netizens' opinions covered a broad range of topics (the breadth). Second, the diversity of netizens' opinions is also reflected in multiple views on each topic, many times with netizens holding opposing views (the depth). Third, the diversity is further reflected in the variances of netizens' opinions given different circumstances. (The variances of netizens' opinions are discussed in chapter 5.) In this chapter we focus on the first two components of the diversity (the breadth and the depth) and survey the most important topics and views expressed by Chinese netizens.

To systematically code and analyze netizens' comments, we relied on a popular qualitative technique: thematic analysis (e.g., Boyatzis 1998). With the exception of netizens' interactions (see chapter 4), we categorized netizens' comments into different themes based on the specific content of each comment. While trying to keep different themes separate to reflect their complexities and nuances, we combined some related themes into broader thematic categories for the purpose of parsimony. When one comment reflected multiple themes, it was counted separately for each theme. The diversity of netizens' comments is very impressive. In table 1 we rank the top ten themes based on the number of netizens' comments in each case. (Note that both the Lin Senhao and Zhao Zhihong cases were reported on multiple times in different months and thus listed multiple times.) In addition to these top themes, many others appeared in netizens' comments (in fact, too many to report!).

Table 1. Top Themes (Number of Comments) by Cases

(January to February 2015)

Top Themes	Lin Senhao	Huang Qinghen	Peng Shu and Hu Haolong	Zhao Zhihong	Liu Han et al.
1	Netizen interactions (57)	Support death sentence (612)	On highway system (33)	Question judicial justice (4)	Death justifications (10)
2	Death justifications (55)	Death justifications (237)	Support death sentence (16)	Netizen interactions (4)	Appease the masses (4)
3	Against defendant (30)	Against criminals (219)	Death justifications (15)	Demand accountability of responsible parties (4)	Appraise the rule by law (3)
4	On defendant's family (20)	For victims (207)	On sentencing (14)	On wrongful convictions (2)	Lessons (3)
5	Support death sentence (18)	Repeat title (79)	Netizen interactions (12)	Zhao's contribution (2)	Support top leaders' actions (2)
6	Sympathy for defendant (17)	Demand harsh punishment (69)	On corruption (9)	Death justifications (1)	(Many "1s")
7	Causes of crime (14)	No leniency (53)	On crime nature (8)	Support Zhao's rights (1)	
8	Ask for leniency (14)	Suggestions (43)	Case comparisons (7)	On appeal procedure (1)	
9	On victim/victim's family (12)	Netizen interactions (4)	Question law (7)		
10	Questioning verdict/ sentence (11)	Cursing (4)	Disbelief of death sentence (7)		

(March to April)

Top Themes	Tuo Heti et al.	Hu "x"	Wang Yuefu	Zhai "x" de	Ruan Fangcheng et al.	Zhao Zhihong
1	Demand harsh punishment (14)	Against victim (26)	Question sentencing (3)	Death justifications (10)	Support death sentence (3)	Support death sentence (16)
2	Demand death sentence (11)	Against defendant (22)	Demand death sentence (1)	Lessons (8)	No leniency (2)	No leniency (6)
3	Death justifications (7)	Netizen interactions (13)	Demand harsh punishment (1)	Against defendant (8)	Discrimination against blacks (2)	Death justifications (5)

(continues)

Table 1.—(continued)

(March to April)						
4	Support defendant to give birth (3)	Against lawyers (11)	Question reporting (1)	Netizen interactions (8)	Others (1)	Case impact (1)
5	Question delay (2)	Support defendant (6)		Suggestions (5)		Question reporting (1)
6	Question sentencing (2)	Support death sentence (6)		Question verdict/sentence (3)		Question verdict/sentence (1)
7	(Many "1s")	On social problems (4)		Support death sentence (3)		Ask for leniency (1)
8		Death justifications (3)		(Many "2s")		
9		Lessons (3)				
10		(Many "2s")				

(May)						
Top Themes	Zhao Zhihong	Wu Qinyuan	Yuan Junkai et al.	Wang Gang	Lian Enqing	Lin Senhao
1	Demand accountability (6)	Causes for wrongful convictions (25)	Netizen interactions (54)	Netizen interactions (38)	Against/question doctors (2,422)	Netizen interactions (2,211)
2	Death justifications (6)	Netizen interactions (13)	Demand death sentence (41)	Question medical system (22)	Netizen interactions (1,968)	Death justifications (1,501)
3	Netizen interactions (6)	Suggestions (11)	Question suspended death sentence (39)	Against defendant (22)	Death justifications (219)	Against defendant (1,324)
4	Support death sentence (5)	Demand accountability of responsible parties (7)	Question parole decision (35)	Support defendant (17)	Support defendant (146)	Support death sentence (891)
5	Seek truth (3)	On compensation (7)	Question law/legal system (30)	Share feelings (5)	Against defendant (138)	Question defense (565)

Table 1.—(continued)

(May)

6	Zhao's contribution (2)	Concern about wrongful convictions (6)	Demand harsh punishment (23)	Jokes (3)	Question reporting (136)	Questioning verdict/ sentence (528)
7	Question death sentence (2)	Share feelings (5)	Demand accountability (22)	Draw societal attention (2)	Against hospitals (81)	On victim/ victim's family (376)
8	Share feelings (2)	Case comparisons (4)	Death justifications (20)	"Think in others' shoes" (2)	Share feelings (73)	On defendant's family (328)
9	(Many "1s")	(Many "3s")	Cursing (18)	Other nations' systems (2)	Support death sentence (67)	Ask for leniency (308)
10			Demand execution (18)	(Many "1s")	Support doctors (66)	Question delay and waste (211)

(June)

Top Themes	Zhang Xiangxi	Lin "x"ping and Ye "x"tian	Sun Zhifu	Liang Kaiwu	Wang Changping
1	Netizen interactions (13)	Netizen interactions (656)	Netizen interactions (7)	Netizen interactions (5)	Netizen interactions (92)
2	Against defendant (11)	Question sentencing fairness (173)	Death justifications (4)	Question delay (3)	Against defendant (33)
3	Cursing (7)	Demand death sentence (122)	Support death sentence (3)	Against defendant (3)	Against police (28)
4	Support death sentence (3)	Against corrupt officials (112)	For victims (2)	Support death sentence (2)	Support death sentence (24)
5	Question delay (3)	Death justifications (110)	Question gendered sentencing (2)	(Many "1s")	Jokes (12)
6	For victims (2)	Case comparisons (95)	Question defendant's mental condition (2)		On TV series *Breaking Bad* (11)
7	Demand harsh punishment (2)	Support death sentence (86)	(Many "1s")		Share feelings (10)
8	Question recidivism (2)	Question death sentence (77)			On police crimes (6)
9	Question government and its officials (2)	On "too late to regret" (59)			Death justifications (5)
10	Appease the masses (2)	Jokes (57)			(Many "4s")

(continues)

(July)

Top Themes	Zhang Weilan et al.	Yang Dazhi	Wang "x"	Fan Jieming	Zheng Dalong and Yang Shengjian
1	Netizen interactions (157)	Support death sentence (81)	Against defendant (3)	Netizen interactions (196)	Support death sentence (7)
2	Against defendant (133)	Against defendant (32)	Support death sentence (3)	Question delay (67)	Netizen interactions (5)
3	Demand death for all defendants (104)	Netizen interactions (27)	Death Justifications (3)	Against defendant (42)	Death justifications (4)
4	Support death sentence (55)	Cursing (25)	Netizen interactions (3)	Support death sentence (32)	Against defendant (4)
5	On movie *Blind Well* (48)	Demand accountability (24)	Cursing (2)	Death justifications (29)	(Many "1s")
6	Death justifications (42)	Regional discrimination (16)	(Many "1s")	Question crime causes (21)	
7	Cursing (41)	Against abolition (10)		Support defendant (19)	
8	Question suspended death sentence (28)	Demand execution (10)		Jokes (18)	
9	Share feelings (27)	Suggestions (9)		Case comparisons (17)	
10	Jokes (21)	Death justifications (8)		Cursing (17)	

(August)

Top Themes	Lin Senhao	Wang Hua et al.	Gu Junshan	Deng Fang	Li Lei
1	Netizen interactions (530)	Netizen interactions (8)	Against corruption (11)	Support death sentence (22)	Netizen interactions (101)
2	Death justifications (400)	Support death sentence (4)	Death justifications (3)	Netizen interactions (19)	Against defendant (20)
3	On defendant's family (299)	Share feelings (2)	Support death sentence (3)	Cursing (16)	Question the elders (20)
4	Against defendant (276)	Demand harsh punishment (2)	Equal treatment of law (1)	Against defendant (9)	Question verdict (13)
5	Support death sentence (267)	Question reporting (1)	Against defendant (1)	Question police inefficiency (5)	Share feelings (13)

Table 1.—(continued)

(August)

#					
6	Questioning verdict/sentence (208)	Question government sectors (1)		For victims (3)	Question defendant's grandma (10)
7	On victim/victim's family (185)	Jokes (1)		Question victims (3)	Question lawsuit (7)
8	Questioning defense (132)	Lessons (1)		Question reporting (3)	Question family relations (7)
9	Question delay and waste (116)	Support judges (1)		Demand execution (3)	Question law (5)
10	Causes of crime (104)			(Many "2s")	Jokes (5)

(September)

Top Themes	Hu Cunbiao and Wang Yong	Yuan Lijun	Chen Yun	Feng Xiujuan	Yang Chaoquan
1	Support death sentence (68)	Question reporting (3)	Jokes (25)	Netizen interactions (91)	Netizen interactions (320)
2	Netizen interactions (68)	Jokes (1)	Netizen interactions (19)	Against defendant (59)	Death justifications (107)
3	Death justifications (23)	Netizen interactions (1)	Support death sentence (16)	Cursing (27)	Against defendant (64)
4	Demand death sentence (23)	Case comparison (1)	Case comparison (16)	Against defendant's paramour (22)	On "too late to regret" (42)
5	Cursing (22)		Against defendant (9)	Against women (18)	Against abolition (28)
6	Against defendant (21)		Question defendant's background (9)	Question defendant's husband (16)	On defendant's "last words" (25)
7	Jokes (20)		Death justifications (7)	Jokes (11)	Support death sentence (25)
8	Case comparisons (12)		Question death sentence (5)	Share feelings (9)	For victim (24)
9	Question crime duration (10)		Make assumptions (5)	Support death sentence (8)	Jokes (22)
10	Demand harsh punishment (7)		(Many "4s")	Question birth control policy (7)	Other nations' systems (20)

(continues)

(October)

Top Themes	Lumei et al.	Wang Jianghua and Wang Jinpeng	Huang "x"	Xiao "x"	Zhao Xu	Wang Zongren
1	Question reporting (6)	Death justifications (1)	Netizen interactions (16)	Demand death for all defendants (2)	Netizen interactions (11)	Against defendant (2)
2	Netizen interactions (4)	Against defendant (1)	Against defendant (10)	Question law (2)	Against defendant (6)	Netizen interactions (1)
3	Demand death sentence (3)	Question low efficiency (1)	Support death sentence (4)	Demand harsh punishment (1)	Suggestions (3)	Discrimination (1)
4	Support death sentence (2)	Support death sentence (1)	Lessons (3)		Death justifications (3)	
5	For victim (2)		Question reporting (2)		Share feelings (2)	
6	Case comparisons (2)		Regional discrimination (2)		Jokes (2)	
7	Against corruption (2)		Jokes (2)		On defendant's mental problems (2)	
8	(Many "1s")		(Many "1s")		(Many "1s")	
9						
10						

(November)

Top Themes	Deng "x"	Ling Ruiming	He Shenguo	Wang Yihuan	Gao Yulun et al.	Liu "x"
1	Share one's experience (9)	Question victim (12)	Netizen interactions (297)	Netizen interactions (17)	Netizen interactions (70)	Netizen interactions (10)
2	Critique bad custom (5)	Netizen interactions (11)	Support defendant (58)	On money and power (9)	Question suspended death sentence (29)	Question sentence (on juveniles) (5)
3	Netizen interactions (4)	Support defendant (6)	Against family planning office personnel (54)	Against both defendant and victim (8)	Demand death sentence (25)	On children from a challenged background (3)

Table 1.—(continued)

(November)

4	Causes of crime (2)	Against defendant (6)	Against defendant (51)	Share feelings (7)	Question deceased prison guard (16)	Question reporting (2)
5	Share feelings (2)	Question death sentence (5)	Question "social maintenance fees" (26)	On background of both defendant and victim (6)	Case comparisons (8)	Regional discrimination (2)
6	Jokes (2)	Regional/national discrimination (4)	Question birth control policy (16)	Support death sentence (4)	Support death sentence (7)	Jokes (1)
7	Victim's fault (1)	Support death sentence (3)	Question death sentence (14)	Lessons (4)	Jokes (6)	On organ donation (1)
8	Lessons (1)	Against defendant's self-surrender (2)	Jokes (13)	Question death sentence (3)	Question prison management (6)	Life imprisonment without possibility of parole (1)
9	Suggestions (1)	Death justifications (2)	Support defendant's children (11)	On "the wealthy" (3)	(Many "5s")	On restitution (1)
10		(Many "1s")	Share feelings (11)	(Many "2s")		Demand death for all (1)

(November, continued)

Top Themes	Song Yongtian et al.	Liu Danao	Yang "x"ping et al.	Wu "x"hua	He Jian	Wang Baiyang
1	Support death sentence (14)	Netizen interactions (659)	Support death sentence (6)	Netizen interactions (89)	Against defendant (23)	Question police (9)
2	On deprivation of political rights (9)	Support defendant (536)	Netizen interactions (3)	Against defendant (45)	Netizen interactions (6)	Crime by law enforcement officers (4)
3	Netizen interactions (9)	Against forced relocation (270)	Question reporting (2)	Cursing (30)	Support death sentence (4)	Cursing (3)

(continues)

Table 1.—(*continued*)

(November, *continued*)

4	Demand death sentence for drug trafficking (3)	Against victims (127)	Question suspended death sentence (2)	Demand death sentence (18)	Cursing (4)	Against gambling (2)
5	Demand harsh punishment (3)	Question fairness (101)	Question delay (2)	Question crime cause (16)	Against government officials (3)	Demand accountability (2)
6	On telecommunication fraud by the Taiwanese (2)	Against defendant (74)	On restitution (2)	Support defendant (12)	Death justifications (3)	Share feelings (2)
7	Disbelief of death sentence (2)	Question verdict (70)	Demand sooner actions (1)	Death justifications (11)	(Many "2s")	Death justifications (2)
8	Regional discrimination (2)	Share feelings (69)	Demand death for all (1)	Against drug addicts (9)		Demand harsh punishment (2)
9	(Many "1s")	Defendants' mental problem (69)	Demand execution (1)	On defendant's mens rea (6)		Netizen interactions (2)
10		On "protection of private property" (62)		(Many "5s")		(Many "1s")

(December)

Top Themes	Wu Youxin et al.	Yang Ruixi	Lin Senhao	Zhang "x"yi	Li "xx"	Pan Guohui	Luo Xiaohua and Chen Rihong
1	Against criminals (25)	Netizen interactions (19)	Death justifications (1,582)	Netizen interactions (30)	Question judges (93)	Case comparisons (2)	Question suspended death sentence (80)
2	Support death sentence (22)	Against defendant (4)	Netizen interactions (1,579)	Support death sentence (9)	Netizen interactions (39)	Support death sentence (2)	Netizen interactions (45)
3	On movie *Blind Well* (17)	Share feelings (3)	Support death sentence (903)	Support victim's heroic behavior (8)	Question suspended death sentence (24)	Regional discrimination (1)	Question judges/court (36)

Table 1.—(continued)

(December)							
4	Netizen interactions (14)	Question delay (3)	Questioning verdict/sentence (647)	Death justifications (6)	Death justifications (21)	Suggestions (1)	Against criminals (21)
5	Cursing (11)	Lessons (2)	Against defendant (637)	Against defendant (5)	Question court (21)		Death justifications (16)
6	Call for "no appeals" (7)	Death justifications (2)	Sympathy for defendant (602)	Question victim's heroic behavior (4)	Support death sentence (19)		Question law/legal system (16)
7	Demand execution (6)	(Many "1s")	On victim/victim's family (580)	Execution suggestions (3)	Against defendant (18)		Question delay and low efficiency (15)
8	Execution suggestions (5)		On defendant's family (528)	(Many "2s")	Question law/law enforcement (13)		Cursing (11)
9	Death justifications (5)		Lessons and wishes (436)		Case comparisons (13)		Support death sentence (8)
10	Crime concerns (4)		Causes of crime (421)		Support prosecutor's protest (11)		Jokes (6) and call for "no appeals" (6)

(December, continued)

Top Themes	Li "x"	Jin Fusheng	Zhao Zihui	Li "x" (#2)	Yang Xueqi	Ou Changsheng
1	Against defendant's wife (2)	Support death sentence (46)	Against defense lawyers (37)	Support death sentence (2)	Question police (306)	Netizen interactions (33)
2	Explain law (1)	No harm of the innocent (18)	Support death sentence (32)	Question defendant's father (1)	Netizen interactions (140)	Against defendant (25)
3		Against defendant (21)	Netizen interactions (26)		Against defendant (130)	Support death sentence (18)

(continues)

Table 1.—(continued)

(December, continued)

4	Cursing (16)	No excuse of mental disorder (17)	Support death sentence (107)	On "wrong target" (15)
5	Netizen interactions (15)	Against mental disorder (15)	Demand accountability (71)	Death justifications (11)
6	Demand crime cause (14)	Against defendant (14)	Cursing (67)	Official corruption (9)
7	Death justifications (13)	Question law/legal system (13)	Regional discrimination (57)	Cursing (8)
8	Jokes (6)	Case comparisons (11)	Question school/principal (53)	Demand death sentence (5)
9	Demand accountability (5)	Death justifications (9)	Question reporting (33)	(Many "3s")
10	Share feelings (5)	Jokes (6)	Execution sooner (32)	

Netizens' Interactions

Netizens' interactions—that is, exchanges of comments by netizens—constituted a major, indeed the largest (measured by the total number), portion of netizens' comments. As shown in table 1, it was ranked a top ten theme in 52 cases (82.5% of all 63 cases). Different from other themes (all coded and grouped based on the content of netizens' comments), netizen interactions constituted a major theme by itself not because of its distinctive content but because of its unique form; it is among these exchanges of comments that we see true netizen interactions. Granted, netizen interactions can be and are indeed further coded based on the content of their discussions and included in our substantive analyses in this and subsequent chapters. Nevertheless, given its significance as a unique theme, a detailed analysis of netizens' interactions is presented in chapter 4. An examination of netizens' interactions displayed four general forms, including netizens' *raising questions and providing answers, counterarguments, concurring arguments,* and *personal attacks.* In netizens' questions and answers, one netizen would post a question and another would provide an answer. For instance, in the Wang Changping case (#19), Wang, a former police officer, colluded with others to manufacture narcotics (over 220 kilograms) and was sentenced to death. One netizen apparently asked about criminal behavior of Wang's accomplices who provided raw materials for drug manufacturing. Specifically, the netizen asked, "Is it legal to sell raw materials for narcotics manufacturing?" A second netizen followed the question and commented, "[If] the police commit no crimes, crime [rates] would drop by half." This reply sounded more like a separate comment rather than an answer to the original question. A third netizen provided a better answer and said, "These black sheep belong to the same group. They have worked together for years, with members from different backgrounds. [They] also colluded with corrupt officials who joined the group."

A total of 4,778 counterarguments were made in 50 cases (79.4% of all cases), constituting the largest proportion of netizen interactions in our sample. The popularity of counterarguments, which fundamentally reflects netizens' different views on each topic, shows one important feature of the diversity of netizens' comments: the "depth" of their comments. As the most extreme form of counterarguments, personal attacks were unfortunately very popular among Chinese netizens' comments. While counterarguments focused on the substance of netizens' arguments, personal attacks targeted individual netizens and often contained foul language and personal threats. To a large extent, the nature of online commentaries (e.g., anonymous, non-face-to-face communication, little consequences attached to one's inappropriate opinions and behaviors) seemingly encouraged netizens' use of personal attacks. A total of 2,057 comments of personal attacks were made in 37 cases (58.7% of all cases) in our sample, trailed only by the number of counterarguments. In comparison, concurrence occurred less frequently and often in simpler forms (e.g., short concurring phrases, a supportive emoticon). A total of 1,012 concurring comments were counted in 46 cases (73% of all cases). The substance of counterarguments, concurrence, and personal attacks is discussed in detail in chapter 4.

Opinions on Death Sentences

Since all cases involved death sentences, netizens' various opinions on death sentences made up a significant portion of their comments. Due to nuances, netizens' opinions on death sentences can be further grouped into several subcategories. First, many netizens *explicitly* supported the death sentence(s) in a particular case. As shown in table 1, supporting the death sentence ("support death sentence") was ranked a top ten theme in 44 cases (69.8% of all cases). Although it is likely that netizens who expressed specific rationales (see the discussion below and chapter 3) for an offender's death sentence could be supporters of the offender's death, we counted in this theme only comments in which support for an offender's death sentence was explicitly expressed (e.g., "Lin Senhao deserves to die," "I support the death sentence"). In the Huang Qinghen case (#2), for instance, Huang (a female) was involved in cross-border child abduction, as a result of which 22 children were abducted from Vietnam and sold to Guangdong province in China. As a principal offender, Huang was sentenced to death while some of her codefendants were spared. One netizen commented on the heinous nature of the crime and said, "Kidnapping children deserves a death sentence!" In the Zhai "x"de case (#9), Zhai (with a lengthy criminal record) tried to borrow 30 *yuan* from his neighbor Zhang. After being rejected, Zhai stabbed Zhang to death. One netizen condemned Zhai as a vicious criminal and lent support to Zhai's death sentence. Specifically, the netizen said, "A death sentence, [is] a correct decision. This maniac dares to rob and kill and has lost his humanity and must pay back with his own life!" In the Ruan Fangcheng case (#10), a case of drug trafficking, a netizen focused on the impact of the crime and said, "50 kilograms [are equivalent to] 100 *jin* (斤), which could destroy so many people and families. It is sufficient to sentence her [Ruan's] whole family to death." In the Wang Hua case (#25), a case involving criminal gangs, a netizen praised the judge and supported Wang's death sentence, saying, "Thumbs up for the judge (为法官点赞)!"

Second, many netizens demanded more death sentences ("demand death sentence"), executions, or sooner executions ("demand execution") in 14 cases in our sample (22.2% of all cases in table 1). In the Zhang Weilan et al. case (#20), Zhang colluded with 20 other codefendants to murder four miners in 2011 and 2012 and claimed fraudulent financial compensation of 1.8 million yuan. Outraged netizens expressed strong condemnation against all offenders, and many demanded a death sentence for all codefendants. One netizen asked, "Why sentenced only three to death? The fact that they committed multiple murders cannot warrant a death sentence for all! This is extremely heinous. [We] don't need to worry how the foreigners would look at China's death penalty now. 21 offenders [should be] all death-sentenced." In a similar fashion, Wu and his codefendants murdered three miners and claimed fraudulent compensation from 2009 to 2011 (Wu Youxin et al. case, #52). Netizens demanded executions and left comments such as "Criminals such as this one should all be sentenced to immediate execution, and [shall use] no suspended death sentences" and "Should affirm the original [death] sentence and carry out execution immediately against criminals who are utterly devoid of any conscience (丧尽天良)." Sometimes netizens called for mandatory death sentences for a particular crime, regardless of the specific circumstances of a case or a particular offender. For example, in the Song Yongtian et al. case (#46), involving Taiwanese drug traffickers, a netizen commented, "Drug trafficking is a felony everywhere in the world! An offender who traffics or possesses 50 grams of heroin or more should be sentenced to death! Knowingly committing a crime, death is not going to be regretted (死不足惜)!"

Third, as a top ten theme, netizens also demanded harsh punishment ("demand harsh punishment") in 10 cases (15.9% of all cases; table 1). In these cases they often questioned and challenged lenient sentences (including suspended death sentences) meted out by the courts and called for harsh(er) punishment. For example, the Tuo Heti et al. case (#6) involved eight terrorists who attacked the crowd at the Kunming railway station and killed 31 civilians. One netizen commented, "Punish criminals harshly, to provide us a peaceful and safe society." In particular, netizens expressed extreme outrage in cases in which released offenders committed new capital offenses. Seeing offenders' old criminal records and their new crimes, netizens strongly questioned decisions of offenders' parole release and its impact on their recidivism (see further discussion in chapter 5). A small but not insignificant number of netizens even called for the revival of ancient, outlawed execution methods to show their "tough stance" against criminals. In the Yuan Junkai et al. case (#12), defendants Yuan, Liu, and Wei all had lengthy criminal records before they were convicted of new crimes and death-sentenced. Yuan, in particular, received a suspended death sentence in 1989 and was paroled in 2007 before he committed another crime in 2012. One netizen called for the revival of ancient execution methods against such criminals and wrote, "[We] should govern society with harsh punishment and tough laws. Revive punishment such as branding one's face (黥面), public execution and body exposure (弃市), cutting one in half at the waist (腰斩), death by a thousand cuts (凌迟), and banishment (充边). [This will] make criminals scared so that their liver and gall are broken (肝胆俱裂) and they are in a constant state of anxiety (惶惶不可终日)."

Fourth, compared to netizens who lent explicit support for death sentences and called for tougher and harsher punishment, at least one netizen questioned and challenged a death sentence in 23 cases (35.6% of all cases; see chapter 3), though "questioning verdict/death sentence" was ranked a top ten theme only in ten cases (table 1). Netizens rejected death sentences/convictions in our sample due to a variety of reasons, including concerns about potential wrongful convictions, the "fairness" of a particular death sentence, sympathy for a defendant given circumstances of a particular case and defendant, and netizens' general questions on law and law enforcement (see chapter 3). In a few cases, netizens rejected death sentences because of their strong criticism of and challenge to existing governmental policies or practices such as the one-child birth control policy (He Shenguo case, #42), China's health-care system and medical malpractices (Lian Enqing case, #14) and the demolition and relocation policy (Liu Danao case, #47) (see chapter 7). Last but not least, a small but not insignificant number of netizens called for outright abolition of capital punishment in 14 cases (22.2% of all cases). Abolition supporters made a number of arguments, including but not limited to the following: (1) the use of capital punishment is no longer acceptable given modern-day civilization; (2) it is rejected by the larger international community; (3) it is, as a form of killing itself, a violation of human rights; (4) it should be replaced with life imprisonment, which serves better utility (e.g., deterrence); (5) abolition would be of great comfort to offenders' family members and friends; and (6) abolition would leave room for offender reformation. Nevertheless, these arguments were countered by abolition opponents (see the discussion in chapter 3). Note that in table 1, netizens' comments against abolition ("against abolition") were ranked a top ten theme in two cases, but the voice of abolition was too weak by comparison to be a top-ranked theme. Netizens' rejection of death sentences (vs. support of death sentences) and their call for abolition (vs. rejection of abolition) again reflected both the breadth and depth of netizens' diverse opinions.

Fifth, it is noticeable that one means through which netizens questioned and challenged court sentencing is case comparison. Such comparisons ("case comparisons") were ranked a top theme in 12 cases of our sample (19% of all cases; table 1). In such comparisons, netizens compared multiple offenders in the same case and challenged their disparate sentencing; more frequently, netizens compared offenders in different cases who committed the same or similar types of crimes but received different punishment; some netizens also compared different crimes and argued that punishment with one crime was unreasonably harsher or lighter than another. Besides domestic case comparisons, some netizens turned to practices in other nations for comparisons ("other nations' systems," table 1) and such international comparisons not only covered issues of sentencing, punishment, and legal procedures but also issues unique to a particular case (e.g., the health-care system in the Lian Enqing [#14] and Wang Gang [#13] cases). Case comparison is a strong indicator of netizens' rational deliberation given its inherent logic, despite the fact that netizens could have reached different conclusions with the same case comparison (see chapter 8). Arguably, it is the most straightforward means for Chinese netizens to see justice in action and compare disparate results of different cases.

Rationales for Death Sentences

Netizens' rationales (i.e., justifications) for death sentences constituted another significant portion of their comments, and as a theme ("death justifications") it was ranked a top theme in 36 cases (57.1% of all cases; table 1). We reserve this important topic to chapter 3 and analyze in detail various rationales explicitly expressed by Chinese netizens in their support of or opposition to death sentences (and China's use of the death penalty in general). For death penalty supporters, major rationales include but are not limited to retribution, deterrence, justice/law requirement, just desert, payback as individual responsibility, social impact (in particular, concerns about public indignation), public order and safety, and respect for lives. In contrast, opponents of death sentences countered and questioned arguments about retribution, deterrence, and public indignation. In addition, as mentioned above, they expressed concerns about fairness of the law and the legal system and wrongful convictions, and some even called for outright abolition. These diverse and sometimes opposing views once again reflect both the breadth and the depth of netizens' opinions.

Opinions on Parties Involved in Death Penalty Cases

Besides their opinions on death sentences and corresponding rationales, netizens' comments focused on a number of key parties involved in death penalty cases. First, as capital offenders, *defendants* were a primary focus of netizens' discussions. As shown in table 1, support and sympathy for defendants ("support defendant" and "sympathy for defendant") was ranked a top ten theme in nine cases (14.3% of all cases). In contrast, the majority of comments on defendants were against them, and such comments ("against defendant") were ranked a top theme in 36 cases (57.1% of all cases). Often, netizens' attitudes toward and comments on defendants were specifically tailored to unique circumstances of each case. In the Sun Zhifu case (#17), for example, due to conflicts with her in-laws, Sun murdered a five-year-old boy and tried to commit suicide by poisoning before police arrived but was saved. Sun's mental disorder was one major issue in this case, though the court ruled that her diagnosed schizophrenia was not severe enough to warrant a reduced sentence. Two netizens commented on Sun's mental disorder specifically. One questioned her mental condition and said, "With mental disorder, she knew how to hide the body and lose all traces (藏尸灭迹), and knew how to commit suicide to escape the punishment (畏罪自杀). . . . It must be that [her mental disorder] was not severe enough." Another echoed that attitude and supported Sun's death sentence, saying, "Her mental condition was normal at the time of murder. A death sentence is correct." Though with only two comments, it was ranked a top theme given the overall small number of comments in this case. In two cases (Jin Fusheng, #59; Ou Changsheng, #63) in which offenders' criminal actions apparently resulted in the death or injury of innocent civilians, netizens openly condemned offenders' crimes against the "wrong targets" (e.g., "This is not heroic. Why targeted ordinary people? Coward, deserve to die!"), and some even encouraged actions against government officials (e.g., "Coward, son of a bitch, you would be a hero if you bomb several corrupt officials").

Whether a defendant can draw sympathy from the netizens depends on the unique circumstances of the case. In the famous Lin Senhao case (#1), Lin was convicted of poisoning his roommate Huang Yang and sentenced to death. Though not the only factor, Lin's status as a highly educated student at a nationally known university gained him much sympathy from many netizens (see chapter 9). Netizens explicitly expressed sympathy for Lin in 757 comments (vs. 53 comments in which netizens explicitly rejected such sympathy) and explicitly called for leniency in 559 comments (vs. 198 comments in which leniency was explicitly rejected). Netizens' call for leniency ("ask for leniency") was ranked a top ten theme in both January and May, respectively, as a result (see table 1). In contrast, in three other cases (Zhao Zhihong, #4; Huang Qinghen, #2; Ruan Fangcheng, #10), netizens explicitly rejected calls for leniency for defendants, and such rejection ("No leniency") was ranked a top theme accordingly.

It is also interesting to note that Chinese netizens often speculated on the socioeconomic backgrounds of defendants and victims and believed that a person with a powerful connection would be able to influence the outcome of a case in China or vice versa, that a powerless defendant would bear the brunt of the use of capital punishment (see the discussion in chapter 5). In the Chen Yun case (#31), Chen was death-sentenced due to his drunk driving, which killed six people. Though Chen's family compensated his victims' families by paying them over 130,000 yuan, he was executed. Netizens left nine comments in this case to lament Chen's lack of powerful connection and background and implied that because of his powerlessness, Chen was death-sentenced and executed. One netizen commented, for instance, "Heh-heh [sound mimicking a sneer], it is a pity that you were not born in Nanjing,[1] and you have no money or connection." Another said, "In China, no money and connection. Drunk-driving and killed six. If you are not death-sentenced, who would be!" In the Wang Yihuan case (#43), defendant Wang stabbed victim Ye to death. Wang was a former member of the political consultation committee of the Liunan district in Liuzhou city, and Ye was a people's representative of the Liunan district. Netizens specifically discussed the background and connections of both Wang and Ye and suggested that Ye's political status might have negated the potential influence of Wang's political status, a reason why Wang was death-sentenced. In both cases, netizens' comments on the

---

1. The netizen was referring to a hit-and-run case in Nanjing. In this case, a BMW vehicle running at a speed close to 200 kilometers per hour crashed into another vehicle and killed two passengers in 2015. The driver, Wang Jijin (王季进), fled the crime scene and was arrested soon after. In 2017 Wang was convicted of endangerment of public safety and sentenced to 11 years of imprisonment. The most controversial issue of the case was related to Wang's psychiatric problem. Two separate evaluations after the accident suggested that Wang suffered from an "acute and transient psychotic disorder (急性短暂性精神障碍)" at the moment of his crime, which might have influenced the final sentencing of the court. This "Nanjing BMW" case was very popular and cited numerous times by netizens in our sample (see chapter 8). To the majority of netizens, the sentence showed inappropriate handling of a case by the Chinese judiciary, who meted out a punishment that was too lenient. Often netizens compared this case to other cases (e.g., the Chen Yun case) in which defendants received much harsher punishment in order to question the fairness of judicial sentencing.

defendant's and victim's backgrounds (or lack of thereof) were ranked a top ten theme (table 1).

Second, a *defendant's family or family members* could be in the spotlight from time to time. In the Lin Senhao case (#1), Lin's family, led by his father, desperately tried everything to save Lin's life and did not give up until his execution. Lin's opponents argued that his family was indeed responsible for their failed parental education (which led to Lin's bad personal character and his eventual crime) and criticized Lin's father's "not my fault and no apology" approach in defending Lin. Some even argued that Lin's father was morally worse than Lin Senhao and called for legal punishment against the Lins for their relentless appeals (which, in the eyes of Lin's opponents, were seen as an abuse of the legal system). In contrast, supporters of Lin's father argued that he did everything that a good father is supposed to do and that his desperate rescue effort, though to no avail, was both legally permitted and morally acceptable. Some expressed great sympathy for Lin's family and pointed out that Lin's parents were victims of his crime as well (see further discussion in chapter 9). Netizens' different positions strengthened both the breadth and the depth of their discussions, as their comments on Lin's family were ranked a top theme in all four months when Lin's case was reported on (see table 1). In a number of other cases, comments on the defendant's immediate or remote family members also broke into the top ten themes, though they were not as dramatic as in the Lin Senhao case. In the Feng Xiujuan case (#32), for instance, Feng reportedly had an affair with her first love and asked for a divorce but was rejected by her husband. She drowned her five-year-old daughter and four-year-old son, strangled to death another eight-year-old daughter, and then tried to commit suicide but survived. Although the majority of netizens condemned Feng for her crime, a number of netizens blamed Feng's husband for the tragic crimes and argued that her husband should have divorced Feng and let her go. Some pointed their fingers at Feng's first love (e.g., "The tragedy was caused by the paramour (奸夫), who should be found guilty [of a crime]"). Both themes ("question defendant's husband" and "against defendant's paramour") were ranked among the top ten in this case. In the He Shenguo case (#42), after his request to register his fourth child was denied by a local registration office due to violation of China's one-child birth control policy, He killed two office workers there with a knife and injured four others. He was sentenced to death and executed. Angry with He's over-quota births, a few netizens left five comments to call for legal punishment against He's children. Fortunately, these were countered by 11 comments supporting He's children, which was ranked a top ten theme in this case.

Third, netizens' comments covered *victims* from time to time. In six cases (9.5% of all cases; table 1), netizens' comments to show their concerns about victims ("for victims") were ranked a top theme; in five cases (7.9% of all cases), netizens left comments against victims ("against victim"), which were ranked a top ten theme. Again, netizens' comments were tailored to unique circumstances of each case. In the Hu "x" case (#7), for instance, Hu detained victim Zhang for over 80 days and eventually drowned Zhang in a lake. Hu's crime was triggered by Zhang's refusal to repay debts owed to Hu (estimated at tens of millions of yuan). The most popular theme of the case, surprisingly, was netizens' comments against Zhang for his refusal to repay debts (26 comments), which might have shown the impact of commercialization in contemporary China (see the discussion in chapter 7). In the Ling Ruiming case (#41), Ling married a Vietnamese lady named Ruan who often lived in other places, using the excuse of work, and there was suspicion that Ruan had committed marriage fraud for money. Enraged, Ling killed Ruan and two of her lady friends and was sentenced to death. The most popular theme in this case was netizens' criticism of the victim, Ruan, as they believed she was at fault for committing marriage fraud. Relative to crime victims, *victims' families* were occasionally reported and rarely focused on in netizens' discussion. The only exception was the Lin Senhao case (#1), in which offender Lin's family and victim Huang Yang's family were often pitched side by side for contrast by the media and thus discussed by netizens (see chapter 9).

Fourth, besides offenders, victims, and their families, an important party in each case was *defense lawyers*. Though netizens' (negative) comments on defense or defense lawyers were ranked a top ten theme in merely two cases in table 1, netizens explicitly discussed the performance of defense lawyers in nine cases in our sample (14.3% of all cases). In six cases, netizens supported lawyers' criminal defense right, and in seven cases netizens questioned and criticized lawyers' defense. The balance was tipped, however, when the total numbers of comments were compared: netizens left a total of 673 negative comments against lawyers, while the number of positive comments was 133, a ratio of roughly 5 to 1. First and foremost, Chinese netizens questioned defense lawyers' morality and believed defense lawyers took on heinous capital cases only for money or fame; many actually launched personal attacks and threats against defense lawyers. Furthermore, netizens questioned defense lawyers' legal strategies. For instance, many pointed out that the "not guilty" defense strategy utilized in the Lin Senhao case (#1) doomed the fate of Lin from the very beginning; they believed that Lin's life might have been spared if the defense were to plead guilty, show sincere remorse, and provide sufficient financial compensation to victim Huang's family (see chapter 9). In contrast, supporters of criminal defense, constituting a minority, all believed in one's fundamental defense rights and lawyers' professional duty to maximize their clients' best interests, even if the clients are capital offenders. It is evident that opponents and supporters of criminal defense held very different views on what proper functions lawyers should and can perform in capital cases in China (see further discussion in chapter 6). It is also noticeable that a small group of netizens openly preached about forgoing proper legal proceedings required by laws. For instance, in the Wu Youxin et al. case (#52), mentioned earlier, Wu and his codefendants murdered three miners and claimed fraudulent compensations from 2009 to 2011. Seven comments called for "no appeal right" for the convicted offenders, a top ten theme in this case (table 1). Different from one's dissatisfaction with extended delays of legal proceedings, we argue that netizens' preaching about forgoing required legal procedures to expedite the legal process and hasten a defendant's death is an irrational behavior (to be detailed in chapter 8).

Fifth, occasionally, netizens' comments focused on various other *third parties* involved in a case. For example, in seven cases (11.1% of all cases; table 1), as a top theme, netizens demanded accountability of relevant parties given the unique circumstances of each case. Two of these cases (Zhao Zhihong, #4; Wu Qinyuan, #11) involved infamous wrongful convictions. Netizens not only expressed deep concerns about wrongful convictions and showed their care for the wrongfully convicted, but they also demanded actions to hold responsible people who were in charge of such wrongful conviction cases. In the Yuan Junkai et al. case (#12), mentioned earlier, Yuan received a suspended death sentence in 1989 and was paroled in 2007 before he committed another capital crime in 2012. Angry about Yuan's new crime and the decision about his parole, netizens pointed their fingers at judges and parole decision makers and demanded to hold them responsible. In the Yang Dazhi case (#21), Yang took advantage of his position as the principal of an elementary school in Guizhou province and molested and raped six students from 2010 to 2014. Reportedly, Yang's family members and the local government officials tried to settle his crimes via financial compensations for his victims. Outraged netizens demanded legal actions against such parties. In the Yang Xueqi case (#62), Yang committed a series of rapes from 1998 to 2012. Many netizens questioned the extended crime duration, blamed incompetence of the police, and demanded actions against responsible parties. Two other special groups of people singled out by Chinese netizens included legal experts and public intellectuals. Both groups were blamed by netizens for their "bad" input and influence over lawmaking, their efforts to promote more legal protections for criminals, and their calls for more lenient and humane punishment—in particular, abolition of capital punishment (see the discussion in chapter 6).

Opinions on China's Law and Legal System and Its Professionals

As death penalty cases involved critical decisions by professionals of China's criminal justice system, netizens' comments also focused on China's law, legal system, and practitioners. In seven cases (11.1% of all cases; table 1), netizens' questions on the law and legal system were ranked a top ten theme. The vast majority of such comments questioned China's laws as being too "soft" on criminals and demanded tougher punishment. Further, netizens questioned the fairness and equity of China's legal system and argued that the system often favors privileged classes (e.g., government officials). In the Peng Shu and Hu Haolong case (#3), netizens questioned laws against corrupt officials (as being too lenient) and demanded harsher punishment. One netizen wrote, for example, "Law against corruption is too lenient. If a death sentence is meted out to anyone who accepts bribe money over 100 million yuan, you will see who dares corruption? It is that the law is too lenient." Another concurred, saying, "Chinese laws are too lenient when used against corrupt officials and much heavier against ordinary people. Time to think about it." The Xiao "x" et al. case (#37) involved drug trafficking. Defendant Xiao and a codefendant were sentenced to death with immediate execution, 5 others received suspended death sentences, and 13 others were sentenced to various non-death prison terms. Again, netizens questioned the law and law enforcement. One netizen commented, "Our nation being so chaotic, it is not certain but a fact (不是一定的而是肯定的). There is something wrong with policy [making]. I suspect that some governmental lawmakers are trafficking drugs and bullying ordinary people to death (欺压百姓致死), and this is why they make such laws." In the Li "xx" case (#55), one netizen expressed concern about the influence of one's wealth and power over law enforcement and put it bluntly: "Laws are made for the wealthy. The 'have-not (穷鬼); out of the way." In the Zhao Zihui case (#60), Zhao attacked 18 people with his knife and caused six deaths. Zhao's defense tried to claim Zhao's psychiatric history as legal mitigation, but the argument was rejected by the court. Netizens left 13 comments to question legally stipulated lenient punishment for people with mental illness. One netizen commented, "[Zhao's] lawyer did not do anything wrong. The key is that the law should stipulate that [criminals with] mental disorder be punished more harshly (罪加一定). It is mental disorder, not God. Why should the criminal be exempted?"

A significant number of netizens' comments were specifically addressed to professionals of China's criminal justice system, including but not limited to judges/courts, police/policing, and corrections/correctional personnel. As shown in table 1, in three cases, netizens' questions on courts/judges/judicial justice were ranked a top theme; in four cases, netizens' questions on police and policing were ranked a top theme; in one case (Gao Yulun et al. case, #44), three inmates broke out of their prison and killed a guard. Netizens questioned management of that particular prison ("question prison management") and the careless (mis)handling of security procedures by the deceased prison guard ("question prison guard"), both of which were ranked top themes of the case. Though some netizens lent their support to professionals (e.g., to appraise their work) from time to time, the majority of netizens' comments questioned the performance of professionals (e.g., judges' wrong decisions and meting out lenient sentences, police officers' low efficiency, incapability of correctional facilities/officers in reforming offenders and reducing recidivism), corruption at various levels, and even crimes by the professionals (e.g., the police). (Given its salience and significance, we reserve further analysis of netizens' opinions on China's criminal justice system and its professionals to chapter 6.)

In addition to their comments on China's law, legal system, and professionals, Chinese netizens expressed a number of specific concerns based on circumstances of cases that were ranked top themes in our sample. First, a significant number of netizens opined about the appeal process in death penalty cases. As the appeals were prolonged, netizens often expressed their frustration with the extended delays and waste of resources. In eight cases (12.7% of all cases; table 1), netizens' questions on *delay and waste* was ranked a top theme, and they demanded more expedient actions. As mentioned earlier, a small number of netizens even openly called for forgoing proper legal proceedings required by the law, such as doing away with one's appeal right. Second, netizens expressed serious concerns about *wrongful convictions*, given the salience of such an issue in recent decades (e.g., J. He 2016). Besides two cases (Zhao Zhihong, #4; Wu Qinyuan, #11) that directly involved wrongful convictions, netizens also expressed deep concerns about wrongful convictions in other non–wrongful conviction cases. In their comments, netizens shared their worries about proper functioning of the criminal justice system, expressed their sympathy for the wrongfully convicted, condemned the real culprit, and demanded accountability (e.g., punish parties who "caused" such wrongful convictions). Third, *questioning fairness* of the legal system (e.g., sentencing, law enforcement) was another major theme. In two cases, questioning fairness was ranked a top theme. In the Lin "x"ping and Ye "x"tian case (#16), three drug offenders were executed. Netizens left 173 comments criticizing sentencing fairness, the second top-ranked theme in this case (trailed only by netizen interactions). One netizen, for example, compared drug trafficking to other crimes and wrote, "Fucked. Is this [drug trafficking] more serious than children abduction and trafficking? Than murder and arson? Than a people's representative stabbing the victim scores of times?[2] Than compulsory acquisition of land which led to human death? If [people] with three kilograms [of drugs] and merely a few hundred grams of sales were [all] death-sentenced, China would have five times as many death row inmates!" In the Liu Danao case (#47), once again, fairness of the law and law enforcement was a primary focal point among netizens' discussions, with 101 comments. As Liu's case involved the disfavored "demolition and relocation" policy, netizens overwhelmingly lent their support to defendant Liu and questioned Liu's verdict and death sentence (see chapter 7). Besides these two cases, netizens' questions on the fairness of the system permeated in many other cases, mainly via netizens' case comparisons as discussed earlier (under the section titled "Opinions on Death Sentences"). Often, it was through case comparisons that netizens contrasted their demand for equal treatment with the reality of contemporary Chinese society, in which unequal treatment between privileged classes and powerless groups was witnessed. In addition, as mentioned earlier,

---

2. The netizen was referring to the Xu Qingyi case cited in note 9 in chapter 8. An official and local people's representative in the Inner Mongolia Autonomous Region, Xu got into a fight with a villager and stabbed the victim 66 times with a knife, killing him. Xu was convicted of murder and received a suspended death sentence.

netizens' speculation (factually founded or unfounded) that a person's background and connection would make a real difference in the outcome of a case was another example of their disbelief of equality and fairness in the existing system.

Opinions on Chinese Government and Its Officials and Policies

Though all of our cases were death penalty cases, netizens' discussions sometimes went beyond the scope of the criminal justice system and covered other general issues involving the Chinese government, its officials, and policies. One salient example is corruption. In four cases, netizens' discussion on corruption was ranked a top ten theme (table 1). Besides two cases that directly involved official corruption (Peng Shu and Hu Haolong, #3; Gu Junshan, #26), netizens shared their thoughts on corruption in many non-corruption cases. With a few exceptions, Chinese netizens lent overwhelming support to anticorruption actions and often demanded harsh(er) punishment against corrupt officials (see chapter 5). Occasionally, netizens raised questions about a particular system or practice that exposed the problem of corruption. For instance, in the Peng Shu and Hu Haolong case (#3), Peng and Hu were in charge of the highway system in Hunan province and reportedly received bribes of 188 and 170 million yuan, respectively, from 2002 to 2010. Besides condemning Peng and Hu, many netizens posted more general questions about managing highway systems in China and made constructive suggestions accordingly; their discussion on China's highway system was indeed the top-ranked theme of the case.

In four cases, though in small numbers, netizens' questions on government and government officials (e.g., "question government and officials," "against government officials") were ranked top themes (table 1). In the Yang Xueqi case (#62), mentioned earlier, Yang committed a series of rapes from 1998 to 2012, and many of his victims were school students. Netizens were outraged by such an extended crime duration, questioned the security measures of schools, and demanded accountability of school officials in 53 comments (a top-ranked theme in this case). One netizen commented, "The security of the school is horrendous, as the criminal suspect could come and go at will." Another concurred: "XX middle school in Changge [city] is almost a reservation (自留地) of this criminal. One crime a month, and sometimes the victims were twice assaulted, every time at will [of the criminal]. [The school] adopted no security measures?" In addition, netizens left 19 comments that questioned the competence of the local government and government officials, such as "Local government and police, an utmost disgrace (丢人是丢到家了)" and "I truly don't know what government officials in Changge [city] were doing (是干什么吃的), speechless!"

Often netizens' comments and discussions of a particular case were embedded in bigger social, systemic, and structural problems. As a matter of fact, the cases in our data that generated the most heated discussions were often those that reflected acute social, systemic, and structural problems of contemporary Chinese society. We reserve discussion of this important topic for chapter 7, which examines the influence of commercialization and power of money (e.g., Hu "x" case, #7); social unrest (e.g., Tuo Heti et al., #6; Wang Hua, #25); power abuse and corruption (e.g., Peng Shu and Hu Haolong, #3); and several disfavored governmental policies, including the one-child birth-control policy (He Shenguo, #42), China's health-care system and practice (Lian Enqing, #14; Wang Gang, #13), and China's demolition and relocation policy and practice (Liu Danao, #47). Netizens' discussions of social problems and their challenge and critique to governmental policies demonstrated not only their keen awareness and active examination of such issues but also their proactive and occasionally bold actions online (though on a limited scale).

On Netizens' Self-Reflections and Unique Features of Online Discussions

Another significant portion of netizens' comments can be lumped together and loosely labeled "netizens' self-reflections." First, netizens openly shared many personal feelings based on what they read from the reported stories. In 17 cases (30.0% of all cases), netizens' *shared feelings* (感叹) was ranked a top-theme (table 1). The content of netizens' shared feelings was very diverse, subject to the unique circumstances of the reported case and various reactions of netizens. Take the Li Lei case (#28), for example. Due to reasons that were unreported, the defendant, Li, murdered his wife, two sons, his younger sister, and his parents in 2009. He was convicted of homicide and subsequently executed in 2011. An inheritance lawsuit (involving an eight-million-yuan legacy) was filed by four surviving relatives afterward, and the people's court in the Daxing district (in Beijing) ruled over this civil lawsuit, which was reported on in August 2015. Seeing

Li's family members fighting over his legacy, netizens shared their feelings in 13 comments. One lamented the tragedy and said, "The death of family members cannot compete with millions of yuan." In the Liu Danao case (#47), Liu drove his vehicle into relocation workers and killed four of them when they tried to carry out demolition and relocation by force. Liu was sentenced to death. Besides being overwhelmingly supportive of Liu (see chapter 7), netizens shared their feelings in 69 comments. One netizen commented on the fierce competition by different parties involved and wrote, "This is society. Humans eat humans. It's likely that some people cannot even figure out who eats whom." In the He Shenguo case (#42), discussed earlier, being sympathetic to He, one netizen commented, "This is what people normally say, 'when desperate, even rabbits would bite people!'" Netizens' shared feelings were popular on two specific topics. One was their lament that a particular offender's regret was coming too late. This "too late to regret" theme, typified by the Chinese phrase "If I had known it would come to this, I would have done things differently (早知今日何必当初)," was ranked a top theme in two cases (Lin "x"ping and Ye "x"tian, #16; Yang Chaoquan, #33). For instance, in the Yang Chaoquan case (#33), one netizen commented, "Too late to regret. *Sharen changming* [a life for a life, see chapter 3]. It is all fate." The other popular topic for netizens' shared feelings was on offenders' "last words." Many of the reported last words contained defendants' regrets and their deep feelings for family members. Thus, one popular Chinese phrase about defendants' last kind words was "When a man is near death, he speaks from his heart (人之将死其言也善)." In the Yang Chaoquan case, one netizen commented on Yang's last words, "When a man is near death, he speaks from his heart. [Say] goodbye to misfortune (再见不幸)."

Second, many netizens reflected on the *lessons* people should have learned from death penalty cases. In nine cases (14.3% of all cases; table 1), lessons drawn by netizens were ranked a top theme. Again, lessons drawn by netizens were diverse, subject to the influence of specific circumstances of the case and netizens' reactions. In the Zhai "x"de case (#9), previously mentioned, Zhai killed his neighbor Zhang with a knife after his request to borrow 30 yuan was rejected. Reportedly, Zhai was a drug addict, which might be a reason for his attempted borrowing. One netizen drew a lesson from the case and said, "Stay away from drugs and cherish [your] life. Once addicted, [one] would completely lose one's human dignity." Another netizen, in contrast, apparently drew a lesson from the victim's perspective and said very succinctly, "Being unyielding is the root of one's trouble (刚强是惹祸之根)." In the Wang Yihuan case (#43), discussed earlier, despite defendant Wang's former membership with the local political consultation committee, Wang was death-sentenced for killing victim Ye, who was a local people's representative. Again, netizens drew different lessons. One netizen said, "It's all because [he] acted on a sudden impulse (一时冲动惹锝祸)." Another said, "Fucked, It's all because of money (他妈的都是钱惹锝祸)."

Third, in many cases, netizens were able to relate what happened in a particular case to their own lives and experiences, and many actively shared their stories. In the Deng "x" case (#40), Deng and his victim, Li (Deng's coworker), got into a fight because Deng did not attend the wedding of Li's daughter due to concerns about wedding gifts. Deng temporarily lost his sanity in a verbal fight and stabbed Li and Li's wife, Luo. Li died at a hospital and Deng was death-sentenced. A number of netizens subsequently criticized the Chinese wedding gift tradition and shared their thoughts and experiences in nine comments. Though a small number, it was ranked the top theme of the case. In the Lian Enqing case (#14), Lian continuously complained about a nasal surgery he received from a local hospital in which he did not receive satisfactory results. Lian eventually lost his composure, went to the hospital, and stabbed three doctors in 2013, one of whom died. Lian was death-sentenced and executed. Nevertheless, the majority of netizens actually supported Lian (see chapter 7), and numerous netizens related his case to their personal negative experiences with doctors or hospitals and shared their stories.

Besides these self-reflections, netizens' online discussions seemingly propelled a few unique features given the nature of the anonymous, non-face-to-face interactions. First, the use of *jokes* was very popular even among discussions of serious capital cases. In 21 cases (33.3% of all cases; table 1), netizens' jokes were ranked a top theme. The substance of netizens' jokes varied greatly. For instance, as described earlier, the Wang Changping case (#19) involved a former police officer who masterminded narcotics manufacturing. Netizens made jokes in 12 comments in this case. One netizen said, "A police officer sentenced to death? The court dared to attack the police. Shoot [the court] to death (毙了)." Another joked, "The government made a wrong decision on this matter. It should be [found as] cooperation between the police and citizens to manufacture flour, which reflected the mass-line policy of the Party to create an official-civilian harmonious situation!" Yet another said, "Manufacturing [drugs] for sale makes money; arresting those who purchase drugs for consumption makes fines. This is a 'win-win' deal."

Second, *use of foul language* was a huge part of netizens' comments and could be directed against any party. In appendix 5, we created a select list of foul words from netizens' comments. As shown in appendix 3, we counted a total of 9,594 comments with foul language based on the list (representing 24.8% of the total number of comments) in 50 cases (79.4% of all cases). It seems that netizens' online discussions aggravated the use of foul language, though such use was almost completely counterproductive in its effect. (We provide a detailed analysis of netizens' use of foul language in chapter 4.) Third, similar to the use of foul language, *cursing* was also popular among netizens' comments. In 18 cases (28.6% of all cases; table 1), cursing was ranked a top theme. Despite its popularity online, we argue that except for venting one's anger, cursing served no other valid purposes and would not help facilitate netizens' communications, and thus is a form of irrational behavior (see chapter 8).

Miscellaneous Themes

In addition to the major themes categorized above, netizens reported many other comments in our sample. Not being able to further group all of them, some major themes with high frequencies (measured by their counts) are briefly discussed below.

First, as critical as they were, a significant number of Chinese netizens made *suggestions* based on specific issues involved in a particular case. In table 1, making suggestions ("suggestions") was ranked a top theme in nine cases (14.3% of all cases), and in 13 other cases, netizens also made various suggestions (though not ranked a top theme). Netizens' suggestions were diverse and tailored to specific issues of a particular case and could be both constructive and destructive. Sometimes facing the same issue, netizens proposed different and even conflicting solutions and suggestions. We argue that making constructive suggestions is a rational online behavior and should be encouraged, as it requires netizens' logical analyses of issues and often critical thinking to propose good solutions (see chapter 8).

Second, if making constructive suggestions represented rational deliberation by netizens, their *discriminatory comments* would be irrational by both the flawed logic and derogatory nature of such comments. In our sample, we witnessed various forms of discrimination (see chapter 8). Among them, the most popular was regional discrimination (地域歧视). Regional discrimination often occurred when a netizen saw the reported hometown of a criminal (or place of the crime) and then generalized the issue to all people from the region, thus showing signs of being irrational. Netizens' discriminatory regional comments were so widespread geographically and targeted people from not only "infamous" and poor regions such as Guizhou and Henan but also prosperous and leading provinces such as Beijing, Shanghai, and Guangdong. Related to regional discrimination, another popular form of discrimination focused on villagers (农民), especially villagers from poor regions. Netizens' derogatory remarks against villagers mainly focused on their moral character flaws (e.g., being dishonest) and crimes (e.g., being crime-prone due to poverty). In contrast, racial, ethnic, and national discrimination rarely occurred. Blacks were targeted in a few racially motivated remarks, and the majority of national discriminatory comments were made against Japanese people, though a few other nations (e.g., India, Vietnam) were targeted as well. Sex and sexual orientation discrimination occasionally surfaced in six cases in which women and homosexuals were blamed for their abnormal (e.g., unladylike) behaviors and crimes based on dominant social norms. In all forms of discrimination, besides unfoundedly generalizing a particular case to a whole class of people, discriminatory remarks often used derogatory or insulting language to attack others, a strong indication of irrationality (see chapter 8).

Third, *question reporting* was also a popular theme among our cases. In 11 cases (17.5% of all cases; table 1), netizens' questioning of reporting was ranked a top ten theme. In another 25 cases, though not ranked a top theme, netizens also questioned and challenged media reporting of the case in point. On the one hand, netizens' questions and challenges of media reporting were critical and comprehensive, catching not only typos and misused terms but also substantive errors of the reports. Moreover, many netizens expressed worries about the way a story was reported and its potential impact on the audience. On the other hand, netizens openly demanded more reporting when they were puzzled by incomplete reporting and unexplained facts. It is interesting to see Chinese netizens demand more information and transparency with a high degree of distrust and suspicion, a potential feature of Chinese netizens' scrutiny in the age of the internet (see chapter 5).

Fourth, in five cases (7.9% of all cases; table 1), netizens' discussion of potential *causes of crime* in a particular case was ranked a top ten theme. In the Lin Senhao case (#1), for instance, netizens' discussion about causes of Lin's poisoning was ranked a top theme in three of the four months in which Lin's case was reported (i.e., January, August, and December). Besides saying it was Lin's own fault, some netizens blamed Lin's parents for their failed parental education, which led to Lin's character flaw (e.g., being selfish and indifferent to others' interests); some targeted Lin's education background as a master's student at a nationally known university and argued that Lin's crime showed potential flaws of the Chinese educational system (e.g., schools aimed only at academic achievement without proper teaching of morality and values); some blamed bad influence of contemporary Chinese society (e.g., societal pressure to become successful by fair means or foul); some attributed Lin's crime to the fault of the victim, Huang (e.g., Huang's bullying triggered Lin's crime); some partially blamed Lin's school (e.g., the school should have taken proactive measures to prevent harmful behaviors such as retaliation by roommates who do not get along) or the hospital where Huang died (e.g., some netizens suspected medical misdiagnosis and mistreatment by doctors as Huang struggled for 15 days before he passed away). Needless to say, netizens holding different views debated over the "real cause(s)," reflecting both the breadth and the depth of their discussion (see chapter 9).

Last but not least, some top themes loomed unexpectedly in a few cases. For instance, in two cases in which criminals murdered miners to claim fraudulent financial compensation (Zhang Weilan et al., #20; Wu Youxin et al., #52), some netizens brought up the movie *Blind Well* (盲井) in their discussion. The movie tells a story in which two criminals planned mine "accidents" to kill innocent miners and claim fraudulent financial compensation, thus mirroring the true crimes in these two cases. In both cases, netizens' discussion of the movie was unexpectedly ranked a top theme. In the Wang Changping case (#19), cited earlier, a former police officer, Wang masterminded narcotics manufacturing. Netizens brought up the American TV series *Breaking Bad* in 11 comments, a top-ranked theme of the case. In the Song Yongtian et al. case (#46), a case involving Taiwanese drug traffickers, cited earlier, some netizens noticed a particular form of additional punishment[3]—that is, deprivation of one's political

---

3. Additional punishment (附加刑) is stipulated punishment in China's Criminal Law to accompany one's principal punishment (主刑). Additional punishment consists of three forms, including fines, deprivation of political rights, and confiscation of property.

rights—meted out by the court against Song and his codefendants and left nine comments. One netizen joked, "The key is 'deprivation of political rights for life', hee-hee-hee [sound mimicking a laugh]." Another netizen questioned, "Can Taiwanese use their political rights in mainland China?" These comments on deprivation of offenders' political rights were unexpectedly ranked a top theme in this case.

In sum, in this chapter we have surveyed major themes and various views reported in netizens' comments in our cases. Netizens' comments reflected a great variety of diversity, and we focused on both the breadth (i.e., diverse themes) and the depth (i.e., diverse views among many themes) of such diversity. As shown, Chinese netizens discussed a variety of topics, both expected and unexpected, and their views on each topic sometimes diverged significantly as well. The breadth and depth witnessed in our data are often lacking in traditional survey studies of public opinion. (A third component of the diversity—the variances of netizens' opinions given different circumstances—is addressed in chapter 5.)

CHAPTER 3

Rationales of Netizens' Decisions
Why Do They Support or Reject Death Sentences?

In this chapter we focus on rationales explicitly expressed by Chinese netizens in their support of or opposition to death sentences (and China's use of the death penalty in general). Past studies have consistently shown that retribution and deterrence are the two most dominant rationales for capital punishment (see the review in chapter 1). As intuitive as it appears, retribution has been interpreted differently by scholars with diverse meanings (see a summary in Bohm 2017, 415–17). In our analyses, we limit retribution to a specific Chinese term, "*sharen changming* (a life for a life, 杀人偿命)," and classified other terms into other categories to document the nuances of netizens' rationales.

In table 2 we display and tally the frequencies (i.e., number of comments) of each major rationale to be discussed in this chapter. For death penalty supporters, major rationales include but are not limited to retribution, deterrence, justice/law requirement, just desert, payback/individual responsibility, social impact/indignation, public order/safety, and respect for lives. In contrast, opponents of death sentences questioned retribution, deterrence, and indignation and expressed concerns about fairness of law and the legal system and wrongful convictions; some even called for outright abolition of the death penalty.

Rationales for Netizens' Support of Death Sentences

Retribution (Sharen Changming)

As a fundamental rule, the term "sharen changming" can be translated literally as "kill people, pay back with life," and the notion is deeply rooted in

Table 2. Top Rationales (Count of Comments) for Support/Rejection of Death Sentences by Cases

(January and February)

Rationales/ Cases	Lin Senhao	Huang Qinghen	Peng Shu and Hu Haolong	Zhao Zhihong	Liu Han et al.
Support					
Retribution (vs. being questioned)	18 (vs. 2)			1	
Deterrence (vs. being questioned)	8 (vs. 1)	133	8		1
Justice/Law Requirement	6				2
Just Desert	6	94	4		7
Payback/Individual Responsibility	10				
Social Impact/Indignation (vs. being questioned)	2	10			4
Public Order/Safety	2				
Respect for Lives/No Killings					
Rejection					
Wrongful Conviction				2	
Question Death Sentence	4	1			1
Abolition (vs. no abolition)	1				1

(March and April)

Rationales/ Cases	Tuo Heti et al.	Hu "x"	Wang Yuefu	Zhai "x" de	Ruan Fangcheng et al.	Zhao Zhihong
Support						
Retribution (vs. being questioned)		2				
Deterrence (vs. being questioned)	1					
Justice/Law Requirement						
Just Desert		1		1		5
Payback/Individual Responsibility						
Social Impact/Indignation (vs. being questioned)	2					
Public Order/Safety	4					
Respect for Lives/No Killings						
Rejection						
Wrongful Conviction						1
Question Death Sentence	2	2				
Abolition (vs. no abolition)						

(*continues*)

(May)

Rationales/ Cases	Zhao Zhihong	Wu Qinyuan	Yuan Junkai et al.	Wang Gang	Lian Enqing	Lin Senhao
Support						
Retribution (vs. being questioned)	2		6		76	472 (vs. 30)
Deterrence (vs. being questioned)			14 (vs. 2)		3 (vs. 4)	346 (vs. 12)
Justice/Law Requirement						194
Just Desert	3				38	89
Payback/Individual Responsibility					5	112
Social Impact/Indignation (vs. being questioned)	1					160 (vs. 9)
Public Order/Safety			6			59
Respect for Lives/No Killings					26	18
Rejection						
Wrongful Conviction		6				43
Question Death Sentence	2				52	104
Abolition (vs. no abolition)	1		(vs. 2)		5	32 (vs. 36)

(June)

Rationales/ Cases	Zhang Xiangxi	Lin "x"ping and Ye "x"tian	Sun Zhifu	Liang Kaiwu	Wang Changping
Support					
Retribution (vs. being questioned)		15	4		
Deterrence (vs. being questioned)		22			
Justice/Law Requirement					
Just Desert	1	71			3
Payback/Individual Responsibility		2			
Social Impact/Indignation (vs. being questioned)					2
Public Order/Safety					
Respect for Lives/No Killings					
Rejection					
Wrongful Conviction		5			
Question Death Sentence		77			
Abolition (vs. no abolition)		35 (vs. 20)			

(July)

Rationales/ Cases	Zhang Weilan et al.	Yang Dazhi	Wang "x"	Fan Jieming	Zheng Dalong and Yang Shengjian
Support					
Retribution (vs. being questioned)	5		2	7	
Deterrence (vs. being questioned)	9	3		3	
Justice/Law Requirement	3	2		1	
Just Desert	22	2	1	12	4
Payback/Individual Responsibility				1	
Social Impact/Indignation (vs. being questioned)	3	1		4	
Public Order/Safety					
Respect for Lives/No Killings				3	
Rejection					
Wrongful Conviction					
Question Death Sentence		1			
Abolition (vs. no abolition)	1 (vs. 2)	(vs. 10)		(vs. 3)	

(August)

Rationales/ Cases	Lin Senhao	Wang Hua et al.	Gu Junshan	Deng Fang	Li Lei
Support					
Retribution (vs. being questioned)	130 (vs. 6)			1	
Deterrence (vs. being questioned)	81 (vs. 1)		3	1	
Justice/Law Requirement	86				
Just Desert	12				
Payback/Individual Responsibility	22				
Social Impact/Indignation (vs. being questioned)	46				
Public Order/Safety	13				
Respect for Lives/No Killings	3				
Rejection					
Wrongful Conviction	11			1	
Question Death Sentence	21				
Abolition (vs. no abolition)	8 (vs. 11)				

(continues)

(September)

Rationales/ Cases	Hu Cunbiao and Wang Yong	Yuan Lijun	Chen Yun	Feng Xiujuan	Yang Chaoquan
Support					
Retribution (vs. being questioned)					28 (vs. 1)
Deterrence (vs. being questioned)	16		5	1	43
Justice/Law Requirement	2				1
Just Desert	3		2	2	25
Payback/Individual Responsibility					13
Social Impact/Indignation (vs. being questioned)	2				
Public Order/Safety					1
Respect for Lives/No Killings					1
Rejection					
Wrongful Conviction					5
Question Death Sentence	1		5	1	1
Abolition (vs. no abolition)	2 (vs. 1)				15 (vs. 28)

(October)

Rationales/ Cases	Lumei et al.	Wang Jianghua and Wang Jinpeng	Huang "x"	Xiao "x"	Zhao Xu	Wang Zongren
Support						
Retribution (vs. being questioned)						
Deterrence (vs. being questioned)						
Justice/Law Requirement						
Just Desert		1	1		1	
Payback/Individual Responsibility						
Social Impact/Indignation (vs. being questioned)						
Public Order/Safety						
Respect for Lives/No Killings					1	
Rejection						
Wrongful Conviction						
Question Death Sentence					1	
Abolition (vs. no abolition)						

(November, Part I)

Rationales/ Cases	Deng "x"	Ling Ruiming	He Shenguo	Wang Yihuan	Gao Yulun et al.	Liu "x"
Support						
Retribution (vs. being questioned)			4		3	1
Deterrence (vs. being questioned)					5	
Justice/Law Requirement					1	
Just Desert			1			
Payback/Individual Responsibility						
Social Impact/Indignation (vs. being questioned)						
Public Order/Safety						
Respect for Lives/No Killings		2	5			
Rejection						
Wrongful Conviction						
Question Death Sentence		5	16	3		
Abolition (vs. no abolition)			1			

(November, Part II)

Rationales/ Cases	Song Yongtian et al.	Liu Danao	Yang "x"ping et al.	Wu "x"hua	He Jian	Wang Baiyang
Support						
Retribution (vs. being questioned)		16		6		
Deterrence (vs. being questioned)	1	(vs. 2)		1		2
Justice/Law Requirement		2				
Just Desert		13		1	3	
Payback/Individual Responsibility				1		
Social Impact/Indignation (vs. being questioned)		2				
Public Order/Safety				1		
Respect for Lives/No Killings		13		2		
Rejection						
Wrongful Conviction						
Question Death Sentence		121		4		
Abolition (vs. no abolition)		1				

(*continues*)

(December, Part I)

Rationales/ Cases	Wu Youxin et al.	Yang Ruixi	Lin Senhao	Zhang "x"yi	Li "xx"	Pan Guohui	Luo Xiaohua and Chen Rihong
Support							
Retribution (vs. being questioned)			615 (vs. 36)	2	9		9
Deterrence (vs. being questioned)	1	2	232 (vs. 12)	1	5		4
Justice/Law Requirement	1		148	2	2		1
Just Desert	3		247				2
Payback/Individual Responsibility			177	1			
Social Impact/Indignation (vs. being questioned)			53		5		
Public Order/Safety			24		1		
Respect for Lives/No Killings			38				
Rejection							
Wrongful Conviction			20				1
Question Death Sentence			203	3	1		
Abolition (vs. no abolition)			55 (vs. 49)		1 (vs. 4)		1 (vs. 3)

(December, Part II)

Rationales/ Cases	Li "x"	Jin Fusheng	Zhao Zihui	Li "x" (#2)	Yang Xueqi	Ou Changsheng
Support						
Retribution (vs. being questioned)		1	6			2
Deterrence (vs. being questioned)		4				
Justice/Law Requirement					2	
Just Desert		8	2		12	8
Payback/Individual Responsibility					1	1
Social Impact/Indignation (vs. being questioned)			1		1	
Public Order/Safety			4			
Respect for Lives/No Killings						
Rejection						
Wrongful Conviction						
Question Death Sentence			3		4	
Abolition (vs. no abolition)					(vs. 1)	2

Note: Blank cells indicate a "zero count" (i.e., no report fits into the category).

Total Frequency in Cases and Total Count of Comments

Top Rationales	Frequency in cases (% of total cases)	Total count of comments
Support		
Retribution vs. being questioned	23 cases (36.5%) vs. 2 cases (3.2%)	1,443 vs. 75
Deterrence vs. being questioned	27 cases (42.9%) vs. 4 cases (6.3%)	958 vs. 34
Justice/Law Requirement	14 cases (22.2%)	466
Just Desert	33 cases (52.4%)	711
Payback/Individual Responsibility	9 cases (14.3%)	346
Social Impact/Indignation vs. being questioned	14 cases (22.2%) vs. 1 case (1.6%)	299 vs. 9
Public Order/Safety	7 cases (11.1%)	116
Respect for Lives/No Killings	9 cases (14.3%)	112
Rejection		
Wrongful Conviction	7 cases (11.1%)	95
Question Death Sentence	23 cases (35.6%)	639
Abolition	14 cases (22.2%) vs. 11 cases (17.5%)	162 vs. 170

Chinese culture. Sharen changming was explicitly mentioned by netizens in 23 cases (35.6% of all cases), and the total number of comments (1,443) significantly surpassed those of other rationales.

In Chinese tradition, sharen changming is taught as "the rule of heaven and the earth (天经地义)." To many, it is easy to comprehend and simple to follow, with little ambiguity. As one netizen commented, "[Anyone who] kills a person needs to be killed; even children know it" (Hu "x," #7). In the Yang Chaoquan case (#33), one netizen said, "There is no soil for abolition of the death penalty in the thousands of years of Chinese culture. We believe in 'sharen changming, qianzhai huanqian (pay the debt if you owe money, 欠债换钱).' Today, fewer and fewer people who owe money repay their debts. If we get rid of sharen changming, then there is basically no more law and heaven (无法无天)." In the Luo Xiaohua and Chen Rihong case (#57), one netizen asked, "When do we insist no more on sharen changming? From its ancient time to the present, China is always [practicing] sharen changming."

Many netizens held this notion as being fundamental and believed it should be enforced without exception, even when there is room for sympathy. In the Liu Danao case (#47), Liu drove his vehicle into a group of relocation workers on purpose and killed four of them when they tried to carry out demolition and relocation by force. Liu was sentenced to death. In their comments, the majority of netizens indeed strongly supported

Liu and questioned the legitimacy of forced relocation (see chapter 7). As sympathetic as they were, however, one netizen commented, "Sharen changming. No matter how much you feel wronged, breaking the law is unacceptable." In the Lin Senhao case (#1), many showed sympathy to Lin given his academic and personal background (see chapter 9). Nevertheless, many netizens supported his death sentence based on the notion of sharen changming. One netizen wrote, "We learned sharen changming from our ancestors. No one is above it, and you [Lin] need to think about it." Another echoed that sentiment, saying, "No matter what Lin's father and his attorneys nonsense-talked, nothing can change the fact that Lin poisoned [the victim]. Sharen changming is fair in any society." In two other cases, supporters of sharen changming would not change their position for defendants' mental incapacity. In the Sun Zhifu case (#17), due to a family feud, Sun murdered victim Yang (a five-year-old) and tried to commit suicide but was saved. Sun was diagnosed with schizophrenia, but her condition was ruled not severe enough to warrant a reduced sentence by the court. Despite her mental problem, one netizen said, "Good! Support [death]! Regardless [whether it is] schizophrenia or depression, killing a person, sharen changming! Do you know how much harm [it is] to the victim?" In the Zhao Zihui case (#60), Zhao's defense tried to claim Zhao's psychiatric history as legal mitigation, but the argument was rejected by the court in meting out Zhao's death sentence. One netizen suggested, "Sharen changming. Our nation should revise laws. One should be held responsible with or without mental problems."

To many, sharen changming, as a golden, ageless principle, is *fair* and *just* punishment to everyone. In the Li "xx" case (#55), one netizen emphasized, "A life for a life is the most just and fairest verdict. Otherwise, anyone can kill to vent one's anger. I always feel that laws today should punish non-severe crimes harshly to be effectively deterrent." Moreover, many netizens believed that sharen changming prevents injustice in contemporary Chinese society, as it denies potential privileges that might be enjoyed by some. In the Lin Senhao case (#1), one netizen commented, "Sharen changming! Hope it works against the second generation of governmental officials and the wealthy (官二代, 富二代)." Another wrote, "I don't believe in laws. I only believe in sharen changming, [and] pay the debt if you owe money."

Sometimes, sharen changming is reasoned along with other justifications. In the Lian Enqing case (#14), one netizen commented, "Sharen changming, the rule of heaven and the earth. If people like Lian are not executed, [I] don't know how many more victims would die in the future." To this netizen, Lian's death was warranted by both sharen changming and concern about public safety (in particular, Lian's future dangerousness). In the Yang Chaoquan case (#33), a netizen emphasized, "Sharen changming, [and] pay the debt if you owe money. If no execution, the killed won't rest in peace. If no execution, are you going to support [financially] them in prison?" In this example, the netizen tied sharen changming with concerns about fairness to the deceased victim and costs of imprisonment.

Deterrence

Deterrence was explicitly mentioned in 27 cases (42.9% of all cases) and generated 958 comments (ranked second by frequency). It shows that Chinese netizens still hold a strong belief that harsh punishment (重刑), particularly capital punishment, deters people from committing more crimes (general deterrence). The idea of "killing one to deter a hundred (杀一儆百)" is favored in Chinese culture. As one put it in the Lin Senhao case (#1), "The meaning of capital punishment is not to execute one individual, but to deter. It forces others to obey the law." Some explicitly expressed concerns about more crimes if Lin's life were spared. One netizen said, "If no death sentence, there would be a Li Senhao, a Zhang Senhao, a Zhao Senhao." Another one wrote, "The influence of bad examples is powerful. If no death sentence is meted against campus poisoning today, it will not [be meted out] in the future. Do you have children who go to school? Aren't you afraid?" Moreover, some expressed concerns that leniency for Lin might open a floodgate and allow more crimes by privileged classes. As one netizen commented, "If [Lin's death sentence is] changed, it will lay a foundation for the second generation of governmental officials and the wealthy who kill. Finding various excuses as defense, they would be sentenced to suspended death, then life imprisonment and reduced prison terms. It won't take long before they are leased."

People's belief in deterrence is so strong and they believe it would work against *all* crimes. Examples of three capital offenses are provided below. In the Huang Qinghen case (#2), Huang was involved in cross-border child abduction. From October 2010 to June 2011, a total of 22 children were abducted from Vietnam and sold to Guangdong province in China. As a principal offender, Huang was sentenced to death while some of her codefendants were spared, including a minor under 18 (at the time of offenses). Many netizens expressed dissatisfaction and argued that more of the codefendants should be sentenced to death. For instance, one netizen suggested, "Kill them all, in order to deter all human traffickers. Strongly recommend to lower juvenile delinquency [legal] age from 18 to 14, at most 16." Another agreed: "A death sentence is correct. Losing a child destroys a family. You are scared when you are sentenced to death, but how come you are not scared when you count the money gained from trafficking children?" Yet another commented, "Those who kidnap and traffic children are all crazy and frantic. No harsh punishment, no deterrence."

For corruption crimes, netizens almost universally demanded harsh(er) punishment. In the Peng Shu and Hu Haolong case (#3), for instance, netizens made comments such as "It's time to kill. To kill big (大开杀戒). Otherwise, there would be more and more corrupt officials" and "Law against corruption is too lenient. If a death sentence is meted out to anyone who accepts bribe money over 100 million yuan, you will see who dares corruption? It is that the law is too lenient."

In the Jin Fusheng case (#59), Jin drove a vehicle into a crowd of 11 people, killing three of them. Jin was convicted of endangering public safety and attempted homicide and was sentenced to death. Netizens again commended harsh punishment against criminals like Jin for deterrence. One netizen commented, "Criminal incidents taking advantage of public transportation occurred frequently. It is absolutely timely and correct for the criminal justice system to punish these criminals. Deterrence is necessary to those who are uncultured and drive wildly!" Another concurred, saying, "Those in traffic accidents who run over the victim(s) twice or more times deserve to be death-sentenced for homicide. To make laws tough, people will obey them. The red line of laws should have a deterrent effect. Raise costs of committing crimes. Lawmaking should not discuss and consider humanitarianism and human feelings. Only in this way does society move toward civilization, the rule of law, and harmony."

In traditional Chinese culture, there is a strong belief in harsh punishment and tough laws (严刑峻法), especially when society is in chaos (乱世). As a result, many netizens argued that the death penalty (especially with lethal injection) is *not* harsh enough and wished for harsher and crueler punishment. They believed that the criminals are rational and that they commit crimes because the costs of crime are too low (成本太低). In the Yuan Junkai et al. case (#12), one netizen pointed out, "[We] should govern society with harsh punishment and tough laws. Revive punishment such as branding one's face, public execution and body exposure, cutting one in half at the waist, death by a thousand cuts, banishment. [This will] make criminals scared so that their liver and gall are broken and they are in a constant state of anxiety. China is a big nation with 1.5 or 1.6 billion people. Whether the crime is corruption, bribe-taking, burglary or rape, society will be in chaos without governance of tough laws." Another one suggested, "[We] should torture them to death. Shouldn't kill by a bullet, which is too lenient for these three bastards." Another concurred, "Death by shooting is anesthesia. People like them should suffer from torture for three days and nights, [so that] they wish they are dead than alive. Then save them and repeat the torture for another 50 years before they die."

Indeed, some netizens recommended various means of torture such as whipping (Huang Qinghen case, #2), North Korean style of "execution by cannon" (Liang Kaiwu case, #18), execution by (using) a meat grinder (Fan Jieming case, #23). In the Lin "x"ping and Ye "x"tian case (#16), several netizens even called for revival of punishing one's close family members, the so-called *lianzuo* (连坐) in ancient China. For instance, one specifically recommended, "Against corrupt officials, [we] should punish one's family members up to nine generations (连坐九族) as [was done] in feudal societies. These corrupt officials follow the feudal rules anyway: when one becomes immortal, his chickens and dogs all rise to heaven (一人得道，鸡犬升天).[1]... No talk of humanitarianism with them. Otherwise, the costs would be too low for corruption and everyone wants to be corrupt instead of being honest."

In the Zhang Weilan et al. case (#20), Zhang colluded with 20 others to murder four miners and claimed fraudulent financial compensation of 1.8 million yuan. Netizens were outraged and expressed strong condemnation against all of the offenders. Again, some recommended extremely cruel punishment. One netizen suggested, "Skin them and cut off their tendons (扒皮抽筋); death by a thousand cuts; rip open the stomach and cut out the heart for the victims (剖腹剜心, 祭奠死者)! To show it to all who think alike. Demand harsh punishment in chaos!" Another said, "It is necessary to use a strong dose against all evils in a chaotic society to stop and heal them. Especially for those who blemish the image of the Party and the government, and those who challenge the bottom line of our society, kill without exception! Call for a revision of the criminal law

---

1. This is a famous Chinese proverb, and its literal translation in the text means that when one gets to the top (e.g., becoming a top official), all family members benefit from his promotion.

to enhance punishment. Otherwise, there is no sufficient deterrence of the laws!" Punishing one's family members was brought up as well. One netizen mentioned, "Even though it is cruel, killing family members up to nine generations has its own reason. These criminals planned to murder others for money, which is most heinous. If death by a thousand cuts [is utilized], see who dares [to try]?"

To strengthen the deterrence effect, many called for public execution. In the Huang Qinghen case (#2), one netizen recommended, "Public execution. To kill the chicken to scare the monkey. See who dares [to try]?" In the Jin Fusheng case (#59), one commented, "For criminals such as Jin, [we] should televise live their execution, and let those who plan to commit crimes see the painful execution, which would prevent many homicides." Similarly in the Yang Dazhi case (#21), one netizen said, "I think that it is more deterrent to televise his death by a thousand cuts. It is even better to use salt. Use water [to awaken him] if he passes out. Keep him conscious throughout [the execution] and do not cover his mouth." It is difficult to gauge the complete sincerity of these proposals, given the nature of online comments (e.g., making jokes). On the one hand, it definitely shows people's outrage against criminals. On the other hand, the diversity and quantity of such proposals to bring back already outlawed execution and punishment methods is still concerning (see the discussion in chapter 8).

Besides the argument for general deterrence, another line of the argument focuses on specific deterrence and suggests that a particular offender would commit more crimes if the offender is not executed and is later released after serving a prison term. For instance, in the Lin Senhao case (#1), one netizen argued, "This type of person cannot be released. Once released, they will harm society. Allowing him [Lin] to become a physician, who knows how many will die at his hands? Someone suggests that 'he can repay society with what he has learned.' What a joke." Another concurred: "Let him walk. He's going to stop killing in the future? Next time, he's going to be more careful [to cover up] and more calculating. Who knows who is going to be the next unlucky victim, who might not even know how one dies."

Justice/Law Requirement, Just Desert, and Payback/Individual Responsibility

Unlike sharen changming and deterrence, which were occasionally challenged by netizens (see the discussions below), the next three rationales—justice/law required punishment, just desert, and payback/individual responsibility—were frequently referred to by netizens but never explicitly questioned in our sample. In our tally, common phrases for justice/law required punishment include *tianli nan rong* (heavenly justice won't tolerate it, 天理难容) and *fa bu rong qing* (law allows no sympathy, 法不容情); the concept of just desert is associated with terms such as *zui you yingde* (crime deserves punishment, 罪有应得), *si you yügu* (one deserves to die, 死有余辜), and *baoying* (karma, 报应); the concept of payback/individual responsibility corresponds to terms such as *changhuan* (repayment, 偿还), *shuzui* (atonement, 赎罪), *daijia* (price, 代价), and *chengdan* (bearing responsibility, 承担). Though often closely associated with the concept of sharen changming, these phrases contain various different nuances.

Justice/law requirement appeared in 14 cases and generated 466 comments. To many netizens, a death sentence is the only fair and just punishment that fits the crimes committed by the offenders, it is "heaven's law," and law has no room for sympathy. As a result, the criminal "deserves to die." For instance, though Lin Senhao's death sentence (case #1) generated much sympathy among netizens, many insisted that the "law allows no sympathy. [A death sentence is] justice and fairness (公平公证)" and "Everyone is equal before the law. Any criminal behavior deserves to be punished."

In the Yang Chaoquan case (#33), Yang burglarized a home and killed the 58-year-old owner on his way out. One netizen said, "After his prison release, [Yang] burglarized into another house and murdered the owner mercilessly. No sympathy for such an evil person. Heaven's law doesn't tolerate it without a death sentence." Similarly, in the Li "xx" case (#55), a netizen commented, "[Li] killed a person publicly in bright daylight and attempted to kill another in front of the police. Heaven's law won't tolerate it if persons like him are not sentenced to death."

To people who believe in heaven's law, laws are sacred, authoritative, and not to be toyed with. Rather, people should respect the law and face severe consequences if a law is broken. In the Yang Chaoquan case (#33), one netizen commented, "If [you] knew it would have ended up like this, you would not have done it. [We] should televise the execution in a proper manner, so that people will cherish lives and freedom and respect law." Note that the notion of "respect for law" is closely related to the concept of deterrence discussed above. It is through deterrence that lessons are learned and laws are respected.

To many netizens, it is often vindictive to see heaven's law answer the call of retribution, though it may come at a later time, and the notion of retribution of heaven's law (天理报应) is deeply entrenched in traditional Chinese culture. In the Wu Youxin et al. case (#52), Wu and his three codefendants murdered three miners and claimed fraudulent compensation, and all four offenders were sentenced to death. One netizen said, "[Victims] unexpectedly became homicide targets of black mines. Alas! Humans are doing it, Heaven is watching it (人在做, 天在看). [You] killed victims and were able to hide it for a while. When retribution comes, you won't escape the heaven's net even if you wear heavenly clothes with no gaps (天衣无缝也难逃天网啊)!" In the Liu Han et al. case (#5), Liu Han and his accomplices were convicted of organizing criminal gangs and committing crimes, including homicide, in 2014 and were executed in 2015. From the 1990s to the 2010s, Liu was able to run his enterprises and criminal gangs with little restrictions or punishment. Netizens demonstrated their strong support for Liu's death sentence. One specifically commented, "There will eventually be an answer for one's good or evil deeds (善恶到头终有报). Heaven's law runs its course and retribution will come without exception (天理循环, 报应不爽)." In the Lin "x"ping and Ye "x"tian case (#16), one netizen said, "They [offenders awaiting execution] were repenting internally though they looked calm. Serious offenders have family members and friends too. It is common [for them to regret]. There will be retribution for one's evil deeds. This is karma. Even if corrupt officials are not caught now, Heaven will bring them in later."

Similar to Western civilizations, the concept of "just desert" is widely accepted by Chinese netizens. In our sample, it was mentioned in 33 cases (52.4% of all cases, the highest percentage of all rationales) and generated 711 comments. The logic of this rationale is straightforward: if one commits a serious crime, one deserves to be severely punished, including the use of capital punishment. To the majority of Chinese netizens, a death sentence is "fit" to the nature of many serious crimes, and in some cases even a death sentence would not be sufficient, and many called for harsher and crueler punishment as discussed above. For instance, in the Huang Qinghen case (#2), many netizens expressed extreme anger about Huang's crimes of child abduction and trafficking and used phrases such as "crime deserves punishment" and "[the crime was] extremely heinous and [you] deserve to die" (罪大恶极, 死有余辜) in their comments. One specifically mentioned, "Your evil destroyed so many families. A death sentence is harsh, but your crime is fit [to such a penalty]." Due to just desert, the offenders' fault is clear: death befalls one only because one commits a heinous crime(s) first. In the Liu Han et al. case (#5), one netizen noted, "Doing evil deeds leads to self-destruction (多行不义必自毙)." In the Peng Shu and Hu Haolong case (#3), one netizen said, "[The crime was] shocking. No *zuo* no die."[2]

The concept of payback/individual responsibility was also popular, as many justified the use of the death sentence as the "price" an offender must pay for their crime and argued that the offender needs to "bear responsibility." Though the concept appeared in only nine cases, it generated 346 comments. In the Lin Senhao case (#1), one netizen wrote, "You [Lin] should have thought about the price you would pay when you did it. When one brings calamities upon oneself, one cannot avoid death (自作孽, 不可活)." Another concurred, saying, "The key is that he [Lin] killed someone. If not, he would not face the death penalty no matter what he did, right? But he did, and he has to bear the responsibility for someone's death." Another spoke directly to Lin's father: "One needs to pay the price for one's mistakes. Your son's life is the price [to pay]. Because he deprived another life without any consideration." Granted, many felt sympathetic to Lin but still insisted on a death sentence because Lin committed an unforgiveable crime. One netizen said, "Lin is not a bad person without any hope. But he made an irreversible mistake. Law allows no sympathy. In tears (挥泪)." In the Yang Chaoquan case (#33), one netizen justified the use of the death penalty from three perspectives and wrote, "From the perspective of law, one should bear responsibility for one's crime; from the perspective of *li* (principle, 理), sharen changming; from the perspective of human feelings, you caused great harm to others for your own interests and hurt your parents too. Not much more needs to be discussed." Another said, "Sympathy today could be continuation of tomorrow's evil. One must pay the price for one's fault!" Another used the term "atonement" and said, "Go and kill yourself. Only death can atone. Go to hell for remorse." Again, some netizens called for harsher punishment as the right "price" to pay for offenders' crimes. In the Wu "x"hua case (#49), one netizen commented, "It's too easy for him to die. Shouldn't we let him suffer [more] from the criminal law? To get a taste of Hell? [So that] he would learn that he has to pay the price for hurting others."

---

2. "No *zuo* no die (不作不死)" is a Chinese internet meme, meaning that "one would not be in trouble had one not asked for it." "Zuo" is a Shanghainese word which means to "act silly." This phrase was originated and included in the Urban Dictionary in 2014.

Social Impact and Public Indignation

Many Chinese netizens justified their support for death sentences because of the potential "social impact" crimes have on society, and in particular "public indignation (*minfen*, 民愤)" generated from the crimes. This rationale generated 299 comments in 14 cases. Two issues raised by netizens were of particular importance to social impact. First, many argued that a particular offender is so dangerous and the damage of a particular crime is so grave that a death sentence is the only option to eliminate such a potential threat. In the Lin Senhao case (#1), many considered Lin's means of committing his crime extremely dangerous. As pointed out, Lin, as a master's student, knew the nature of N-Nitrosodimethylamine (the poison used for his crime) and even tested its effect in experiments. Nevertheless, Lin poisoned the water in the drinking water dispenser. Potentially more victims could have been poisoned besides the actual victim, Huang. During Huang's hospitalization, Lin had numerous opportunities to turn himself in and disclose the source of the poison (which might have saved Huang's life), but he chose not to and simply hoped to get away with it. Many netizens argued that Lin's "no rescue" during Huang's hospitalization was equivalent to his murder intent. Committed by a highly educated individual with a high IQ, Lin's crime was unforgiveable to many netizens, and copycats of Lin would pose extreme danger to campus safety if Lin's life were spared, therefore setting up a bad precedent. One netizen wrote, "Lin must die. Poison others if you don't like them. Then the impact is immense. Where is the bottom line of ethics?" Another commented, "Sharen changming. Lin chose to poison after planning to avoid detection. Highly educated people with high IQs don't need to follow the principle of sharen changming?" Note that the argument of social impact is different from that of deterrence (both general and specific deterrence), though they often go together. While the deterrence argument focuses on crimes, the social impact argument often goes beyond crime control and covers other aspects of the impact of one's crime to the society (e.g., minfen).

A second explicitly expressed concern of social impact is the potential use of vigilante justice (私刑) by victims (or bystanders). In the Lin Senhao case, one netizen suggested, "If [Lin's death sentence is] changed, the victim's parents can only seek justice via vigilante justice." Others concurred and made comments such as "The meaning of a death sentence to the victim's family is irreplaceable by other means of punishment. If the victim's family members see the murderer still alive who might be paroled out someday, they won't accept it mentally. People will lose their trust to the government on crime control, which leads to overuse of vigilante justice" and "Mercy to the poisoner is merciless to the victim and his parents. . . . This is to push them to Mount Liang (梁山).[3] No wonder some don't report crimes to the police but take things into their own hands."

Minfen, or equivalent concepts such as *minxin* (public will, 民心), often appeared in netizens' comments to show how people have become so angry with an offender's crime(s), and a death sentence is necessary to appease people's indignation. Many netizens who supported death sentences also urged the courts to consider such minfen in meting out harsh punishment. The following are some select examples:

> "Crime [is] inexpiable, [a death sentence] to the great satisfaction of the people (恶贯满盈 大快人心)." (Lin Han et al., #5)

> "Without death, it is not enough to assuage public indignation and uphold the law (不杀不足以平民愤, 正国法)." (Huang Qinghen, #2)

> "It would mean betrayal to the people if [we] sentence Zhao lightly." (Zhao Zhihong, #4)

> "Cannot let a single corrupt official go free. Ordinary people (老百姓) would applaud." (Gu Junshan, #26)

> "Crime deserves punishment. Execution soon by shooting to reassure the citizenry (安民心)." (Gao Yulun et al., #44)

> "[We] should kill with no exception dregs of the society who endanger public safety and harm the innocent. This is to get rid of the evil on behalf of people." (Jin Fusheng, #59)

---

3. Mount Liang, a mountain in Shandong province, was made famous by Shi Nai'an's novel *Shui Hu Zhuan* (Water Margin, 水浒传). The story, set in the Song dynasty, tells of a group of 108 outlaws who gathered at Mount Liang to fight the corrupt government and officials. Many of these outlaws were forced to give up their normal lives to join the group. The term *bi shang liang shan* (driven to join the Mount Liang rebels, 逼上梁山) has been a popular phrase.

Minfen can go beyond offenders and target family members or parties who are close to offenders. In the Lin Senhao case, not only Lin himself was called a "skunk (人渣)" who "deserved to die 10,000 times!!!!" but his family (particularly his father, who was doing everything to save Lin's life) and defense team were also targeted by indignant netizens. One netizen criticized Lin's father and said, "Shameless, Lin's animal (畜生) father! Your son's life is a life, but Huang's is not? Homicide, the evidence [is] clear. If no death sentence [is meted out] for this maniac (变态) [referring to Lin], where is heavenly justice?" Some attacked Lin's lawyers by using phrases such as "Dog fart lawyer(s), if no death sentence [is meted out], I'm going to go and kill soon," and "If no execution [by shooting], the next to die will be family members of the defense lawyers." Note that netizens' calls to punish innocent family members and parties raise a concern for rationality, a topic we address in chapter 8.

Public Order/Safety and Respect for Lives/No Killings

The last two major rationales, public order/safety and respect for lives/no killings, generated 116 comments (in seven cases) and 112 comments (in nine cases), respectively. Though often tied to deterrence, the emphasis of public order/safety is on public order and security. For example, the Tuo Heti et al. case (#6) involved terrorist attacks, and netizens specifically mentioned public safety in their comments, such as "Punish criminals harshly; to provide us a peaceful and safe society" and "Punish criminals who endanger public order without mercy." In the Yuan Junkai et al. case (#12), one netizen wrote, "Get rid of those who harm people; it is the right thing to do for the entire society! It is God's decision whether to show mercy. What we need to do is to rid all wrongdoers and build a peaceful environment! Order sometimes needs to be safeguarded by blood and bloodshed. Criminals are not endangered species! No need to protect [them]!" In the Hu Cunbiao and Wang Yong case (#29), one person commented, "Wish for several rounds of national 'strike hard' campaign. Drug users, maniacs (变态狂), hoodlums (二流子), criminal gang [members] (黑社会), corrupt officials, all be executed by shooting!"

To many netizens, a death sentence has a special role to play in maintaining societal stability and harmony, especially when China today is plagued by social unrest and arising crimes. For instance, as one netizen put it in the Lin Senhao case (#1), "I think that we need harsh punishment in this society full of disorder and chaos. Only when the costs are more than the benefits does deterrence work. . . . If leniency is granted to murderers, [criminals] would get away with all kinds of excuses and society will be in chaos."

A small group of people used "respect for others' lives" (尊重生命) in their justifications for death sentences. To them, life is sacred, nothing can justify murder, and capital punishment is the last defense line in society. Even when a particular defendant is wronged to some extent, nothing justifies his or her crime of murder. In the Lin Senhao case (#1), one netizen wrote, "Humans may make mistakes. Nevertheless, no forgiveness for an educated [person] who knew the law and willingly poisoned when the price is another's life. Life is not a joke. Support [his] death sentence." In the Lian Enqing case (#14), Lian had received a nasal operation at the number one people's hospital in Wenling city (in Zhejiang province) in 2012. Lian complained about the result of his operation afterward, despite being informed that the operation had been a success. In 2013, without receiving satisfactory results after multiple rounds of complaints and negotiations, Lian lost his composure, went to the hospital, and stabbed three doctors, one of whom died. He was convicted of homicide and sentenced to death. Lian's case generated much sympathy from the netizens, many of whom criticized the Chinese health-care system and blamed doctors for purposeful malpractice (e.g., overtreating and overcharging patients). Despite such sympathy, one netizen who supported Lian's death sentence said, "The problem is multifaceted, and the hospital was at fault to some extent for sure. But [remember] the old saying: a human life has the priority over Heaven (人命大于天). No one has the right to deprive another's life. This is the bottom line." In the Ling Ruiming case (#41), one netizen commented, "No death sentence for killing two people? Homicide; facts and evidence clear. Though those [victims] are Vietnamese, they are humans. No one can deprive others' lives."

Rationales for Netizens' Rejection of Death Sentences

Netizens rejected death sentences for a variety of reasons. For some, they questioned popular rationales accepted by death penalty supporters, such as sharen changming, deterrence, and minfen; for others, they questioned the appropriateness of death sentences in particular cases due to concerns about wrongful convictions and fairness in sentencing and the law/legal system; lastly, some netizens outright rejected capital punishment and called for its abolition.

Questioning Sharen Changming

Despite the dominance of sharen changming, a very small but not insignificant number of netizens openly questioned this rationale (about 5.2%, based on the ratio of the number of comments that questioned and supported sharen changming in table 2). In the Lin Senhao case (#1), some netizens expressed sympathy for Lin and openly rejected sharen changming. They argued that sharen changming is a belief in the past and should be abandoned in contemporary society. For instance, one netizen said, "Sharen changming was taken for granted in ancient laws. In today's society, [it is] difficult to judge if it reflects the spirit of contemporary law." Another concurred: "Sharen changming is a product of uncivilized eras (愚昧时代). There is never an end of taking revenge (冤冤相报何时了). Evil persons (恶人) should be killed, but stupid persons (愚昧的人) should be spared." Others questioned the utility of sharen changming, pointing out that not all murder cases in China ended up with death sentences, and refuted the concept of sharen changming in practice. One netizen lamented that "sharen changming only hurts those who are alive now." Another argued, "A life for a life is sometimes not a good medicine (良药). Sentence [Lin] to life without the possibility of sentence reduction in 30–40 years (I don't know if the law has this option). This would maximize Lin's punishment and comfort Huang's father, and Lin's father won't be broken. To forgive others is to bless oneself." Another asked, "What I don't understand is the popularity of the revenge psychology of a life for a life. . . . Only can his [Lin's] death pay back [his crime]? Would another person come back to life with his death? Is it true that only death by shooting can discharge your hatred?" Sometimes netizens outright rejected this principle. One netizen commented, "Huang's father so demands. He's going to mourn for the rest of his life. They only demand sharen changming. How sinister humans are." Another said, "Depriving another [of] life cannot save one's soul. It is just another killing."

Questioning Deterrence

Again, a very tiny group of netizens rejected the notion of deterrence (about 3.5%, based on the ratio of comments that rejected and supported deterrence in table 2). Often these contenders questioned the claimed deterrence effect of capital punishment either in a single case or in general. In the Lian Enqing case (#14), one netizen commented on a letter written by Lian in which he expressed no remorse: "This letter shocked me. What is the death penalty? Isn't it meant to deter criminals? This criminal showed no remorse: was he deterred at all by the death penalty?" Another netizen also worried about the deterrence effect in this case when so many netizens openly expressed sympathy for Lian or even supported him and condemned China's health-care system and doctors' malpractice. This netizen said, "Don't even talk about deterrence. Just look at the ratio of those who show support to the doctors to those who support the patients [such as Lian]."

In the Wu "x"hua case (#49), Wu murdered three people, injured another, and resisted police officers before he was arrested. Wu had a history of drug use for over 10 years and served a three-and-a-half-year sentence for drug trafficking. Wu reportedly expressed little remorse during his trial and was apparently fearless about his coming death. One netizen commented, "It is meaningless to sentence him to death. He's not afraid, and what purpose does this death sentence serve? The best punishment is to jail him alone for life without the possibility of sentence reduction. It is only meaningful to let him suffer from the remaining life without seeing daylight."

In comparison to worries about specific deterrence effect (to a particular offender such as Lian and Wu above), more netizens cast doubt on the general deterrence effect of capital punishment. In the Lin Senhao case (#1), one netizen refuted the argument that many people would imitate Lin's crime if Lin were spared from death. This netizen said specifically, "If we replace the death penalty with life imprisonment in murder cases, how many would commit murders because of no more death sentences? Normal people wouldn't. From the perspective of crime prevention, the [deterrence] effect of the death penalty is debatable. This is also the reason why [courts] demand caution in death sentencing." Because empirical studies that test the deterrence effect in China are lacking, netizens turned to other nations for comparison. One netizen said, "I'd like to ask those who argue that no death sentences would lead to more poisoning: are there more killers in Western nations that have abolished capital punishment?" Another pointed to China's high execution number and said, "If execution can solve all problems, the world would have been in peace already. Look at our country [China], how many executions every year? What's the effect [of these executions]? Check out yourself."

Occasionally, netizens pointed out some negative "side effects" of the overuse of capital punishment. In the Yuan Junkai et al. case (#12), one netizen said, "This is belief in harsh punishment. Do you know criminal psychology? . . . If [we] adopt harsh punishment for all, some criminals who know they will be death-sentenced anyway would commit even more crazy crimes. Do you prefer living in a dangerous environment or a more dangerous one? Besides, [our] society discriminates against released inmates, and unfair treatment won't allow them to integrate back into society but force them to go to the opposite side of society, which leads to new crimes." Some further argued that "social order/safety of a particular society depends on the civilization level of the society, not the severity of punishment" and that "punishment such as a suspended death sentence and life imprisonment carries sufficient deterrence."

Granted, opponents to the deterrence argument were outnumbered by deterrence supporters and were often countered by supporters who would emphasize China's uniqueness (e.g., a huge population, with low level of economy, low level of education and citizen quality) or turned to examples in which deterrence worked in other nations (e.g., Singapore, USA), sometimes with incorrect facts.

Questioning Minfen

In the Lin Senhao case (#1), netizens left nine comments to express their reservations about minfen, as the case generated tens of thousands of comments, and many netizens were emotionally charged and committed to securing Lin's death or saving his life. Specifically, these netizens worried about irrational emotional charges under the excuse of minfen; they were concerned about judicial independence in China and did not want judges to be influenced by such minfen. For instance, one netizen argued, "The argument of minfen is wrong . . . public opinion cannot determine courts' rulings. The use of the death penalty is not to assuage minfen. Both [the] Hu'ge and Yao Jiaxin cases are tragedies."[4] In some major cases, Western

---

4. Hu'ge (Huugjilt 呼格吉勒图 as his full name) was wrongfully convicted of homicide and executed in 1996 at the age of 19. From the moment when the deceased was found (April 9, 1996) to Hu'ge's execution (June 10), the whole legal process (including his trial and appeal) was completed in two months. Only in 2014 was Hu'ge officially exonerated. Yao Jiaxin was convicted of murder after a car accident in 2010 and executed in 2011 at the age of 21. In Yao's case, minfen played a significant role in his death sentence (see Belkin 2017).

nations such as Great Britain often forbid media reporting before a court reaches a ruling to avoid the influence of the media." Another netizen lamented the influence of minfen in Lin's case and said, "This case apparently generated minfen. It is impossible to save Lin's life. This is obviously wrong. We don't need indignant 'red guards' [referring to Red Guards in the Chinese Cultural Revolution period]. We need law, pure law." Still another called for caution in reviewing Lin's appeals and said, "Is a verdict of a national exultant celebration what we pursue as ideal law? Information received by ordinary people is filtered and interpreted by relevant personnel, and such an interpretation is often biased. But this interpretation becomes the dominant one because of [the influence of] the carnival celebration. But what if it is wrong? Celebration then becomes an accomplice. Let the professionals study and debate it. Not being anxious to know the result should be the right attitude for us, the ordinary people. We are not reading a story. To kill him [Lin] is easy. Please use caution." Lin was eventually death-sentenced and executed. Some suspected that the huge pressure by netizens' "call for kill" online might have played a role in the judges' decisions, albeit that is impossible to prove (see further discussion in chapter 9).

Wrongful Convictions

In recent decades, cases of wrongful convictions and executions have been exposed in China and received serious attention from the government and the public (e.g., He 2016). Two cases in our sample (Zhao Zhihong, #4; Wu Qinyuan, #11) directly involved wrongful convictions. Besides lengthy and detailed comments on these two cases, a small number of netizens expressed concerns about wrongful convictions in seven cases, with 95 comments. For instance, in the Lin "x"ping and Ye "x"tian case (#16), one netizen commented, "Cannot abolish the death penalty. But be more humane with executions. Besides, it is undisputable that wrongful convictions exist in the world. Do our best to minimize the number [of wrongful convictions]. Alas." In the Yang Chaoquan case (#33), one netizen wrote, "An ironclad case with foolproof evidence (铁证如山) cannot rule out the possibility of a wrongful conviction. Be cautious with capital punishment."

Granted, it is extremely difficult to prove a wrongful conviction in China. Often such cases were proven by fortuitous and unexpected turnarounds (e.g., the supposedly 'deceased' came back alive[5] or a true criminal was caught years later and confessed[6]). With many notorious but well-publicized cases (e.g., Hu'ge) in mind, netizens who commented on the likelihood of wrongful convictions were often concerned about grave consequences of wrongful convictions and executions. For instance, in the Gao Yulun et al. case (#44), despite calls by many netizens to expedite and shorten the legal review process, one netizen supported lengthy reviews to avoid potential mistakes and said, "If [we] expedite the trial and execution because the evidence is clear, then the evidence in the Hu'ge case 'was clear' too. But for the expedited trial and execution, a violation of law, Hu'ge would not have been wrongfully executed. No case should follow a special [expedited] procedure, and [all cases] should follow the legal procedure step by step. Though some criminals would live longer, this would minimize privileges to the greatest extent and allow more Hu'ge to live."

Questioning Death Sentences

In our sample, death sentences were questioned and challenged in 639 comments and by at least one netizen in 23 cases (35.6% of all cases; table 2). In our tally, we counted only comments that questioned death sentences *explicitly*. Granted, this calculation may have underestimated the number of people (and their comments) who actually had questions about or disliked death sentences in a particular case. For instance, in cases that generated great sympathy for defendants, such as the Liu Danao (#47) and Lian Enqing cases (#14), many more netizens supported the defendants in their comments even though they did not explicitly reject the death sentence(s). In the Lian Enqing case, 67 comments explicitly supported Lian's death sentence, and 138 comments judged Lian negatively; in comparison, 52 comments explicitly questioned Lian's death sentence, 146 comments supported Lian, and 40 more showed sympathy for him

---

5. For example, in the infamous Teng Xingshan (腾兴善) case, Teng was wrongfully convicted and executed in 1988. Years later, the supposedly 'deceased' victim was found still alive, thus proving Teng's wrongful conviction. In a similar vein, She Xianglin (佘祥林) was convicted of murdering his wife and death-sentenced in 1994. Only in 2005 did She's wife resurface after years of missing, thus proving She's wrongful conviction.

6. For example, in the Hu'ge case, it was in 2005 that the real culprit Zhao Zhihong confessed to the crime of which Hu'ge was convicted, nine years after Hu'ge's wrongful conviction and execution.

explicitly. In other words, our counts of cases and comments that explicitly questioned death sentences are conservative measures.

Netizens rejected death sentences in our sample for various reasons. One popular reason was questions on the "fairness" of a death sentence, often in comparison to other offenders or other death sentences. In the Lin "x"ping and Ye "x"tian case (#16), for instance, one netizen commented, "[I] feel that [out of three offenders] only the third offender, Ye, who murdered two people for money is fit for the death penalty with immediate execution. The other two trafficked drugs of 100 grams and committed robbery which led to human deaths. [Death sentences are] a bit harsh." In the Zhao Xu case (#38), Zhao suspected that his wife, Hu, had an affair. In November 2013 Zhao strangled his son and stabbed Hu to death. Zhao was convicted of homicide and sentenced to death. One netizen compared Zhao's death sentence to corruption and said, "This kind of things caused little damage to society. Death sentences should be used with caution in these cases. The harm done by him [Zhao] is much less than that of corruption of tens of millions of yuan. How come those legal experts shut their mouths this time?" In fact, netizens almost universally condemned corruption in our sample, and it was rather common for netizens to compare a non-corruption case with corruption cases and argue for leniency of the former and harsher penalty for the latter.

A second popular reason for netizens' rejection of death sentences was sympathy for a defendant given the circumstances of a particular case (e.g., the offender was wronged in the first place). In the Ling Ruiming case (#41), Ling married a Vietnamese lady, Ruan, in 2004. Nevertheless, Ruan often lived in other places (supposedly) because of her work, and there was suspicion that Ruan had committed marriage fraud. Enraged, Ling killed Ruan and two other ladies at Ruan's place and injured two more. Despite his self-surrender to the police, Ling was sentenced to death. Some netizens expressed their sympathy for Ling. For instance, one netizen commented with specific facts (which were *not* verified by the official news reports), "It is because Ling's marriage money was saved by his mother through hard farm work. Ruan took the money and ran way. In the meantime, she cheated another guy from Shandong province. She committed marriage fraud for money everywhere.————There is a reason for it (事出有因); Ling should not be sentenced to death! Anyone who was cheated would have done it. The dog-fart law protects a swindler. Vietnamese women targeted Chinese men for fraud."

A third popular reason for netizens' rejection of death sentences involved netizens' strong criticism and challenges to existing governmental policies or practices such as the one-child birth control policy (He Shenguo case, #42), China's health-care system and medical malpractice (Lian Enqing case, #14), and the demolition and relocation policy (Liu Danao case, #47). In such cases, the death sentence of a particular offender was embedded within netizens' discussions of bad governmental policies. Due to their dislike of the policies, netizens lent their support to the defendants and rejected their death sentences (see chapter 7). In the Liu Danao case (#47), for instance, Liu drove his vehicle to attack demolition and relocation workers and killed four of them. Nevertheless, many netizens called Liu's behavior "self-defense" and his death sentence a "wrong decision." One said specifically, "[It is] obvious that he was protecting his private property against intruders. How come it became endangering public safety?" Another went even further and argued, "Protecting his home, Liu should be found not-guilty and released."

A fourth popular reason for netizens' rejection of death sentences involved their general questions on law and law enforcement. In the Peng Shu and Hu Haolong case (#3), for instance, one netizen questioned the lack of specificity in China's criminal law, which leaves ample room for sentencing disparities in corruption cases. Specifically, the netizen wrote:

> Our nation's law is based on criminal law? Criminal law is like a rubber band! In the last two years, there is no stipulated upper threshold in the amount [to trigger the use of capital punishment] in criminal law: it is possible to sentence someone to death for a million or 10 million yuan; it is also possible to receive no death sentence with 50 million, 100 million or 200 million yuan. It is no wonder for a corrupt official of 16 million yuan to claim: someone with 20 million was sentenced to life imprisonment but I was sentenced to death?! I am not defending these corrupt officials, but laugh at what is laughable! Maybe you all understand why.

In comparison, in the Lin "x"ping and Ye "x"tian case (#16), netizens questioned the fairness of law enforcement. For instance, one netizen argued that "the majority of death-sentenced people are indeed ordinary people. Very few of those with power and money were death-sentenced. Lawmakers are all people with power and money and they leave a way out for themselves." Moreover, a few were not happy in this case with the reported parade of death-sentenced inmates right before their execution.[7] One netizen said, "Not to talk about the legitimacy of execution by shooting yet. But practicing parade at present goes too far." Another said, "Only when China is able to stop this type of public punishment does society make real progress."

Last but not least, netizens rejected death sentences due to defendants' mental conditions in a small number of cases (e.g., Feng Xiujuan, #32; Wu "x"hua, #49). In the Zhao Zihui case (#60), for instance, Zhao stabbed a number of people and caused six deaths. Zhao was convicted of homicide and sentenced to death. His defense tried to claim his psychiatric history as legal mitigation, but the argument was rejected by the court. Three netizens believed that Zhao's death sentence was too harsh given his mental condition. One commented, "Sentencing him to death is like sentencing an animal to death. Ridiculous." Another wrote, "Given his psychiatric problem, [he] should be sentenced more leniently or bear no criminal responsibility. Isn't it how it goes with the mentally retarded?" As discussed earlier, however, there were others who called for harsher punishment for those mentally challenged, based on their presumed dangerousness to society.

Abolition

As shown in table 2, netizens called for outright abolition of capital punishment in 162 comments in 14 cases (22.2% of all cases), by no measure insignificant numbers. At the same time, death penalty supporters opposed abolition explicitly in 170 comments in eleven cases, comfortably matching the force of the abolitionists.

Chinese netizens called for or opposed abolition for a variety of rea-

---

7. It should be noted that public parade of death-sentenced inmates before an execution is already outlawed in China. For instance, Article 48 of the "Opinion on Further Strictly Enforcing the Law to Ensure the Quality of Death Penalty Cases (关于进一步严格依法办案确保办理死刑案件质量的意见)" jointly issued by the SPC, the Supreme People's Procuratorate, the Ministry of Public Security, and the Ministry of Justice in 2007 stipulates that "public parade or other behavior to humiliate dignity of the executed is prohibited." It is restated in the 2012 "Interpretations of the Criminal Procedure Law of the PRC (最高人民法院关于适用《中华人民共和国刑事诉讼法》的解释)" by the SPC (Article 426).

sons. We provide below some quotes from two cases to highlight some of the nuances. First, in the Lin "x"ping and Ye "x"tian case (#16), a number of comments called upon abolition as follows:

> "The death penalty, a punishment of depriving a life, is no longer appropriate for civilized society at present."

> "Use the death penalty with caution. Bring [China's practice] in line with international practice (向国外接轨). Life imprisonment instead for death-sentenced inmates. [Ask them to] work and receive education until [their natural] death."

> "Our country should abolish capital punishment. To those drug traffickers and murderers, sentence them to life imprisonment without the possibility of sentence reduction. It carries more deterrence than a death sentence and it complies with requirements of humanitarianism."

> "[We] should build a factory and ask them to work there for free! At least they are alive. How heart-breaking it is for their parents, brothers, and sisters to learn [about their death sentences]."

> "In this world, no one could deprive another's life with any excuse, unless it is governance in feudal societies and fascism."

> "It is a world trend to abolish the death penalty. Compared to criminals, [governmental] killing with organization and planning is equally cruel and inhuman. It might be more sinister and evil at a deeper level. It is easy to kill a person physically; it is difficult to save a soul. To reform an unforgiveable criminal in prison, without the possibility of parole and sentence reduction, still shows the dignity and seriousness of law and works to deter criminals."

> "Everyone has the right to live in this world. Recommend abolition of capital punishment. Deprivation of another life on purpose is not acceptable. This is a means of curbing violence with violence (以暴制暴), a vicious cycle. [We] should change it to incarceration with different terms proportionate to the nature of one's crime. Everyone makes mistakes in life, and [we should] allow criminals an opportunity to reform."

As shown in these examples, abolition supporters argued the following points: (1) the use of capital punishment is no longer comparable to modern-day civilization; (2) it is rejected by the larger international community; (3) it is, as a form of killing itself, a violation of human rights; (4) it should be replaced with life imprisonment, which serves better utility (e.g., deterrence); (5) abolition would be of great comfort to offenders' family members and friends; and (6) abolition would leave room for offender reformation.

Second, in the Yang Chaoquan case (#33), many of these reasons were echoed and expanded as follows:

"[We] should move toward civilization. Abolish capital punishment, but life imprisonment must be life imprisonment!"

"Correct, sentence those who commit the most atrocious crimes to life imprisonment without the possibility of sentence reduction. If so, the deterrence effect is not weaker than that of death sentences."

"Scientists hurry to invent a machine to test human brains. For those who are sincerely remorseful for their crimes, it is more meaningful to keep them alive than death sentences."

"I believe death sentences are not as good as life imprisonment—ask them to learn a skill in prison and split their monthly earnings: one third goes to the victim, one third goes to their parents and children, and one third is saved to cover their expenses when they can no longer work."

"Life is precious, which is agreed! Given so, since one family has already suffered, why let another family suffer the loss as well? Law is a tool to suppress the evil and encourage the good (惩恶扬善). Isn't it [capital punishment] aggravating people's suffering? Wish for sooner abolition of capital punishment!"

Facing abolitionists' arguments, death penalty supporters countered with their justifications. The following quotes are also borrowed from the two cases above:

(From the Lin "x"ping and Ye "x"tian case)

"A death sentence is a good deal to them. Life imprisonment until [one's natural] death is real torture. Abolition of capital punishment, how many prisons are needed? How much resources and manpower? Does [our] nation have the capability? The concept of 'a life for a life' has been existed in China from its ancient time to its present. Can it be changed overnight?"

"For a population of 1.4 billion people, it is nothing to kill several."

"How come there are always idiots (二货) who call for abolition and treat themselves as saints? . . . Don't compare to other nations. China [has] so many people. Without capital punishment society would be in chaos. What do you mean 'deprivation of another's life on purpose'? What do you mean '[a nation has] no right [to kill]'? Only criminals have the right to deprive others' lives??? [We] already use the death penalty with caution. Only after approval by the Supreme People's Court [SPC] can an execution be carried out. I would say: we not only retain capital punishment, but also expand its use against those who kidnap children, rape women, drunk drive and injure innocent people, and flee crime scene after accidents, and manufacturers without a license (黑作坊) who harm people's health. The costs of crimes are too low."

"It is possible to abolish the death penalty, but it must be accompanied with increased terms of imprisonment—for instance, life imprisonment without the possibility of sentence reduction (which is crueler than capital punishment to some extent), 30, 40, or even longer years of imprisonment. Our nation faces now a dilemma: the death penalty is too harsh but prison terms are too lenient."

(From the Yang Chaoquan case)

"Death sentences are cruel. But the characteristics of Chinese society include population density, a huge gap between the wealthy and the poor, complex social classes, an entrenched notion of classed society, sharp social problems and conflicts, distributive inequality, and inequality in utilization of social resources. It would be a long road for abolition."

"Even now society lacks a feeling of safety. Why abolish the death penalty? Get shit for brains (脑子进屎了)!"

"Whether to abolish the death penalty depends upon the competence of the population (国民素质)! If they have a strong sense of shame, they would feel shamed for even one year imprisonment, not to mention the death penalty; they would dare not raise their heads when they go out, and their self-esteem would be harmed greatly. Then, [it is time to] abolish capital punishment. At present, the competence of our Chinese population is far worse than that of developed nations. You will know when you compare environmental protection."

"[We] should abolish the death penalty, not for humanitarianism!!! Sharen changming! [We] should change changming to asking criminals to work on dangerous jobs. This is to make them live in fear and make their lives worse than death."

"Based on the conditions of our nation, I don't support abolition. Life imprisonment is difficult to enforce in our nation. People with power and money always find a way to get themselves out of prison. Eventually, punishment will be reserved for ordinary people without money and power. Therefore, given the current conditions of China, [we] should put those atrocious criminals to death immediately."

"Don't call without any shame Western nations' abolition of the death penalty 'progress of humanitarianism.' The facts are in front of us: just look at the worsening public security in Western nations, the more heinous and younger criminals, and the impact of inhumane terrorist organizations.... Where is the progress of modern humanitarianism compared to the past?! Humans have always gained more knowledge about humanitarianism and made progress in relentless fights with all sorts of crimes, fraud, and reactionary thoughts (反动思想). But the facts that humans have created countless disasters are in front of us. These so-called Western human rights standards self-claim to have reached the highest level in human history, the very top? Disasters continue. It is impossible to fool people for a thousand or ten thousand years (千秋万代)! Only to recognize and get rid of the hypocritical and evil false humanitarianism soon would make humans suffer less and avoid destruction!"

As shown in these examples, abolition opponents first called upon some popular rationales such as sharen changming, public safety, and deterrence to counter abolitionist arguments; second, they refuted the viability of abolition by referring to special conditions of China (e.g., a huge population, low citizen quality, various inequalities, privileges enjoyed by special classes) and thus rejected the relevance of the international trend to China; third, they questioned the viability of an alternative in case of abolition—that is, life imprisonment as punishment—and pointed out that China does not have "real" life imprisonment without the possibility of sentence reduction, which leaves room for power abuse; lastly, they worried about increased resources when death-sentenced inmates have to be kept alive behind bars in case of abolition. The heated debate, matched in both frequency and depth, clearly showed the confrontation between these two camps.

In this chapter we have reviewed major rationales explicitly embraced by netizens for their support of or opposition to death sentences. It is evident that Chinese netizens in our study supported capital punishment for a variety of rationales, and traditional Chinese culture plays a significant role in shaping people's justifications (e.g., the idea of sharen changming, the emphasis on deterrence with harsh punishment). At the same time, though representing a small group compared to the majority, counter voices (e.g., opposition to death sentences in particular cases or to capital punishment in general, including calls for abolition) can still be heard. A key distinction should be made between netizens' support for capital punishment in general (as a concept) and its application in particular cases. Data showed that the majority of Chinese netizens approve of the use of capital punishment in general but may well question its use in specific cases. In other words, besides the breadth and the depth of netizens' rationales, their opinions are subject to changes given the unique circumstances of cases, a topic we address in chapter 5.

CHAPTER 4

Interactions

How Do Netizens Respond to Each Other?

In this chapter we focus on netizens' interactions—that is, exchanges of comments by netizens. Our examination focuses primarily on two overarching research questions: (1) How do netizens respond to and interact with each other (the "forms")? And (2) do we witness a rational deliberation process in which people holding different or even opposing ideas may gain better understanding of the issues from interacting with each other (the "rationality")? In our sample, out of 38,512 total comments, 11,318 (29.4%) were replies (跟帖, 回复) by netizens (see appendix 3). When measured by counts, Lin Senhao (case #1, with 5,683 replies), Lian Enqing (case #14, with 2,433 replies), and Lin "x"ping and Ye "x"tian (case #16, with 928 replies) were the top three cases producing the most reply comments; when measured by the percentage of the number of replies out of the number of total comments, the Lian Enqing case had the highest percentage, 52.5% (2,433 replies out of 4,660 comments). A number of other cases, such as Lin "x"ping and Ye "x"tian, Feng Xiujuan (#32), Yang Chaoquan (#33), and He Shenguo (#42), generated a reply percentage above 40% (that is, over 40% of comments in these cases were replies).

An examination of netizens' interactions displayed four general forms, including netizens' *raising questions and providing answers, counterarguments, concurring arguments,* and *personal attacks*. In our analyses below, we focus on the last three forms but leave out netizens' questions and answers for two primary reasons: First, counting netizens' questions and answers creates some methodological challenges. Specifically, our analyses focus on replies by netizens. In its design, the comments section of Sina.com.cn allows netizens to directly reply/answer to a particular comment or a string of comments. As a result, the reply immediately follows the last comment. In appearance, in the case of multiple replies, the messages create a series of tiers, often being numerically numbered in sequence. In Chinese, netizens use the term "floor (楼)" as in a high-rise building to refer to the sequence of replies, such as the first floor or 1F (一楼, referring to the first comment or commenter), the 2F (the second comment), and the 3F (the third comment). In our counting, netizens' replies are exact measures of their interactions and therefore data for our analyses. In the case of questions and answers, however, they do not necessarily come as replies. On many occasions a question was raised by one netizen; many comments later, another netizen left a comment, which was seemingly answering the question posted earlier. Nevertheless, the answer was not directly provided immediately after the last question as a reply. Rather, it appeared as a new comment. Though logically this new comment could be shown as a reply, it was not. Such scenarios created methodological problems in our counting, as it required accurate reading of such messages substantively to figure out whether it was a true new message or a mere reply to previous messages. Since such reading and judgments could be subjective, we decided to focus exclusively on replies.

Second and equally important, the substance of netizens' questions and answers was often lacking. In many cases, when a question was posed by a netizen, it was not certain that an answer would be provided by another. It is likely that a question was passed without any answer (and thus without any interaction). Further, it was sometimes not clear if an answer was even purposefully sought by a posted question. When an answer was provided, it was often very short and followed no further interactions. Given these two concerns (one on methodology and the other on substance), we decided to leave out netizens' questions and answers in our analyses below. However, if questions and answers were provided in replies, we included them and further grouped them into either counterarguments, concurring arguments, or personal attacks if they fit.

In addition to these three general forms, three specific recurring netizen exchanges were observed, including the argument of "*putting yourself in the other person's shoes* (换位思考)," the practice of *questioning others' motivations and identities*, and netizens' *reactions to "online violence* (网络暴力)." In table 3, we categorize netizens' replies into six groups accordingly, including three general reply forms and three specific themes.

Table 3. Netizens' Interactions by Cases

Cases/Interactions	Counter arguments	Personal attacks	Concurrence	"Putting oneself in others' shoes"	Question netizens' motives and identities	Reactions to online violence
Lin Senhao	2,300	1,073	347	434	170	99
Huang Qinghen	2		2	1		
Peng Shu and Hu Haolong	2		13			
Zhao Zhihong	6		2			
Liu Han et al.						
Tuo Heti et al.						
Hu "x"	10	2	1			
Wang Yuefu						
Zhai "x"de	5	1	2			
Ruan Fangcheng et al.						
Wu Qinyuan	2		4	3		
Yuan Junkai et al.	15	8	12	1		
Wang Gang	20	13	3	2		
Lian Enqing	1,149	370	188	20	32	10
Zhang Xiangxi	8	1	1			
Lin "x"ping and Ye "x"tian	310	127	73	8	20	15
Sun Zhifu	6		1			
Liang Kaiwu	2		1			
Wang Changping	37	18	11		5	2
Zhang Weilan et al.	58	16	26		1	
Yang Dazhi	3	6	10	2		
Wang "x"	2		1			
Fan Jieming	68	26	27			
Zheng Dalong and Yang Shengjian	1		1			
Wang Hua et al.	1	1				
Gu Junshan						
Deng Fang	9	5	2			
Li Lei	27	6	4		1	
Hu Cunbiao and Wang Yong	20	12	13		1	1
Yuan Lijun						
Chen Yun	6		8			
Feng Xiujuan	38	12	6		3	
Yang Chaoquan	149	59	31	10	2	1
Lumei et al.						
Wang Jianghua and Wang Jinpeng						

Table 3.—(*continued*)

Cases/Interactions	Counter arguments	Personal attacks	Concurrence	"Putting oneself in others' shoes"	Question netizens' motives and identities	Reactions to online violence
Huang "x"	1	1				
Xiao "x"						
Zhao Xu	5	4	1			
Wang Zongren	1					
Deng "x"	1		1			
Ling Ruiming	6		1	1		
He Shenguo	117	57	33	3	2	3
Wang Yihuan	7	1	4			
Gao Yulun et al.	27	9	17			
Liu "x"	1	3	1			
Song Yongtian et al.	2	2	1			
Liu Danao	183	120	107	18	21	30
Yang "x"ping et al.	3					
Wu "x"hua	28	22	15	1	1	1
He Jian	2	2	1			1
Wang Baiyang						
Wu Youxin et al.	7	1	2			
Yang Ruixi	4	4	2			
Zhang "x"yi	21	5	1		2	
Li "xx"	11	18	3	3		
Pan Guohui						
Luo Xiaohua and Chen Rihong	11	17	6	2		
Li "x"						
Jin Fusheng	9	1	5	1		
Zhao Zihui	7	2	6	2		
Li "x" (#2)						
Yang Xueqi	50	22	12		2	5
Ou Changsheng	18	10	3	1	3	1
Total	**4,778**	**2,057**	**1,012**	**513**	**266**	**169**

Note: Blank cells indicate a "zero count" (i.e., no report fits into the category).

Counterarguments

The largest group of netizens' replies consisted of counterarguments. A total of 4,778 counterarguments were made in 50 cases (79.4% of all cases). Counterarguments can be made about almost anything. First, counterarguments can be made against a particular fact, subject, or issue. In the Zhang Weilan et al. case (#20), Zhang colluded with 20 others to murder four miners and claimed fraudulent financial compensation. Some netizens brought up the 2003 movie *Blind Well* in their discussion. The movie tells a story in which two criminals plan mine "accidents" in order to kill innocent miners and claim financial compensation on behalf of the deceased miners. Netizens pointed out how Zhang et al.'s crimes copycatted the movie. As the movie was banned in mainland China, a few netizens speculated on the reason why it was banned. One netizen (1F) commented, "Maybe 'Blind Well' was banned due to fear, fear of more people being killed, and more being executed by shooting." Another (2F) countered, "Wrong. 'Blind Well' was banned because it is too real, with no celebration (歌颂)." Another (3F) re-countered, "There are many [movies] without celebrations. What a weird (奇葩) comment!" One netizen (1F) specifically blamed the movie for its bad influence and wrote, "It is the movie 'Blind Well' that taught people the crime. TV should be subject to strict censorship in the future." Another (2F) immediately countered, "Pure fart. This kind of thing [has been] in existence in China for so long. Putting the cart before the horse (本末倒置). Don't know what [he] is talking about." A third netizen (3F) also countered, "How many villagers have seen 'Blind Well,' do you think? What a joke. It is a problem of the system, but you have to blame it to the influence of 'Blind Well.' Moreover, 'Blind Well' was not released. ZF [the initials of *Zheng Fu*, i.e., 'government' in pinyin] only tried to save the fig leaf (遮羞布)."

Second, a counterargument can be made against a particular netizen because of his or her "faulty" comment. In the Zhang et al. case above, one netizen (1F) posted a simple question: "What is the reason that made these old men murder for money?" A netizen (2F) replied, "Genes. The genes of each family are different. Their next generations will pass on the same genes. Therefore, [the punishment] should be extermination of the entire family. If it were a different person, no matter what was offered, he would not do this kind of things against humanity (反人类)." Offended by this particular netizen, a third netizen (3F) countered, "Son (孩子), [I] only want to say, going back three generations, your family was also [made of] farmers. Did you have a gene mutation? Exactly because of people like you, [we have] the source of discrimination! Everywhere there are good people and bad people!"

Third, counterarguments were often made against certain arguments or suggestions. Take the Yuan Junkai et al. case (#12), for example. Defendants Yuan, Liu, and Wei all had lengthy criminal records before they were convicted of new crimes and death-sentenced. Yuan himself received a suspended death sentence in 1989 and was paroled in 2007 before he committed another crime in 2012. Looking at their lengthy records and new crimes, many netizens were angry with their releases. One netizen (1F) commented, "A suspended death-sentenced inmate released and killed again???!!! Who released [him]???!! Accepted [bribe] money???!!!!! Corruption!!!!" 2F countered, "China [produces] so many suspended death sentences!! Not everyone who was released recidivated, right??? The odds are very low!! Don't take a part for the whole (以偏概全)!!!" Another netizen (1F) asked, "A suspended death-sentenced inmate released and killed, the prison and the court bear no responsibilities?" 2F countered, "A court has to bear responsibility for the recidivism of released inmates who served their time? If so, a doctor treated a disease but the patient got sick again, should the doctor be held responsible too?"

In the Lin "x"ping and Ye "x"tian case (#16), one netizen (1F), self-named "North Hall Woodman (北堂樵夫)," was sympathetic to defendants and proposed, "Recommend abolition of capital punishment! Send all these criminals to desert in the northwest region to plant trees. Stipulate that one who successfully plants 100 acres of trees will be released." Woodman's suggestion generated a number of counterarguments. One netizen (2F) self-named "Change the Low Costs of Crime (改变犯罪成本低)" countered, "It is too simple and naïve to the extent of being unbelievable. When you send them there, what are you going to do if they refuse to plant trees? Or what if they escape on their way? When there is no death sentence for a murderer, what can you do with a prison breaker? And [do we] need two guards for every inmate who plants trees? When inmates fetch trees, guards follow; when they get water, guards follow too. No death sentences for murder anyway, [they will] find an opportunity to kill the guards." Woodman countered back (3F), "What a pity for your ignorance. There is no water and human habitation within hundreds of kilometers of the desert region in the northwest, not even grass! At the labor camp, one armed soldier can guard hundreds. No one tries to escape, because it means death!" Low Costs of Crime again countered with a long message (4F), further blaming Woodman for his "low intelligence" and "no brain" and arguing that desperate inmates may kill the guards and arrange someone to pick them up. Woodman replied with personal knowledge (5F): "My good buddy served five years as an armed soldier, three of the five years in a condition like that. It is very common for a soldier to guard 150 inmates! . . . You go and learn about the labor camp conditions in Xinjiang, conditions and environment even worse! It is a joke to ask them to plant trees! Grass won't live there, not to mention trees! You know many people in Gansu need to use muddy water for drinking water! Don't talk nonsense when you don't know." Then another netizen intervened and suggested (6F), "Put a self-explosion necklace around their necks, which would self-explode [when it is] out of a fixed range." Another one (7F) countered, "You [6F] and 1F [Woodman] match in intelligence! It is not easy to raise you this big (能活这么大真不容易, insulting language in Chinese). 2F [Low Costs of Crime], I have to blame you too. You have way too much free time (闲的蛋疼)! One look at the comment from 1F, you can tell that he is not using his brain. You still argue with him, you have way too much time!"

Most such exchanges were relatively short, but they occasionally went into detail. For instance, in the Lin Senhao case (#1), one netizen self-named "Reincarnation of Baogong (包公显圣)"[1] questioned the evidence and verdict of Lin's case in January 2015 after the Shanghai High Court (the court of second instance) affirmed Lin's death sentence meted out by the intermediate people's court (the court of first instance). Baogong argued that Lin's death sentence was not scientific and accurate, as there was no direct evidence to prove Lin's poisoning besides his own confession. If Lin recanted his confession, Baogong pointed out, the court would have to uphold the principle of presumption of innocence (that is, to find Lin not guilty without sufficient evidence for a conviction). Baogong suggested that it is problematic for the court to adopt one version of Lin's story (confession) but not the other version (Lin's April Fool's story, which implied that Lin was simply pulling a prank). Instead, the court should have accepted Lin's April Fool's story (given Lin's credibility due to his confession to the poisoning), which would have negated Lin's murder

---

1. Bao Zheng, commonly known as Baogong (Lord Bao) was a government official in the Song dynasty, known for his great honesty and uprightness and his ability to solve difficult cases. He gained the honorific title "Justice Bao (包青天)" because of his fight on behalf of the powerless against the powerful.

intent. Baogong's comment generated heated discussions among netizens. Besides supporters who concurred with Baogong, many countered, based on reasons such as retribution, public safety, and evidence (e.g., evidence refuting Lin's April Fool's story, and other corroborating evidence). Others questioned Baogong's motive (e.g., "[you have] no sense of justice"), and asked Baogong, "What if you were Huang Yang (or Huang's parents)?"

It is difficult to predict *when* and *why* some comments or cases generated discussions that were much more heated than others. It appears that a number of factors may have played a role. First, more discussions, including debates, were often generated when netizens demonstrated vested interest on issues reported in a particular case. A glance at cases with the most counterarguments shows that many such cases involved critical issues of contemporary Chinese society, such as crimes committed by people with high IQs and education levels (Lin Senhao case), China's health-care system (Lian Enqing case, #14), the one-child birth control policy (He Shenguo case, #42), and the demolition and relocation policy (Liu Danao case, #47).

Second, when netizens held different or opposing views on certain issues, more discussions and debates were likely generated. Take the Wang Gang case (#13), for example. Wang was arrested three times for drug trafficking and claimed he had committed his crimes in order to raise money to cure his uremia (e.g., receiving necessary treatment, including kidney transplant). Based on the circumstances of the case, the Inner Mongolian High Court eventually reduced Wang's death sentence to a suspended death sentence. Wang's suspended death sentence generated heated discussions among netizens. On the one hand, many questioned the reduction and argued that Wang's medical condition should not be an excuse for his serious drug crimes. For instance, some pointed out that "getting a fatal disease is random, but drug trafficking is a harmful action to others. Cannot save one to harm hundreds and thousands" and "If anyone who is seriously ill commits crimes, can you still be here and talk nonsense (喷)? Life and death, it's all destined. Does one have to live until 100? Which nation promises full treatment of serious illness for free? If you go to a developed nation, you cannot even afford treating a cold." On the other hand, many others expressed their sympathy for Wang; some even concurred with Wang's crimes as a means of raising money for his treatment. For instance, some made comments such as "Life or death (生死攸关), no time to worry about others. All species live for survival. Haven't you seen animals eat their own due to lack of food? Though not seen, you have heard [that] humans eat humans. As a living being, he did it for survival, and [I] cannot say his crimes [are] extremely heinous. If it were you, ask yourself, can you do it? Bear the pain [of the disease] until death" and "If I were diagnosed with cancer, I would have robbed the bank too." Others also questioned the utility of "morality" in Wang's circumstances and asked questions such as "What are you going to do when your relatives are in crisis??????? Give up or give it a desperate shot (拼死一博)? This is a tough decision! Morality means nothing on such a decision! The opposite of morality is evil."

Third, media reporting could have played a role in two ways, through detailed follow-up reports and by tailoring a particular report to trigger people's interest. For instance, the Lin Senhao case was reported on numerous times in 2015. Each time Lin's case moved through a different legal phase (e.g., appellate trial, final review and approval by the Supreme People's Court [SPC], execution), more reports came out and rekindled netizens' discussions. In contrast, both the Lin "x"ping and Ye "x"tian case (#16, with 928 replies and 310 counterarguments) and the Yang Chaoquan case (#33, with 149 counterarguments) were reported only once but generated quite high numbers of debates. As pointed out by netizens, reporters in both cases seemingly succeeded in drawing people's sympathy for offenders. In the Lin "x"ping and Ye "x"tian case, specifically, it was reported and shown in videos that a few women chased the "death van" in tears when three offenders (including Lin and Ye) were taken away to the execution site, a scene that drew sympathy from many. In the Yang Chaoquan case, on his day of execution, Yang reportedly bowed to his prison guard and thanked him for his help during Yang's incarceration. Yang then kneeled down toward the direction of his home and kowtowed several times, apologized to his parents in tears, and said, "If there is a next life, I would be a good man, a good son." Such a moving story drew great sympathy from many netizens and generated discussions and debates accordingly.

Last but not least, as typified in the Lin Senhao case, two particular types of comments seemingly generated more replies and counterarguments. One was arguments with extreme positions and strong language, such as that of Baogong in favor of Lin. For another example, one netizen (ID "229488296") posted three questions in May 2015 after the SPC kicked off its final review of Lin's death sentence:

> Answer me three questions: (1) Can capital punishment truly deter criminals . . . and lower crime rates? . . . (2) Police investigation

cannot ascertain all facts. Please use your pig brain to reflect upon Hu'ge, whose death everyone was demanding back then [see chapter 3 for the Hu'ge case]. (3) Do those who demanded Hu'ge's death feel guilty and regret? Now everyone demands [Lin's] death. Are you going to regret it if [Lin's] execution turns out to be wrong in the future? I'll answer you the third answer: No! Because *penzi* [喷子, see discussion below] like you are a group of numb onlookers who are wearing a fake name tag of justice by watching [Lin's] head being decapitated and [his] blood to achieve sensation and excitement! Onlookers! Onlookers!

This comment went viral in the comments section, and numerous netizens provided replies (e.g., many strings of replies contained over thirty comments). Despite such pressure, this netizen demanded hard evidence to prove the presumed deterrence effect of capital punishment and raised serious concerns about a potential wrongful conviction.

Another type of comment that generated a high volume of feedback came from someone who claimed to be very close to Lin and pleaded leniency for him. For instance, in May 2015, a netizen nicknamed "Noble Lady (高贵女子)" claimed to be Lin's girlfriend. In her comment, she appraised Lin as "kind and optimistic, and welcomed by other students (this is why hundreds of Fudan students petitioned for Lin's life)," but criticized the deceased victim, Huang, as a "bad-mouthed person, well known in his college." Noble Lady believed that Lin was merely teaching Huang a lesson, but Huang died due to his poor physical condition. She pointed out that Lin's parents were peasants with little money and therefore could not financially compensate Huang's parents. She eventually pleaded for Lin's life so that Lin could repay society with his knowledge. Noble Lady's "close relationship" to Lin and her strong position generated many discussions. Many netizens countered her and questioned her true identity.

Personal Attacks

As the most extreme form of counterargument, attacking netizens was unfortunately very popular among Chinese netizens' comments. While counterarguments focused on the substance of arguments, personal attacks focused on particular individuals and often used foul language and personal threats. As shown in table 3, 2,057 comments of personal attacks were made in 37 cases (58.7% of all cases), trailed only by counterarguments. As a matter of fact, any party can be a target of personal attacks due to its "popularity." First, attacks can target offenders, their family members, lawyers, and friends. In the Yang Dazhi case (#21), Yang took advantage of his position as the principal of the Xianjin elementary school in Tianba village in Guizhou province, and molested and raped six students (between the ages of 8 and 13) from 2010 to 2014. His family members and the local government reportedly tried to "settle" his crimes via financial compensation (ranging from 50,000 to 100,000 yuan) with the victims and asked them to sign an agreement not to expose Yang's crimes. Yang was convicted and sentenced to death. Angry netizens expressed their indignation against Yang, people who helped cover up his crimes, and even their family members. One netizen commented, for instance, "Severe punishment against this kind of 'trash'! And the assisting sectors and personnel behind him, all [deserve to be] punished! Or, learn from India, get rid of (处理) their family members and children as well!"

In the Lin Senhao case (#1), Lin was labeled "skunk," his father an "old fool (老东西)," and his defense attorneys "pettifoggers (讼棍)" by netizens against Lin. Sometimes even Lin's supporters or sympathizers were not exempt from such comments. For instance, in the heated discussion with Baogong, one netizen attacked Baogong's argument that Lin had no intention to kill but to play a prank on victim Huang and said, "Don't dog fart here. Why not use Oreo toothpaste, but lethal poison? Still find excuses on behalf of Lin. If the deceased were your son, you would not have nonsense-talked and confused black with white. To me, you are just S.B. [original in English] like Lin's lawyers." Another jumped on Baogong's argument that Lin would be better off not to confess to the crime, and wrote, "Based on your comment, you are an experienced criminal. No self-confession? [That's] excuses to avoid responsibilities. You should go and talk to Huang Yang's father, who can kill you to vent his anger. In this way there will be one fewer animal on earth."

Second, personal attacks sometimes were launched against victims and their close family members and friends. In the Lian Enqing case (#14), numerous netizens related Lian's case to their negative personal experiences with doctors and hospitals and expressed their anger against not Lian but doctors and hospitals. For instance, one netizen said, "[I] respected doctors very much before. Since my family members were coaxed into hospitalization twice, I've been wanting to beat them every time I see doctors. Treat minor symptoms (小病) as major diseases (大

病), so overpriced (太黑了)—animal." Another concurred: "[I] support killing doctors. My father got a minor heart problem. An immoral hospital ordered and placed two stents in him. To date, my father suffers a lot. For my father, I also want to kill these immoral animals." When one netizen (1F) seemingly questioned media reporting and asked, "Why not pose heartbroken pictures of family members of the deceased doctor?" 2F attacked, saying, "Because family members of the deceased are not humans, but animals. It's all because of the sin of the dog doctor (狗医生做的孽). [You] still have the guts to mention him (还有脸提他)!"

Third, attacks are often made against one particular netizen, a group of netizens, or their family members and friends. In the Wang Gang case (#13), discussed earlier, Wang's experience divided netizens into two camps—one that showed sympathy for Wang and even concurred with his crimes, and the other that supported Wang's death sentence and rejected his "raising money for medical treatment" excuse. In heated debates, netizens' attacks also escalated. For instance, one netizen countered the argument raised by others that Wang should not commit drug trafficking crimes to raise money for his uremia treatment and said, "Those who pretend to be a God of morality (道德帝) . . . see if you got the fatal disease." In another exchange, one netizen (1F) expressed sympathy for Wang and commented, "Without reform of the health-care system, if I got cancer and was dying, I would perhaps derail a light rail transit car (轻轨) or a high-speed train (高铁) to draw people's attention, which would hopefully do something good to others. Because our opinions would not be heard by decision makers at the top under normal circumstances." Three netizens immediately attacked 1F: 2F countered 1F, saying "If you'd like to be a German pilot who tried to find a company (拉人垫背) when dying, wish you die tomorrow, and take [with you] all of your family members and relatives. Then the top [decision makers] will investigate your nine generations, which creates more attention." 3F attacked 1F, saying, "You are an sb [see discussion below]. Tell me your address, and I'll take you when I die." And 4F commented, "A stupid person (二逼) like 1F should get a fatal disease soon and go and see the King of Hell (阎王爷)[2] before finding a company! So that innocent people won't get hurt by you, a blackheart devil (黑心鬼)."

Fourth, a few special groups of people were singled out and attacked

---

2. According to Chinese religious culture, the King of Hell is in charge of the 18-floor hell.

by netizens in our sample. For instance, humanitarians—and in particular abolitionists—were often attacked by their opponents. Sometimes they were given bad names such as "holy mothers (圣母)" to emphasize their "holy noble work." Another related group being singled out from time to time was public intellectuals. Though the term should represent a group of experts who possess special knowledge about certain subjects, it was seemingly denigrated in the context of China's death penalty discussion and referred to as a group of self-claimed experts who preach for decriminalization and softening of criminal punishment, in particular abolition of capital punishment, to serve their own personal agenda. In the Yuan Junkai et al. case (#12), for instance, one netizen (1F) commented, "The public intellectuals mentioned China [produces] too many death sentences, and should be cautious in using death sentences." 2F immediately attacked, writing, "If criminals rape or murder wives and daughters of the public intellectuals, they would show different countenance." Another also asked, "What do you say, holy mothers who preach for abolition every day?" In the Yang Chaoquan case (#33), one netizen (1F) called for rehabilitation and made a suggestion: "Scientists hurry to invent a machine to test human brains. To those who are sincerely remorseful for their crimes, it is more meaningful to keep them alive than death sentences." 2F countered with an attack: "A stupid holy mother bitch (圣母婊). A typical example of 'easier said than done (站着说话不腰疼)'. [I] suddenly realized that it will take a long time to eliminate people like this one genetically." Another added, "Those who asked for abolition are all trash." Sometimes radical netizens singled out a few celebrities who are known for their criticism of Chinese social problems and their call for more humanitarian measures in Chinese society. In the Ou Changsheng case (#63), for instance, a netizen specifically called out Bai Yansong (白岩松), a nationally known TV host: "Where is Bai Yansong, the moral bitch? [Is he] lying on the bed of his lover in a villa and working on his commentary that criticizes inhuman actions by the police, the procuratorate, and the court?"

Last but not least, personal attacks could be launched against seemingly unexpected parties, such as governmental employees. This occurred when netizens were not satisfied with the performance of these employees. For instance, in the Li "xx" case (case #55), defendant Li, a fugitive at large, ran into victim Wang and Wang's son on the street. Wang called the police and tried to stop Li from taking off. Li stabbed Wang to death and was arrested by the police as he went after Wang's son. Li was charged with homicide and assault and received a suspended death sentence from the court. It was reported that the people's procuratorate decided to protest the court ruling and tried to change the suspended death sentence to a death sentence with immediate execution. Many netizens sided with the people's procuratorate and expressed their dissatisfaction with the court ruling and called for harsher punishment. Some pointed their fingers at the judges and made comments such as "Two prior criminal records, hurting and killing people in front of the police, sentenced [only] to suspended death? How chivalrous the judge is. Is the defendant your real father? Or your head was kissed by a pig?"; "If the son of the deceased is doughty, go and kill the judge"; and "It's OK. Kill family members of the judge after release. No death sentence anyway. The evidence is so clear and [Li is] a serious felon. The judge does not know the law. Dog-fart judge."

Often verbal attacks occurred in two forms, including the use of foul language and direct personal threats. Use of foul language was a huge part of netizens' attacks and could be directed against any party as detailed above. Given the nature of online discussion, we noticed a few features of netizens' comments related to the use of foul language. First, as online comments were made anonymously, without face-to-face interaction, netizens seemed to be more willing to adopt strong, extreme language, including foul language, which is evident in the high frequency of such language. As shown in appendix 3, we counted a total of 9,564 comments with foul language based on a select list of foul words (representing 24.8% of all comments) in 50 cases (79.4% of all cases). Note that this sum included use of foul language in all types of comments, not just replies. Second, thanks to their creativity, Chinese netizens used foul language in a variety of forms (see appendix 5). Specifically, foul language could come in commonly known foul words in Chinese such as fart (屁), shit (屎), dog (狗), pig (猪), skunk (人渣), and animal (畜生); it could also come in abbreviations of Chinese pinyin such as "b,"[3] "sb," "2b," "tmd,"[4] or seemingly irrelevant words with the same pronunciation of a dirty term

---

3. Normally a foul word, "b" is the abbreviation of *bi* (逼) in pinyin. Literally it can be translated into "cunt." When it is used in combination with other words, it could carry many negative meanings such as "sb (asshole, 傻逼)," "2b (stupid asshole, 二逼)," and *zhuang bi* (being pretentious, 装逼). Note that "sb" is different from "son of a bitch" in English. We use "sb" to represent the Chinese term and "S.B." to represent the English term throughout the manuscript.

4. A foul word, "tmd" is the abbreviation of *ta ma de* (他妈的) in pinyin and can be translated into the dirty word "fuck."

such as "煞笔, 沙比, 砂壁"⁵ and "几把"⁶; it could occasionally come in original English terms such as "S.B." and "asshole." Third, as popular as it is, the effect of using foul language was completely negative; it seemingly only aggravated the issues being discussed and often led to further negative exchanges among netizens. For instance, in the Wang Changping case (#19), Wang, a former police officer, colluded with others to manufacture narcotics. Wang was found to be a principal offender of the group and sentenced to death. Commenting on Wang as a dirty cop, one netizen (1F) wrote, "This is exactly a good servant of people, a good cop! Heh-heh [sound mimicking a sneer]. [We need to] raise the salary of such an animal? How much more power [do we] need to give them?" Though apparently 1F used foul language against only dirty cops, 2F countered with more foul language against 1F and said:

> You fart "heh-heh." Which nation and which profession do not have bad apples (败类)? This cop is a bad cop; a death by shooting would be great satisfaction to the people. But did all cops do drug trafficking? Since it is not [true], you blamed the whole police force for one bad cop and called them all 'animals.' As you are blaming innocent police, aren't you an animal? Since you are an animal, can we say your whole family is made of animals? If you deserve to die, is it true that your whole family deserves to die? How much power possessed by the police is governed by national laws. No matter how much you cry as if you've lost loved ones (如丧考妣), you cannot do anything [about it]. Why don't you die? Then you won't be annoyed (闹心).

On many occasions, netizens were making valid points in their comments. Nevertheless, their use of foul language changed the nature of the discussion and turned it into unnecessary personal attacks. For instance, in the Zhai "x"de case (#9), defendant Zhai (with a lengthy criminal record) stabbed his neighbor Zhang to death after his attempt to borrow 30 yuan was denied. Zhai was convicted of homicide and death-sentenced. One netizen (1F) asked, "Do you lend money when facing such a desperado

---

5. All of these Chinese terms used characters with the same pronunciation as "sb," as their literal meanings are irrelevant indeed.
6. A meaningless term used characters with the same pronunciation as "鸡巴" (penis or dick).

(亡命之徒)? If [you] lend the money, [he] will come back and borrow more; if [you] don't, he will stab you. If [you] call the police, [the police] won't arrest him if he has not done it; you would have been dead if he has already done it; if you strike first and stab him, you will be arrested. Who tells me what to do????" 2F suggested not to take the first strike, and if the victim were killed (as happened in this case), the killer would himself be punished and killed. 3F turned to the use of foul language and said, "Die together with such a skunk, really fucked (真TMD操蛋)!" In the Hu Cunbiao and Wang Yong case (#29), one netizen (1F) commented, "Reducing the use of capital punishment represents progress of society." While 3F and 4F countered 1F with arguments about deterrence and necessity against corruption crimes, 2F and 5F used foul language. Specifically, 2F blatantly attacked 1F: "If a rapist raped your mother, you wouldn't report to the police! Sb." In contrast, 5F made a valid point but ended with foul language: "All nations without the death penalty can sentence [the criminal] to prison terms of hundreds or thousands of years. China only learned how to reduce the use of capital punishment, but not to enhance prison terms. Do you think this is right? Sb."

Besides foul language, direct personal threat was another popular form of attack, and again, it could be directed against any party. In the Lin Senhao case (#1), many threats were directed at Lin and his family. For instance, one netizen threatened both Lin and his parents: "Son [referring to Lin], death sentence. [Lin's] Parents, re-education through labor (劳教), because they did not teach their son right with disciplines (教子无方 教子不严), which led to the loss of a son by another family." A fair share of these threats was directed against Lin's supporters, such as "Public execution! Whoever claims sympathy for the murderer, sentence to one month to one year!" and "I think that one family member of those who signed the petition [of mercy for Lin] should be poisoned. Then they can talk about leniency." Unhappy with the media reporting, some even threatened the reporters. One netizen said, "Lin Senhao [should be] quickly reborn, then poison the little editor of the report; then what is he [the editor] going to say?"

In the Lin "x"ping and Ye "x"tian case (#16), as cited earlier, one netizen (1F) suggested the abolition of capital punishment and sending death-sentenced inmates to plant trees in a remote region. Another netizen (2F) countered with foul language and made a threat against 2F's enemy: "You are an sb. If [we send them to] plant trees, I'll kill the whole family of my enemy tomorrow. I mean it (说到做到)." Another netizen (1F) expressed sympathy for offenders and commented, "Being death-sentenced for trafficking a small amount of drugs is a bit too cruel! Those who prey on (坑害) ordinary people for tens of millions of yuan truly deserve to die!" 4F personally threatened 1F: "1F is a drug trafficker, and his IP [computer IP address] has been identified by the police as a suspect."

Besides threats against netizens themselves, personal threats could be made against netizens' family members. For instance, the Gao Yulun et al. case (#44) contained examples of both. One netizen (1F) commented, "Police died, then many [offenders] were death-sentenced; ordinary people died, then it was nothing (就一文不值). Because cops were killed." Then 2F countered with "I want to TM curse you.[7] When serious felons [referring to Gao et al.] got arrested, you called for 'kill, kill, kill' without going through judicial procedure! When they got rearrested after a prison break, you became sympathetic. Are you God or TM bipolar (精神分裂)?" Another netizen (1F) appraised Gao and said, "I think Gao Yulun is a true man (是条汉子)!" 2F immediately countered: "[We] will talk about it after [he] kills your family." Threats against females were often made using sexually offensive words. In the Yang Xueqi case (#62), one netizen (1F) questioned if a death sentence fits rape crimes and said, "Rape is a serious crime, but it does not deserve death by shooting. It is a life regardless. It [rape] is not murder or arson, and does not deserve death." 2F countered, "Rape your mother, your wife, your sister, your woman, what do you say then? Skunk!" In the Fan Jieming case (#23), one netizen (1F) expressed sympathy for Fan and said, "Social inequality [leads to] angry of an ordinary man (匹夫) [referring to Fan]. How detestable and what a pity!" 3F countered with personal attack against 1F's wife: "Social inequality occurs because the pay to your wife's prostitution is low? How much?" 1F cursed back: "No. Borrow your wife first!"

Concurring Comments

Compared to counterarguments and personal attacks, concurrence occurred less frequently and often in simpler forms. As shown in table 3, a total of 1,012 concurring comments were counted in 46 cases (73% of all cases). Concurring comments were usually made in one of two forms. First, netizens may agree with one another with some simple concurring

---

7. Original in pinyin, it is equivalent to "tmd" (see note 4).

phrases or an emoticon (e.g., a "thumbs up," a "national flag"). A list of select concurring phrases is provided as follows:

"Agreed (赞同)" (Huang Qinghen, case #2)
"A sensible person (明白人)" (Peng Shu and Hu Haolong, case #3)
"I think so too" and "Truth being told. Support." (Zhao Zhihong, case #4)
"An erudite person (高人), sharp minded (想问题好深刻)" (Zhai "x"de, case #9)
"Agree with what you said" (Lian Enqing, case #14)
"Well said (说锝太好了)" (Lin "x"ping and Ye "x"tian, case #16)
"Right" (Li Lei, case #28)
"Well reasoned (有理)" (Chen Yun, case #31)
"Very precise (很精辟)" (Yang Chaoquan, case #33)
"My view is the same as yours" (Deng "x," case #40)
"Completely agree with you" (Ling Ruiming, case #41)
"Good" (Song Yongtian, case #46)
"Certainly" (Li "xx," case #55)
"True" (Yang Xueqi, case #62)
"An excellent point (有水平)" (Ou Changsheng, case #63)

Second, some netizens provided further information to support and concur with others, and such concurrence often needed to be read within a specific context. In the Wang Gang case (#13), discussed earlier, one netizen (1F) commented briefly, "I would do it [the crime] if I were him [Wang]; [it would be] death either way." 2F concurred: "If I were him, maybe I would too, death anyway.... Though it [crime] may be punished by death by a thousand cuts, it is nothing compared to life." In the Sun Zhifu case (#17), one netizen (1F) commented on gendered punishment and said, "Men would be treated as normal even with mental problems. Women would be punished more leniently if they have some very minor mental issues. This is China's 'gendered law' (性别法律)." 2F concurred, saying, "Agreed. Equality before the law, only a phrase (听听就算了)." In the Liu "x" case (#45), Liu (20 years old) committed the crimes of kidnapping, robbery, and homicide and was death-sentenced. His accomplice, Du, being a minor, was sentenced to a 16-year imprisonment. 1F commented on Du's sentence, "16 years, worse off than death by shooting. Don't know how many vices [Du] would learn during 16 years and [he] would harm more people after release." 2F concurred: "Correct. 16 years,

[if] behaving inside, [Du] maybe get paroled in 10 years. Don't know how many will be killed [by Du]. Maybe no one can catch him anymore." Again, netizens' concurrence may carry a negative effect only to aggravate the situation. For instance, in the He Jian case (#50), 1F commented on He's crime, "If [you] kill, kill leaders at the deputy levels (局长) or higher. I would do so." 2F concurred: "True. Why [did you] kill non-related ordinary people? If to kill, kill your enemy or those corrupt officials. Moreover, if to kill, [you'd better] kill big: kill, kill, kill."

In addition to these two forms of concurrence, there is a special game played by some netizens, which is labeled "the rule of the 2F (二楼定律)." The rule was originated and designed to mock 2Fs who often rush to criticize 1Fs without carefully reading the substance of 1Fs' comments. When the rule is followed, one netizen (the initiator) would call for the rule by mentioning the first character of a fixed phrase, and then other netizens would follow to add the next character of the phrase one by one (i.e., "to build it floor by floor" 盖楼) until the phrase was completed, which would be read as *zi gu er lou chu sha bi* (自古二楼出傻逼, which could be translated into "since the beginning, 2Fs generate sb"). The use of foul language ("sb") is meant to mock and insult 2Fs. Nevertheless, the rule has been overused or abused to the extent that anyone can initiate this rule and try to attack a 2F whose opinion the initiator disagrees with. In a number of cases, netizens tried to play this rule, sometimes successfully and other times being disrupted (e.g., by inserting a wrong character on purpose to thwart the meaning of the phrase) by dissenters who would favor 2Fs. It appears that many netizens knew the rule and could play it well. At the same time, a small group of "hard-core fans" of the rule more actively participated in these plays (e.g., being an initiator and a follower from time to time). The design of the rule itself and the way netizens played it all reflected certain features of online comments (e.g., not being afraid of using foul language, being playful, and calling for support from others).

Three Recurring Themes

Noticeably, three specific themes reoccurred among netizens' exchanges, including "putting yourself in the other person's shoes," questioning others' motives and identifications, and reactions to "online violence." First, encouraging netizens to "put themselves in others' shoes" was made in 513 comments in 18 cases (28.6% of all cases), and the majority of such comments (434 comments, 84.6%) were made in the Lin Senhao case (see table 3). To reflect the nuances of such thinking, the argument was presented in three different ways. First, some netizens tried to put themselves into the shoes of others, and the typical logic is therefore "If I were . . . , what would I do?" For instance, in the Wang Gang case (#13), one netizen commented, "If I were diagnosed with cancer, I would have robbed the bank too." In the Yang Dazhi case (#21), one netizen tried to put themself in the shoes of the victims and wrote, "What is [it] going to do to our daughters! How dangerous in a dangerous school! Are you going to report [it] if your daughter is raped??? Certainly!" Second, more netizens (measured by the number of such comments) tried to ask a second party to put themself in the shoes of others in order to convince them, and the cliché is therefore "If you were . . . , what would you do?" In the Lian Enqing case (#14), one posted such a familiar question: "If you were the patient, what would you do? Put yourself in the other person's shoes." Often, in the context of crimes and death sentences, emotionally charged netizens could have used this thinking provocatively, which produced most likely a countereffect. In the Wu "x"hua case (#49), one netizen countered another who expressed sympathy for Wu, saying, "If I killed your entire family, would it be all right for you to be sympathetic to me?" In the Ou Changsheng case (#63), one netizen called for a careful review of Ou's death sentence, especially the reason(s) why Ou committed his crime (creating a public explosion). Another countered with "Fart further review! If someone killed your entire family and were death-sentenced, would we pose and think why your entire family was killed?" Third, occasionally netizens would ask a third party to put themself in the shoes of others. For instance, in the Luo Xiaohua and Chen Rihong case (#57), one netizen criticized the suspended death sentence meted out by the judge(s) and asked the judge(s) to think about what it would be like to be in the shoes of the victims. Specifically, the netizen wrote, "I was merely hateful when reading [about the crime], but was tearful when I saw the suspended death sentence. Two lives, at the age of flowers (花朵般的年龄), so young, one 15, one broken family. Your honor, what if they were your daughters? If this crime does not warrant a death sentence [with immediate execution], are there more heinous crimes on earth?" In the Zhao Zihui case (#60), one netizen pointed fingers at Zhao's defense attorney and commented, "This defense lawyer is a skunk, and loses [his] basic moral values for money. What if he himself or his family members were stabbed, then what would he think?"

The effect of the argument is difficult to predict and most likely depended on the context and how the argument was utilized. On the one hand, encouraging others to "put themselves in others' shoes" could bring out useful information and provide a different perspective. In the Lin Senhao case (#1), for instance, many pointed out that Huang (the victim) was the only child of his family, but Lin had sisters and brothers. Therefore, as one netizen noted, "Resentment cannot be forgiven. Huang's parents are old and have lost the only hope of their lives. The remaining days of their lives are going to be quite difficult." Nevertheless, because both sides used the same logic, it was not clear whether their arguments would help bridge the gap among netizens. For instance, to the argument of "What if you are Huang (or Huang's parents)?" a netizen countered, "But you should put yourself in the shoes of Lin's father too. What if you were him?" To counter the argument that Lin's poison was not lethal, one popular proposal from some netizens was to "let Lin try his poison. If he turns out to be all right, find him not guilty." One frustrated netizen openly questioned the usefulness of such an argument and wrote, "Everyone has the right to share one's thoughts. You may disagree and refute. But [there is] no need to say that 'you drink the poison and come back alive and then we talk' or 'if I kill your father, I won't repay with my life.' These assertions obviously won't happen. What can they prove? Nothing." On the other hand, when the "putting yourself in others' shoes" argument was delivered with anger and foul language, it only aggravated the situation. For instance, one netizen commented, "Be careful with your mom's egg (慎重你妈个蛋, a foul term in Chinese). If your mother is killed in this way, you don't want the killer to face a death sentence?" This line of argument would be unlikely to convince others.

A second recurring theme involved questioning others' motives and identities. Such a theme was made in 266 comments in 15 cases (23.8% of all cases). Two popular online phrases, *Shuijun* (water armies) and *penzi*, were specifically tied to this recurring theme and widely shared by netizens. "Shuijun" refers to someone who is hired to post comments to serve specific purposes. Shuijun often flood the comments section with aggressive postings to draw the attention of others and achieve the desired effect. A specially known group of shuijun hired by Chinese governments at all levels are nicknamed "50-cent party members (五毛党)" because of how much they are reputed to be paid for each positive posting (i.e., 50 cents in Chinese yuan). It is clear that the Chinese netizens in our study were well aware of the existence of shuijun (and the "50-cent party members"), and this is partly the reason why they had constant doubt about and often questioned others' motives and identities. "Penzi," a new term that has appeared online, refers to netizens who attack others verbally. Often they disregard the content of specific comments, jumping to quick conclusions and attacking netizens they dislike without rational deliberation. It seems netizens agreed that *pen* (verbal attack) is bad. Nevertheless, netizens may easily point fingers at each other and call each other "penzi," especially when they suspect that the other party is a shuijun.

Questioning others' motives and identities can be very specific, such as the examples of Baogong (whose motive was questioned) and Noble Lady (whose self-claimed identity as Lin's girlfriend was questioned) in the Lin Senhao case. Other times netizens simply raised the possibility either in a positive sentence (e.g., "This guy is a shuijun") or in a question (e.g., "Is [he] a shuijun?"). Though there might be some circumstantial evidence of aggressive posting by some netizens (see chapter 1), there was hardly any direct proof that one was truly a shuijun. Comments such as "Too many henchmen (狗腿子)," "Hard work for 50 cents" (Ou Changsheng case, #63), or "Don't know why [there are] so many penzi" (Zhang "x"yi case, #54) only showed how suspicious Chinese netizens were with online discussions, since it was difficult, if not impossible, to ascertain the true identity and motive of netizens. In the Lin "x"ping and Ye "x"tian case (#16), for instance, one netizen self-named "Mao Xicai, the son of the biggest nouveau riche," posted a very provocative comment to defend the second generation of governmental officials and the wealthy. Specifically, he said:

> You useless losers (废柴), what's the use of daily cursing against us, the second generation of officials and the wealthy online? [You'd] better off use this free time to move several bricks and bags of cement [implying blue-collar hard labor]. Let me tell you: humans are born into different classes. If you don't have a dad who is an official with money, and you don't have skills to make money, you are doomed at the bottom of the society, being dregs! You deserve to live in slums and eat pig food! Accept your fate. Even if you work ten thousand times harder, [you are] no match to the second generation of the official and the wealthy who do nothing. This is fate, got it? Everything on earth is karma, predetermined.

Immediately after this comment, four netizens questioned Mao Xicai's motive and identity and believed he was merely denigrating the second generation of the officials and the wealthy. In particular, 5F said, "How pretentious (装逼) 1F is! A real wealthy kid (富家子弟) would not have time to talk nonsense here!"

With little trust, netizens' questions about one's motivation could easily lead to calling each other "shuijun." In the Liu Danao case (#47), one netizen (1F) questioned the "forced" nature of the demolition and relocation incident that triggered Liu's crime (i.e., driving his vehicle into relocation workers) and argued that "302 out of 320 families in the village signed demolition and relocation agreements and received financial compensation, including Liu's family. [The workers] tried to tear down houses of the agreed parties, and the murderer [Liu] agreed too and received compensation. From A to Z, I don't see any 'forced' relocation. Therefore, [we] don't expect penzi to be smarter (涨脑子), but to read the full news report." 4F countered back and questioned 1F's identity and said, "1F, are you from a demolition and relocation office? If so, see how many would believe you even if you were telling the truth. Liu Danao would be crazy if he agreed to relocation and received compensation and killed people. Use your feet (脚丫子) to reason, is it possible?" In the Wang Changping case (#19), one netizen (1F) questioned others' suggestion to equip police officers with guns and called them shuijun. 2F countered with foul language: "Fuck your shuijun. Which nation does not have several bad cops? You are so hateful of the police, you are fucking definitely not a good guy." 3F instantly reacted, saying, "Captured alive a shuijun dog (水军狗) [likely referring to 2F]! Also a scum supported by public funds." 4F commented, "Anyone is said to be a 'shuijun.' Does it have to be cursing irrationally and verbally attacking to not be a shuijun? Make rational comments and don't be an online mob member (网络暴民)."

Concerned with netizens' emotional outbursts, their verbal attacks, their use of foul language, and, more importantly, the potential impact of such irrational online behaviors on the outcome of particular cases or on China's legal system in general, a very small number of netizens expressed deep worries about those behaviors (sometimes labeling it as "online violence") and "called for rationality" (呼唤理性) from time to time, as a third recurring theme in our sample. As shown in table 3, a total of 169 such comments were made in twelve cases, most of which occurred in the Lin Senhao case (#1). First, some netizens were deeply troubled by what they saw and left comments expressing their concerns, such as "Alas, [netizens become] so emotional and impulsive once being instigated! When would Chinese netizens grow up?" (Lin "x"ping and Ye "x"tian, case #16), "Check out comments, full of rage (戾气), mocking and distrust" (Hu Cunbiao and Wang Yong, case #29), "How many in the comments [are] extremists such as the ISIS [i.e., Islamic State of Iraq and Syria, original in English], serious potential trouble for society!" (Ou Changsheng, case #63), and "Read the comments, [I] feel that the rule of law has a long way to go (任重道远)!" (Lin Senhao, case #1).

Second, some netizens tried to pinpoint reasons for Chinese netizens' irrational and immature behaviors. In the Lin Senhao case, some pointed out that the composition of Chinese netizens itself may have had a role to play. One netizen said, "I support 1F. There are 500, 600 million Chinese netizens. Among active users, those who received higher education are less than 5%.[8] Most internet platforms are occupied by 'losers' [original in English] who share no spirit of the 'rule of law,' but curiosity (猎奇), apathy (冷漠), lack of spirit (颓废), and no-where-to-release resentment. Hope public opinion won't be kidnapped by them." Another commented, "Nowadays, netizens who spend time online daily are basically those unemployed (most of them villagers) with primary or secondary education. China's online cursing is the world number one, exactly because of these low-quality netizens. If government decisions are kidnapped by netizens, which leads to 'punishment or no punishment, depending upon fellow villagers (老乡) [implying a connection between a defendant and a decision maker],' that would be a new disaster for China!" Yet another said, "I bet most death sentence supporters are young women, minors, the extremists, or emotionalists; those who oppose the death sentence are the mature and prudent. Please publicize age and gender compositions of the commenters." A number of netizens also looked for reasons at the societal level. One netizen criticized the current restless (浮躁) nature of society and wrote, "A restless society that produces a big group of restless angry young men (愤青). I was one once, and even became a 'behind-the-curtain pusher' to call for the execution of Yao Jiaxin [see chapter 3]. But when I looked back? Check and see if the victims gained any benefit? The joy of Yao's immediate execution satisfied the claimed justice of angry young men? But eventually, have to face the pain of losing a family member." In the Wu "x"hua case (#49), one netizen argued for more transparency: "[I] don't understand why so many comments lent support to the apathetic murderer, [I] wonder (纳闷)! Only because the character-

---

8. CNNIC data showed that 18.6% of Chinese netizens received college education or higher, slightly higher than the 13.9% of overall national population who received college education or higher (see chapter 1).

istics are too unique (特色太奇葩) [likely implying the so-called Chinese characteristics] and would like to hide everything, [so that] truth won't be publicized under the sun. As a result, all of us lose patience and trust and are in a constant stage of doubt. Sad, very sad."

Lastly, some netizens openly called for rationality. In the Lin Senhao case (#1), for instance, one netizen called for rational reasoning but not verbal bashing and wrote, "If you think another's reply is irrational, you may counter. For example, why did you claim (in your reply) that I'm a penzi? I disagree. The reply by 3F, why is that a penzi? If you don't accept his argument, you can reply after his comment. Don't leave your comment here, where 3F cannot see." Another netizen encouraged all netizens to build a healthy environment and said, "Lastly, call for all netizens and the masses: don't curse Lin's father because that's his responsibilities as a father; don't curse Huang's father because that's his responsibilities as a father; don't curse the courts. Three years. It shows caution by the courts. What should we curse? I think we should curse everyone in society. [We should] build, maintain, and safeguard societal ethics, moral values, and consciousness of the rule of law. We all did so little, particularly those who hype themselves via this case!"

In sum, netizens' interactions made up nearly 30% (29.4% to be exact) of all comments in our sample. As past studies in this field (especially survey studies) often failed to capture interactions by research subjects, our study provided invaluable data. It should be acknowledged, however, that netizens' online interactions could be very different from interactions in a different context (e.g., a focus group; see Sato 2014). Largely because of the anonymous nature of online interactions, we witnessed the dominance of counterarguments and personal attacks in our data, along with netizens' questioning of others' motives and identities. In this chapter we have focused primarily on three general and three specific forms of netizens' interactions. Besides the forms, we are also interested in learning if such interactions involved a process of rational deliberation. Though online interactions and exchanges could be potentially developed into a platform where netizens engage in civil dialogues and deliberations, Chinese netizens' heated (and sometimes intimidating and violent) debates cast serious doubt about the effectiveness of such potentials, a topic we return to in chapter 8.

CHAPTER 5

Variances of Netizens' Opinions
*Crime Types, Defendants and Victims,
Legal Procedures, and Media Reporting*

In this chapter we focus on variances of netizens' opinions, another important component of the diversity of their opinions in our study. Consistent with results from other nations, Chinese netizens' opinions on death sentences are *not* immutable. Rather, their opinions often change given different circumstances. We focus on four key factors that have influenced netizens' opinions (as evident from our data). First, we examine how different crime types influenced their opinions. Second, we examine how different defendants and victims generated different responses from the netizens. Third, we examine the impact of legal procedures and explore potential different netizen responses accordingly. Lastly, we focus on media reporting and examine how media reporting might have affected netizens' comments and how Chinese netizens openly questioned and challenged media reporting.

Crime Types

Among many concerns about China's use of the death penalty, the extremely high numbers of annual death sentences and executions (never publicly disclosed by the Chinese government) are one of the top worries of the international community. Moreover, the variety of capital offenses is another major concern. As reviewed in chapter 1, when the first Criminal Law was adopted in 1979, 28 capital offenses were stipulated legally. When the Criminal Law was revised in 1997, the total number of capital offenses had already been increased to 68. In the 21st century, efforts to reduce and limit the use of China's death penalty have been gradually introduced, including the reduction of capital offenses by law. In 2011 and 2015, the 8th and 9th Amendments of the 1997 Criminal Law eliminated 13 and nine capital offenses, respectively (with 46 remaining now). As data about China's death sentences and executions remain "state secrets," no past studies have been able to accurately depict a full picture of China's actual use of the death penalty. Available empirical evidence (e.g., Liu, Xiong, and Liang 2019; Xiong, Liu, and Liang 2018; M. Xiong 2016), nevertheless, witnessed China's willingness to mete out death sentences based on various capital offenses, led by homicide and drug offenses.

Appendix 2 tallies the total numbers of officially charged capital offenses and offenders in our sample. As shown, in 2015 death sentences were issued by Chinese judges in at least 13 different types of capital offenses, including violent crimes against individuals (e.g., homicide, sexual offenses, kidnapping, robbery), crimes against public security (e.g., public explosion, criminal gang activities, terrorism), drug offenses (e.g., trafficking, manufacturing), and corruption offenses. Homicide and drug offenses were the two leading capital offenses in our sample: among 123 death-sentenced offenders, 48 were convicted of homicide and 32 were drug offenses. Our sample thus dovetails previous studies and confirms an extensive use of the death penalty in China across a variety of capital offenses, led by homicide and drug offenses.

Violent Crimes against Individuals and the General Public

As shown in appendix 2, a number of violent crimes against individuals and public security subjected 88 offenders to death sentences in our sample. Three features loom when we examine netizens' comments across these violent crimes. First, though Chinese netizens were heavily influenced by notions such as sharen changmin based on Chinese culture (see chapter 3), we seemingly observed more room for debate on one's death sentence in violent crimes against individuals than crimes against the general public. In our examination, we created one simple measure to see if any netizen expressed sympathy for a defendant in a particular case. Out of 63 cases, at least one netizen expressed such sympathy in 17 cases (30%). Out of these 17 cases, two involved drug offenses, 13 cases involved crimes against individuals, and two cases involved crimes against public security. In the last two cases, both Liu Danao (#47) and Jin Fusheng (#59) were charged with "endangerment of public security." The Liu Danao case involved the disfavored demolition and relocation policy (see chapter 7). As a result, netizens offered overwhelming support to Liu and disapproved of his death sentence. In the Jin Fusheng case, Jin drove his vehicle into a crowd of 11 people and killed three. Allegedly, Jin's crime was due to economic disputes, but no details were revealed about the disputes. Only one netizen explicitly appraised Jin's courage but condemned his crime against the innocent. Specifically, the netizen said, "A warrior! A real man is sure to take the revenge (有仇不报非君子)! But you cannot harm the innocent. If Chinese ordinary people all have your courage, [there is] no need to worry that migrant workers (农民工) won't get their [deserved] pay. No corrupt officials would dare harm ordinary people." Except for these two cases, compared to crimes against individuals (in which circumstantial factors may elicit sympathy for offenders), Chinese netizens condemned crimes against the general public consistently and called for harsh punishment, be it public explosion, criminal gang activities, or terrorist attacks. For instance, the Tuo Heti et al. case (#6) involved a group of eight terrorists who attacked a crowd at the Kunming railway station and killed 31. Given her pregnancy at the time of the offense, a capital sentence was not applicable to Tuo Heti by law and she was sentenced to life imprisonment instead. Netizens condemned this terrorist act and made comments such as "Severe punishment for terrorists, to provide a peaceful and safe societal environment!" and "As long as it involves terrorism, offenders all [deserve] death regardless of being a principal or not. This is an obligation to our future generations." Some even called for Tuo Heti's death after she had given birth. In addition, as shown in the quote from the Jin Fusheng case above, netizens often condemned offenders' crimes against innocent people. In the Ou Changsheng case (#63), Ou bombed a bus, killing two and injuring many others. Netizens condemned Ou's bombing of innocent people and left comments such as "The majority of bus riders are the poor. Why does a poor person harm another poor person? Don't do things that sadden your friends and gladden your enemies (亲者痛仇者恨)"; "This is not heroic. Why targeted ordinary people? Coward, deserve to die!" and "Coward, son of a bitch, you would be a hero if you bombed several corrupt officials."

A second feature of comments made by netizens on violent crimes is how they were specifically tailored to particular crimes. Take rape, for example. Though made by a small number of netizens, a constant theme was "calling for castration." In six out of eight rape cases, castration was called for. The two exceptions were the Zhao Zhihong and Wu Qinyuan cases (#4 and #11), both of which involved wrongful convictions and homicide, therefore bigger issues indeed. Some netizens used euphemisms and suggested "confiscat[ing] the tool of the crime," implying castration, and some further proposed tailored punishment against rapists (e.g., "rapists should get a sense of being raped" in the Yang Xueqi case, #62).

A third feature of comments on violent crimes is how these crimes mirrored emerging social and legal problems in present Chinese society (a topic we address in chapter 7). For instance, partially due to the one-child birth control policy, demand for children (especially boys) has arisen over the last three decades, and child abduction as a new crime has emerged and worsened (Jiang and Sánchez-Barricarte 2013; Shen, Antonopoulos, and Papanicolaou 2013). In the Huang Qinghen case (#2), 24 offenders committed cross-border child abductions from 2010 to 2011 involving 22 children. Netizens vehemently condemned such offenses and called human traffickers "lunatic," "non-humans," and "demons," saying they "deserved to die," as "so many families are broken." Another example is the criminalization of drunk driving. As more and more people have purchased their own vehicles in China, drunk driving has become an increasing problem. The 8th Amendment of the Criminal Law in 2011 criminalized drunk driving, which previously was subject only to administrative penalties. In our sample, Chen Yun (case #31) was death-sentenced because he killed six people due to his drunk driving. After the accident, Chen called 120 (the emergency number in China) for help, took a taxi home to see his family, but eventually surrendered himself to the police. Chen's family compensated each victim's family with 23,000 yuan (a total of over 130,000 yuan) and pleaded for another chance for Chen but to no avail. Though a few questioned Chen's death sentence, netizens overwhelmingly supported tough punishment against drunk driving. Some netizens made rather emotional comments such as "Don't wait until an accident to use death sentences. Death-sentence all who are found drunk driving. It is obvious that [drunk drivers] are driving disregarding others' safety. China has a big population, and it is to do away with the evil if [we] shoot to death tens of thousands of drunk drivers" and "A life for a life if drunk driving kills victims. More so for the mentally retarded offenders."

Drug Offenses

China's drug use history and its regulation efforts represent a unique case to Chinese people and to the world (Lu, Miethe, and Liang 2009). The

PRC government has adopted a zero-tolerance approach to drug offenses since the very beginning and often tied its fight against drug crimes to the "fate of the nation." A total of 32 drug offenders in nine cases were death-sentenced in our sample, trailed only by homicide offenders. Besides "ordinary" domestic offenders, offenders from other regions and nations (e.g., the Song Yongtian et al. case [#46] involved Taiwanese offenders; the Huang "x" case [#36] involved a Hong Kong resident who smuggled drugs from Brazil; the Ruan Fangcheng et al. case and Lumei et al. case [#10 and #34] involved Vietnamese citizens) and people with special status (e.g., the Wang Changping et al. case [#19] involved a former police officer) were death-sentenced as well.

Consistent with the Chinese government's stance, Chinese netizens overwhelmingly demanded tough punishment against drug offenses. Often they recognized harms not only to individuals but also to families, communities, and society in general, and many related present drug problems to historical problems suffered by the Chinese people in the 19th and 20th centuries (e.g., the "Opium Wars," the "Sick Man of Asia [东亚病夫]"). In the Lin "x"ping and Ye "x"tian case (#16), for instance, netizens pointed out: "Drug trafficking is worse than homicide. It is harmful to a whole family or several families"; "Drugs are the most heavily regulated in China. Because China suffered so much from drug uses and was almost destroyed, China adopts the toughest regulation. I support"; "For manufacturing and trafficking drugs, capital punishment must be retained. Otherwise, the Chinese nation (中华民族) will be completely destroyed"; and "Nowadays, the thoughts of penzi [see chapter 4] are weird! Are they defending severe crimes such as drug trafficking? Is the tragedy of 1840 [referring to the Opium Wars] not enough?" In the Song Yongtian et al. case (#46), netizens supported tough sanctions against Taiwanese drug traffickers, bringing up historical lessons and making comments such as "Drugs were eradicated when the new China was founded. Zero toleration for its resurgence. No matter who is the offender, punish severely without mercy!" and "Nowadays, more and more people traffic and use drugs. If it continues, Chinese people will become the 'Sick Man of East Asia' again. For drug traffickers, regardless what nation he is from, how much he traffics, and whether he only does trafficking or traffics to support his use, he will be killed upon arrest. This will keep users from reaching drugs and thus avoid China becoming once again the 'Sick Man of East Asia.'"

Another justification for China's tough laws against drug offenses by netizens stems from international comparison. Netizens argued that China's tough laws are consistent with other nations and if China does not stop drug offenses, it would become like those nations that are notorious for their drug problems. For instance, one netizen pointed out that "drug trafficking is a felony in the whole world! Death-sentence all who traffic or possess 50 grams of heroin or more! [Offender] knowingly committed a crime, no mercy for his death!" (the Song case above). Another demanded tough regulations and warned against the lack of thereof and said, "Drugs require absolute severe punishment. Otherwise, it cannot resist the temptation of money. And it is very harmful to society. A negative example is Mexico" (the Lin and Ye case above).

Note that China's Criminal Law makes capital punishment applicable to drug smuggling, selling, transporting, and manufacturing (Article 347), while personal drug use is regulated by the Law of the PRC on Public Security Administration Penalties (中华人民共和国治安管理处罚法). In other words, though personal drug use is subject to administrative punishment (e.g., a drug user is subject to up to 15 days of administrative detention based on Article 72), it is normally not subject to criminal sanctions. Nevertheless, drug users were often targeted by Chinese netizens as well. In the Zhai "x"de case (#9), netizens made comments such as "Drug users, shoot to death too. Society will be in order"; "Mentioned already: drug users and traffickers are not humans. Better to wipe them out"; and "So many people still commit drug offenses, an indicator of not enough progress in our nation. To build China a drug-free nation, it is necessary to stick to 'any offender related to drugs is to be killed,' that is, to wipe out all people who are addicted and who manufacture and use drugs. Install surveillance cameras in all rooms at every entertainment facility, which would help curb prostitution and gambling by the way." In the Wu "x"hua case (#49), Wu had a lengthy drug history. After his release from prison, he sneaked into a house and murdered three people. One netizen commented, "For skunks with a lengthy drug history [like Wu], his life is no different from that of a pye dog, no longer a human!" Another agreed, saying, "It is the best to force drug users to go through detox. Release back to society after they get rid of their addiction. Otherwise, send them to desert to work, or direct execution, to avoid further harm to society!"

Counter opinions occasionally appeared. In the Lin and Ye case cited above, one netizen, sympathetic to Lin and Ye's deaths, commented, "Being death-sentenced for trafficking a small amount of drugs is a bit too cruel! Those who prey on ordinary people for tens of millions of yuan [likely referring to corrupt officials] truly deserve to die!" A real debate broke out in the Wang Gang case (#13). As discussed in chapter 4, Wang's story divided netizens into two camps—one that showed sympathy for Wang and even concurred with his drug crimes, and the other that supported Wang's death sentence and rejected his excuse of "raising money for medical treatment." It showed that netizens' general support of tough punishment for drug offenses could be subject to change given some unique circumstances.

Corruption

Official corruption has become a huge problem in contemporary Chinese society, and it has drawn significant attention from people from all walks of life (e.g., Deng, Zhang, and Leverentz 2010; Gong 1997, 2002, 2003, 2006; Guo 2008; Z. He 2000; Ko and Weng 2012; X. Lu 2000; Ren 2008; Y. Sun 2004; Wedeman 2005, 2008, 2012). Two cases in our sample directly involved official corruption. In the Peng Shu and Hu Haolong case (#3), Peng and Hu were in charge of the highway system in Hunan province and reportedly received bribes of 188 and 170 million yuan, respectively, from 2002 to 2010, and both were sentenced to death. In the Gu Junshan case (#26), Gu was a military lieutenant general and served as deputy minister of the general logistics department. He was convicted of a series of corruption-related crimes and received a suspended death sentence. In both cases, netizens lent their overwhelming support to their death sentences and expressed high hopes. For instance, netizens made comments such as "This is an important signal: the time for corrupt officials is running out. Once arrested, they would be put to death!" (Peng and Hu case); "Excellent! Don't let one single corrupt person walk away, even if from the military. The central government showed great determination, which ordinary people applaud!" and "Very deterrent. Xi Dada [referring to President Xi Jinping], a good job. As long as there is a problem, [we] need to uncover it, which serves as a warning to those who are in [important] positions and who will be promoted to such positions. What you do, Heaven is watching, and ordinary people are watching. Don't let down people's hopes!" (Gu case). In the meantime, critical comments were made as well. In the Peng and Hu case, one netizen wrote in a cynical tone, "So many corrupt officials found, finally see two being death-sentenced." Another netizen concurred: "Chinese laws are too lenient when used against corrupt officials and much heavier against ordinary people. Time to think about it."

Netizens' questioning about lenient or no punishment at all for corrupt officials was very common and echoed in many non-corruption cases. In the Lin and Ye case (#16) cited earlier, one netizen pointed out specifically that "nowadays, there would be different voices online about drug use, drug trafficking, and even homicide. Only when it is about official corruption, is [the voice] surprisingly the same: kill . . . [repeated eight times]. Why? Shouldn't the administration rethink about it? The biggest reason is that the light punishment against these 'spies and animals' hated by all does not assuage public indignation!" Further, some netizens argued that corruption does more damage to Chinese society than many other capital crimes. In the Wang Gang case (#13), discussed in chapter 4, Wang committed his crimes to financially support his uremia medical treatment. One netizen, a uremia patient himself, shared his medical suffering and compared drug trafficking to corruption, writing, "When there is hope to live, drug trafficking is a children's game (小儿科). . . . Why are people who receive bribes of tens or hundreds of millions of yuan only sentenced to a few or a dozen years of imprisonment? Who does more harm?" In the Zhao Xu case (#38), one netizen compared Zhao's double homicide to corruption and said, "This kind of things caused little damage to society. Death sentences should be used with caution in these cases. The harm done by him [Zhao] is much less than that of corruption of tens of millions of yuan. How come those legal experts shut their mouths this time?"

The condemnation against Chinese corrupt officials was almost universal in our study. However, there were a handful counter voices arguing that the harm of corruption is not as severe as other capital crimes. In the Lin and Ye case, a few made comments such as "Excuse me, would a corrupt official endanger your life?" "What's the use of cursing corrupt officials daily? Running a red light is more dangerous than corrupt officials"; and "[We] may put corrupt officials under arrest and seize their property, and [corruption] is only economic. But drug trafficking could make one become addictive, almost impossible to get rid of the addiction. One's life and even a family is destroyed. You tell me which one is more harmful? Without deterrence of the death penalty, more people will use and traffic drugs." In the Peng and Hu case, one netizen even boldly acclaimed the "achievement" of corrupt officials and wrote, "Worth [the death sentence]! [The offender's] life is not long, but he himself and his family had a high-quality life! One's loss benefited a whole family!!!" Despite such counter opinions, official corruption was overwhelmingly condemned by Chinese netizens.

Defendants

As shown in appendixes 1 and 2, a total of 123 offenders were death-sentenced in our sample. When broken down by gender, there were merely six females (4.9%), compared to 117 men (95.1%). Two of the six were Vietnamese citizens (Ruan Fangcheng, #10; Lumei et al., #34, both involved in drug trafficking); one was convicted of a series of child abductions (Huang Qinghen, #2); one was an ethnic minority and convicted of terrorism (Tuo Heti, #6); two others were convicted of homicide (Sun Zhifu, #17; Feng Xiujuan, #32). The two homicide cases, in particular Feng's case, to some extent reflected features of a gendered society. Feng reportedly had an affair with her first love and asked for a divorce but was rejected by her husband. Afterward, she drowned her five-year-old daughter and four-year-old son, strangled to death another eight-year-old daughter, and took rat poison and cut her own wrist to commit suicide but survived. In Sun's case, due to conflicts with in-laws, Sun murdered a five-year-old victim and tried to commit suicide via poisoning but survived. Sun's diagnosed schizophrenia was ruled not severe enough to warrant a reduced sentence.

An examination of the defendants' socioeconomic background showed that the majority of them seemingly came from ordinary backgrounds, with a few exceptions in cases such as corruption (Peng Shu and Hu Haolong, #3; Gu Junshan, #26) and criminal gangs (Liu Han et al., #5; Wang Hua, #25). In one homicide case (#43), defendant Wang Yihuan stabbed victim Ye to death. Ye was a people's representative of the Liunan district in Liuzhou city, and Wang was a former member of the political consultation committee of the Liunan district. Despite his political background, Wang was sentenced to death. It is interesting to note that in 15 cases (23.8% of all cases), Chinese netizens specifically discussed defendants or victims' backgrounds and connections (背景), and the cliché is that "if the defendant had powerful connections, he would not have been death-sentenced." In the Wang Changping et al. case (#19), which involved a bad cop, netizens questioned Wang's lack of connections. For instance, one netizen said, "It's all because he was just a local police officer. If he was an official at the deputy level, he wouldn't be death-sentenced. Many experts would have pleaded mercy for him, and he would have been sentenced to a prison term of several years. Then when the media is no longer interested, you know . . ." In the Wang Yihuan case, one netizen commented, "Heh-heh [sound mimicking a sneer], it seems that he would have been saved if the deceased was not a people's representative," which implied that the victim's political status might have negated potential influence of defendant Wang's political status. When netizens commented on one's connections, they were fond of making analogies between the case in point with fictional figures or well-known contemporary examples. For instance, in the Lian Enqing case (#14), one netizen wrote, "Have a good [death] journey. It's because your father is not Li Gang (李刚)." The Li Gang case happened in 2010. When a driver named Li injured two victims in an accident (one of whom later died), Li reportedly claimed, "You dare sue me. My father is Li Gang." The father, Li Gang, turned out to be the deputy chief of the local police department. Eventually the driver, Li, received a six-year sentence, but since the incident, "My father is Li Gang" has become a popular phrase used to mock the second generation of Chinese officials. Another popular analogy netizens used in this context was the famous novel *Journey to the West* (西游记) by Wu Cheng'en (吴承恩). Netizens pointed out that just like what is written in the novel, demons with strong backgrounds and powerful connections were all saved and converted, but those without were all killed by the Monkey King (孙悟空). This analogy implies that those defendants without connections were all death-sentenced.

As mentioned earlier, in 17 of 63 cases (30%), at least one netizen expressed sympathy for a particular offender. A logical question, then, is who generated more sympathy from Chinese netizens and who did not? By the total number of comments demonstrating sympathy or support for defendants, seven of the 17 cases generated merely one or two such comments, four other cases had fewer than 10 such comments, and three other cases generated dozens of such comments. The top three cases (Lin Senhao, #1; Liu Danao, #47; and Lian Enqing, #14) all received hundreds of such comments. Lin's case generated 757 such comments, but more comments (2,079 to be exact) actually supported Lin's death sentence. Due to multiple news reports over time, along with Lin's status as a highly educated master's student at a famous university and his poor family background, Lin's case generated much sympathy (see chapter 9). In contrast, both the Liu and Lian cases, along with the He Shenguo case (#42, ranked #4 with 60 sympathy comments), generated more comments that showed sympathy or support for defendants than comments that supported defendants' death sentences! These three cases, forming a unique group, dealt with systematic social, political, and legal problems—namely the demolition and relocation policy in the Liu Danao case, China's health-care problems and doctors' malpractice in the Lian Enqing case, and the one-child birth control policy in the He Shenguo case. All three cases served as merely catalysts for bigger issues embedded in contemporary Chinese society, and netizens' discussions clearly went beyond the scope of the cases in point (see chapter 7). Unfortunately, sympathy and support by the majority (or even supermajority) of netizens was not able to save their lives.

Apparently, in a few cases, Chinese masculinity culture played a role in netizens' offering sympathy and support for defendants. In the Gao Yulun et al. case (#44), for instance, Gao and two other cellmates (Li Haiwei and Wang Daming) broke out of prison and killed a guard. All three were rearrested soon after, and Gao and Wang were death-sentenced. Five comments appraised Gao for his "courageous," manly criminal acts. One netizen said, "I on the other hand feel Gao is a real man!" Another elaborated:

> Actually Lao Gao [i.e., 'old Gao,' a common term in Chinese] is quite respectable. One death inmate [referring to Gao, who was serving prison time for previous homicide convictions] killed a malfeasant guard [the deceased guard], which led two fatuous prison officials to prison terms and uncovered shady deals of jails and prisons, and propelled progress of judicial reforms. During his escape, he smoked cigarettes, drank strong liquor (白酒), ate mooncakes, celebrated the mid-autumn festival,[1] broke the record of 'even if you have dodged the Lunar New Year's Day, you cannot make it to the fifteenth day (躲过初一躲不过十五),[2] tested a whole army of police, made it to the top news yearned day and night by Wang Feng (汪峰),[3] and left behind 150,000 award money to family members!

Though it is not clear whether facts stated in this quote were all accurate or even true, the netizen's admiration was obvious. In another case (#53), Yang Ruixi stabbed six people to death. Yang's motive was not reported, and his alleged mental and personality problems were ruled irrelevant by

---

1. It is a traditional holiday in China, held on the 15th day of the eighth month of the lunar calendar with a full moon at night. It is typically celebrated as a family reunion day and mooncakes are traditionally consumed.
2. A Chinese idiom that means you will never escape things that are destined to happen.
3. A famous contemporary pop singer in China.

the court. One netizen briefly commented, "Salute! A real man is sure to take the revenge!" though the story about Yang's revenge is unclear (if there is one). Granted, netizens who appraised criminals' manly acts constituted only a tiny number.

Contrary to defendants who gained sympathy, a few groups of defendants were singled out and condemned. First, some death-sentenced defendants (Yuan Junkai, #12; Zhang Xiangxi, #15; Wang "x," #22; Yang Chaoquan, #33; Gao Yulun et al., #44; Yang Xueqi, #62) carried previous criminal records, and their new capital offenses were thus considered "recidivism." It was common for netizens to point fingers at these recidivists and argue that they did not deserve a second chance. In the Zhang Xiangxi case (#15), Zhang served prison terms twice, for kidnapping and child molestation. Five months after his last release, Zhang battered three elementary school students with an iron stick, killing two of them and seriously injuring the third. Zhang was death-sentenced. Angry netizens made comments such as "[He] should have been shot to death a dozen years ago, then he would not be able to harm these three children"; "Check his prison record as an adult; this is not a person who should be allowed to live"; and "The bloody lesson told us that whoever served prison times before would recidivate sooner or later." A netizen in the Yang Chaoquan case (#33) went even further and argued, "Whoever served prison time is not a good man. His children will become criminals as well. This is called 'piglets depend upon mom's seeds (捉猪崽看娘种).' If the seeds are not good, it would turn out to be bad!" In two other cases (Zhai "x"de, #9; Wu "x"hua, #49), defendants were drug users, and netizens were not hesitant to tie their capital offenses to their drug use. In the Wu "x"hua case, Wu had a drug use history of over 10 years and served time for drug trafficking before he killed three people and was death-sentenced in 2015. One netizen commented, "The brains of drug addicts are severely damaged. Once the addiction is triggered, the only thing on his mind is drugs. He would have killed his parents or children, let alone his neighbors. No other reasons. He needed money for drugs. That's the reason. Thus, drug addicts are useless and done (废人). The sooner they die, the sooner they reincarnate."

A second group singled out by netizens for condemnation included offenders with mental health problems. In the Zhao Zihui case (#60), Zhao stabbed six people to death and injured many others, and his claim of psychiatric problems was rejected by the court. One netizen commented, "Mental disease, [we] should allow him to die. Chinese law that punishes the mentally disordered leniently is meant for corrupt officials and the wealthy. Don't know how many times it [law] was cursed, but it has never been changed. [Offenders with] mental diseases should be death-sentenced, with immediate execution."

A third group singled out by netizens included offenders who attacked the "wrong targets" in their crimes. Beside offenders who harmed innocent people (see the Jin Fusheng and Ou Changsheng cases discussed earlier), netizens also condemned offenders who targeted vulnerable victims. In the Zhang Xiangxi case, one netizen commented on the fact that Zhang had targeted elementary students and said, "[You] had no guts and were bullied. You then bullied the weaker and more vulnerable. You are good for nothing (没出息). If you had guts, you would have killed officials you disliked. Trash." In the Feng Xiujuan case, Feng's crimes against her own children were condemned by netizens. One netizen said, "Why does she have the right to take her children to the 'free world' [implying death]? She can die if she wants to. . . . Children do not need such a mother. She has no right to be a mother. Regardless the reason, it is unforgivable to harm children. It is more shameful and heinous than harming others."

One last group singled out by netizens for condemnation included offenders with special social status. For instance, two cases involved former police officers, and many netizens pointed fingers at bad cops; some even tied the rampancy of crimes to a corrupt police force. In the Wang Changping et al. case (#19), former police officer Wang masterminded drug manufacturing. Cynical netizens made comments such as "Finally [I] understood why illegal drug business is doing better and better with tougher and tougher punishment!" and "No wonder drugs become more and more rampant with punishment. This is why. This police is crazy for money, and lost the bottom line of being a human." In the Yang Dazhi case (#21), Yang was the principal of an elementary school and took advantage of his position to molest and rape six students. One angry netizen commented, "Being the school principal, he should have been a role model, but committed crimes against young girls, including rapes. He was so reckless (胆大妄为) and behaved worse than animals (畜生不如). His death sentence is good!" In the eyes of netizens, police officers and teachers are in unique positions to serve the best interests of the public. Their dereliction—or, even worse, taking advantage of their positions to commit crimes—triggered netizens' anger and resentment.

Victims

A total of 129 victims died as a result of capital offenses (other than those involving corruption and drugs) in our sample. Twenty-two crimes involved a single victim, but multiple deaths were caused in 25 crimes (see appendix 1 for more information). On the one hand, criminals were condemned and victims (and their family members) received sympathy from netizens. To many netizens, a death sentence was often viewed as the only proper punishment to satisfy the victims and their families. In the Lin Senhao case (#1), for instance, one netizen commented, "Sharen changming; death deserved for committing a sin. Lin poisoned Huang, no forgiveness for his crime. For Huang and his family, Lin deserves to die." Granted, the most vulnerable group of victims, children, drew the most sympathy. Besides cases in which offenders killed their own children (e.g., Feng Xiujuan, #32; Li Lei, #28; Zhao Xu, #38), netizens universally condemned crimes against children or young students. In the Huang Qinghen case (#2), netizens expressed their indignation against human traffickers and made comments such as "Kidnapping one child destroys a whole family. The hope and dream of the family is all broken" and "[The offender] deserves to die, good sentencing. The emotional damage to the abducted child and the family is more than physical suffering!" In the Yang Dazhi case (#21), discussed earlier, besides condemning Yang's sexual offenses against students, some netizens expressed deep concerns about "children left behind (留守儿童)."[4] For instance, one netizen asked, "Children left behind . . . why [are they] left behind? . . . what do left-behind families gain? Parents of 'children left behind' are probably working hard in a city, [but] what does society give them in return? Peaceful and contented life and work? An equal opportunity for education?" Another concurred: "The Chinese government should pay attention to children of our migrant

---

4. In contemporary China, the phrase "children left behind" refers to children whose parent(s) moves out of town for work for an extended period of time. Often such a phenomenon occurs in rural areas. When a single parent or both parents migrate to cities for work, their children are left behind and taken care of by older generations or family relatives. It is reported that the total number of "children left behind" had reached 22 million in 2012 (https://baike.baidu.com/item/留守儿童/1968574). For studies of "children left behind," see Biao 2007; S. Cao 2006; X. Chen 2017; X. Chen et al. 2009; X. Chen and Jiang 2018; X. Chen, Liang, and Ostertag 2017; Fan, Su, Gill, and Birmaher 2010; H. Hu, Lu, and Huang 2014; Lee 2011; Qin and Albin 2010; Tian, Ding, Shen, and Wang 2017; M. Zhou, Murphy, and Tao 2014.

workers. Children should be able to attend schools where their parents are working. Beg netizens to help spread the word."

On the other hand, crime victims were blamed in a number of cases for various reasons. First, in a few cases, victims were viewed as being "at fault" to some extent. In the Ling Ruiming case (#41), discussed in chapter 3, Ling married a Vietnamese lady, Ruan, who might have committed marriage fraud. Enraged, Ling killed Ruan and two of her lady friends and was sentenced to death. Several netizens expressed their sympathy for Ling and blamed Ruan. One argued, "Those swindlers deserve to die!" Another concurred, saying, "[Ruan's] Self-committed sin. [We] should deter them. Otherwise, they would bully the honest (老实人好欺负)." In the Hu "x" case (#7), due to business disputes, Hu detained victim Zhang for over 80 days and eventually drowned him in a lake. Surprisingly, among netizens' comments, the most popular theme targeted and blamed Zhang for his refusal to repay his debts to Hu (estimated at tens of millions of yuan). Netizens called Zhang a "deadbeat (老赖)" and made comments such as "[He is] not repaying his debts, [he] is also a swindler" and "Repaying one's debts, the rule of heaven and the earth." Another argued, "[Zhang] knew that his life would be in danger if he did not repay it when he borrowed the high-interest loans, [he] still borrowed it. Deserve to die! Not to mention that he had spent and enjoyed the money that could have supported [Hu] for several generations. Deserve to die. People die for money and birds for food! Alas."

Second, in a number of sexual offense cases, female victims were blamed for their failure to put up resistance efforts and to report crimes. In the Yang Xueqi case (#62), Yang committed eight rapes and 10 attempted rapes from 1998 to 2012, but only two of his 14 victims reported crimes. Many netizens commented on victims' lack of crime reporting. One asked, "What is the mentality of not reporting the crime after being raped? They shouldn't feel ashamed. It is not your fault. You [victims] should feel painful and angry and report to the police promptly so that the offender won't walk free unpunished (逍遥法外)." One netizen pointed out the potential revictimization effect if the victims chose to report the crime, writing, "Have you ever thought about [this]: even for these victims, there are people who tend to question why you were targeted and raped among so many girls? Besides sympathy, most people would talk about these crimes as jokes. . . . As a result, these victims suffered once by rape and suffered another time when their reporting was publicized." Another netizen suggested that an important reason for victims' decision not to report crimes is because of a lack of action from the police. Specifically, the netizen commented, "Only two out of 14 promptly reported crimes to the police. You think it is because victims don't want to contact the police? In many occasions it is no action (不作为)! There is no action once a crime is reported." Another netizen countered that suggestion and said, "This offender was arrested in 2013. The reason for this delay was that no witnesses were willing to identify [the suspect]. It is the offender himself who confessed about his previous crimes. Even when the police asked, witnesses would not testify. Many of them were students, felt ashamed, and wouldn't be willing to testify! It took two years of hard work for the police to collect evidence!" In the Luo Xiaohua and Chen Rihong case (#57), Luo and Chen met their two female victims (19 and 14, respectively) at a train station, managed to gain their trust, tricked them into getting off the train, and eventually led them into woods in a remote area before raping and strangling them to death. A few netizens blamed both victims for their naïvety and lack of resistance. One asked, "How stupid these two ladies were, with no sense of personal safety? What good was going to occur once they were led to the woods?" Another concurred and gave a bad name to the victims, saying, "Tarts (骚货), there were many opportunities and [there was] time. If [victims] shouted [for help] a few times, how could they [offenders] manage to take them to such a remote area?"

Third, in a few cases, elements of Chinese traditional culture and habits seemingly played a role in netizens' negative reactions to the victims. In the Deng "x" case (#40), Deng and his victim, Li, were coworkers. Deng was invited to attend the wedding of Li's daughter but chose not to go due to concerns about wedding gifts. As a result, both families ended up in a verbal fight, and Deng's wife, Xia, had a heart attack and was sent to a hospital. Deng asked Li to reimburse him for Xia's hospital bills but was rejected. On a second day, Deng went out of control in another verbal fight with Li and stabbed Li (who died) and his wife, Luo. Deng was death-sentenced. A number of netizens criticized the wedding gift custom, and one directly blamed victim Li and said, "No gifts, let it be (不随份子就不随吧). Make no more contact [with Deng]. It is not right to go after Deng and argue with him." In the Jin Fusheng case (#59), Jin drove his car into a crowd of 11 people, killing three. After watching a video of the crime scene, one netizen blamed pedestrians who did not obey the traffic rules. Specifically, the netizen commented, "Before watching this video, I took it for granted that this son of a bitch drove his vehicle onto the sidewalk and committed this heinous crime. After watching the video, I found this skunk acted crazily almost entirely on the vehicle road. On the contrary, it is the victims who walked on the wrong road. This skunk deserves to die. But if people obeyed traffic rules, not so many would have been victimized." In the Feng Xiujuan case (#32), besides condemning Feng for killing her own children, netizens commented on Feng's husband and her first love (with whom Feng had an affair). On the one hand, a number of netizens blamed Feng's husband for the tragic crimes and argued that he should have divorced Feng and let her go. One netizen said, "It's all the husband's fault. A woman asked for a divorce. It [the crime] wouldn't have happened if a divorce was granted. Don't pluck an immature fruit since it won't be sweet (强扭的瓜不甜) [a Chinese idiom that means 'an unwilling relationship is doomed to be unhappy']. Likely this husband has a history of domestic violence. Otherwise, how come the mother tried to kill herself and the children?" Another concurred: "The husband is at fault too. His wife had an affair and no longer wished to be with him. He still insisted wearing a green hat (戴绿帽子) [a Chinese idiom that means 'to be a cuckold'] and did not grant a divorce." On the other hand, some netizens pointed their fingers at Feng's first love (the home wrecker) and pointed out that "the tragedy was caused by the paramour, who should be found guilty [of a crime]." A few netizens even encouraged Feng's husband to take actions. One netizen suggested, "The husband go and knife to death the first love. Otherwise, you are not a man." In all of these examples, notions of Chinese culture (e.g., gendered roles of men and women in a marriage), customs (e.g., wedding gift as a "must"), and (bad) habits (e.g., not following traffic rules) were singled out and commented on by netizens in their discussions about the victims.

Last but not least, a few victims, unfortunately, were denigrated and even demonized in a few cases, such as those of Lian Enqing (#14), Liu Danao (#47) and He Shenguo (#42). These cases, as mentioned above, dealt with systematic social, political, and legal problems—namely, China's health-care problems and doctors' malpractice, the demolition and relocation policy, and the one-child birth control policy. When netizen critics opened fire at these policies, victims of crimes had become symbols of such policies and therefore lost their meaning as individuals. For instance, in the He Shenguo case, one angry netizen commented, "A contraceptive ring would be forced for the first pregnancy and tubal ligation for the second pregnancy, though laws and regulations do not make them mandatory. The birth control workers who force them deserve to die even if they are knifed." It is obvious that this netizen's condemnation against birth control workers went beyond the scope of the case, and He's specific victims were deemed no longer worthy of sympathy after they became and were denigrated as part of the birth control team. (These cases are discussed in further detail in chapter 7.)

Legal Procedure

In discussing variations of the legal procedure, we are primarily interested in whether netizens' opinions would vary at different stages of the procedure. Unfortunately, only two cases (Lin Senhao, #1; Zhao Zhihong, #4) were reported on more than once in the news, and all other cases were reported on at one point in 2015 (thus reflecting no variation of the legal procedure). Specifically, the Zhao Zhihong case was reported on twice: in January, Zhao was death-sentenced by the court of first instance (i.e., the trial court), and on April 30, Zhao's death sentence was affirmed by the court of second instance (i.e., the appellate court) with two reports, on April 30 and May 1, respectively. Only slight variations were witnessed between the two times for a few reasons. First, Zhao's case produced a relatively small number of comments at both times (20 in January and 84 in April/May), thus making variations less likely. Second, as Zhao's case involved the infamous wrongful conviction and execution of Hu'ge (see chapter 3), his case was portrayed as (and had to be) "ironclad" this time around, thus leaving little room for arguments. Third, the affirmation of the trial court's death sentence by the appellate court did not allow much room for further debate. As a result, by relative rankings based on the number of comments, the observed variations showed only that more comments (four comments) questioned the proper functioning of the criminal justice system in January, but more comments applauded Zhao's death sentence (21 comments), and justified his sentence (11 comments) in April/May. At these times, a number of other themes stayed constant, such as netizens demanding truth, condemning wrongful convictions, and demanding accountability of the personnel who were in charge of Hu'ge's wrongful conviction and execution.

By contrast, the Lin Senhao case provided a rich source for analyses of variations. First, Lin's case generated the largest number of comments in our sample (n = 17,611). Second, it was reported on at four different times: in January the Shanghai High Court (the appellate court) affirmed Lin's death sentence; in May, during the mandatory review and approval process by the Supreme People's Court (SPC), a three-judge panel held a hearing with Lin's defense attorneys, who questioned evidence of Lin's case; in August an SPC judge met Lin's father to listen to his opinions, an unprecedented move as it is not required by law, while Lin's father and Lin's attorneys submitted legal documents to SPC judges; and in December, despite signs of hope in May and August, Lin's death sentence was approved by the SPC, a last meeting between Lin and his father was arranged, and Lin was executed promptly afterward. Such twists and turns grabbed netizens' attention and rekindled their discussions each time. Third, the public interest stimulated the media, which focused on every move made by Lin, Lin's family, his attorneys, and the victim's family and produced many follow-up stories. The synergy among legal proceedings, the media, and the public (i.e., netizens) allowed much variation over the full year.

In our observation, the progress of legal proceedings (and the media reporting) generated variations in two significant ways in Lin's case. First, the relevant *prominence and ranking of major themes* of netizens' discussion was affected, measured by the popularity (i.e., the total number) of such themes. For instance, when Lin's death sentence was affirmed by the Shanghai High Court in January, a common theme (ranked fourth) appeared in comments that either showed netizens' sympathy for Lin or explicitly rejected such sympathy. Nevertheless, this theme was not dominant and fell out of the top ten rankings in May and August when the SPC reviewed Lin's death sentence. Rather, netizens were anxiously awaiting the final outcome, and both Lin's supporters and opponents presented their case passionately online while being suspected by the other group, who called their comments foul plays (i.e., trying to influence the SPC's final decision) (see chapter 9). The "sympathy" (or lack of thereof) theme loomed again as dominant (ranked fourth) in December after the SPC approved Lin's death and Lin was executed. Another example is netizens' comments that questioned "delay and waste" in Lin's legal proceedings: timing was not an issue in January ($n = 0$) but became a major concern in May, August, and December (with 211, 116, and 252 comments, respectively). To many netizens, as the legal proceedings dragged on, the appellate reviews turned into unnecessary delays and waste of resources. For instance, one netizen commented, "[I'm] puzzled. How many years [passed] already? How come Lin has not been executed? Since when has our nation's criminal justice system become so slow?" Another theme that shows the impact of legal proceedings is comments in which netizens expressed their wishes to Lin or learned lessons from his case. This theme, not ranked among the top in May and August, was a top theme in January (ranked eighth) and December (ranked seventh) when Lin's death sentence was affirmed by the Shanghai High Court and the SPC, respectively, as netizens saw the "finale" of the case. (Note that many believed that the decision by the Shanghai High Court was the final decision, not aware of the mandatory SPC review by law.)

Second, the progress of legal proceedings also affected the *substance* of some themes. For instance, two popular themes involved comments directed at both Lin's family and victim Huang's family (both ranked as top ten themes in all four months). Despite such consistency, the substance of these themes was subject to change with the progress of the legal proceedings. In May and August, while Lin's father was desperately doing everything to save Lin's life, netizens who supported Lin's death sentence blamed his father for his "selfish love," his little care for Huang and Huang's family, and his "improper" efforts (e.g., turning to the media) to influence the SPC's death sentence review. In December, after Lin's execution, one new issue arose with regard to Huang's family. It was reported that Huang's father was exploring the possibility of a civil compensation lawsuit. Netizens weighed in on this issue with 120 comments. Unlike the majority support for Lin's death sentence witnessed in previous months, the majority of netizens indeed opposed the idea of civil compensation (85 out of 120 comments). Netizens who supported the idea argued that seeking civil compensation was "a legal right" for the Huangs and that "Lin's death was the payback to Huang's death, but nothing has been paid back to the harm done to the Huang's family." In contrast, many more argued that "Lin's family owed nothing to the Huangs, and Lin, who had a debt to the Huangs, is already died." They pointed out that "it is Huang's family that demanded Lin's life instead of compensation, and it would offend the feeling of the public if the Huangs would press for more after Lin's death," and it would be like "dropping down a stone on the man who has fallen into a well" (落井下石). Substantive changes among netizens' comments were also evident in Lin's progress when news broke out such as a letter exposed in July in which Lin admitted the poisoning of his victim, his last interview in December with the media, and his last meeting with his father before execution. Each time when new stories developed, netizens responded and the substance of their discussion changed accordingly.

In sum, though we have only two cases that allowed us to examine variations due to the impact of legal procedures, we witnessed some significant changes in netizens' discussions as the legal proceedings progressed. Such changes affected not only the relative ranking of popular themes but also the substance of some major themes.

One final observation about legal procedures in our study was netizens' willingness to *forgo* proper legal proceedings required by law. In 25 of all 63 cases (39.7%), netizens made comments to express their dissatisfaction with extended delays of trials and appeals, and some openly advocated forgoing legal procedures. For instance, in some cases, netizens argued that no appeals should be made, such as "Forgo the [SPC's] review and approval stage, and [go to] execution directly" (Tuo Heti case, #6) and "Correct sentencing! Don't fart bother with the appeal, you two, sons of bitches!" (Wang Changping case, #19). In the Zhang Weilan case (#20), angry netizens pointed out that "these animals still have guts to appeal. Sharen changming, let alone you killed three people. Even if you die ten times, it is not too much." They argued that "for those who were sentenced to life imprisonment and chose to appeal, change [the life sentence] to a death sentence with immediate execution!!! For other appellants, enhance their punishment!!!" In the Yang Dazhi case (#21), one even suggested forgoing trials and said, "In my opinion, no need to waste resources on trials. Directly cut off his head (取下项上人头). No one will question [it] in ten thousand years." These comments, apparently made with strong emotions, raised concerns about the rationality of netizens' comments, a topic we address in chapter 8.

Media Reporting

Our analyses of media reporting focus on two related issues: (1) how reporting affected netizens' comments, and (2) how netizens questioned and challenged media reporting. In general, media reporting could have influenced netizens' comments in two fundamental ways: the substance (i.e., content) provided to netizens, and the way the substance was delivered. Substance-wise, in contemporary Chinese society, the media (both public and private) and all sorts of media outlets, including new social media such as Wechat (微信), are still subject to heavy governmental control and censorship. What is reported in capital cases is no exception. Stories about death sentences often tended to be short and the language formal. With a few exceptions (e.g., the Lin Senhao case), very few follow-up stories were reported in our sample. From the perspective of netizens, they responded to what was reported and tailored their comments based on information provided on crime types, defendants and victims, and legal proceedings. At the same time, what is *not* reported could also affect netizens' discussions. In particular, in many cases, unsatisfied with a lack of information, netizens demanded further reporting (see discussion below). Sometimes they even supplemented facts with their own comments (e.g., a netizen's comment appraising Gao Yulun [case #44] as a "real man" cited earlier), though such facts were not authenticated officially. Granted, netizens' interest could prompt further media reporting, as seen in the Lin Senhao case.

Delivery-wise, the media (e.g., reporters) have some latitude in how to report stories in order to tailor them to people's interest. Other than the sensational Lin Senhao case, stories were rarely followed up on with every major player involved. Sometimes reporters managed to find a particular angle to tackle the story. As discussed in chapter 4, for instance, reporters were successful in both the Lin "x"ping and Ye "x"tian case (#16) and the Yang Chaoquan case (#33) to draw people's sympathy for these offenders (and therefore prompted netizens' interactions). In the Lin and Ye case, it was done by the media's focusing on family members of the soon-to-be-executed inmates; in the Yang Chaoquan case, it was done by their providing a detailed description of Yang's activities on the last day before his execution. Unfortunately, such cases were few. The majority of cases were formalistically or even formulaically reported (e.g., description of crimes, sentencing information) with little room or effort to expand on other aspects of the story (e.g., bringing in a humanistic perspective as in the Lin and Ye and Yang Chaoquan cases). Other than the Lin Senhao case, follow-up information on victims and their families was provided in only two other cases (see appendix 4). The lack of creativity in delivery may reflect lack of efforts by editors/reporters or might be related to limitations of the substance based on valid reasons and concerns (e.g., information control and censorship).

In 34 of the 63 cases (54%), netizens questioned and challenged media reporting of the case in point. Such questioning and challenging is comprehensive, indicating the great attention paid by netizens to these stories. First, a challenge could be as simple as a typo or a term used. In the Huang Qinghen case (#2), one netizen caught a typo and commented, "There is a typo in the title. One [is] found, cool." In the Gao Yulun et al. case (#44), one netizen commented on a misused term and said, "The quality of the editor is poor, who wrote that a 'criminal suspect' is death-sentenced. It should be that a 'defendant' is death sentenced." Second, many netizens found errors in the substance of stories. In the Zhai "x"de case (#9), one netizen pointed out two seeming contradictions in the report, including "to confiscate his properties" and "Zhai had no money even for food." In the Yang Chaoquan case (#33), one netizen challenged pictures that accompanied the story and said, "Little editor, is this a jigsaw puzzle (拼图)? It was summer to begin with, then suddenly it snowed and people wore an army-style heavy coat (军大衣)!" In the Zhang "x"yi case (#54), one netizen found a simple math error and wrote, "I'm impressed with the math of the little editor. The old man is 68 this year, and had his son at 30. The son died this year at 35. Moreover, how come the deceased police has two sons [probably suggesting a violation of the 'one-child birth control' policy]?"

Third, many netizens worried about how a story was reported and its potential impact on society. In the Zhao Zhihong case (#4), one netizen argued that the way Zhao's story was reported might have misled people. Specifically, the netizen wrote, "Zhao Zhihong confessed his crime back in 1996. His sentence has been long decided. The media should not overemphasize his crime and the sentencing, because it is under the sun and everyone knows it. The media should not mislead people and shift the focus to Zhao Zhihong but cover the crime of Feng Zhiming (冯志明) [a leading official who was in charge of Hu'ge's wrongful conviction and execution case]." In the Wu "x"hua case (#49), one netizen criticized the one-sided reporting of the story, saying, "This report could have been biased. [I] only see how bad the suspect was for his misdeed and how innocent the victims were. Certainly the victims bribed [the editor] in order to put the suspect to death immediately! I always believe in one phrase: whoever is pitiful must have a cause to be despised (可怜之人必有可恨之处) [implying the victims' fault]!" In the Yang Xueqi case (#62), one story used a title that said, "A man raped 18 women and his death sentence approved: he retaliated because his wife was homosexual." A number of netizens challenged this story for its biased reporting on homosexuality. One said, "The story [was] quoted out of context. They got divorced many years ago, [a fact] not explained. This is to mislead people against the homosexuals. Don't you know how it affects the homosexuals?" Granted, given the different positions of netizens, the reporting of a particular story might look "positive" to some but "negative" to others. Nevertheless, suspicion about the media's biased reporting was rather common among netizens, as one netizen summarized in the Wang Changping case (#19): "We are all victims of media consumption. China's media is the director behind the scene. For the same story, they may choose how to report it and tell the 'truth' in different ways with different results!"

On the other hand, it was popular for netizens to demand more reporting when they were puzzled by incomplete reporting and unexplained facts. Again, it could be as simple as demanding a plain fact. In the Liang Kaiwu case (#18), Liang killed a security guard and took a semiautomatic machine gun and killed another victim a few months later. One netizen asked, "How did he bring the gun onto the train? Please explain, little editor." In other cases, especially sensitive cases, netizens were apparently dissatisfied with unreported key facts (e.g., motive of crime). In the Liu Danao case (#47), many netizens believed that some key facts were hidden deliberately, which might have explained (or even justified) Liu's crime of killing four demolition and relocation workers. For instance, one netizen said, "Not reported in detail (语焉不详), covered by cloud, mountain, and fog (云山雾遮), hiding the head but showing only the tail (藏头露尾). Dare you show all details? Where is the conflict, a very important element—motive?" Another concurred: "Why only official stories? There are no arguments from Liu Danao; neither are there defense arguments." In the Fan Jieming case (#23), it was reported that due to financial disputes, Fan killed a coworker (and four more people on his killing spree). Nevertheless, no specifics were provided about the financial disputes. One netizen demanded, "Explain first what financial disputes were, OK?" It is interesting to see Chinese netizens demand more information and transparency with high degrees of distrust and suspicion, a feature of Chinese netizens in the age of the internet.

In sum, in this chapter we have focused on variations of netizens' comments based on four factors, including crime types, information about defendants and victims, the impact of legal procedures, and media reporting. Our examination showed that although Chinese netizens showed strong support for death sentences in general, their opinions were *not* immutable but were subject to changes given the circumstances of a particular case, an important finding and lesson consistent with results from other nations (e.g., Hood 2018). As we have argued, these variations represent an important part of the diversity of netizens' opinions, along with the breadth and the depth of their discussions (see chapter 2). Taken together, the diversity of netizens' opinions on death sentences casts legitimate doubt on the "overwhelming public support" claimed by the Chinese government.

CHAPTER 6

Criminal Justice System and Its Professionals in the Eyes of Netizens

In this chapter we focus on Chinese netizens' explicit comments about the criminal justice system and its professionals. As death penalty cases often involve the most difficult decisions of the criminal justice system, how the system functions and how professional players of the system perform in the eyes of netizens in our study made up a significant portion of their discussions. In sequence, we examine netizens' challenges and questions to the judicial system (i.e., courts and judges), the police (and policing), the correctional system, criminal defense lawyers, and other players (e.g., lawmakers, legal experts, and public intellectuals). Our examination covers both positive and negative comments made by netizens.

Challenges to the Judicial System

Since all of the comments in our study were generated by real cases, netizens' comments on the judicial system outnumbered comments on other branches. Specifically, in 36 cases (57.1% of all cases), netizens made explicit comments about judges or the courts. In nine of these cases, they appraised judges on their performance. Almost invariably, these short, positive comments were made in order to support judges' death sentences in certain cases, as shown in the following examples:

"A fair decision by the court!" (Tuo Heti et al., #6)

"It gladdens people's hearts (大快人心). Thumbs up for the judicial system in Guangzhou." (Lin "x"ping and Ye "x"tian, #16)

"A good example by the court in Guizhou" (Yang Dazhi, #21)

"Judge [is] righteous, applaud." (Deng Fang, #27)

"Support! Support! A good precedent! A wise judge!" (Chen Yun, #31)

"Applaud for fair, equitable and transparent sentencing" (Wang Yihuan, #43)

"This judge [is] wise" (Zhao Zihui, #60)

It is evident that Chinese netizens' strong belief in heavy penalties and harsh punishment (see chapter 3) played a significant role in their evaluation of judges' performance. The only exception appeared in the Lin Senhao case (#1), when netizens commented on the attitude of judges (e.g., "Regardless the sentence, the attitude of judges, thumbs up"). Nevertheless, in Lin's case appraisals of judges' attitude were outnumbered and outweighed by netizens who insisted on a death sentence. For instance, one netizen said, "If a death sentence is meted out, we will believe in judges! [And] believe China's law still has hope!"

In 32 cases (88.9% of 36 cases), negative comments were made against judges or courts. In terms of substance, netizens' questions and challenges can be grouped into six categories. First, consistent with their preference for heavy penalties, netizens strongly challenged non-death sentences or suspended death sentences meted out by judges in many cases. In the Gao Yulun et al. case (#44), Gao, Li Haiwei, and Wang Daming broke out of prison and killed a prison guard. While Gao and Wang were death-sentenced, Li was sentenced to life imprisonment. Some netizens challenged Li's non-death sentence. One netizen said, "One life imprisonment, what fucking laws? All should be shot to death, including judges." Another concurred: "It would be death by a thousand cuts in ancient times, but only life imprisonment now. What a heart of a holy mother (圣母心), judge." Comments on the Li "xx" case (#55) revealed sharp contrasts in netizens' different attitudes toward judges and prosecutors given their positions in sentencing. In this case, defendant Li stabbed victim Wang to death in public and was going after Wang's son when he was arrested. Li received a suspended death sentence from the trial court. Reportedly, the people's procuratorate decided to protest the trial court's ruling and demanded an immediate death sentence. Among netizens' comments, the two most popular themes (by the number of comments) were their questioning of judges' performance (93 comments) and Li's suspended death sentence (24 comments). For instance, one netizen asked, "Homicide on purpose, why not a death sentence? Do you [judges] own and run the court? [Are you] still representing the national judicial system? It is obvious that judges don't know the law and accepted bribes favoring the defendant. Sentencing like this makes people bitterly disappointed!" In contrast, 11 comments supported the procuratorate's decision to lodge a protest. A typical comment among them was "Thumbs up for the prosecutorial protest! Strict investigation of reasons for judges' lenient sentence!" Demands for harsh punishment were sometimes made in the name of fairness and equity. In the Wang Yuefu case (#8), a group of seven offenders was charged with arson, in which one villager died and three others were seriously injured. The principal offender, Wang, was death sentenced but the others were spared. One angry netizen asked, "Why is Du Qunshan (杜群山) not a principal offender? Is this sentence fair and just? If Du Qunshan does not die, how can Geng Fulin (耿福林) [the deceased victim] close his eyes [a Chinese idiom, equivalent to 'rest in peace']?" Named as the second offender after Wang, Du was sentenced to life imprisonment, and the news report did not detail roles played by each offender and the court's sentencing justifications (e.g., why Wang was the only person found as a principal offender).

Netizens' preference for capital punishment was not universal (see chapter 3 for their questioning of death sentences). In a few cases, such as those involving Liu Danao (#47) and He Shenguo (#42), netizens strongly challenged relevant governmental policies (the demolition and relocation policy and the one-child birth control, policy, respectively; see chapter 7). As a result, many of them believed that the judges who sentenced Liu and He to death made a wrong decision. In the Liu Danao case, they asked, "Whom does law serve?" and argued that Liu's death sentence was "legitimate but not reasonable (合法但不合情理)." They also blamed the court, saying, "This court is very IS [Islamic State, original in English]" and "This court will be facing a guillotine," and claimed that "To death-sentence Liu Danao shows the incompetence of the Zhengzhou intermediate people's court and the shamelessness of the Henan Provincial High Court." In the He Shenguo case, one netizen argued that "a court is not a place for ordinary people to argue (不是给老百姓讲理的地方)." By all means, netizens demanded tough laws against true criminals but were not afraid of supporting defendants against bad governmental policies.

Second, Chinese netizens expressed some concerns about the appeal process in death penalty cases. Often, as the appeals process went on, netizens expressed their frustration with the extended delays and waste of resources. Many believed that such delay and waste is not necessary, and some even called for an expedited process and said they would be willing to forgo proper legal procedures, as discussed in chapter 5. In the Yang Ruixi case (#53), one netizen pointed out, "[Yang was] death-sentenced in July 2013. More than two years of delay by the Supreme People's Court (SPC)? Where is law's fairness and equity given such efficiency?" Another immediately concurred: "Cases in China, efficiency is always low. It occurred in 2013 but execution carried out today. Was it death by shooting or lethal injection?" Besides delay and waste of resources, another common concern, associated with their belief in heavy penalties, was netizens' strong suspicion that an offender's death sentence could be changed and reduced with appeals. In the Chen Yun case (#31), one netizen commented, "A second trial would change [the death sentence] to life imprisonment, a third trial would change [it] to 15 years, and a fourth trial would declare [the defendant] not guilty and released. To favor and protect criminals is a good tradition of the criminal justice system." Similarly, in the Yang Dazhi case (#21), a netizen said, "[The outcome of] a first trial is a death sentence, a second trial life imprisonment, and a third trial 10 years." Such a suspicion showed netizens' lack of trust of the Chinese judiciary and their suspicion was tied to specific problems of the judicial system identified by netizens (detailed below).

Third, founded or unfounded, jokingly or seriously, some netizens tied their criticisms in specific cases to judges' self-interests, in particular their financial interests. In the Zhao Zhihong case (#4), one netizen very briefly commented, "How much is the costs of appeals? The court is laughing," which implies that the appellate court would make money from the appeal. In the Hu "x" case (#7), defendant Hu murdered victim Zhang due to Zhang's refusal to repay debts owed to Hu (estimated at tens of millions of yuan). Sympathetic to Hu, one netizen questioned the role of the court in cases when one party refuses to repay debts owed to another party. Specifically, the netizen said, "Refusal to pay debts; the murderer doesn't deserve to die, right? With regard to one's refusal to repay debts, what role does a court play? Litigation fees alone would cost several hundreds of thousands of yuan. Can you afford it? [Even so,] it is still uncertain whether you would get your money back. They killed Zhang; it was forced [due to Zhang's refusal to pay debts]. The police cannot find the murderer [deserving] a death sentence."

Among the most controversial reform measures in recent years is the practice of "cash for clemency." Couched in criminal reconciliation practice (Z. Li 2012; Ng and He 2017; Xiang 2013), since the mid-2000s the SPC has been encouraging judges to mediate between defendants and families of homicide victims to secure financial agreements that would allow courts to sentence defendants to suspended, instead of immediate, death sentences (Trevaskes 2015; Weatherley and Pittam 2015). Though the goal of "cash for clemency" is to reduce the number of death sentences, its practice in the eyes of netizens has turned into a means with which the wealthy can afford "buying more justice" for themselves at the expense of the poor. In the Yuan Junkai et al. case (#12), Yuan had a lengthy criminal record, received a suspended death sentence in 1989, and was paroled in 2007 before he committed another capital crime in 2012. Many netizens expressed their anger with Yuan's release and pointed their fingers at the court. Some specifically tied their accusations to the financial interests of the court. For instance, one said, "Heh-heh [sound mimicking a sneer], [Yuan] fucking gave money to the court. Otherwise, how could he be released after [committing] homicide?" Another concurred, saying, "As long as you have money, a death sentence turns into a suspended death sentence, and a sentence of 10 years into 5 years." Yet another commented, "Replacing incarceration with financial fines; more for money but less for sentencing (重钱轻判); sentencing alteration and reduction; huge corruption in the circle of law." In the Yang Chaoquan case (#33), Yang burglarized a home and killed the owner. As discussed in chapter 4, a detailed description of Yang's last-day activities on his execution day drew great sympathy from many netizens. One particular netizen compared Yang's death sentence with others who were spared, and suspected that Yang's lack of resources for clemency was the primary reason for his execution. The netizen wrote specifically, "[Yang] should not be sentenced to death. What's the reason that many who deserve to die were not death-sentenced? This one was death-sentenced because of no money? Nowadays, everything is about money." In contrast, another netizen questioned the delay in the case but also tied the issue to money: "Cases like this one with a simple process, clear facts and accurate evidence, [waited] more than two years for execution!!! My God, our nation's judicial efficiency is so low. In my view, as long as the evidence is sufficient, an immediate execution should be ordered. Without an immediate execution, they might be waiting for the party to send money!!! Raising salaries for judicial personnel was discussed lately, [I'm] speechless! Even if the party compensated [the victim] and gave money to judicial personnel in charge of the case, does it justify more lenient punishment nationwide?"

Fourth, many netizens expressed concerns about judicial misconduct and corruption.[1] In the Zhao Zhihong case (#4), one netizen suspected "behind-door deals" between Zhao and the judges and commented, "Is [Zhao] considering an appeal? Shouldn't this result [a death sentence] expected? Why [he] needs reconsideration? In my view, it is to get a permission [for Zhao's death sentence]? Maybe someone has promised him that he wouldn't die if he confessed in this case." As Zhao's case involved the wrongful conviction and execution of Hu'ge (see chapter 3), many netizens suspected more problems with the trial court. One said, "The Inner Mongolian Court has 'hidden dragons and crouching tigers'! Feng Zhiming [one of the leading officials in charge of Hu'ge's case] was only the spearhead (枪头), and there are more behind him." Another netizen commented, "Only Zhao's confession proved Hu'ge's innocence. If [Zhao is] sentenced to death, no one would confess anymore. Chinese courts are a major base for corruption, and there are basically few good judges, and the wrongfully convicted are countless. Who should be harshly sentenced is the police in charge." In the Luo Xiaohua and Chen Rihong case (#57), despite their heinous crimes (rape and homicide), only Luo was sentenced to immediate death, and Chen received a suspended death sentence. Netizens challenged Chen's sentence. One netizen said, "Something is wrong with the judge who meted out the suspended death. Rape plus two lives only sentenced to suspended death. But for the review and approval by the SPC, these two murderers might escape death. Judges in charge did it for hidden facts (隐情), and they should quit from the criminal justice system." Another simply asked, "Judges accepted bribes? Why one received only suspended death, [I'm] baffled."

Though the majority of such comments showed merely netizens' suspicions, in a number of cases, several whistleblowers apparently named judges in real cases to expose issues (though such accusations were *not* verified officially). In the Liu Danao case (#47), one wrote, "Corruption permitted? Power and glory (威武雄壮)! The precondition of corruption is the protection of the Party. How many wrongful convictions has the SPC reviewed and approved? Judicial corruption has led to a total loss of public trust! Please search 'the homicide case by the Qidong village offi-

---

1. As corruption has become ubiquitous in China, the Chinese judiciary is no exception. See, for example, L. Li 2012.

cial' (启东村官杀人案)!" The Wu Qinyuan case (#11) involved another wrongful conviction, and one netizen argued, "I don't think this wrongful conviction was caused by judges' oversight. It was framed by judges. Even powerful DNA evidence cannot stop the wrongful conviction. What other wrongful convictions cannot be produced by them?" In the Feng Xiujuan case (#32), one netizen referred to a specific case and questioned the ruling of a particular court. The netizen wrote, "Li 'x'qiang in Maoming was involved in criminal gang activities, including longtime kidnapping, two homicides, and numerous injuries (including serious injuries). The Maoming intermediate court sentenced Li to 16 years of imprisonment. Two lives, numerous injuries, killing with guns and knives in bright daylight, is 16-year sentence fair and just? Only Heaven knows." In the Fan Jieming case (#23), one netizen pointed out that "judges also forged signatures. . . . Check the Micropole (东望秘珀软件) back pay (欠薪) case in which judges Zhang Yiling (张依琳) and Zhang Junye (张骏烨) from the Putou district court forged signatures." Granted, the mere fact that netizens named real judges does not prove that the judges were involved in professional misconduct. But such bold statements did lend more credibility to these netizens' accusations. Occasionally netizens also expressed frustration with the fact that no formal sanctions were taken against exposed judges. For instance, one netizen discussing the Lian Enqing case (#14) called for actions against two judges and said:

> Killing is not right for sure. How to deal with it fairly? Court, letters and visits (信访),[2] fair and just? Two judges, Zhu Xingui (朱新桂) and Zhang Lingyan (张凌燕) from the Linzi district people's court in Zibo city in Shandong province have been reported in real names for two years for their collusion in high-interest loans, corruption, and forcing people to go broke (逼人死命). Relevant departments and courts at all levels have not dealt with it, why? Hope an immediate investigation of these two judges and bring back to ordinary people a blue sky (晴天) [implying 'justice'].

Similarly, in the Jin Fusheng case (#59), a netizen shared his own experience in Beijing and expressed his frustration that no formal official actions

---

2. The "letters and visits" system is a practice that allows ordinary people to present their complaints, via means such as mails (i.e., letters) and visits, to relevant departments at all levels of the government. For studies of the "letters and visits" system; see, for example, Gao and Long 2015; L. Li, Liu, and O'Brien 2012; Minzner 2006; Paik 2011.

had been taken even after he exhausted all legal procedures (e.g., procuratorate protest, letters and visits). He openly solicited ideas and suggestions from others to help him with his case and to expose judicial corruption.

When netizens commented on incompetent or corrupt judges, they referred to two well-known fictional figures for an analogy. One is from the famous novel *Dream of the Red Chamber* (红楼梦) by Cao Xueqin (曹雪芹). In chapter 4 of the novel, titled "An Ill-Fated Girl Happens to Meet an Ill-Fated Young Man—The Hulu Bonze Adjudicates the Hulu Case," a corrupt official mishandles a case on purpose to give favor to the well-connected defendant. As a result, "Hulu Bonze (葫芦僧)" has been coined as a name for corrupt and incompetent judges ever since. In the Luo Xiaohua and Chen Rihong case (#57), unhappy with Chen's suspended death sentence, one netizen commented, "[A] Hulu Bonze misjudged the Hulu case." The other analogy is from a famous Henan opera (豫剧), *The Small Official at the Seventh Rank* (七品芝麻官). The opera tells of a story in which a county official at the seventh rank (a very low rank) dares to fight well-connected defendants to vindicate justice. One famous line spoken by the county official is "If an official is not working for the people, he would rather go home and sell yams as a profession (当官不为民作主不如回家卖红薯)." In the Liu Danao case (#47), one netizen challenged Liu's death sentence and wrote:

> This sentence, legitimate but not reasonable, can only arouse people's indignation. Any person with a good sense (明眼人) should know the darkness behind this sentence. As a powerless minority, [Liu] sacrificed his life for others, which shows something wrong. The court did not investigate the reason that triggered this case and the truth behind the case, which let down the reputation of the government once again! In fact, [Liu's] death is not worth it, not to mention only for a few skunks [implying workers killed by Liu]! Don't count on your death to awaken society, and there are too many events of the same nature. An agreement should be secured before tearing down one's house. The few deceased were merely assistants. Cannot wipe them all out. What I want to ask is why the government tolerates such behavior? To tear down people's house should first provide compensation to their satisfaction! This judge should go home and sell yams!

Fifth, many netizens made personal comments directly against judges. For instance, many of them called for accountability against misbehaved judges. In the Yuan Junkai et al. case (#12), one netizen questioned Yuan's parole and argued that judges who made the decision should be held responsible for Yuan's recidivism. Specifically, the netizen wrote:

> If he was shot to death on his first offense, how would there be a new innocent victim? Those judges who tried to reform a natural-born criminal are stupid and too naïve, or tried to protect the criminal, and ignored personal safety and property rights of law-abiding citizens. If a suspended death-sentenced criminal kills again, the court bears significant responsibilities. A person deserved to be killed should be killed, as long as evidence is sufficient! One crime is enough! If the evidence is sufficient but a criminal is sentenced leniently, a judge should bear responsibilities for future victims who suffer [from more crimes].

Similarly, a netizen addressing the Yang Xueqi case (#62) demanded accountability from the president of the court and said, "Before his arrest in this case, he [Yang] served prison time five times!! Who is the president of the court? He should have joint liability." In a number of other cases, netizens even blatantly attacked and threatened judges. In the Yuan Junkai et al. case (#12), one netizen who questioned Yuan's parole decision threatened the judge and said, "[Yuan committed] homicide, still paroled out? Judge, you are not afraid of a visit by the deceased at night?" In the Li "xx" case (#55), not satisfied with the suspended death sentence meted out by the judge, some netizens called for "a cyber manhunt of this judge, a typical wrong sentence" and said, "If the son of the deceased is doughty, go and kill the judge."

Sixth, a tiny number of netizens tried to analyze the root causes for judicial problems and proposed constructive solutions. In the Li "xx" case (#55), one netizen elaborated on reasons why judges issue more lenient sentences and wrote:

> Nowadays, completely one-sided, law, court, and judges would favor criminal suspects, and find excuses for them to mete out more lenient sentences. For one, this is for self-protection so that they don't bear responsibilities; for another, sentencing more leniently without harsh punishment would avoid many troubles. In particular, in death penalty cases, in the name of 'killing cautiously,' many judges would sentence a great number of offenders who deserve

immediate death sentences to suspended death sentences, in order to avoid responsibilities. Moreover, they are afraid of bad karma; many of them accepted money from the criminals or their families, so why not? This has become the unwritten rules. As a result, laws have become soft noodle when used by judges.

In the Wu Qinyuan case (#11), one netizen suggested that "judicial independence and judges to be elected by people is the solution." This was echoed by another netizen commenting on the Lin Senhao case (#1), who proposed that "we need judicial independence and guarantee of judicial practices not being hampered by administrative expenditure. All lawsuits [should be] free, to be covered by national budgets."

Challenges to the Police

In 25 cases (39.7% of 63 cases), netizens made explicit comments about the police. In merely two cases, netizens appraised the police for their performance. In the Zhai "x"de case (#9), one netizen said, "Thanks to the police for catching this criminal!" In the Zhang Weilan et al. case (#20), one netizen commented, "The people's police work hard throughout the year (常年如一日) and hold their positions without being noticed (默默坚守). Thank you for your hard work. To protect people's safety, thumbs up for the front-line police!" Another concurred: "It is hard work for the front-line police officers. Those who get injured are always front-line officers."

In three other cases, netizens also supported the police in response to others' critiques. In the Wang Changping et al. case (#19), one netizen expressed concern about police officers' low salary and said, "The salary for the police is low, with little money to support one's family. Tell your family members: don't become a police officer and not even for the next life, [because] one cannot even support one's wife!" In the Luo Xiaohua and Chen Rihong case (#57), one netizen countered some netizens' criticism of police officers' low efficiency in cracking the case and said, "sb [cursing words, see chapter 4], you can even verbally attack this? Can you do it? If not, shut your filthy mouth. I'm tired of a sb like you who only turns to verbal attack. At least the police was chasing the criminal after 12 years, which was good." In the Yang Xueqi case (#62), one netizen suggested, "I think that our nation should pay attention to police's salaries and benefits, allow normal working hours, strengthen the force, establish a reasonable retirement system for the police, and get rid of nepotism. This is to strengthen their sense of belonging, raise their professional pride, and improve their combat skills. As the saying goes: you want the horse to run fast but don't want the horse to eat much, is it realistic?"

In 24 cases (38.1% of 63 cases), netizens made negative comments to criticize the police and policing, which can be grouped into three categories. First, in two infamous wrongful conviction cases, netizens expressed their resentment toward corrupt police officers and demanded that those who were responsible be held accountable. In the Zhao Zhihong case (#4), netizens pointed their fingers at Feng Zhiming, a leading official in charge of Hu'ge's wrongful conviction and execution, and made comments such as "People like Feng Zhiming who self-claimed an expert in cracking cases are true killing devils. They are more dreadful, sinister, and detestable! If people like Feng don't get their deserved harsh punishment, running the nation according to law won't get an effective kickoff!" and "People like Feng Zhiming only want to be promoted and become rich and they would disregard others' lives at will (随心所欲地草菅人命) in exchange for their fame (换取功名). Such low skunks deserve to be severely punished." Many others openly shamed the police, though they did not name a particular person, and left comments such as "Zhao Zhihong [committed] a great sin and deserves to die. But who ignored the 4.9 case [Hu'ge case] and who insisted [on Hu'ge's death]? But for the publicity, is the court going to continue ignoring the 4.9 case?"; "Don't the Chinese police feel shamed?"; and "I only pay attention to the police who caused [Hu'ge's] wrongful conviction." In the Wu Qinyuan case (#11), netizens again called for punishment of those who were responsible for the wrongful conviction of Yu Yingsheng (于英生). One netizen commented, "I just don't understand: how come the fake one became the true one after being handled by the police? The semen inside the female body was not from her husband [referring to Yu, the wrongfully convicted husband]. Why did the police 'point to a stag but call it a horse (指鹿为马)'?[3] Moreover, the cooperation

---

3. "Calling a stag a horse" is a famous historical story recorded in the *Records of the Grant Historian* (史记), written by Sima Qian (司马迁). The story occurred during the reign of the second emperor of the Qin dynasty (221–207 B.C.). According to the story, in order to test his power and control over subordinate officials, the prime minister Zhao Gao brought a stag to the emperor and told him that it was a horse. When the emperor corrected him, Zhao turned to other officials. While some officials, afraid of Zhao's power, concurred with Zhao, some kept silent, and still others were brave enough to speak the truth. Afterward, Zhao managed to get rid of those who dared to challenge

among the police, the prosecution, and the court was smooth. Someone wanted Yu dead, and it cannot be done by a low-rank official." Another commented, "Heaven is watching. What happened to officials in charge then??? The public should crack down on these corrupt bastards and send them to 8-year imprisonment!!! Otherwise, Heaven's law won't accept it."

Second, in a great number of cases, netizens expressed concerns about incompetence among Chinese police. Such concerns often pointed to inefficiency and incapability of cracking crimes, especially when the investigations lasted a long time. In the Liang Kaiwu case (#18), for instance, one netizen said, "[Liang] self-surrendered twice and escaped twice, but [it] did not draw enough attention from the local police. Only until it became a huge case was it treated seriously. What's the use of the local police?" In the Hu Cunbiao and Wang Yong case (#29), netizens commented on the eight-year crime spree during which Hu committed a string of sexual offenses and robberies. One netizen said, "Between 2004 and 2012, defendant Hu Cunbiao stopped en route women and female students who were not accompanied by parents numerous times at Zaozhuang city, Jining city, and Tengzhou city in Shandong. He committed rapes, robberies, and molestations by means such as force or threat with a knife. A total of 11 rape victims, including seven minors under the age of 14. And it required 7–8 years to catch and sentence him. No need to talk about public security anymore." Another concurred with a sarcastic tone, "From 2004 to 2012, eight years, finally caught [Hu], a full display of the extraordinary power of the police." Similarly, in the Yang Xueqi case (#62), Yang committed a series of rapes from 1998 to 2012. One netizen commented, "Cannot take it anymore (实在看不下去了). It would be different if [Yang] fled and committed his crimes hither and thither and covered his crimes well. Serial local crimes over the years. A repeat offender, with the same method within a clear boundary. Remained at large for so long. Nothing more to comment. Even a pig using its brain would be able to narrow down suspects. A dog would be able to deter criminals. This place raises such a group [of incompetent police], truly unfortunate to the local people." Another concurred sarcastically, "The capability of the Chinese police in solving cases is so strong: caught [Yang] in merely 18 crimes." In the Luo Xiaohua and Chen Rihong case (#57), one netizen argued that inefficiency in solving cases could be due to the low priority set by the police. The

---

him and speak the truth. Since then, the phrase "calling a stag a horse" is used to refer to one's deliberate effort to manipulate facts and confound right and wrong.

netizen compared prostitution cases (which could be financially lucrative to solve) with murder cases and said, "Fucked, it takes an hour to crack a case of prostitution, but it takes dumb luck (狗屎运) to crack this murder case." Granted, many netizens demanded accountability. For instance, in the Deng Fang case (#27), Deng raped and murdered two victims—one in 2013 and another in 2014. One netizen asked, "How come the police did not catch him in his first murder? Only until the second murder after more than a year? If this murderer did not commit the second murder, he would not even be caught? The police department deserves punishment! Incompetence in solving cases!"

In addition to general comments on police incompetence, netizens questioned some specific police behavior (or the lack of thereof) in a few cases. In the Fan Jieming case (#23), Fan killed a number of victims with his hunting gun, and one netizen questioned why the police did not use lethal force against him. One netizen commented, "[In a desperate situation where] either the fish dies or the net splits (鱼死网破), why did [the police] not use guns! Only use guns against people without guns! How pathetic the Chinese police are!" Similarly, in the Li "xx" case (#55), a few questioned why police did not use weapons and made comments such as "[Li] passed three police to go after [the victim's son]. Why not shoot [him] to death?" and "Who can tell me: why the police did not draw their guns this time? Are there reasons behind it?" In the Zhang "x"yi case (#54), victim Liu was a 35-year-old police officer who witnessed a crime and tried to stop offender Zhang. Zhang stabbed Liu 16 times, and Liu died at a hospital later. A couple of netizens questioned Liu's combat skills specifically. One said, "Speaking candidly, deep condolences for the death of Liu Yong. But this is the competence of our police? Being stabbed 16 times? Where are police's combat skills? How do we expect you [police] to protect ordinary people?"

Third, two cases in our sample involved former police officers who turned into leading criminals, and many netizens blasted bad cops; some even tied the rampancy of crimes to a corrupt police force. In the Wang Changping et al. case (#19), Wang, a former police officer, masterminded drug manufacturing. A total of 28 comments targeted bad cops in general, the third most popular theme in this case, trailed only by counterarguments (37 comments) and comments against Wang himself (33 comments). Specifically, netizens commented on the severe nature of crimes involving bad cops (e.g., "Police participated in drug manufacturing; the nature is extremely severe"), called for harsh punishment (e.g., "Knowing the law but breaking it. How audacious! Shoot to death and flog the corpse"), questioned the lifestyle of bad cops (e.g., "Police in our place all drive good cars. Where do they get the money?"), suggested a connection between drug crimes and police corruption (e.g., "Finally [I] understood why illegal drug business is doing better and better with tougher and tougher punishment!"), and demanded investigation of police corruption (e.g., "Police corruption does the most damage to society. Suggest strict investigation of the police system"). One angry netizen described the worsening image of the police and even cursed them, writing, "Fucking police, how degraded they are these days! Speaking the truth: ordinary people have the worst image of police in their minds! Their eyes redden (眼红) [a Chinese idiom that means 'being jealous'] when the police see others' business do well. . . . How many cases of shooting ordinary people [by the police] have occurred this year? Only because of your bandit skin (匪皮) [likely referring to police uniform]. So it serves one right when sometimes police are killed! Retribution!" In the Wang Baiyang case (#51), to pay his gambling debts, Wang, a former police officer, abducted victim Yuan, asked for ransom money, and strangled Yuan to death. After his incarceration, Wang planned a prison break with three cellmates but failed. Though it received only nine comments, questioning bad cops was the most popular theme in this case. Again netizens pointed out the severe nature of such cases (e.g., "Bad cops are the stumbling blocks of the progress of legalization"), argued for police involvement in many crimes (e.g., "If police do not commit crimes, public security will improve by half. Behind the back of criminal gangs there is always people's police!"), and warned future bad cops (e.g., "Faced much pressure? Finally send one bad cop to the execution site. Have a good journey, and there might be more followers on the road to hell [黄泉路]. The alarm bell is ringing for those bad cops who put their faith in luck [心存侥幸])."

In addition to these two cases, netizens occasionally shared stories about bad police and policing. In the Wang Changping et al. case (#19), one netizen asked, "What happened to the police officer who broke the neck of a migrant worker Zhou Suyun (周素云)? How come there is no news? Is it national secret?" Another shared a different case and said, "In order to protect the interests of the Dehui Office of the Charoen Pokphand Group (正大集团德惠分公司) in illegally occupying forest land, and building houses and drilling wells, the police department of the Dehui city in Jilin province arrested many civil rights fighters who opposed the drilling and tried to refill the drilled wells. [Police] forced confessions through torture. The first trial sent the case back to the procuratorate for more investigation? The arrested have been detained for over four months. Guilty or not, seeing flowers through the mist (雾里看花) [a Chinese idiom implying the murky nature of the case]." In the Yang Xueqi case (#62), many netizens were angry with the incompetence of the police in Changge city (where Yang's crimes occurred); one shared a personal story about Changge police and said, "Absolutely no action from Changge police. There was a robbery once on the 107 national highway. A male truck driver was beaten by a couple and was bleeding and motionless. Several Changge police were present but dared not intervene. [They are] a group who only know how to eat (吃干饭) but do nothing. The local rascals become wild! As a result, the reputation of Changge is not good." Again, these stories were not officially verified, but the whistleblowing did lend more credibility to such stories.

Challenges to the Correctional System

Compared to their critical comments on the judicial system and the police, netizens challenged China's correctional system in merely five cases (7.9%) in our sample. All comments made were negative and criticized various problems detailed below, thus being typical examples of "critique when problems loom but no comments when no issues are reported."

Netizens' critique against China's correctional system focused on three specific issues. First, netizens were extremely angry with new capital crimes committed by people with criminal records. In four of the five cases in which netizens commented on the correctional system, defendants carried prior criminal records and their new capital offenses would thus be considered "recidivism" (Yuan Junkai et al., #12; Zhang Xiangxi, #15; Gao Yulun et al., #44; and Yang Xueqi, #62). Given the recidivism, netizens questioned sentence reductions and parole decisions in these cases that allowed offenders another chance to commit new crimes. In the Yuan Junkai et al. case, one netizen asked, "Why was he paroled? On what conditions? Why allowed him to be out and harm others again?" Another questioned if corruption was involved and asked, "A murderer who was sentenced to suspended death could be paroled? How much money did law enforcement personnel collect? Strict investigation. Allowing these skunks out to harm society, corrupt officials who released them should be doubly guilty (罪加一等) and harshly punished." In the Zhang Xiangxi case, one netizen commented on Zhang's new crime, "The bloody lesson told us that whoever served prison time before would recidivate sooner or later." Netizens again demanded accountability from the responsible personnel. In the Yuan Junkai et al. case, one wrote, "A suspended death-sentenced inmate out to kill. Shouldn't the prison and court bear responsibilities?" Another netizen was more direct and said, "The director of the labor camp should be removed, investigated, and sentenced. Judges, lawyers, and other involved personnel in [Yuan's] first sentence should all be removed and never employed again. Those who caused serious consequences with bad societal impact should be removed and sentenced accordingly." In the Hu Cunbiao and Wang Yong case (#29), neither Hu nor Wang had prior records. Nevertheless, one netizen countered another's suggestion to reduce the use of capital punishment and said, "Recidivism after reeducation occurs very often. Reeducation? Or you bear full responsibility? This is not our disregard to lives; it is their disregard to our rights, lives, and properties . . . should have ended their lives earlier."

Second, related to recidivism, many netizens questioned the rehabilitation function of the prison system. In the Yuan Junkai et al. case, one netizen argued, "A second time in prison, still not reeducated. It shows that prison education has a problem, which leads to the third fatal behavior. It is a long road for rehabilitation of criminals. Laws should be revised." Another wondered, "Why [Yuan showed] no repentance? And most of those reported nowadays are recidivists and repeat offenders who received prison education! Is prison system appropriate and prison education plausible?" Many openly rejected the idea of prison rehabilitation. For instance, one strongly argued, "Life imprisonment for those who commit a second crime. The so-called reform of criminals is impossible!!!!" Another concurred: "The prison does not have the effect of rehabilitation but only continues their recidivism. [Inmates] are isolated from society for a long time and have a difficult time finding jobs, as they are rejected by employers; [they] are doomed for abandonment by society, and the odds of going back to the wrong road are extremely high." In the Yang Xueqi case, one netizen pointed out that "the recidivism of Chinese released inmates is very high, which shows that our prison system fails to function as reform, but only makes them worse." Another agreed, saying, "Five times in prison, isn't prison supposed to reform criminals? Why makes them worse? Since when has Chinese prison become a refuge (收容所)? Put together a pile of bad apples. No one cares and it is difficult to not get rotten." Yet another wrote, "Criminals in prison are there for a retreat (休养生息). They learn criminal lessons, communicate with others, reflect on why they fail, draw lessons, improve criminal skills, and recidivate after release!" Occasionally, frustrated netizens called for harsher punishment in prison. In the Yuan Junkai et al. case, one netizen suggested, "Prison should be like hell! Serious offenders should not be allowed to come out alive, [and this is] to deter criminals! Nowadays, prison humanization (人性化) [is discussed]. Aren't they comfortable enough? How many of the released are reformed? Or is this a future plan for corrupt officials?"

Third, the Gao Yulun et al. case, in which Gao and two other cellmates managed a prison break and killed a guard, exposed some management issues (at least at that particular facility). On the one hand, netizens blamed the deceased prison guard for his careless handling of security procedures. For instance, one netizen asked, "How careless the prison guard was: how could he allow himself alone to face three offenders? Other guards? Not enough hands? How dangerous! The death of the guard should not have happened! His family members must be heartbroken! Be vigilant! Should be careful when dealing with those desperados!" Another echoed that sentiment: "The deceased does not deserve to die, but he was mainly responsible for his own death. From the released video, he apparently talked and laughed together with the offenders like friends. He forgot they are criminals, and his failure to distinguish right from wrong caused his death." On the other hand, some netizens took the discussion beyond the deceased guard and questioned the daily operation and management of the prison system. For instance, one sharply pointed out, "There is no explanation at the deeper levels, [and] this sentence has no meaning! One, why was one guard able to interrogate [three] serious offenders at midnight? Two, how did three offenders walk out of the prison, like strolling in a courtyard (闲庭信步)? Three, are there other holes in prison management?" Another netizen tried to explain why prison guards seemingly befriended inmates, tying it to the low social status of prison guards. Specifically, the netizen commented, "The group that is looked down upon the most by police in the public security system is prison guards. Once befriended, they would tell you that inmates have a term limit but they would stay in prison for the rest of their lives. Prison guards don't have any connections or are not treated well by their superiors. Thus they don't have any pride in front of the inmates. Seeing each other every day would make one familiar with another. It is normal to talk and laugh together, because neither one is doing well."

Criminal Justice System and Its Professionals in the Eyes of Netizens 157

Challenges to Criminal Defense and Defense Lawyers

Criminal defense has always been a risky business for defense attorneys in China, despite its strengthened role in recent decades (e.g., S. Liu and Halliday 2016). Given the grave nature of capital offenses, what defense lawyers can offer in capital cases is extremely limited, and they often tread a thin line (e.g., H. Lu, Trejbalova, and Liang 2019; M. Xiong, Liu, and Liang 2018). In our sample, netizens explicitly discussed defense lawyers' performance in nine cases (14.3% of all cases). In six cases, netizens supported lawyers' right to criminal defense, and in seven cases netizens questioned and criticized lawyers' defense. However, when the total numbers of comments were compared, the balance was tipped: the total number of negative comments against lawyers reached 673 while that of positive comments was 133, thus a ratio of roughly 5 to 1. The Lin Senhao case (#1), with the most comments in our sample, generated 616 comments against lawyers and only 126 comments supportive of lawyers.

Content-wise, netizens' challenges to defense lawyers can be grouped into three categories. First, many netizens questioned defense lawyers' morality, as they defended the worst offenders, and believed they took the case for money or fame. In the Hu "x" case (#7), one netizen blasted Hu's defense lawyer and said, "Order that animal lawyer can no longer conduct lawyering for the rest of his life! In bright daylight, [he] called black white! Nonsense talk! A righteous lawyer would decline representation for these animals [capital offenders]." Another asked, "This lawyer, for money, his conscience was eaten by a dog?" Yet another specifically used the lawyer's name and said:

> How fucking you dare do this? Do you need money? The money paid by hundreds of millions of people in the nation for your sacrificial money (冥币) [false paper money burned as an offering to the dead] could feed you for several generations. You animal, worse than pigs and dogs (猪狗不如的东西). [Do you] know why reporters would like to interview you? It is for the Chinese people to see that some animals in the world would be willing to take on representation for money. [You] even did it with great confidence and made faces. Do you have any professional ethics?

In the Zhao Zihui case (#60), one netizen commented, "Lawyers are 'speaking on behalf of those who pay them.' Sometimes [they] used lame arguments and perverted logic (强词夺理) and nonsense-talked (无稽之谈), which could piss off people. Fortunately, it is up to the judges whether they would accept [lawyers' arguments]." In the Lin Senhao case (#1), many netizens called defense lawyers "pettifoggers" "with no morality" and argued that defense lawyers are to "help with collusion" and "call a stag a horse."

Second, Chinese netizens frequently questioned defense lawyers' general or specific strategies. For instance, related to the argument about lawyers' lack of morality, many claimed that defense lawyers are just "finding holes of the law" (钻法律空子) to defeat the law. In the Hu "x" case (#7), one netizen commented, "I studied law too. However, this lawyer is not only challenging the bottom line of morality, but also finding holes of the law. Law is not a time machine, and cannot reproduce the crime 100%. As long as the evidence is accurate, [we] may find guilt! This lawyer is so bigoted!" In the Lin Senhao case (#1), one said, "I don't even know what law is supposed to do now. When I was young, I believed that it is meant to safeguard justice, reward the right and punish the wrong, and protect legal interests of law-abiding citizens. Only until I grew up did I realize this is not true. When dealing with a case, lawyers are not relying on the law, but finding holes of the law." Another questioned how defense lawyers in Lin's case handled evidentiary flaws specifically and wrote:

> It is all right to take advantage of the flaws. But [you] cannot talk nonsense and make something out of nothing to mislead the public. Once finding a flaw, lawyers should inform the court, not to publicize it online to mislead the public. Because what you submitted is not evidence, it should be decided by the court. [You should] not announce in advance that it is a mistake of the investigators and the court. You found a problem, and it is one-sided story. However, you immediately announced to the public that it is the problem of the court. What are you planning to do? Netizens don't know the details of the case. Your announcement is misleading.

In two cases, netizens challenged lawyers' specific defense strategies. In the Zhao Zihui case (#60), Zhao's lawyer tried to claim Zhao's psychiatric history as legal mitigation, but the argument was rejected by the court. Netizens left 22 comments to reject the mental problem argument (the third most-popular theme in this case). For instance, one commented, "[Zhao's killing] method is cruel. People with such a mental disorder should have died long time ago. The lawyer doesn't have [lawyering] skills (没本事), and always used mental disorder as the defense." Others demanded, "[We] should evaluate the lawyer's mental condition and see if it is normal" and "This lawyer has mental disorder and should be disbarred." In the Lin Senhao case (#1), Lin's lawyers argued that Lin simply meant to teach victim Huang a lesson as a prank on April Fool's Day and had diluted the poisoned water; thus, the quantity of the poison was not sufficiently lethal. Angry netizens rejected and ridiculed the defense. One netizen said, "I think that Lin should poison his lawyers to make them dumb. What do you mean 'not reaching a sufficient lethal quantity'? Have you tried it? Some people are physically weak and might die on a small quantity. Is there such a standard?" Another argued, "Lawyers defend the criminal to perform their duties. Sometimes to win the case, they don't rule out the possibility of turning to inappropriate means such as coaching the criminal in favor of the defense. From start to finish, I believe Lin's insistence of the prank story is what the lawyers coached him." One netizen summarized the arguments against the defense lawyers' strategies, saying, "The so-called defense by the lawyers is just adding fuel to the flames. It produced no positive functions but a disservice (帮倒忙)." After Lin was executed, some netizens strongly argued that his defense chose a wrong overall strategy, which backfired and ended the last hope of saving Lin's life. One netizen left a long message to summarize the case:

> Thanks to Si and Tang, two defense lawyers who successfully sent Lin to the wrong path with no return (不归路). As a lawyer, it is his duty to fight to maximize the interests of the client, and for the most favorable sentencing outcome for the client. There were two options in dealing with the trial of second instance: first, to plead guilty, show remorse to the Huang's family and compensate to obtain their forgiveness, and argue for more lenient sentences; second, what you two actually did was to plead not guilty and try to completely overturn Lin's conviction. As renowned lawyers in the judicial circle who knew the media well, of course [you] knew that the success odds for the first option are very high, which would maximize the likelihood of saving Lin's life. The disadvantage, however, is that you two big-name lawyers wouldn't be able to show off your capabilities to the media and it would not generate high publicity for you. Option two is very difficult, and its success odds are almost zero given the current Chinese judicial system. (Don't

say that you don't know. To overturn the whole conviction is to challenge the whole system of the police, the procuratorate, and the judiciary, the odds very low.) But it would be easy to fool Lin's family and give them hope. At the same time, it would maximize the publicity of you two. If successful, you two would have become the number one criminal lawyers in China. Even if [you] failed, your publicity would be strong. The choice of yours we all see: the Huangs and the Lins are not the winner, but you two are. Congratulations for becoming winners of life.

Third, many netizens took their criticism to the next level and launched personal attacks and threats against defense lawyers. Here are some examples:

"What a bird [insulting language in Chinese] is this lawyer? Fuck"; "This lawyer is in danger. If the case is lost, he [referring to defendant Hu] would drown you to death in a pig cage." (Hu "x" case, #7)

"Wish the whole family of the lawyer would die for defending that animal." (Wu "x"hua case, #49)

"Why would a lawyer on earth defend this kind of man? Once [defendant] got out, it's likely that he [lawyer] would be the next one to be stabbed after [defendant] getting drunk." (Zhang "x"yi case, #54)

"Sentence the lawyer too"; "How come this lawyer can run a train all over his mouth (满嘴跑火车) [a Chinese idiom, meaning 'talk nonsense']. He would do anything for money. Once released, this kind of man [defendant] would kill the whole family of the lawyer. See what the lawyer will do"; "Don't let me run into this lawyer. Otherwise, [I'll] stab him to death. I have mental disorder anyway." (Zhao Zihui case, #60)

"If an inmate's death sentence was changed to a suspended death sentence and [he was] eventually released, then is it all right to ask defense lawyers and witnesses to bear joint liabilities? If recidivism occurs, is it all right for you to go to prison too?" "That dog lawyer should be sentenced to death too!!" "How come we don't have knights-errant (侠客) anymore? If so, the parents of this murderer and that rogue lawyer would perhaps have already gone to see the King of Hell [see note #2 in chapter 4]"; "China must reform the lawyering system and punish those who talk nonsense." (Lin Senhao case, #1)

These examples show clearly that Chinese netizens have their own standards in their judgments of lawyers' performance. To the majority of them, it is the outcome (i.e., evildoers get punished) that matters.

Compared to opponents, supporters of criminal defense all believed in one's legal defense rights and lawyers' duty to maximize their clients' best interests, even for capital offenders. In the Hu "x" case (#7), one netizen pointed out, "It is the lawyers' duty to defend. Even if one commits heinous crimes such as patricide, matricide, rape and robbery, he still has the defense right. A lawyer is not a judge." Another said, "Don't comment on lawyers [negatively]. Lawyering is a great profession. It is to maximize the interests of one's client." In the Wu Youxin case (#52), one netizen countered another and said, "Don't be stupid. How many people who commit crimes need lawyers to defend them? Everyone has the right to fight for one's rights before the end of the trial." In the Zhang "x"yi case (54), one netizen pointed out that "defense is the duty of the lawyer, and it has nothing to do with who is the client."

Supporters of criminal defense also countered netizens' specific criticisms against lawyers. In the Lin Senhao case (#1), one answered the suggestion that lawyers are just "finding holes of the law" and said, "Although I support a death sentence too, . . . law needs lawyers to split hairs (钻牛角尖). Lawyers defending their clients, what is there to be accused of?" A few others concurred and made comments such as "The existence of lawyers is to force the prosecution to look for ironclad evidence. Don't verbal attack [lawyers] if you don't know" and "The duty of lawyers is to try his best, within the framework of the law, to exonerate or reduce the punishment of clients. . . . If this principle is broken, he is not a lawyer, but a pettifogger." In the Zhao Zihui case (#60), answering the critique of many netizens on Zhao's mental disorder defense, one netizen explained, "This defendant would have no money to hire a lawyer. It should be an appointed lawyer from the judicial department. According to the law, lawyers can only plead no guilt or lesser degree of guilt. Thus it is not easy to plead lesser degree of guilt for him [Zhao]."

It is evident that opponents and supporters of criminal defense held very different views on what proper functions lawyers should or can perform in capital cases. In contrast to the minority supporters, the majority of Chinese netizens held a negative view of defense lawyers and did not believe in their contributions to the criminal justice system. In the Zhao Zihui case (#60), one netizen questioned the sincerity of the defense and commented, "The so-called defense by the lawyer was simply to take one's money and say a few clichés. Defendant's death or not, is he going to care? What a joke." In the Lin Senhao case (#1), one netizen equated defense lawyers to hatchet men of criminal gangs (黑社会打手) and wrote, "Nowadays, what almost all lawyers do is the same in nature as that of hatchet men of criminal gangs, except one relying on 'knowledge (文)' and the other on 'force (武).' We need now special laws against 'illegal debates' by lawyers." Another wrote, "Overall, lawyers in China play obviously negative roles, leading society to moral decline and to the direction of using law against morality, trumpery, and deceit." Despite such negativity, in a couple of cases, some netizens specifically called for lawyers to defend capital offenders. In the Liu Danao case (#47), one netizen called for more defense and said, "Whether he [Liu] was at fault, why not go and ask villagers?! Guilty but not sufficient for death!! Why cannot he petition for a psychiatric evaluation of momentary delusion? Defense lawyer, Wang Cailiang, what did you do?" In the Lin "x"ping and Ye "x"tian case (#16), one netizen suggested turning to lawyers for help despite holding a negative view of lawyering. Specifically, the netizen suggested, "You don't know the profession of lawyering? If you have money, you may hire a team of lawyers to fight for you. [If] you kill someone, your lawyer may say you have mental problems or raise some other defense. Anyway, lawyers will take advantage of all holes of the law to help lessen [one's] degree of guilt." These examples suggested that Chinese netizens knew that good lawyering may potentially help one's case, though they may disapprove of what lawyers do in their defense and how they do it.

Challenges to Other Players

Besides the challenges to major players discussed above, Chinese netizens challenged a number of relatively peripheral players in their comments, including lawmakers, legal experts (法律专家), and public intellectuals (公知).

Netizens' challenges to lawmakers focused on both *lawmaking* and *law enforcement*. Influenced by their strong belief in heavy penalties, netizens often called laws "too lenient" when it comes to punishing criminals. For instance, one police officer commented in the Yuan Junkai et al. case (#12), "As a police, [I] know it very well. It is not the police that lacks the force (不给力). It is the law. Finally caught [a criminal], the court sentenced [him] to three-month imprisonment.... The costs [of committing crimes] are too low." In the Zhang Xiangxi case (#15), one netizen lamented, "This is China's law. Once, twice, three times, to tolerate criminals until [they] commit all sorts of heinous crimes!" Netizens also questioned two other related issues: "humanization (人性化)" of penal sanctions and the policy of "killing fewer and killing cautiously (少杀慎杀)." In the Fan Jieming case (#23), one netizen questioned humanization of the law and wrote, "The humanization of Chinese laws brings harm or death to innocent ordinary people. Is it fair and reasonable?" In the Wu "x"hua case (#49), one commented, "This is China's humanized law, neither fish nor fowl (不伦不类). It does not allow Chinese laws to be based on China's conditions. To get rid of those lawmakers who do not consider national conditions is the right question we should reflect upon." In the Li "xx" case (#55), one netizen pointed out the influence of the "killing fewer and killing cautiously" policy on Li's suspended death sentence and said, "This is the other extreme of the notion of 'killing fewer and killing cautiously': one who deserves to die is spared. One who deserves to die should be killed. Otherwise [we] might just revise the law to abolish capital punishment. Suspended death sentences [should] restrict sentence reduction, with a minimum of 27 years. Or give him the immediate death sentence."

Another constant theme of such challenges was aimed at China's unique suspended death sentences. Almost universally, netizens questioned the "soft and changing nature" of the law, and many proposed to do away with the law. In the Luo Xiaohua and Chen Rihong case (#57), one wrote, "In China, suspended death = life imprisonment = 10 years = 5 years = ..." to express dissatisfaction with the "changing nature" of suspended death sentences. In the Yuan Junkai et al. case (#12), one netizen commented, "Suspended death, without a term, is not imprisonment with a fixed term. Supposedly, one would be executed after the [two-year] suspension. However, basically [there are] no executions [in reality]. Thus recommend abolition of suspended death, which might stop judicial corruption."

In questioning law enforcement, Chinese netizens expressed several major concerns. First, they argued that the laws are not enforced evenhandedly but are tough on ordinary people and lenient with the privileged classes. In the He Shenguo case (#42), one netizen simply said, "Laws are made to regulate ordinary people." In the Liu Danao case (#47), one netizen put it the opposite way: "Law is to serve the privileged classes." Another elaborated by saying, "Alas, you don't know [our] national conditions. Laws are not made by ordinary people. Once made and ready to be enacted, there is no requirement for acceptance by ordinary people. We cannot choose officials helpful to ordinary people and cannot decide their salaries and promotions either. They ask us to supervise. Without rights by ordinary people, how to supervise?" In the Yuan Junkai et al. case (#12), one netizen observed, "The precondition of the rule of law is to have no privileged classes. In our society where everyone wants to be an official, get rich and be a friend of a tycoon (土豪), very difficult." Second, some netizens pointed out the fact that Chinese laws are often heavily influenced by governmental and Party policies, given the lack of judicial independence. In the Yuan Junkai et al. case (#12), one netizen commented, "Chinese laws are basically made out of policies. Those who truly understand laws do not have a say. Even if they do, it is a cliché. The final say lies in the hands of politicians who are law-ignorant amateurs. As a result, the laws faced by ordinary people always bully them but are riddled with a thousand wounds against criminals (千疮百孔) and useless (无计可施)." In the Lin "x"ping and Ye "x"tian case (#16), one netizen bluntly pointed out, "Chinese laws cannot wrestle with the leg of the crotch (裆) [the word 'crotch' here implies 'the Party' as they share the same pronunciation, 'dang']."

Third, netizens also expressed concerns about the influence of one's wealth and power. In the Li "xx" case (#55), one netizen put it very bluntly: "Laws are made for the wealthy. The 'have-not,' out of the way." In the Luo Xiaohua and Chen Rihong case (#57), one netizen described the impact of "cash for clemency" and said, "[If] one buys off sufficiently (疏通打点到位了), 'killing fewer and killing cautiously' would be applied; [if] one has no money or connection, 'killing more swiftly and severely (从快从严)' would be applied. Law in China is a joke." One netizen in the Chen Yun case (#31) disbelieved Chen's death sentence, since Chen financially compensated families of the victims killed by his drunk driving, and asked, "[Chen, who] financially compensated [his victims,] is sentenced to death? Sentencing of Chinese laws keeps up with *renminbi* [i.e., Chinese currency]!" In the He Shenguo case (#42), one netizen commented on ordinary people's lack of financial resources to use the law and wrote, "For issues that cannot be solved by the nation, we often have to handle it ourselves. Don't mention turning to legal resorts. Ordinary people cannot afford it. Do you know how much are attorneys' fees? Do you know how much time and energy is involved in a trial? Don't mention legal assistance. I've experienced it. When ordinary people have nowhere to complain their grievances, they have to rely on sacrificing themselves to defend their families. Government, think about it!" As discussed in chapter 5, many netizens compared lenient punishment for corruption offenses to harsh punishment for other crimes and demanded more action against corrupt officials. In the Fan Jieming case (#23), one netizen said, "Sentencing [regular] criminals to death is quick and straightforward; corrupt officials are not sentenced to death even if they take bribes of the whole nation. What kind of law is it?"

Two other special groups of people were also targeted by Chinese netizens: legal experts and public intellectuals. Legal experts were blamed by netizens in nine cases, with 92 comments for their input and influence over lawmaking, as a result of which more humanized and lenient laws are adopted, at least as viewed by netizens. For instance, in the Yuan Junkai et al. case (#12), one netizen argued, "Legal experts and scholars lead a comfortable life (养尊处优) and see songs and dances to extol the good times (歌舞升平). They are not connected with the reality of society. Laws made by them are too lenient, a major reason for rising crime rates of society. China needs to revise laws to punish criminals harshly!" In the Fan Jieming case (#23), one netizen contrasted laws in other nations with Chinese laws and hinted at the negative roles played by legal experts and scholars. Specifically, the netizen asked, "Isn't it integration (接轨)? [For crimes that] foreign nations sentence hundreds of years, China has life imprisonment (bullshit) which ends with over ten years of incarceration? In other nations, juveniles could be sentenced to life imprisonment, but China released murderers after a few days in jail? More bullshitting? Yelling animals (叫兽) [implying professors, as both share the same pronunciation] and brick-makers (砖家) [implying experts, as both share the same pronunciation], what do you think? Don't ask Yuan Fang (元芳).[4] Yuan Fang was died long time ago??!!" In the Luo Xiaohua and Chen Rihong case (#57), one netizen blamed legal experts for promoting abolition and said,

---

4. Yuan Fang is a fictional figure in a famous TV series that featured Di Renjie (狄仁杰, 630–700), who served as a prime minister in two dynasties. Di is known for his righteousness and his capability to solve complicated cases. Yuan Fang is Di's primary assistant in the TV series, and a popular phrase in the show is a question posed by Di to Yuan: "Yuan Fang, what do you think?"

"The most detestable is abolition of capital punishment proposed by the so-called legal brick-makers. Without deterrence of capital punishment, it will be chaos. Sharen changming. To kill two if two are killed is the most fundamental notion. All others pale." Another suggested the influence of legal experts on judges and said, "It is not that judges are taking bribes. It is that legal brick-makers proposed using caution in capital punishment to minimize killing. To save their job, judges have to follow! The reason lies in lawmaking and has little to do with adjudicating judges!"

Some netizens attacked experts directly. In the Yuan Junkai et al. case (#12), one netizen commented, "As a legal servant (法律民工) who has been working at the bottom of society on legal affairs for years, I always believe that the existing legal system is dog fart. Most legal experts and scholars are hypocrites who dress their ill deeds with fine words (满口仁义道德一肚子男盗女娼)." In the Lin Senhao case (#1), one challenged the authority of legal experts and said, "[This is] to hire an expert to fart. Nowadays, as long as experts show up to participate, most of them are hired to produce inequality, because experts nowadays have lost their conscience and public authority (公信力)!" In the Hu Cunbiao and Wang Yong case (#29), one netizen even labeled experts "traitors" and said, "Not knowing our national conditions but pretending to be experts, most Chinese experts are essentially traitors sided with the West. Our law allows people to kill, no fucking death anyway. Who fears whom?" Rarely netizens called for help from legal experts. In the Zhao Xu case (#38), one netizen compared Zhao's double homicide to corruption and said, "This kind of things caused little damage to society. Death sentences should be used with caution in these cases. The harm done by him [Zhao] is much less than that of corruption of tens of millions of yuan. How come those legal experts shut their mouths this time?"

Similar to legal experts, public intellectuals were also attacked by netizens in three cases, with 19 comments for their promotion of human rights for criminals and their call for abolition of capital punishment. In the Lin Senhao case (#1), one netizen said, "A great cause that public intellectuals are most interested in is to fight for human rights on behalf of criminals. This is [why] crime rates are higher in recent years. Your criminals' human rights rhetoric put a lot of pressure on judges at local courts. Shameless public intellectuals!" In the Yang Dazhi case (#21), one netizen attacked public intellectuals in a vicious hypothetic case and wrote, "Look, some public intellectuals, from the perspective of a holy mother, demand to abolish the death penalty. When your fucking daughter were raped by others, would you still talk about abolition? Shameless maniacs, must be death sentenced. What happened to Chinese people?" Another concurred: "The most detestable are those who raise a flag for human rights and call for abolition. He and his family members, with good luck, never experienced such tragic misery, and they will never feel the mental suffering by victims and their relatives. It is easier thus for you to say (站着说话不腰疼) and call for abolition."

In summary, this chapter has focused on Chinese netizens' comments on key players of the criminal justice system. The majority of comments were indeed negative, as netizens tended to share their feelings and express their opinions when issues and problems were detected. An overall review of netizens' comments showed a number of dominant features. First, the majority of Chinese netizens demanded tough punishment against heinous criminals and thus supported capital punishment. They questioned the practice of suspended death sentences and reform policies in recent years such as "cash for clemency" and "killing fewer and killing cautiously," as they were viewed as being too lenient to criminals and left too much room for manipulation. This "get tough" mentality is consistent with values and beliefs of traditional Chinese culture and evident in some other nations (e.g., the United States) too. Second, netizens questioned prison rehabilitation (i.e., the lack of thereof) and were extremely emotional when released offenders committed new crimes. This phenomenon is, of course, not new and unique to China either. On the contrary, China has been known for having one of the lowest recidivism rates in the world (Liang and Wilson 2008), despite its struggle in recent years. It is likely that the publicity of notorious cases in the media exaggerated the degrees of the problems and overshadowed successful stories. Third, netizens expressed deep concerns about corruption and misconduct by players in the criminal justice system, and it is probably fair to say that all branches of the Chinese criminal justice system are facing challenges of public trust (e.g., Hsieh and Boateng 2015; M. Hu and Dai 2014). Though it appears that most of the time their concerns were based on suspicion and not on officially verified evidence, Chinese netizens were not afraid of "spreading rumors" and blowing the whistle when they learned about real cases. To a large extent, netizens' concerns reflected sharp social issues faced by China at deeper levels (see chapter 7). Last but not least, netizens' negative comments about criminal defense and defense lawyers are especially concerning. The majority of netizens questioned lawyers' morality and their "true purposes" of lawyering, and some even outright rejected the functions of criminal defense. With a landslide emphasis on the outcome (i.e., criminals get deserved punishment), the majority of Chinese netizens in our study apparently undervalued the importance of procedural justice. Within such an environment, it is no wonder that Chinese criminal defense lawyers often run a high risk in defending their clients, especially in capital cases.

CHAPTER 7

Social, Systemic, and Structural Problems
How Are Netizens' Opinions Embedded within the Framework of Contemporary Chinese Society?

> "The occurrence of a typical case is not only an issue of individuals but also reflects social problems."
> —"5274720819" (Suzhou, Jiangsu)

As quoted in this chapter's epigraph (Zhang Weilan et al., #20), a great number of cases and cases that generated the most discussions in our sample indeed reflected conflicts and struggles in contemporary Chinese society. In this chapter we examine in sequence cases that typify some major social, systemic, and structural problems in China, including that of money, commercialization, power abuse and corruption, social unrest, the one-child birth control policy, the health-care system, and the demolition and relocation policy.

Money, Commercialization, Power, and Corruption

Since the late 1970s, China has witnessed rapid economic development, and millions of people have been lifted out of extreme poverty. While its economic feat has impressed the world, China has suffered from many side effects of such development, including widened economic and social inequalities, worsening environmental problems, and rising crime rates. In our sample, a number of cases directly reflected the influence of money and commercialization.

In the Hu "x" case (#7), Hu detained victim Zhang for over 80 days and eventually drowned him in a lake, triggered by Zhang's refusal to repay debts owed to Hu (estimated at tens of millions of yuan). Surprisingly, the most popular theme in this case targeted and blamed Zhang for his refusal to repay debts (26 comments). Netizens called Zhang a "deadbeat" and made comments such as "not repaying his debts, [he] is also a swindler" and "Repaying one's debts, the rule of heaven and the earth." Sympathetic to Hu, some believed that he should be spared, arguing, for instance, that "considering the harm done to the offender due to the victim's refusal to repay debts, the offender does not deserve to die." Such comments only make sense when netizens' lack of sympathy for the victim is examined within the background of China's economic development and commercialization. In particular, as borrowing and lending, from either banks or individuals, has become increasingly popular, a common problem arises when the lender falls behind with the loan or even refuses to pay it back. In Hu's case we witnessed the strong condemnation against such borrowers by Chinese netizens. The interest rate charged by Hu was not reported (a high percentage perhaps), but it was seemingly not an issue to the netizens. Rather, their comments focused on the dishonesty of some borrowers and the difficulty of collecting such debts in China. One netizen commented, "Don't ask whether the suspect charged high-interest loans. In China, borrowers nowadays are living like a powerful don (大爷)! Don't repay debts but bully you!" Another said, "One not paying back debts, another not getting money back. Nowadays, debts with documentation and evidence, you try to collect it reasonably, but to little avail. Sometimes [the borrower] is tougher than you. Therefore, if you have money, better save it for food than loan to others." Compared to the majority opinion, a few people worried about neglecting Hu's crime and loss of humanity while focusing on economic calculations. One netizen commented, "So cruel his killing method [is], [and he] smiled during the trial as if nothing had happened. Only one word to describe the offender: inhumane! However, some netizens are not condemning the cruelty of the murderer but calculating gains and losses of the murder: [I] only shake my head. The loss of humanity in society is not an issue of merely a few crimes. Refusal to repay debts by the deceased should of course be held responsible, but cannot be a justification for the creditor's murder." Another concurred in a counterargument: "Not discussing murder but calculating gains and losses, what humanity is this?"

While Hu tried to recover what he was entitled to, offenders in a number of other cases committed their crimes purely for pecuniary purposes. In the Huang Qinghen case (#2), crimes of child abduction were committed for profit. One netizen lamented, "Beg the mercy of God. Human souls are swallowed by money." Both the Zhang Weilan et al. case (#20) and the Wu Youxin case (#52) involved offenders who murdered miners to claim fraudulent compensation. Netizens blamed a decline of morality and attributed it to marketization. In the Zhang et al. case, netizens made comments such as "Except money, Chinese people lost their belief, trust, credibility, and morality"; "[After] the reform and openness, belief is completely gone. Making money becomes easy, by fair means or foul. Pleasure seeking, humanity lost. Spiritually barren, with sorrow left only!"; and "Human desires for materials know no bounds, [and] will destroy humanity, with society filled with sin and filth." One netizen even quoted Karl Marx from his famous work *Capital: Critique of Political Economy* and wrote, "[With adequate profit, capital is very bold. A certain 10 percent will ensure its employment anywhere. . . .] 50 percent, positive audacity; 100 percent will make it ready to trample on all human laws; 300 percent, and there is not a crime at which it will scruple, nor a risk it will not run, even to the chance of its owner being hanged." Others were reminiscent of the old times (e.g., "This is the blessing of a harmonious society. Did we have such a phenomenon during Mao Zedong's time?!!!!!"), demanded self-reflection (e.g., "In front of money, justice and morality become silent. Humans lost their principles. Isn't it time for Chinese education to reflect?"), and even sent out a strong warning ("The bottom line of Chinese morality is lost! No conscience! Need a big war to change it! Wait and see, China will experience a war in five years!"). In the Deng "x" case (#40), cited in chapter 5, the feud between Deng and victim Li was triggered by Deng's decision not to attend the wedding of Li's daughter because of concerns about wedding gifts (that is, giving money based on contemporary Chinese tradition). One netizen lamented the tradition and compared it to practices in other nations, writing, "Because of money, humans become demons. As a matter of fact, we replaced friendship with money. In other nations, a bouquet would be all right."

Netizens attributed such crimes to different causes and thus proposed different solutions. To some it was about a decline of morality and loss of humanity when money dominates people's lives in contemporary China. To others it was about increasing gaps between the haves and the have-nots and a lack of effective solutions to deal with conflicts. In the Wu Youxin case (#52), one netizen commented, "As the gap between the wealthy and the poor widens, there will be more and more cases of 'getting rich' by fair means or foul. 'Laws' integrated with the West cannot solve the rising crime rates of 'Chinese characteristics.'" Another netizen focused on (the lack of) regulation in mining business and wrote, "Regulation is in chaos for a significant number of privately owned mining companies. Desire for profits is the main cause for frequent occurrence of such evil incidents! This is evident to people! There, it is also the hiding place for gangs and criminals."

Still to some others, the rising crime rates were due to judicial corruption and declining public trust in the government and the Party. In the Fan Jieming case (#23), Fang killed a coworker (and four more people on his killing spree) due to financial disputes, though no specifics were provided about the disputes. One netizen discussed systemic failures and wrote:

> Sharen changming, the same rule in thousands of years, no need to comment. But his financial disputes with others, why cannot it be solved timely? Too many such financial disputes. It is fair to say that financial disputes of society make up the majority of social conflicts. If [they] don't get mediated timely or fairly, social conflicts will sharpen and this case won't be the last! I don't mean to defend the murderer, but just comment on the case. Old cases accumulated, wrong cases not corrected, judicial corruption, taking bribes from both parties (两头通吃). What can ordinary people do? Cannot rely on law, no results with mediation, no one answers the call, and finally fight with death! Killing one is enough, killing two earns one, and killing more earns more. Does [our] nation expect this? What have you done earlier?

In the Zhang Weilan et al. case (#20), one netizen argued that "the serious problem faced by Chinese society is a crisis of trust and morality. To fundamentally cure the problem requires to rebuild polity and the Party, fight corruption and uphold integrity, rebuild a good image of the Party in the hearts of people and give them hope. This is the fundamental to solve social problems."

A serious challenge to the image of the government and the Party is the proliferation of official corruption. Netizens made explicit comments about corruption in 26 cases (41.3% of all cases). In addition to two corruption cases (discussed in chapter 5), comments on corruption sometimes even dominated netizens' discussions in non-corruption cases. For instance, in the Lin "x"ping and Ye "x"tian case (#16), the number of comments on corruption reached 122, ranked the fourth most popular theme of the case. The "popularity" of this theme indicated netizens' keenness of this problem. Besides commenting on reported cases, some netizens shared what they knew about other cases to demonstrate the ubiquity of the problem. In the Peng Shu and Hu Haolong case (#3), one netizen commented, "There are many like these [Peng and Hu]. Check out Fujin city in Heilongjiang [province]: the former police chief [has] hundreds of millions of yuan; the mayor is not simple." Another wrote, "[Among] village officials in our place, who does not have tens of millions [of yuan]? For those who are bolder, heh-heh [sound mimicking a sneer], no need to mention!"

As discussed in chapter 5, the most popular comment about corruption was the lack of harsh punishment—in particular the use of capital punishment—against corrupt officials. Applauding Peng Shu's and Hu Haolong's death sentences (#3), netizens made comments such as "The Heaven dynasty (天朝) glorious!!! Finally see death sentences. Must support this!!!" and "Caught so many corrupt officials, [and] finally see two death-sentenced." Netizens often compared lenient punishment of corrupt officials with harsh punishment of ordinary criminals. In the Peng and Hu case, one netizen compared robbery with corruption and said, "You dare try robbery? Corruption is equivalent to robbing people's money of the whole nation. But [he] doesn't face shooting, because he is an official in a nation with characteristics." Another netizen, commenting on the Gao Yulun et al. case (#44), agreed:

> I cannot figure it out. Is it easy for them to face such a high risk to rob? Look at those corrupt officials. Few got themselves into serious trouble, but only disciplinary sanctions. Those who rob are sentenced directly. Different treatment. Maybe corruption is more polished (文艺) than robbery. Robbery directly threatens people's interests, property and safety, but corruption is only indirect robbery based on forced voluntariness of bribers. This leads to the outcome in which corrupt officials receive only disciplinary sanctions but robbers received imprisonment. There are two kinds of perpetrators: one killing people with blood and the other without blood.

In the Yuan Junkai et al. case (#12), one netizen compared Yuan et al.'s death sentences for rape with sentences of the wealthy and the powerful and said, "With money and power, even gang rape is nothing; without money and connection, stealing a snack faces five years. This is our fucking rabbit government (兔政) [likely a degrading term]." Another concurred, saying, "Heh-heh, normally this is not done by people living at the bottom of society. Those at the top who control money and power may legally own more women." Similarly, netizens in the Yang Xueqi case (#62) compared Yang's death sentence to that of officials and made comments such as "Please answer why officials who sexually assault young women are not death-sentenced?" "If [he were] an official, raping 28 would not be a crime," and "Raping how many people would be subject to death sentences? Though this person deserves death, corrupt officials who rape young girls would only be found guilty of engagement in prostitution with a minor (嫖宿幼女) and sentenced leniently.[1] Such laws are not fair."

In the eyes of netizens, power and money often go together in contemporary China, and corrupt officials are therefore in a perfect position to wield both to buy themselves more justice. In the Wang Yihuan case (#43), both defendant Wang and victim Ye had some political background (Wang being a former member of the political consultation committee and Ye being a people's representative of the Liunan district in Liuzhou city). Netizens noticed such political background and made comments such as "Political consultation members all come from wealthy people. Never heard about a poor person being elected a member," "Those with money all become officials and those officials all become wealthy!" and "Nowadays, how many representatives are representing the interests of people at the bottom? And how many are representing the interests of the wealthy?" In the Yang Chaoquan case (#33), netizens lamented the privileges received by officials in sentencing. One netizen wrote, "In fact, [I] don't dislike capital punishment. But there are privileges in China's death sentencing, and officials and ordinary people are not using the same set of laws." Another asked, "Why big-time corrupt officials are not death sentenced? [Their] social harm is much greater than this, but with no death sentence? China's law is a joke, and others are all nonsense. Just wash and sleep (洗洗睡吧)." Yet another called for revival of ancient punishments

---

1. Engagement in prostitution with a minor was made a unique crime by the Criminal Law in 1997 (Article 360). Different from both rape and sexual molestation, this crime targeted male clients who have sex with female minor prostitutes and would potentially subject them to lesser punishment compared to either rape or molestation. The law faced tremendous challenges in practice, and many argued that the law aimed to favor people with wealth and power (e.g., officials). In 2015 the revised Ninth Amendment of the Criminal Law rescinded this law and integrated it into rape laws (see, e.g., M. Hu, Liang, and Huang 2017).

against corrupt officials in the name of justice and equity, writing, "Since the ancient time, China has had 'sharen changming, qianzhai huanqian.' This cannot be changed and is the only power lines by touching which leads to death. To corrupt officials, [we] should revive penalties such as death by a thousand cuts, disembowelment, and skinning, which suit these animals. Don't thank me and please call me Lei Feng (雷锋)."[2] In the Lin "x"ping and Ye "x"tian case (#16), one netizen pointed fingers at Party members and said, "If corrupt officials are expelled from the Party and death-sentenced, that is good. Don't use expulsion from the Party as the death-free indulgence (免死金牌). In addition, the second generation of the officials who do car race and disregard others' lives should be directly shot to death." In the Lin Senhao case (#1), one netizen commented on differential prison treatment based on one's official rank and wrote:

No joking. Even the treatment after sentencing for senior officials is different from that of ordinary wealthy people. [The imprisonment facility] for the premier level (正国级) officials is a villa (别墅); for the vice premier and ministry (副国和正部级) levels, a foreign-style house (洋房); for the deputy minister (副部) levels, a suite; for deputy levels (局级), a standard room. Don't mention corruption and decadent sex lives, that's nothing. Only when lining up [implying political lineup], if [you] don't obey the rules, it would potentially trigger serious trouble including death.

Netizens attributed rampancy of corruption to different causes. For instance, a number of them blamed declining morality and temptation of money. In the Peng Shu and Hu Haolong case (#3), one netizen commented, "Corruption in over 30 years harmed several generations! Good times of half of our lives were ruined and spent in a society of darkness, cruelty, decline of morality, corruption, degeneration, and loss of humanity!" Another commenter, on the Zhang Weilan et al. case (#20), echoed that idea, writing, "Greed swallows humanity, same with corrupt officials, except that corrupt officials kill people without blood and eat people without spitting out bones (吃人不吐骨头) [a Chinese idiom implying 'cruelty and greed']." One netizen in the Yuan Junkai et al. case (#12) said, "The

---

2. Lei Feng (1940–1962) was a role model established by the Chinese Communist Party in the 1950s and 1960s. He was known for his willingness to help others at any costs, and his deeds were highly praised by the government.

declining morality of Chinese people is due to the declining morality of governmental employees, who serve only mammon. There is a system, but no enforcement. Money is the system. It leads astray benevolent people!" In contrast, some people blamed corruption as systemic failure and suggested structural solutions. In the Wang Changping case (#19), one netizen commented, "Anti-corruption as said. But I believe there is still a fundamental problem: where is supervision? It is missing. It is a problem of passing the buck (踢皮球), and turning a blind eye (睁一只眼闭一只眼), and moral education." This was echoed by another netizen in the Peng Shu and Hu Haolong case (#3) who proposed that "only after establishing an effective supervision system, especially via participation by the public, can corruption be effectively stopped." In the same case, netizens also suggested punishing the bribers (e.g., "Shouldn't the bribers be sentenced too?") and cutting off sources of corruption (e.g., "Firmly abolish the tolls of highway roads and bridges," as this case involved corruption by officials who were in charge of the highway system).

Social Unrest

It is well documented that China has witnessed rising crime rates along with its economic development in the last four decades (L. Cao 2007; Cheong and Wu 2015; X. Deng and Cordilia 1999; Liang 2005; J. Liu 2005, 2006). Though all crimes are harmful, a number of cases in our sample in particular reflected increasing social unrest in contemporary China, such as terrorism (e.g., Tuo Heti et al., #6), endangerment of public security (Ou Changsheng, #63), underground criminal gangs (Liu Han et al., #5; Wang Hua, #25), drunk driving (Chen Yun, #31), abuse of drugs and drug offenses (Song Yutian, #46; Pan Guohui, #56), and sexual offenses against minors (Yang Dazhi, #21). Many of these crimes were either rarely seen or almost eradicated from the 1950s to the 1970s, but they reemerged in the reform era, and some showed signs of rampancy (e.g., drug use and offenses, H. Lu et al. 2009).

An overall examination of these cases showed rather consistent opinions by Chinese netizens. First and foremost, many netizens lamented worsened public security in China. In the Wang Hua case (#25), for instance, one netizen commented, "The underground criminal gangs, after thirty years of disappearance, reemerged." In the Yuan Junkai et al. case (#12), one netizen said, "Let's have a 'strike hard' campaign. Society is in chaos!" Another was reminiscent of the "good old days" and wrote, "All rapists were shot to death in the 1980s. The public security then was so good! Nowadays, laws are too lenient on these SOBs (孙子). As a result, society is more and more chaotic." This was echoed by another netizen in the He Jian case (#50), who commented, "Nowadays, the way of the world (世道) is too chaotic, all because laws are too lenient. Only one word [to describe] China's public security these days: Chaos."

This feeling of insecurity and chaos was well reflected in crimes of special natures. Take drug offenses, for example. In the Song Yongtian et al. case (#46), one netizen lamented, "In China, drugs already [have become] so rampant. Soldiers in the army use drugs, teachers in schools use, celebrities use, the second generation of the wealthy use, and many in villages use." In the Wu "x"hua case (#49), one netizen named a well-known singer, Yin Xiangjie (尹相杰) who was arrested and convicted of possession of illegal drugs in 2015. The netizen commented, "It is drugs again. Drug traffickers are the primary culprits, and drug users are accessories to a tyrant's crimes (助纣为虐). How are you doing, Yin Xiangjie?" In the Wang Changping et al. case (#19), Wang, a former police officer, masterminded drug manufacturing. One netizen commented, "The current society calls white black and black white, confuses right and wrong, and holds human lives cheap, and corruption is rotten to the core. Even people's police is manufacturing drugs. Darkness. It was reported that migrant workers delivered a 'no-action' banner [to the police]. No action, because [police are] busy manufacturing drugs? The current government, pathetic, alas!" In two cases, capital offenders managed to get hold of guns to commit their crimes, a rare phenomenon given China's tight gun control. In the Liang Kaiwu case (#18), one netizen said, "Many years ago, the two Wang brothers were killed by the police![3] How come it happened again? Alas, the government [is] incompetent. Killing everywhere, it seems that society has some problems." In the Fan Jieming case (#23), one netizen wrote, "The reincarnation of vicious Satan! Call for relevant

---

3. The case of two Wang brothers shocked the conscience of the nation in the 1980s. The brothers, Wang Zongfang and Wang Zongwei, committed their first quadruple murder in February 1983 in Shenyang in northeastern China and killed six more people as they fled to southern China, where they were eventually captured and killed in September in Jiangxi province. Their six-month killing spree and their access to guns made the case extremely notorious and even caused panic in society, which triggered the first round of the "strike hard" crime campaign in 1983 (https://baike.baidu.com/item/二王/10542294).

sectors to mete out harsh punishment against illegal gun possessors (including hunting guns). There are many holes in existing gun controls. All relevant sectors should set in place a system of accountability in jurisdictions where illegal gun possession or cases occur!" Another expressed similar concerns and said, "Fortunately China's gun control is fairly tight. Otherwise, someone would suddenly shoot at your back while [you're] walking on road. [You] still don't know who shot you at your funeral. How pathetic your death would be." The Yang Dazhi case (#21) involved Yang's sexual offenses against students by taking advantage of his position as a school principal. Looking beyond Yang's crimes, some netizens expressed deep concerns for "children left behind," which has become a unique phenomenon in rural areas (see note 4 in chapter 5). One netizen boldly asked, "Children left behind . . . why [are they] left behind? . . . what do left-behind families gain? Parents of 'children left behind' are probably working hard in a city, [but] what does society give them in return? Peaceful and contented life and work? Equal opportunity for education? . . . Chinese government . . . Chinese policies . . . Chinese officials . . . not far from demise."

In addition to security concerns, netizens demanded harsh punishment against criminals to protect the safety of society. The Tuo Heti et al. case (#6) involved a group of eight terrorists. Given her pregnancy at the time of the offense, Tuo was sentenced to life imprisonment while three others were death-sentenced. Netizens condemned this terrorist act and made comments such as "Severe punishment for terrorists, to provide a peaceful and safe societal environment!" and "No death sentence due to pregnancy. [If] more crimes in the future, don't know [if you will get] life or death." A few even called for Tuo Heti's death (e.g., "Once the birth is given, [we] should carry out execution. [She] must die"). In the Ou Changsheng case (#63), Ou bombed a bus, killing two and injuring many others. Netizens condemned Ou's bombing of innocent people and made comments such as "Bombing a bus to kill innocent people is purely a terrorist act. Kill [Ou] without mercy!" In the Hu Cunbiao and Wang Yong case (#29), one netizen proposed the following:

> To improve China's social morale, [we] must strengthen laws. In particular, against rape, kidnapping, robbery, burglary, bullying ordinary people, bribery, and being arrogant and domineering (飞扬跋扈), enhance the punishment; against underground criminal gangs, deals between power and money, and bullying others with

bad impact by taking advantage of one's authority or family connection, strike harder and more harshly. Set up grievance centers nationwide, and one may petition across provincial borders without the necessity of visiting the central government. Conduct firm investigation of government departments which ignore serious grievance. Severely punish those who intercept and sanction petitioners midway. Only in this way can China's social morale improve.

Moreover, many netizens proposed specific measures tailored to the nature of crimes. For instance, addressing sexual offenses, one netizen in the Yuan Junkai et al. case (#12) targeted people who have many mistresses and commented, "Support harsh sentences against these criminals. If [we] can punish those who can afford a second, third, fourth or fifth mistress (二奶三奶四奶五奶) and mistresses no longer exist, then everyone can afford a wife and this type of crime will decline greatly. This is the fundamental solution." Another concurred: "Now the male-female ratio is severely imbalanced. It would be a surprise if [there were] no rapes. Those with power and money can afford eight or ten mistresses, while those without money cannot afford a wife. Not to mention campaigns against prostitution. How about male sex hormones and how [do you] allow them to live? Don't be prudish and curse others. These are social facts." In the Hu Cunbiao and Wang Yong case (#29), one netizen blamed the lack of sex education in schools, which aggravates sexual offenses, and wrote, "It's impossible to describe how serious China's school education problem is! What should be covered by schools is not taught: education about law, self-protection, biological sex, and social cognition, all ignored. The so-called quality education (素质教育) is nonsense! Is it truly unpreventable for criminals to harm so many victims? Only until spotting the crimes by chance can [we] stop crimes? Besides, China's police work so hard on catching gambling and prostitution. They should do more to protect people's lives, properties, and safety!" In the Yang Xueqi case (#62), one netizen proposed a data bank to match suspects' information and said, "Recommend the judicial system establish a data bank that records individual blood types, genes, fingerprints, and other individual information so that we have them on record, which would be helpful to crime prevention. Once a crime occurs, we may quickly find the true culprit and avoid waste of national resources. It would help in the medical field too." Another countered with a legitimate concern: "I think criminal record should not be registered. It would help them find jobs and the odds of recidivism would decrease. With record, employers would ask for it. Without jobs, how to survive? Only going back to their old games (老本行) [implying more crimes]. To improve societal systems and reforms needs to look for causes and to solve [issues] from their causes." In the Yang Chaoquan case (#33), one netizen called for self-reflection and said, "Actually we should reflect rationally: why a person committed burglary and murder for merely 200 yuan? We need to reflect on the social roots that lead to such behavior, to avoid more tragedies. Not just critique, verbal attack, and use harsh words. If so, society would go into irreversible despair." Another agreed, saying, "The whole society needs to calm down and ponder. Behind the restlessness is taunt and sneer, pushing the wall when it is about to collapse (墙倒众人推), or even taking another's life. It took China several decades to go through what the West has gone through in several hundreds of years. It is unavoidable to have many conflicts. How to deal with them requires wisdom."

In sum, despite China's impressive economic progress, rising crime rates and worsened public security have become major concerns for Chinese netizens, which seemed to justify their support for harsh punishment, including the use of capital punishment. Many netizens attributed crimes of social unrest to widened economic and social inequalities, mammonism, declining morality, and rampant official corruption, and some were not afraid of boldly challenging governmental policies, three of which directly impacted the cases discussed below.

Challenges to the "Birth-Control" Policy: He Shenguo Case (#42)

In December 2015 the Standing Committee of the National People's Congress passed a new amendment to China's Population and Family Planning Law, which kicked off a universal two-child policy effective in 2016. This new policy replaced the well-known one-child policy after its implementation of three and a half decades.[4] Unfortunately, the new law seems to have come too late for He Shenguo. On July 22, 2013, He tried to register his fourth child with a local registration office, but his request was

---

4. There is a rich body of literature on China's one-child birth control policy. For studies of the policy implementation and its impact, see, for example, Ebenstein 2010; Goodkind 2017; Q.Jiang, Li, and Feldman 2013; Q. Jiang and Liu 2016; B. Li and Zhang 2017; J. Li 1995; Nie 2011; X. Wang and Zhang 2018; H. Zhang 2007.

denied. On the second day, He came back with a knife and killed two workers of the office and injured four others. On June 19, 2014, He was convicted of homicide and sentenced to death by the intermediate people's court in Fangchenggang city in Guangxi province. On November 16, 2014, the Guangxi High Court affirmed his death sentence, which was subsequently approved by the Supreme People's Court (SPC). He was executed on November 12, 2015, a month and a half before the official amendment of the new family planning law.

Netizens' comments in He's case centered on the one-child birth control policy, and two camps were formed, one challenging the policy and the other supporting it. Netizens' challenges to the policy and its implementation can be categorized into several groups. First, netizens targeted the family planning offices (FPO, 计划生育办公室) and blasted FPO personnel for their brutal enforcement against couples who dared to have multiple children in violation of the one-child policy (a total of 54 comments). For instance, netizens made comments such as "[Victims] being knifed to death, deserved it! Payback. How many women with 7–8 month pregnancy were forced to abort?" "From whom do so many lost souls seek revenge because of forced abortions by the FPO?" and "How many FPO personnel torn down others' houses and took away their properties and pigs? Where do they go to petition and seek justice?" Some cursed FPO personnel based on the belief of karma. One netizen commented, "The next generations of many FPO personnel met with mishaps (出事) [because of] too much damage to one's virtue (太损阴德). There are several examples in our place: a son of one FPO person in our village was born deformed." Another related that "in the 1990s, the FPO personnel in our village directly dropped dead a 10-day baby who was born over quota (超生). Back then, there was no legal consciousness and no pursuit of legal liabilities, because they were governmental employees. The mother went crazy and missing, and the father raised the older child alone. The life of the murderer who killed the baby went downhill afterward: his wife got ill and died, and his only son was killed by a car accident. Therefore, humans are doing it, Heaven is watching it. Sooner or later retribution comes."

Second, many netizens pointed out how FPOs and their personnel took advantage of the national policy to serve their own interests. One netizen commented, "[Victims] deserved to be killed. No matter what business you do with the FPO, it would find a way to make things difficult. Ask for bribes or ask you to treat them meals. No FPO personnel is good.

Deserved to be killed, and the more, the better." Another netizen shared real-life experiences and wrote, "There is a reason for [He's] killing. I have seen women with 7-month pregnancy being forced to abort by FPO personnel. To those who gave birth already, [FPO personnel] would take away their properties if no fines are paid. They would take away everything they can. This is FPO personnel." Yet another implied that some FPOs "created" local policies to their own advantages that were not designed by national laws and regulations. Specifically, the netizen said, "The real culprit of He Shenguo and the two FPO workers was the local policy (土政策). Which law or regulation stipulates that household registration (上户口) is tied to family planning [which justifies no registration for babies born over quota]? Whoever knows shows the document. Everything is caused by the local policy." In fact, a number of netizens (11 comments) blasted the FPO's denial of household registration for children born over quota. One strongly condemned this practice and said, "The [central] government has published regulations that claim that household registration should not be tied to fines for over-quota births. The little lives have their right to live. Household registration is the government's obligation. Why does it have to be tied to fines to make it difficult for the masses? For fines, you should fine the parents, and it has nothing to do with children. Anger of an ordinary man leads to bloodshed in five feet (匹夫一怒, 血流五步)! Tragic!!!"

Third, netizens in 10 comments argued for one's procreation right as a fundamental human right and made comments such as "Procreation is humans' most fundament right!" and "Procreation is a natural process. Neither [should we] encourage more births nor limit it to one! China has survived thousands of years [without a one-child policy]. Why do our generations have such bad luck [with such a policy]?" Netizens holding such a belief strongly challenged the brutality of forced abortions and asked, "Forced abortions, isn't it killing?" and "Procreation is humans' most fundamental right! Shouldn't the government self-examine this practice given countless FPO tragedies?" One netizen even compared the one-child policy to Hitler's genocide and said, "The record of population killing was created by 'xx' (某人) in China, leading Hitler by several blocks."

Fourth, netizens in 26 comments questioned the so-called social maintenance fees (社会抚养费). As a euphemism for fines, social maintenance fees were institutionalized in 2002 by the Measures for Administration of Collection of Social Maintenance Fees promulgated by China's State Council, and the actual fees collected varied from one region to another. Netizens challenged the legitimacy of the fees and made comments such as "[We] paid social maintenance fees, [but] society raised whom?" and "The most despicable is to collect money from [mothers'] wombs. Which dynasty had collected social maintenance fees?" One boldly argued, "Social maintenance fees raised FPO personnel. They are the true murderers. Killing them gladdens people's hearts. The more, the better!" Another compared He to corrupt officials and said, "A big-time corrupt official would harm tens of thousands but [is] not death-sentenced. To collect social maintenance fees by holding whose flag (打着谁的旗号)? Who in society is going to raise his [He's] children? [He's] death sentence [is] too harsh." Another concurred: "What are social maintenance fees?! Isn't it true that we as parents raise our children?! When does the government provide to ordinary people resources and means to raise their children? It raises a group of corrupt officials and mistresses (小三)!"

Last but not least, some netizens argued that He's tragic crime was the outcome of an abnormal society. One netizen wrote, "The perpetrator and the deceased were all victims of an abnormal society. We are all liable. Those who pay the fines feed the officials' arrogance, those who choose not to give births make the officials feel self-important, and few of those who do not pay the fines come out and fight but sacrifice the growth of their children. The fact that each takes what he needs leads to an abnormal society." Another commented, "Giving more births leads to death, and call it law-breaking; so many who visit prostitutes, gamble, use drugs, and commit crimes thrive. Tragedy of society. Ordinary people living at the bottom are meat on an anvil."

Netizens who explicitly supported the one-child policy or the FPOs made three arguments. First, they challenged over-quota births by people such as He and his wife (e.g., "Why have so many births?"), questioned a lack of effective enforcement of the policy, and some even demanded actions (e.g., "Arrest people who have over-quota births to show force to the public"). Second, some expressed concerns about the "quality" of over-quota births, particularly those by poor people. For instance, one netizen commented, "In China, the lower their education level is, the more births they have. Villagers have more births. In contrast, full-time master's and Ph.D. students and the highly educated only have one child or none. If this situation lasts long, the Chinese nation will be destroyed, with intelligence getting worse and worse. I think full-time master's and Ph.D. students should be awarded 10,000 yuan for each birth." Another expressed similar concerns and said, "Those with money can have as many births as they want, which is reasonable. They can afford raising and educating their children who can land good jobs. It is beneficial to themselves and the nation. 'The poorer, the more births' [and they] cannot provide a good living environment and education to children, which is a crime to children. Living without dignity is worse than a dog." A few (five comments) even threatened actions against He's children (e.g., "Kill his whole family. Children of this kind of people won't end up being good people in the future"). Third, a couple of netizens explicitly supported the social maintenance fees. One argued, "I have two children and you have four. Resources are limited. It is already tough for my two to compete with your two. Your extra two now are competing with my two. I am definitely not happy with the disadvantage of my children. Would I allow you to act so recklessly and care for nobody (肆无忌惮)? Therefore it is justified for you to pay social maintenance fees!" Another concurred: "[It is] normal to pay social maintenance fees for [your] over-quota births. [You] use more national resources overall. No money to pay fines but to kill people, why so many netizens applauded?"

By all measures, the camp challenging the one-child policy overwhelmed the camp supporting the policy: 58 comments explicitly supported He versus 51 against him; 54 comments were posted against FPOs and their personnel versus six supporting comments; 16 explicitly questioned the one-child policy versus seven that supported it; 14 comments questioned He's death sentence versus nine supporting it. It is obvious that to the majority of netizens, He's case is no longer about He's killing of two FPO workers. Rather, it is about the legitimacy of the one-child policy and FPO practices. To be fair, troubles presented to He's family due to the one-child policy do not justify his killings, and He's attempt to register his fourth child won't benefit from the revised two-child policy either. As one netizen commented, "History will give us an answer." The history of the one-child policy seemingly came to an end, but He's tragedy and his own life cannot be reversed.

Challenges to the Health-Care System and Practice: Lian Enqing (#14) and Wang Gang (#13) Cases

Along with its economic reforms since the 1980s, China has initiated profound reforms to its health-care system.[5] Two cases in our sample, both

---

5. The literature on China's health-care reforms is rich. See, e.g., Blumenthal and

broken out in May 2015, reflected serious challenges to China's health-care system. In the Wang Gang case (#13), discussed in chapter 4, Wang committed drug trafficking to raise money for his uremia treatment. Given Wang's circumstances, the Inner Mongolian High Court reduced his initial immediate death sentence to a suspended death sentence. Ranked the second most popular theme of the case, 22 netizens' comments challenged China's health-care system. Specifically, netizens echoed Wang's justification for his crimes—that is, the existing medical system is too expensive for ordinary people. Without proper means, "being driven to join the Mount Liang rebels" (see note 3 in chapter 3) is the only desperate way. Netizens made comments such as "Nowadays, seeing a doctor is so expensive. An ordinary illness would cost 500, and sometimes thousands of yuan at a major hospital, but it costs 10 or 8 yuan at a clinic! National health-care reform is just talking, officialese everywhere" and "From this case, we see that ordinary people cannot afford medical treatments with major illnesses! Many occurred around us! Hope [our] nation will adopt more policies benefiting ordinary people." Further, netizens demanded better assistance from the government. One wrote, "Our nation's capability to assist patients who are seriously ill is too weak. Committing crimes for survival, he [Wang] is responsible, but don't the nation and local governments bear any responsibilities? If we have a good system of medical assistance, is he going to commit crimes?" Another commented on Wang's suspended death sentence, "Suspended death? This disease is no different from suspended death. A friendly gesture (顺水人情), this is China's laws. This is forced by China's medical system. Because of this system, countless patients are left to take their chances (自生自灭). In China, 'You can have anything but illness' (有啥别有病). This phrase has multiple meanings: one is to wish everyone good health, and the other is what everyone understands [referring to financial burden]."

If Wang's case exposed the expansive nature of China's health-care system, which could be out of reach by ordinary people, the Lian Enqing case pushed the challenge to the next level. In this case, Lian suffered from empty nose syndrome (空鼻综合症) and received a nasal operation at the number one people's hospital in Wenling city in Zhejiang province in 2012. Despite being informed about the success of the operation after con-

---

Hsiao 2015; Hsiao 1995; S. Hu et al. 2008; Y. Li et al. 2012; Y. Liu 2004; Y. Liu, Hsiao, and Eggleston 1999; Meng et al. 2015; Wagstaff, Yip, Lindelow, and Hsiao 2009; Yip and Hsiao 2008, 2009; Yip et al. 2012.

sultations at different hospitals, Lian complained about the result of his operation and believed that the hospitals colluded to cover up the "truth." Without receiving satisfactory results after multiple rounds of complaints and negotiations, in 2013 Lian lost his composure, went to the hospital, and stabbed three doctors, one of whom died. Lian was convicted of homicide and sentenced to death in January 2014 by the intermediate people's court in Tanzhou city, and his death sentence was approved in April by the Zhejiang High Court. After the SPC's approval, Lian was executed in May 2015.

With a total of 4,660 comments, Lian's case generated the second highest number of comments in our sample. Unlike Wang, Lian killed one doctor and was thus a murderer; Lian was apparently able to afford his nasal operation, but his case exposed serious issues with China's healthcare system at different levels involving various parties (e.g., relationships among patients, doctors, hospitals, drug manufacturers, governments at various levels). First, Lian's case revealed an abnormal and strained relationship between Chinese doctors and patients. In 305 comments, netizens explicitly questioned doctors and their practices. Their primary argument was that Chinese doctors have lost their morality and work for financial interests. For instance, one netizen commented, "Nowadays, doctors have lost their basic morality. 'Look, listen, question, and feeling the pulse (望闻问切) [four basic ways of diagnosis in traditional Chinese medical science]' are gone. The first thing is to run tests. A cold would cost you four or five hundred yuan at a hospital. This is Chinese characteristics and Chinese medical insurance." One netizen lamented the loss of virtue from the past and said, "Doctors in ancient times would heal the wounded and rescue the dying. Now after health-care reforms, doctors won't treat patients without money and only treat them after paying." Another commented on how helpless patients often feel: "Patients are treated like fish and meat (任人鱼肉), with no options. Thus, corrupt doctors are so arrogant: alienated, cold, hard, confronting, pushing, tricky, challenging, demanding, and cheating. [They] disregard people's lives in operations as practice and experiment, make money with people's lives, and do all evils without any fear!" Some even openly cursed doctors, making comments such as "Based on harmful behavior of the animals in white cloaks [implying doctors] and drug dealers, they deserve to die" and "If doctors maintain their [low] level of morality, tens of thousands of Lian Enqing[s] would follow suit. Doctors deserve to die."

In addition to concerns about doctors' morality and ethics, netizens disliked the way patients were treated. For instance, one argued that doctors often don't keep patients informed about their illnesses and treatment options but insist on their suggested treatments. Specifically, the netizen wrote:

> When a patient visits a doctor at a hospital, the doctor won't tell the patient if the illness can be cured after tests. Normally they would say it is curable and ask you to pay bills. If the illness is not cured eventually, doctors would say they are not omnipotent. The patient paid under the assumption that the doctor would cure the illness. If not cured, the patient would believe that the doctor did not fulfill his responsibility. If the doctor explains well to the patient after tests and tells the patient [about the illness], even if the illness is incurable, the patient can make a decision. If you don't say anything but insist on treatments, the patient would of course believe you can cure the illness. But the patient paid and the illness was not cured. As a result, the patient would blame the hospital and the doctor.

Another criticized doctors' attitudes and wrote, "Nowadays, doctors are the boss, very arrogant. Patients would queue for a whole day. [You] need to book several days in advance for a B-mode ultrasound test. If the doctor is not available on your appointment date and your diagnostic results cannot be examined, you have to do it again. Why do ill patients have to bear this? That person who killed the doctor [Lian] was hapless and got nowhere to complain. When can doctors put themselves in the shoes of patients? Can you show a good attitude when a patient visits you?" Further, some netizens pointed out that the strained relationship between doctors and patients is due to a lack of communication and proper procedures to handle disputes. One netizen said, "There lacks good communications between doctors and patients. If everyone can deal with conflicts patiently and peacefully, things won't go to the extreme." Another said, "We are not asking that doctors repay with their lives if the illness is not cured. It is because nobody would comfort the patient when there is an issue and conflict. No one is solving the issue for the patient. If the hospital timely solves [Lian's] problem, would we have such a tragedy?"

In 66 comments, netizens supported doctors, and many of them seemed to be doctors themselves (or worked as doctors) or family members of doctors. They complained about doctors' hard work, irregular hours, mistreatment by patients (e.g., the so-called medical chaos professionals [医闹]), and lack of sympathy and understanding from the masses. Some were so disappointed to see the overwhelming negative comments against them and vowed not to allow their loved ones (e.g., spouses and children) to enter the medical profession. Nevertheless, their voice was overwhelmed by the majority who condemned doctors and their practices (plus 149 shared personal stories). The apparent divide is indeed alarming (see Liebman 2013).

Second, netizens explicitly criticized China's hospital system (81 comments) and medical system (53 comments). One netizen commented, "Thank you [Lian] for your contribution to society. People should remember you and build a monument. Regarding doctors, they are victims of our times and medical system. No choice. [Lian] should not be death-sentenced. It is the medical system that should pay the costs. Amen." Many netizens directly blamed marketization of the health-care system, in which pecuniary gain has become the primary goal. For instance, one commented, "The marketization of hospital system means that doctors and meat vendors of the market are no different. Their ultimate goal is to instill more water into their business to maximize profit. In such an environment, low-class and poor people cannot receive medical assistance. Doctors in a market won't be willing to spend more time on patients who have no money or power. This is the root cause of frequent occurrence of medical disputes." Another shared similar concerns and said, "Healthcare reforms make hospitals like business. Only aim for money and would immediately stop treatment without money. Disregarding people's lives, where is professional medical ethics?" Some netizens showed how pressure from the hospital to generate more revenues forces doctors to adjust their practices. As one pointed out, "Today's doctors in hospitals, they are not all bad. But compared to doctors in the past, fewer embrace professional medical ethics. It is not all their fault. Today, everything needs money. A hospital's evaluation of a doctor is based on how much revenues a doctor generates. Doctors who generate revenues will be rewarded with money and prices. Every doctor therefore endeavors to make money. To make money needs to visit more patients. A day has only so many hours. Within such hours, [doctors] need to make money and treat illnesses carefully, which is very difficult." Another said, "It is God's will if no problem looms; but problems surely present. Hospitals are holy places to treat diseases and save people. How come to evaluate doctors with revenues? Hospitals nowadays won't answer my question. That's all right. It is no longer a secret. Health-care reforms, we anticipate."

In addition, netizens discussed other systemic reasons why China's health-care system fails to respond to concerns by ordinary people. For example, one netizen mentioned the lack of an effective insurance system and said, "The bottom line is that the health-care system has problems. If all treatments are covered by insurance, who would worry how much money to spend? If doctors overprescribe medicines and perform unnecessary operations, insurance companies would fight them in lawsuits." Another discussed the lack of media supervision, pointing out that "in essence, China's medical system receives no supervision, including media supervision. Therefore it is a vicious cycle. Many medical malpractices were committed willfully, because no one was held responsible and the media cannot expose them. Thus there is no costs for crimes by corrupt doctors. As soon as ordinary people enter a hospital, laws are no longer effective." Yet another lamented over the powerless status of ordinary patients and their incapability to challenge the medical system and wrote, "In Shanghai Zhongshan hospital, every doctor collects money [implying illegally or immorally]. In China's medical system, ordinary people are the disadvantaged minority, who cannot win cases of medical malpractice. This is not a problem of individuals but the system. It never changes." In 16 comments, netizens compared China's system to foreign nations and called for reforms. One netizen commented, "Nowadays at hospitals, doctors check on what you ask for: it is patients who see doctors, not doctors who see patients. In advanced nations, however, it is doctors who see patients. [They] would treat all your illnesses, [under] a notion of maintaining your health." Another mentioned the famous Dr. Norman Bethune (白求恩), who lost his own life while serving Chinese people in the 1930s, and said, "Dr. Bethune is forever gone. Even if he lived today, he would likely not be awarded 'the champion of internationalism,' because he would have blocked the wealth of other doctors and be rejected by the medical system and the government. He would be charged with some unknown crimes (莫须有) and made disappeared."

Third, although drug manufacturers were not directly involved in Lian's case, netizens condemned them in three comments for their collusion with doctors and hospitals to fix medicine prices. One netizen commented, for instance, "Doctors and patients are fighting each other, even with loss of human lives. Drug manufacturers are laughing instead. The small kickbacks received by doctors are nothing. In my view, some unethical drug manufacturers should be killed."

Fourth, netizens criticized the lack of actions by the Chinese government to ease and deal with medical disputes via proper interventions (in 30 comments). As one netizen commented, "This young man had courage but no brain. Who should be killed is not doctors but government officials, or government employees of those sectors who passed him around like a ball. There is no guarantee that an operation would be successful even if doctors gave 100% of their energy and fervor. But if government employees do the same, this kind of tragedy won't happen!" Another demanded accountability and asked, "When disputes arise between doctors and patients, what should the government and relevant sectors do? For this case, I wonder what responsibilities the local government and health management departments should bear?" Another concurred: "It is not that the government stayed far away, but it stayed far away to merely look. Only until a conflict breaks out does it come forward to deal with it. This is inaction and corruption. Should hold relevant personnel responsible." Some criticized specific governmental measures that made patients' challenges to medical disputes even more difficult. For instance, one netizen argued how centralized medical evaluations make the results more likely to favor doctors and hospitals. Specifically, the netizen wrote:

> Doctors and governmental employees similarly regard themselves superior to others! Do not allow others to challenge their authority! Therefore whoever killed doctors and urban management officers (城管) are all death-sentenced![6] The hospital systems control much power and other sectors do not offend them. Medical disputes are supposed to follow the judicial procedure, but courts all defer to evaluation outcomes, and evaluations can only be done by official medical associations (医学会). "A father evaluates a son," the phrase has been in existence for a long time, known by everyone. Isn't it true that it [evaluation] changed nothing? After the enactment of the Tort Liability Law (侵权责任法), people believed that it would change the situation for medical dispute resolutions. A notice by the Ministry of Health directly sent patients to ice holes [implying 'being made disappointed'], and courts at all levels follow suit and send patients to medical associations for evaluations! Before [the

---

6. *Chengguan* (i.e., urban management officers) are para-police who are responsible for the enforcement of urban regulations. First established in the late 1990s, the practice of chengguan has been quickly developed to cover all major cities in China. For studies of chengguan, see Caron 2013; Hanser 2016; Swider 2015; J. Xu and Jiang 2019; Zang and Musheno 2017; Zang and Pratt 2019.

notice], patients were able to demand judicial evaluations. The situation is worse for patients. Is this judicial progress or regress? Isn't it forcing ordinary people to go to the extreme?

Another netizen called for establishment of an independent evaluator: "Hope the government soon introduces a third party to investigate medical disputes and to facilitate [communication among] companies, organizations, and sectors in medical disputes. With nowhere to petition, daily suffering from the illness, and no psychological comfort, a patient would eventually vent with harms."

Fifth, similar to other cases, netizens attributed medical disputes to increasing conflicts of contemporary Chinese society. For instance, one netizen argued, "Building trust is the key. Doctors should work conscientiously and explain to patients with authority issues arisen from the treatment. Patients should believe outcomes of investigation. Now problems lie in three parties: doctors who collect red envelopes [implying illegal or immoral money collection], patients who do malicious medical disputes, and unconvincing medical evaluations. There is only one reason: money. When the first case of gaining illegal interests goes unpunished, more and more cases follow." Another commented on the 'side effects' of China's economic development and said, "Our only pride is that we've achieved in 30 years what the West has accomplished in 200 years. The price of 'pulling up the crop to help it grow (拔苗助长)' is evident:[7] environment damaged severely, corrupt officials, being rich but heartless, mammonism. The Chinese nation has lost its belief and morality and is under a mutually harmful state." Again, netizens called for systemic reforms and governmental actions (in 42 comments) and made comments such as "If there is a system of the rule of law and a normal channel to petition grievance, this tragedy wouldn't have happened. This is an extremely abnormal society" and "This is a social problem, which should be collectively dealt with by the government and society. Governmental agencies and society still carry an irresponsible mentality of 'you may choose not to!' Once this mentality dominates, our society will become a society of 'men eat men': Goods expensive, you may choose not to buy! Phone bills expen-

---

7. "Pulling up a crop to help it grow" is a story by the Chinese philosopher Mencius (孟子 公孙丑上). In this story, a man in the Song Kingdom (宋人) tried to pull up his crops a few inches to help them grow faster but later found only dead crops. The lesson is that hastening things without following their natural course can lead to the opposite effect.

sive, you may choose not to use! Tolls expensive, you may choose not to go out! Conflicts sharpened. Regarding this, governmental agencies are the primary leaders and should endeavor to solve issues and bear primary responsibilities!"

Challenges to the Demolition and Relocation Policy and Practice: Liu Danao Case (#47)

With rapid economic development, land has become increasingly lucrative in China. To facilitate real estate development, the demolition and relocation policy was enacted (see J. Chen and Lai 2013; Y. Deng 2017; Feng 2009; Han, Shu, and Ye 2018; Huang, Dijst, and Weesep 2017; Shih 2010; Yu et al. 2017). Within such a background, the Liu Danao case arose and generated the third most comments in our sample ($n = 3{,}221$). Liu was employed as a driver by a chemistry engineering company and lived in Nan Liu village of the Chengguan district in Zhengzhou city in Henan province. According to the court findings, a company, Zhengzhou Yutong (宇通) Bus Co. Ltd., was in charge of a real estate development project, because of which the Nan Liu village was about to be removed and relocated. Reportedly, 302 of the total 320 families of the village signed relocation agreements and received financial compensation, including Liu's family. However, on the morning of June 1, 2010, dissatisfied with the relocation deal, Liu tried to stop a team of relocation workers from entering the village in his white car and drove his car into the crowd a few times. Four people were killed and many others injured. Liu fled the crime scene but self-surrendered in the afternoon. Liu was death-sentenced by the intermediate people's court in Zhengzhou city in November 2010, and the Henan High Court subsequently affirmed his death sentence. On November 20, 2015, Liu was executed after the SPC approved his death sentence.

Like the He Shenguo and Lian Enqing cases, netizens condemned the evil policy in this case—that is, the demolition and relocation policy, and overwhelmingly supported Liu: in 536 comments, netizens explicitly supported him (versus 74 against him), plus 55 comments in which they expressed sympathy for him (versus two comments in which sympathy was explicitly rejected); in 70 comments, netizens openly questioned Liu's guilty verdict, and in another 51 comments they rejected his death sentence (versus 39 supportive of his death sentence). One netizen commented on such lopsided support for Liu, "We all see it: after Liu's killing, how many people hated it? How many people showed sympathy for the relocation workers? This is what the public wanted (民心所向)!"

The majority of netizens' comments can be categorized into several groups. First, netizens condemned relocation workers in 127 comments (versus 18 comments in which netizens supported them). In the eyes of the majority of netizens, relocation workers were not really helping the relocated; instead they were helping developers at any cost to destroy the families and lives of the relocated. One netizen second-guessed the evil plan of the relocation workers in Liu's incident and wrote, "Fire trucks and ambulances were present. It is evident that if running into [villagers'] self-defense, [they] would have burned the village and put out the fire, and hauled away corpses via ambulances. Only when perpetrators who cruelly killed the relocated were death-sentenced, would [owners'] defense with force stop!" Another called them rascals and said, "Relocation workers, we all know them! Normally they are hooligans and skunks hired by the government or evil-minded developers! Such a system of laws! Always make true heroes and martyrs feel guilty.... Don't abuse public trust. You think that you would be able to cross the sea under camouflage (瞒天过海) while cloak it [demolition and relocation] with legitimacy? There is a scale from heaven to earth! Ordinary people are the weights, and don't force them to stop playing with you. You would be nothing then!" One netizen directly contrasted relocation workers with Liu and wrote, "Those SOBs who forced demolition and relocation deserved to die even if they were killed. They go to hell. To defend one's family, even if [Liu] killed relocation workers, [he] is a hero in an era of the rule of law! Heaven is waiting for you, take care!" Many netizens questioned why few legal actions were taken against relocation workers and their practices, making comments such as "Don't see many relocation officials who caused deaths punished" and "I think the government should examine itself. Why did the relocated often take on extreme behavior? Why did relocation team often run into resistance? It is said that nothing would have had happened if the relocation team caused deaths or injured others. Is it because of money?" Besides relocation workers, netizens also condemned police (in 29 comments) and urban management officers (in six comments) who assisted demolition and relocation. One netizen cursed these people, writing, "The most valuable is a person who sacrificed gloriously for the truth. I'm crying for you, who will be remembered forever (永垂不朽)! Those police or urban management officers who assisted the relocation, guilty of a crime for which one deserves to die ten thousand times (罪该万死)! Die without any descendants (断子绝孙)!"

Second, netizens blasted the demolition and relocation policy itself in 270 comments (versus five comments supportive of the policy) and made comments such as "In China, the most sharpened conflict is demolition and relocation! Defenseless villagers are the most hapless! The rule of law in villages is so pale and weak!"; "He [Liu] and people whom he killed are all victims of society. But for the undisclosed, various demolition and relocation policies, there would not be such tragedies"; and "Wish there is no demolition and relocation in Heaven." Netizens particularly detested demolition and relocation by force (强拆). One netizen said, "To ordinary people, 'forced relocation' is the most detestable. [Ordinary people] curse with mouths, hate in hearts, are ready to swing fists, but have to suppress their outrage and accept it. In a reality of lawlessness, they have no choice. This man with his extreme behavior is appraised as a 'hero' by ordinary folks, and it shows how much Chinese ordinary people at the bottom of society hate relocation workers. But for the dictatorship in China, we would have seen an uprising already." Against forced relocation, many netizens called for the enactment of further laws to protect people's private property rights (in 62 comments) and considered Liu's behavior "self-defense" (in 30 comments). One netizen said, "What is self-defense? This is. [Liu is] people's hero." Another agreed: "Those relocation workers are not ordinary people who can be defined 'ordinary.' They are hatchet men. Forced relocation without permission of the owners is a crime. To protect one's legal rights, he [Liu] should be [found guilty of] over-defense!"

Third, dismayed by Liu's death, many netizens questioned China's laws and legal system (in 51 comments) and courts and judges (in 25 comments). They consistently expressed their dissatisfaction with unequal treatment of the law and made comments such as "The Chinese judiciary protects first and foremost law enforcers, second the powerful, third the collective, fourth citizens, and last villagers. Forever true" and "It is always true that the weak stand as an easy prey to the strong. The government will compensate if law enforcers commit crimes; powerless people like ants (蚁民) would serve longtime imprisonment, or lose all their properties or even their lives. That a prince who violates the law should be punished equally as ordinary people is just a phrase to fool ordinary people." Others argued that there are no laws and legal protections for the poor and made comments such as "Not to discuss whether it is wrong to run over people, there is no sense of security nowadays! . . . Likely tomorrow your house happens to block the wealth of powerful people! . . . Where is law? Does anyone see a powerful person being sentenced for destroying others' houses and injuring others? Or serving prison time? . . . Laws are games for the wealthy [and] have nothing to do with poverty!"

Netizens strongly demanded fairness and equity (in 101 comments) and called for transparency in demolition and relocation policies and practices (12 comments). One netizen asked, "Why is relocation not transparent? Local compensations should be publicized online." Another commented, "In fact, ordinary people support national development. Compensations should be transparent, even if it is only one yuan. It is fairness that matters. Those with power and connection get compensated for ten thousand; those without get one hundred. This is the root cause for conflicts." Almost universally, netizens believed that the relocated people did not receive fair and equitable treatment. For instance, one netizen commented, "The government always says equity and fairness. For relocation policies, is equity and fairness done to the forcefully relocated? Nail households (钉子户)[8] who refuse to move become so because of the unequal treatment they received. It is because compensations are not disclosed publicly. The collusion between local governments and developers is in the news all the time. The victims are, however, people and not officials. [We] need to learn from the history." Another said:

> You don't know how dirty it is. According to a madam from Xingyang city [located 15 kilometers west of Zhengzhou], relocation [team] took their land and destroyed their grass and trees. When asked about compensation, they were told by their village that the land belongs to the nation, road construction is to their benefit and asked instead why they insist on compensation!? Villagers further asked why relocation in other places including the airport received compensation. The village official said: it is different from one region to another, from one village to another, thus different results! But for coming here, you won't believe how corrupt it is!

---

8. Nail households refer to those that refuse to move or relocate during removal and relocation projects. They are viewed as "nail households" by the developers because of their determined resistance. See Y. Deng 2017.

To answer the concern that some nail households purposefully took advantage of the relocation and demanded unreasonably high compensation, one netizen called for proper legal procedures to handle the disputes and wrote, "Maybe the relocated people are asking too much [compensation]. Even if they do, it should be brought to a court to prove their excessive demands after debate and let the court decide a fair amount. If the relocated still refuses to move after these proper procedures, then forced relocation can be carried out. Besides, forced relocation needs armed police to maintain order and prevent violence. It is all right to do forced relocation, but it needs to follow proper procedures."

Fourth, netizens questioned the government (in 53 comments) and government officials (in 34 comments) at all levels for their roles in demolition and relocation. Many believed that the government sacrificed villagers' interests for those of others. For instance, one netizen wrote:

> After the 2000s, the government opted for the interests of business or governments but neglected villagers' interests, a key to conflicts between villagers and the governments. With or without consent, the governments normally turn to forced relocation. Farmland is the same, and there are many farmers and vegetable growers who lost their land. The number of farmers who petition yearly is not small. This bloody case shows indeed: killing one is easy and deserved too. But the governments cannot bully the weak in the future and go against the will of people. It is smart not to vie for interests with ordinary people! This case is tragic and a bloody lesson worthy of reflection.

Another shared how one's workplace pressed employees for relocation purpose and said, "The workplace asked its employees to persuade their family members to relocate. Otherwise, the annual evaluation of the employees wouldn't be passed, which prohibited pay raises several times, plus quarterly merit-based salary deduction and annual bonus deduction. This practice to tie demolition and relocation with employees' annual appraisal is not a policy from the central government. Please leave your comment." Many outraged netizens indeed left bold challenging comments such as "Where is oppression, where is revolt!"; "An oppressive government drives people to rebellion,"; "ZF [the initials of 'government' in pinyin] officials and developers take the lead to endanger public security, what should we do?"; and "After 70 years, they [referring to Communist Party members] always do things in their own way with no supervision."

Last but not least, netizens embedded their discussions of the demolition and relocation policy within contemporary Chinese society (33 comments) and demanded self-reflection of societal problems (30 comments). For instance, one taunted the so-called harmonious society and said, "Speaking of a 'harmonious society.' For some people's interests, they don't care about ordinary people's lives or deaths." Another echoed the concern that the majority interests are sacrificed for the minority: "[I] don't support killing! But in society without law but only power, what else can ordinary people do to protect their basic rights except use violence against violence? Only hope this society ends soon! [We] cannot allow the so-called flourishing age (盛世) to be a flourishing age of the minority, but a purgatory for the majority."

In this chapter we have examined a number of social, systemic, and structural problems reflected in our cases. Despite China's tremendous economic growth in the last four decades, a string of issues such as mammonism, decline of morality, loss of (socialist) faith and belief, rising crimes and social unrest, corruption, and increasing distrust in the government and the Party have all plagued contemporary Chinese society and fundamentally influenced people's lives. At the same time, governmental policies (e.g., the birth-control policies, the demolition and relocation policy) and reform measures (e.g., on the health-care system), if viewed as problematic to the public, could have faced continued and rekindled challenges. It is evident that netizens' comments in specific cases are indeed embedded in those bigger issues and problems of Chinese society, and many netizens are not afraid of speaking up online. Capital offenders and victims of our discussed cases represent extreme stories, while the masses may face, experience, or suffer from those issues and problems at different levels. To some extent, cases discussed in this chapter function as colored pieces of a kaleidoscope and collectively highlight some problems in Chinese society. Unfortunately, instead of forming mesmerizing pictures, all of these cases are tainted with real people's suffering and blood.

CHAPTER 8

Netizens' Discussion of Death Sentences
Rationality or Irrationality?

In this chapter we take on the issue of rationality. As intuitive as it may sound, the concept of rationality carries different definitions across different fields, and each theory makes various assumptions. For instance, in the field of economics, rational choice theory makes the assumption of the *homo economicus* who aims to maximize one's self-interests. In sociology, Max Weber (1968) famously distinguished various types of rationality and emphasized the role that formal rationality plays in the emergence of bureaucracy and modern capitalism in Western societies. Without restricting rationality to a specific field, we first examine Chinese netizens' perspectives—that is, their explicit usage of rationality. Then we turn to Jürgen Habermas's (1984/1987) concept of communicative rationality to analyze netizens' interactive communications. Accordingly, we identify a number of irrational and rational examples.

Rationality as Logical Reasoning

The corresponding Chinese term for rationality is *lixing* (理性) or *lizhi* (理智). Granted, *none* of the netizens who used this term defined or explained it explicitly. An examination of their usage suggests a broad and general definition of rationality, which often ties the concept to reason. For instance, Sen (2002, chapter 1) defines rationality as one's deliberate effort to utilize reason and scrutinize one's choices in making decisions. In his view, rational deliberation of choices should cover many things, such as one's actions, objectives, values, and priorities. Sen further argues that any pre-specified axioms such as "internal consistence of choice," "intelligent pursuit of self-interest" (e.g., rational choice theory), or "maximizing utilities" (e.g., utilitarianism) are *not* necessary and could even generate problems in conceptualization and application of rationality. When the emphasis of rationality is placed on careful scrutiny of one's choices based on reasoning, the process of one's evaluation or analysis is expected to take in all available relevant information (knowledge) and be highly logical, analytical, objective, and independent of one's emotions, personal feelings, or instincts.

Such features seem to fit how Chinese netizens used the term in our sample. For instance, one netizen in the Lian Enqing case (#14) expressed deep concern about people's support for Lian's killing and wrote, "I am sympathetic to Lian's experience but don't support Lian's approach [killing] to solve his problems. His doctor was at fault but did not deserve to be killed. Where is law with such killing? Seeing so much support from netizens, I feel [it is] absurd. [This is] societal collective *irrationality*, which leads to chaos." In the Lin Senhao case (#1), one netizen questioned people's unquestioned support for sharen changming and said, "A just legal system is based on *rationality*. The idea of 'a life for a life' is no doubt to express one's anger for a lost life. I think that not everyone would insist paying back with a life as a punishment, as a necessary way to regulate people's behavior." In both of these examples, the netizens explicitly turned to rationality (or irrationality) to question the lack of deliberate reasoning by their criticized counterparts.

Netizens' discussion of penzi (see chapter 4) also sheds light on features of irrationality from their perspectives. First, the defining feature of penzi is verbal attack. In the Wang Changping case (#19), one netizen expressed frustration with relentless verbal attacks by penzi and commented, "Anyone is said to be a 'shuijun' [see chapter 4]. Does it have to be cursing irrationally and verbally attacking to not be a shuijun? Make rational comments and don't be an online mob member." Second, some questioned oversimplified and flawed reasoning by others. One netizen in the Wang case commented, "Always going to the extremes when looking at issues is a feature of Chinese netizens. . . . It shows that Chinese netizens' reasoning tends to be oversimplified and crude without organization (简单粗暴, 毫无章法)!" One netizen in the Lian Enqing case (#14) summarized penzi's reasoning as follows: "Penzi enjoys confusing and misleading people (混淆视听), making digressions (东扯西拉), taking a part for the whole, and making exaggerations (夸大其词)."

Third, netizens pointed out that penzi tended to be emotional and involved rushing to quick decisions without careful deliberation. In the Lin Senhao case (#1), one netizen lamented, "Those penzi online . . . so emotional. Is this 'ruling the country by law'? The Supreme People's Court [SPC] is not supposed to approve Lin's death sentence. Being verbally attacked by you like this, [Lin is] doomed." Another said, "They [penzi] all make an assumption (臆斷) based on their emotions and then judge." Last but not least, it was pointed out that penzi often preferred extreme actions, including killing. One netizen who commented on the Lin Senhao case criticized penzi's demand for quick actions and wrote, "After reading these comments, [I feel] China is far from a society of the rule of law. A group of online mob. Do you have a right to order the SPC what to do? Do you have a right to demand extreme punishment against a person? [You] should learn to respect the law."

Rationality in Communicative Interactions

While a broadly defined rationality dovetails with Chinese netizens' usage, we turn to Jürgen Habermas's (1984/1987) concept and theory of communicative rationality (TCR) to help guide our further inquiry. Habermas's TCR specifically deals with social interactions as a form of verbal communication and locates rationality in structures of interpersonal linguistic communication. The theory's framework rests on the assumption that all speech acts have an inherent purpose—to achieve the goal of mutual understanding—and that human beings possess the communicative competence to bring about such understanding. In Habermas's words, communicative rationality "carries with it connotations based ultimately on the central experience of the unconstrained, unifying, consensus-building force of argumentative speech, in which different participants overcome their merely subjective views and, owing to the mutuality of rationally motivated conviction, assure themselves of both the unity of the objective world and the inter-subjectivity of their lifeworld" (1984, 10).

To Habermas, the central question is how one can justify moral commands, norms of action, ethical evaluations, and the like through rational discussions. The key is to clarify the norms and procedures by which an agreement can be reached, and this is done through intelligent deliberation of validity claims as a form of public debate and justification. Habermas envisioned that any individual engaging in communication would be accountable for the normative validity of the claims raised. In making a validity claim, a speaker is ready to claim three *validity dimensions*, including normative rightness (WE), theoretical truth (IT), and expressive or subjective truthfulness (I). Thus, the speaker is obligated to defend that a claim is true (IT, i.e., propositional truth in the objective domain of culture and science), and normatively right (WE, i.e., moral rightness in the social domain of society), and honest (I, i.e., sincerity in the subjective domain of personality). Moreover, if challenged, the speaker would justify these claims with good reason. Open deliberation and debate is the procedure by which people arrive at an unconstrained, unifying consensus, and the rational character of validity claims thus derives from their capability to be criticized and grounded within an argumentative exchange. Inherent in such rational deliberations are components such as equal opportunity for one's communication, one's capability of communication, and logical consistency of one's claims.

Granted, Habermas's theory is projected in an ideal speech situation and subject to many criticisms (e.g., Cummings 2002; Gunaratne 2006). Nevertheless, its power as a form of interactive communication oriented toward mutual conflict resolution through understanding, compromises, and consensus-building based on the intersubjective recognition of criticizable validity claims sheds significant light on evaluating Chinese netizens' interactions online, if a civil, open, and public debate and deliberation of one's claims and reasoning is desirable in such a context. Compared to a broadly defined term, we argue that Habermas's TCR is better suited for analyses of Chinese netizens' comments for several reasons. First, the nature of the TCR fits online communicative interactions nicely. Second, the TCR inherently encompasses the requirement of logical reasoning (Dallmayr 1988) and is more specific in both the context and measures of rationality. Third, while the objectivity of rationality has always been controversial, especially in making moral and ethical judgments (e.g., Strandberg 2017), the TCR allows us to make normative judgments within its defined domain.

Habermas's TCR can be extended to the legal field. For instance, Feteris (2003) applied Habermas's theory to legal discourse and argued that the TCR could be useful as both a heuristic instrument for reconstructing processes of legal decision making and a critical instrument for evaluating decision-making procedures and legal outcomes. For the former, Habermas's (1989) advocacy of "deliberative democracy" suggests that a government's laws and institutions should be a reflection of free and open rational discussion in the public sphere; for the latter, communicative rationality could function as a tool for determining the legitimacy of law (e.g., congruence with moral discourse of society), though the complementary relationship between law and communicative rationality works in both directions to influence each other.

In our study, netizens' discussion of death sentences represents communication about legal issues (e.g., moral support for or challenge to capital punishment). Applying Habermas's theory, we may evaluate the rationality of netizens' comments from at least three aspects. First, each comment can be evaluated on the three validity dimensions as outlined above (i.e., WE, IT, and I). Therefore, if an argument is not based on sound facts (e.g., is fabricated), not congruent with existing social and legal standards, or not made truthfully or sincerely, a question can be raised about its rationality. Second, because open and public debate and deliberation is necessary to establish the validity of each claim, any endeavor conducive to such a process could be viewed as rational (or vice versa). Third, because the overall goal of rational deliberation is enriching the discussion and mutual understanding and building consensus, any comment with a disruptive effect on such a goal could be viewed as irrational. Based on these measures, we found a number of specific irrational and rational examples in our study.

Personal Attacks: Use of Foul Language, Threats, and Curses

As detailed in chapter 4, personal attacks were unfortunately very popular among Chinese netizens' interactions. A total of 2,057 comments including personal attacks were counted in 37 cases (see table 3). Personal attacks focused *not* on the substance of netizens' comments but on individuals, thus a strong indicator of irrationality. Verbal attacks generally occurred in two forms: use of foul language and direct personal threat. Note that the counts we discussed in chapter 4 included only comments of interactions between netizens. To measure netizens' overall use of foul language, we created a select list of foul words among *all* comments (appendix 5) and counted a total of 9,594 comments with the use of a single or multiple foul words (representing 24.8% of the total comments) in 50 cases (79.4% of all cases) (appendix 3). This high frequency reflects one typical feature of netizens' online discussions, given the nature of anonymous, non-face-to-face interactions.

Personal attacks could be made against any party. Depending on the actual target, the effect could vary. First, when foul language did *not* target a specific party, the damaging effect was arguably the least, even though one could have used foul language consistently as part of one's virtual language. For instance, in the Zhai "x"de case (#9), Zhai stabbed his neighbor Zhang to death after his attempt to borrow 30 yuan failed. One netizen commented on the unexpected tragedy, "Fucked, 'woe befalls the one who sits at home (无事家中坐, 祸从天上来)'!" In the Yang Dazhi case (#21), Yang took advantage of his position as a school principal and molested and raped six students. One netizen showed admiration for Yang's sexual offenses and commented, "Worth his death, fucked (泥妈)." In both examples, as vulgar as they were (especially in the second example), the use of foul language was to express one's feelings, and neither intended to harm a specific party.

Second, when personal attacks were made against a particular defendant, the damage seemed to be limited and justified in the views of the majority of netizens given the heinous crime(s) committed by the defendant. In the Peng Shu and Hu Haolong case (#3), Peng and Hu were convicted of receiving bribes of 188 and 170 million yuan, respectively, and both were death-sentenced. One netizen commented, "Fucked, these sons of bitches deserve to die." Foul language against guilty offenders such as Peng and Hu would likely be viewed as acceptable by the majority of netizens, as it offends no one else but the deserving offenders. Take the Yuan Junkai et al. case (#12), for another example. Defendants Yuan, Liu, and Wei all had lengthy criminal records before they were convicted of new capital crimes and death-sentenced. Angry netizens questioned their recidivism and wondered why they had been given a second chance in the first place. One netizen used foul language and said, "Have a good journey. Go to India for your reincarnation, animal!" In this example, though the foul language used against the defendant(s) (i.e., "animal") was likely non-offensive to most netizens, its implication of India as a deserving place for sex offenders was offensive as a form of national discrimination (see the discussion below).

Third, aside from the last two scenarios, when attacks were lodged against any other party, the damaging effect was evident. Some select examples of such offensive usage are provided below:

> "Stupid pig, you may use violence. Given your comment, you must be a youth. You may use violence just like the ISIS and the Taliban. Wait and see if you can solve the problem?" [A netizen criticizing

another who supported Lian's use of violence against doctors; Lian Enqing case, #14]

"Too many dogs who verbally attack others. Reform is accomplished step by step. Fucked, [they] only know how to verbally attack others." [A netizen targeted netizens who verbally attacked others; Lian Enqing case, #14]

"sb [a Chinese cursing word, see chapter 4], you can even verbally attack this? Can you do it? If not, shut your filthy mouth. I'm tired of a sb like you who only turns to verbal attack. At least the police was chasing the criminal after 12 years, which was good." [A netizen countered others' criticism of police low efficiency; Luo Xiaohua and Chen Rihong case, #57]

"Fucked, why spare one criminal? Sharen changming! If [the offender] raped the daughter and wife of the judge, would the judge have spared him? Kill them all! To mourn for the deceased!" "Let's all rape the judge's wife and daughter. A suspended sentence at most and might get paroled out with good behavior! Once out, [one becomes] a hero again!" [Netizens targeted the judge(s) who spared an offender's life; Luo Xiaohua and Chen Rihong case, #57]

"Since the beginning, 2Fs generate sb." [One netizen attacking another in the Yuan Junkai et al. case, #12; for the "rule of the 2F," see chapter 4]

"What do you say, holy mothers who preach for abolition every day?" [A netizen attacking abolitionists; Yuan Junkai et al. case, #12]

"Where is Bai Yansong, the moral bitch? [Is he] lying on the bed of his lover in a villa and working on his commentary that criticizes inhumane actions by the police, the procuratorate, and the court?" [A netizen targeted Bai, a TV host known for his criticism of Chinese social problems and calling for more humane measures; Ou Changsheng case, #63]

"This defense lawyer is a skunk, and loses [his] basic moral values for money. What if he himself or his family members were stabbed, then what would he think?" [A netizen targeted Zhao's lawyer; Zhao Zihui case, #60]

"A herd of animals in the comments section! He killed four people!!" [A netizen showing anger with netizens who supported Liu despite Liu's killings; Liu Danao case, #47]

"Those sons of bitches who turned to forced relocation and were killed by [Liu's] vehicle deserved to die. Go to hell. To protect one's family, even if [you] killed relocation workers, [you are] a hero in an era of the rule of law! Heaven is waiting for you. Good-bye!" [Netizens targeted relocation workers—that is, the victims of Liu's crimes; Liu Danao case, #47]

In all of these examples, it is ostensible that personal attacks in the form of either foul language or personal threat were directed at a specific target, be it a netizen, a group of netizens, a crime victim, a judge, a lawyer, or abolitionists. Comments of an offensive nature such as these would have most likely produced only a negative and disruptive effect in one's communication with others. Sometimes a netizen may have a valid point. However, the use of foul language could have spoiled one's effort. For instance, in the Hu Cunbiao and Wang Yong case (#29), one netizen commented, "Reducing the use of capital punishment represents progress of society." Another disagreed and countered with a valid point but ended the argument with foul language. Specifically, the netizen said, "All nations without the death penalty can sentence [the criminal] to prison terms of hundreds or thousands of years. China only learned how to reduce the use of capital punishment but not enhance prison terms. Do you think this is right? Sb."

Similar to the effect of foul language and personal threat, another popular but irrational theme was cursing (泄愤), often used to express one's outrage. Such cursing occurred in 35 cases (55.6% of all cases) in our sample (see table 4). In the Lin Senhao case (#1), many cursed Lin for his crime with comments such as "Only one way [to punish him]: Kill! Kill! Kill!"; "[Lin] deserves to die a thousand times!!!!!!!!"; "This person [Lin] deserves death by a thousand cuts"; and "Must die! Otherwise, people of the nation won't accept it! Must kill [his family members of] nine generations!" Though such comments were directed at Lin (and his family members), cursing in these examples served no real purpose except to vent one's anger.

Moreover, calling for revival of outlawed forms of harsh punishment (e.g., death by a thousand cuts, killing one's family members up to nine generations) used in ancient China is another indicator of irrationality, as such punishment has already been abandoned based on contemporary moral and legal standards. Besides cursing Lin, another group of netizens turned to threats and made comments such as "I don't care anymore. If Lin is not death-sentenced, I'll go and kill him. I won't be death-sentenced anyway"; "Fucked, if no death sentence [is meted out], I'll buy some poison and feed to some who have argued with me"; and "If [Lin is] not shot to death, the next to die would be family members of his lawyers." Some angry netizens even pointed their fingers at people who called for leniency (e.g., "You fart! [I'm] cursing you!! According to Buddhism you preached, you should be killed 10,000 times by others and reincarnated 10,000 times") or people who argued for abolition ("If capital punishment is abolished, I'll buy a gun immediately and kill scores of people because I hate them!"). In all of these examples of threat cursing, it is unlikely that the cursing netizens would take any real actions. Nevertheless, online commenting had become an easy outlet for their venting. One netizen deeply worried about such irrational venting and said, "If law is all about emotional venting, this world would be dire. Is it progress of the world? Is it progress of the legal system? It would be the collapse of the legal system, the dominance of the 'rule of man,' and regression of society. It would lead to more cases of Nian Bin and Hu'ge [see chapter 3].[1] [It is] a group of shuijun and angry young men with no brains who'd like to impose their emotions upon the law. [It is] laughable, pathetic, and lamentable."

Punishing Innocent People and Forgoing Legal Procedure

Another example of netizens' irrational comments was to call for legal punishment of innocent people, which occurred in eleven cases (see table 4). Most of the time, such comments were made against family members of a defendant, either categorically or specifically. In the Peng Shu and Hu Haolong case (#3), one netizen suggested, "Wipe out nine generations

---

1. The Nian Bin (念斌) case is another infamous wrongful conviction case that occurred in recent years. Nian was initially charged with the lethal poisoning of two of his neighbor's children in 2006. From 2006 to 2014, Nian was death-sentenced three times by the trial court and once by the provincial high court, until he was eventually exonerated (see, e.g., Lu, Trejbalova, and Liang 2019).

[of defendant family members]; kill the whole family!" In the He Shenguo case (#42), some netizens were angry with He's over-quota births and made comments against He's children such as "Kill his whole family. Children of this kind of people won't end up being good people in the future" and "These four children are eggs of a murderer and should be all arrested." In the Lin Senhao case (#1), many netizens blamed Lin's parents for their selfish love for Lin; some particularly disliked Lin's father due to his relentless effort to save Lin's life. To them, Lin's father was simply playing the system to cover up Lin's homicide. One netizen commented, for instance, "Son [Lin], death sentence. [Lin's] parents, reeducation through labor, because they did not teach their son right and with proper discipline, which led to the loss of a son in another family." Another added, "Lin's answering for the death [of victim Huang] is to serve heavenly justice. This animal is so evil and should have been decapitated during the month of his murder! His father is a despicable man. Speaking impolitely, giving birth to a murderer is committing a crime!" Moreover, Lin's opponents went further and even pointed fingers at whoever supported Lin. One commented, "Public execution [of Lin]! Whoever spoke on his behalf [should be] sentenced to imprisonment of one month to a year!" Another netizen targeted people who petitioned for mercy and said, "I think that one family member of those who signed the petition should be poisoned. Then they can talk about leniency." Note that such irrational calling for punishment was made not just by Lin's opponents but by his supporters as well. For instance, one supporter of Lin launched an attack against judges who sentenced him to death, saying, "I believe we should rescind Lin's death sentence and change it to three-year imprisonment. And at the same time [we should] sentence executing judges to five-year imprisonment each."

There is a fine line between morally blaming a defendant's family members (debate) and calling for legal punishment (action). In the Zhao Zihui case (#60), three netizens vented their anger specifically at Zhao's mother. One questioned her effort to launch an appeal on Zhao's behalf and commented, "Zhao's mother gave birth to such an animal and dared to appeal. How do they face the spirit of the deceased (怎能对得起死去的亡灵)?" In contrast, another went further and suggested, "To counter his mother's non-apologetic, non-compensatory, and hiding attitude, [we] should burn down his house." Though both comments were made against Zhao's mother, the call to burn down the defendant's house presents a stronger argument for irrationality.

Table 4. Counts of Cases with Unique Circumstances

Cases (marked with "X") in which netizens ...	Made curses	Called to punish innocent people	Called for no appeals	Made discriminatory remarks	Made case comparisons	Compared with other nations	Made suggestions
Lin Senhao	X	X	X	RD	X	X	X
Huang Qinghen	X				X		X
Peng Shu and Hu Haolong	X	X	X		X		X
Zhao Zhihong					X		
Liu Han et al.				SD			
Tuo Heti et al.			X				
Hu "x"					X		
Wang Yuefu					X		
Zhai "x"de							
Ruan Fangcheng et al.				RED			
Wu Qinyuan	X				X		X
Yuan Junkai et al.	X			RD	X		X
Wang Gang						X	
Lian Enqing	X	X		RD; AV; ND	X	X	X
Zhang Xiangxi	X		X	ND		X	
Lin "x"ping and Ye "x"tian	X		X	RD; AV	X	X	X
Sun Zhifu				SD	X		X
Liang Kaiwu	X				X		
Wang Changping	X		X		X		X
Zhang Weilan et al.	X		X	RD; AV	X	X	X
Yang Dazhi	X	X	X	RD; SD	X	X	X
Wang "x"	X		X				
Fan Jieming	X			RD	X	X	X
Zheng Dalong and Yang Shengjian							
Wang Hua et al.							
Gu Junshan							
Deng Fang	X		X	RD; ND			
Li Lei	X		X	RD			X
Hu Cunbiao and Wang Yong	X		X	ND	X	X	X
Yuan Lijun					X		
Chen Yun		X			X		
Feng Xiujuan	X			RD; AV; SD; ND	X	X	X
Yang Chaoquan	X	X		SD; ND	X	X	X
Lumei et al.					X		
Wang Jianghua and Wang Jinpeng							

Table 4.—(continued)

Cases (marked with "X") in which netizens...	Made curses	Called to punish innocent people	Called for no appeals	Made discriminatory remarks	Made case comparisons	Compared with other nations	Made suggestions
Huang "x"				RD			
Xiao "x"							
Zhao Xu	X				X		
Wang Zongren				AV			
Deng "x"							X
Ling Ruiming				RD; ND	X		
He Shenguo	X	X		AV; ND; RED; RD	X	X	X
Wang Yihuan	X			RD	X		
Gao Yulun et al.	X			RD; ND	X		
Liu "x"				RD; AV			
Song Yongtian et al.				RD	X		
Liu Danao		X		RD; ND	X	X	X
Yang "x"ping et al.							
Wu "x"hua	X	X		RD; ND	X		
He Jian	X			RD		X	X
Wang Baiyang	X			RD			
Wu Youxin et al.	X		X		X		
Yang Ruixi	X				X		
Zhang "x"yi	X						
Li "xx"	X	X		RD	X	X	X
Pan Guohui				RD	X		
Luo Xiaohua and Chen Rihong	X	X	X	RD	X		
Li "x"							
Jin Fusheng	X		X		X		X
Zhao Zihui	X	X	X	AV	X	X	X
Li "x" (#2)							
Yang Xueqi	X	X		RD; SD; AH; ND	X	X	X
Ou Changsheng	X		X	RD; AV; ND	X	X	
Total	**35**	**11**	**17**	**RD: 26; AV: 9; RED: 2; ND: 13; SD: 6; AH: 1**	**39**	**18**	**24**

Note: RD: Regional discrimination; AV: Discrimination against villagers; RED: Racial/ethnic discrimination; ND: National discrimination; SD: Sex discrimination; AH: Discrimination against homosexuals.

Granted, netizens reacted differently to such irrational comments. Some adopted a "tit for tat" strategy and countered back, while others called for rational reasoning. In the Lin Senhao case (#1), one netizen attacked Lin's father, saying, "Old fool, [he] is not a good bird [insulting language in Chinese] either." One netizen countered, "You are not a good bird either. What makes you qualified to insult Lin's father! Trash!" In contrast, another replied with a mild and rational tone, writing, "Lin's father is the biggest victim of this case and has to bear the pain at his age. Looking at his hopeless expression in the first picture, it is really sad! Lin deserves to die and has received his punishment. But please do not go after his family. Those who accused Lin's father should not have done it. Humans are species with feelings, not to mention [the loss of] a person closest to oneself. Can anyone feel the pain of a father who has to witness his son's death! Everything started with Lin Senhao, and let's end it with Lin Senhao! Poor parents."

Another example of netizens' irrational reaction was their willingness to forgo proper legal proceedings required by laws, as discussed in chapter 5. It is one thing to express one's dissatisfaction with extended delay of trials and reviews, but it is another to openly advocate forgoing legal procedures to expedite the process and hasten a defendant's death. In 17 cases (table 4), netizens specifically called for "no appeals." For instance, in the Wang Changping case (#19), one netizen wrote, "Correct sentencing! Don't fart bother with the appeal, you two, sons of bitches!" In the Zhang Weilan et al. case (#20), one suggested that "for those who were sentenced to life imprisonment and chose to appeal, change [the life sentence] to a death sentence with immediate execution!!! For other appellants, enhance their punishment!!!" At the same time, many rational netizens insisted on following proper legal procedures. One netizen in the Fan Jieming case (#23) commented, "First and foremost, the law should follow procedural justice. Even with capital offenders, [they] should have appeals, until the final review and approval by the SPC." Another reminded others about Hu'ge's wrongful conviction and execution and said, "Law is based on procedure and evidence. Proper procedures need to be followed, and necessary evidence cannot be overlooked. Hu'ge was executed so fast. What a wrong decision! If [the] Hu'ge case was reviewed for two more years, the outcome could have been very different."

Discrimination in Various Forms

In our sample, we witnessed various forms of discrimination (see table 4). The most popular of these was regional discrimination, which occurred in 26 cases (41.3% of all cases). Often it occurred when a netizen saw the hometown of a criminal (or place of the crime) and then generalized the issue to people from a whole region, thus showing signs of being irrational. Some select examples are as follows:

> "You know, all private hospitals in China are made a mess by Putian people [from Fujian province], who have almost become known as 'rats crossing streets and chased by all (过街老鼠人人喊打)'"; "[Solve the issue] this way: All Fujianese... died! No need for treatment!... The doctor-patient relationship would be improved significantly!" [Lian Enqing case, #14]

> "So many crimes in Beijing"; "So many sex predators in Beijing!" [Yuan Junkai et al. case, #12]

> "Beijing has produced several cases in which family members were killed. How could they do it? Beijingnese are weird." [Li Lei case, #28]

> "Guizhou is not rich,[2] but poor. So many evil officials." [Yang Dazhi case, #21]

> "As expected, it is the Sichuanese [who are the criminals]!" [Zhang Weilan et al. case, #20]

> "[He's] from Guangdong [province], abusing drugs." [Deng Fang case, #27]

> "It's a Cantonese again!!!! Beg you Cantonese not to eat placenta and dead babies anymore. Your genes have already mutated. You are a group of uncivilized people who refuse to change (顽固不化)." [Feng Xiujuan case, #32]

---

2. Note that the netizen intended to use the first character of Guizhou (贵, richness) to make a pun.

"Hong Kong people fear death the most." [Huang "x" case, #36]

"Shanghai dogs are biting people again." [Lin "x"ping and Ye "x"tian case, #16]

"Why do Guangxi people enjoy killing people? It is descendants of the reactionary militia (反动民团) trained by Bai Jiansheng that committed these crimes!"[3]

"It is Liuzhou news again! Liuzhou [city] is the true leader of Guangxi news" [He Jian case, #50]

"So many bizarre judges in Shandong, who handled cases like this." [Li "xx" case, #55]

"Fully support: Henan is not a living place for people. In barren mountains and dangerous waters live the rogues (穷山恶水出刁民)! Societal environment and public security is extremely poor!" [Yang Xueqi case, #62]

"[It is] a Henan bird (河南鸟人) [referring to defendant Liu]"; "Big Holland [produces] all sorts of weird news!"[4] [Liu Danao case, #47]

"Hunan people would kill fellows from Hunan." [Luo Xiaohua and Chen Rihong case, #57]

It is evident from these examples that provincial and regional discriminations were quite prevalent among netizens' comments, targeting not only infamous and poor regions such as Guizhou, Guangxi, and Henan but also prosperous and leading provinces such as Beijing, Shanghai, and Guangdong. Facing such discrimination, netizens reacted differently. In

---

3. Bai Chongxi (白崇禧 1893–1966), also named Jiansheng (健生), was a Chinese general in the National Revolutionary Army of the Republic of China. From the mid-1920s to 1949, Bai and his ally Li Zongren (李宗仁) ruled Guangxi province as regional warlords with their own troops.

4. It appears that some netizens used Holland (the Netherlands) to represent Henan in their comments, as the pronunciation of "Holland" in Chinese (荷兰) is very close to that of "Henan."

the Yang Xueqi case (#62), Yang committed multiple sex crimes in Henan. One netizen made a discriminatory comment in an ironic tone, saying, "Henan is truly a remarkable place with beautiful mountains and clear waters that produces outstanding people (山清水秀, 人杰地灵), heh-heh [sound mimicking a sneer]!" Another concurred: "Big trucks are all afraid of breaking down on highways [in Henan]! All thieves and robbers are from Henan." Some netizens countered with comments such as "After hearing the two words 'Henan,' your rabies started" and "The Sichuanese are truly the worst of the worst" (countering a Sichuanese who made derogatory remarks against Henan people). And then there were others who pointed out the problem of discrimination (e.g., "Everywhere there are good and bad people. This is ostensible attack based on one's region") and used rational reasoning with comments such as "Every province has people like this. Don't take a part for the whole" and "Facing such a heinous crime, people [like you] cared only about 'regions.' I want to say when you [make yourself] feel good based on 'regional disparities,' then you are so low and can only comfort yourself with sneers against others based on their regions." Last but not least, there were netizens who lamented netizens' regional discrimination. For instance, one netizen commented, "Regional discrimination is a bad habit of Chinese people." Another wrote, "Reading netizens' comments, so many filled with regional discrimination in China. Which region does not produce some black sheep? Is it necessary to denigrate people from all regions? [We are] all Chinese! When you denigrate our ancestors, aren't you talking about yourselves? Such people don't deserve to be Chinese and [they would] be traitors in a time of wars!"

Second, related to regional discrimination, another popular form of discrimination focused on villagers, especially villagers from poor regions, which occurred in nine cases (table 4). Netizens' derogatory remarks against villagers mainly focused on two things: their moral character flaws and their crimes. Many netizens blamed villagers for their moral character flaws such as dishonesty and low quality (低素质). In the Lian Enqing case (#14), one netizen commented, "I know many villagers who are not honest (淳朴), to be candid. They cannot get along with each other and fight for some small interests. Each family would like to gain more benefit and to show off when they get some money. Speaking the truth, [being labeled] honest and kind is merely self-deception." In the Ou Changsheng case (#63), one netizen criticized the quality of poor people and said, "Speaking the reality, the poor treat the poor very badly. The wealthy would give some in charity, but the poor wouldn't accept the fact that someone like them lives a better life." In the He Shenguo case (#42), one criticized over-quota births occurring among poor villagers and expressed concerns about the quality of such babies. Specifically, the netizen wrote, "In China, the lower their education level is, the more births they have. Villagers have more births. In contrast, full-time master's and Ph.D. students and the highly educated only have one child or none. If this situation lasts long, the Chinese nation will be destroyed, with intelligence getting worse and worse."

In addition to blaming villagers for their character flaws, many netizens blamed them for their crimes. In the Zhang Weilan et al. case (#20), several netizens left comments such as "Villagers are so evil. It would be difficult for urbanites to do things so completely without conscience that would doom [them] with no descendants"; "Nowadays, criminals are basically all coming from villagers"; and "Barren mountains and dangerous waters produce rogues." Another netizen tied villagers to a specific region and said, "These Sichuan villagers would do all necessary evils for money." Some netizens traced villagers' crimes to poverty. For instance, one commented, "Though it is sad for the poor [to realize] . . . but the fact is not that villagers are honest but poverty produces evilness and wealth leads to conscience (穷生奸计富涨良心) . . . thus it is important to develop economy and raise education levels for all." In the Liu "x" case (#45), one netizen compared children from different family backgrounds and wrote, "It's obvious. Nowadays, children from poor families, families with multiple children, and families located in remote regions don't have financial resources to match but envy comfortable lives of children who are from the cities and who are the only child of their families. Therefore, they commit extremely high levels of property crimes. You go and check, cases of theft, robbery, burglary, telecommunication fraud, and street swindle, almost all of them are committed by children from these families. Children who are the only child living in cities, few of them were involved in these property crimes."

Unlike the case of regional discrimination, very few netizens countered back when it came to discriminating against villagers. The only exception occurred in the Liu "x" case (#45), when one netizen questioned the title of the report, which was "Villagers born after 1995 kidnapped and murdered: one [was] death-sentenced and the other [received] 16-year imprisonment." The netizen asked specifically, "Why highlight 'villagers' in the title? Why not do the same to urbanites who commit crimes? Little editor, your villager ancestors are asking you to burn joss sticks[5] at your family grave [insulting language in Chinese]!"

Compared to regional discrimination and discrimination against villagers, racial, ethnic, and national discrimination rarely occurred in our sample. Only in the Ruan Fangcheng et al. case (#10) did two netizens make discriminatory remarks against black people. One commented, "Black people, [with] low intelligence, don't want to work but turn to crimes. Holy mothers don't verbally attack me: just look at Detroit and [you should] know. Some Chinese women are stupid. Black people from Africa have no money, but they are willing to go with them. I feel so uncomfortable as if I were drunk (我也是醉了)."[6] Another immediately followed with a short but blunt accusation and said, "Blacks are not good people." In the He Shenguo case (#42), one single netizen brought up the issue of differential treatment based on one's ethnic origin and said, "Here is the question: our nation only enforces the birth-control policy against Han people?" Nevertheless, no one followed up on this comment.

Nationality was discussed in 13 cases by a small number of netizens (table 4). In 11 cases, netizens made derogatory remarks against Japanese people. Such remarks were mainly made in two forms. First, some comments implied that the Japanese are people of low and evil quality and nature. In the Wu "x"hua case (#49), one netizen commented about defendant Wu, "Maybe he is a Japanese descendant, with an evil heart." Similarly, a netizen commented in the Feng Xiujuan case (#32), "Are you a descendant of Japanese dogs in China?" In the Deng Fang case (#27), one netizen compared defendant Deng with the Japanese and said, "Fuck his mother. To kill him is nothing, but what a loss for the two victims!!! This skunk is worse than the Japanese!" Second, some netizens openly called for actions against the Japanese. In the Gao Yulun et al. case (#44), one netizen said, "Don't kill them [defendants]. Send them to a suicide squad to bring back the head of Abe [Shinzo, the Japanese prime minister] and the dark horse [meaning unknown] for redemption." Though this remark may sound like a joke, it was definitely derogatory with and in bad taste. In the Ou Changsheng case (#63), one netizen commented on Ou's crime and wrote, "Bombing a bus is not ideal. [You should] kill foreigners, ideally

---

5. Slender sticks of incense burned before a Chinese god worshipped in the form of an idol.

6. A popular Chinese phrase in recent years that means "I'm speechless" or "Are you kidding me?"

the Japanese. I'm planning so." Besides Japan, a few cases targeted other nations. The Ling Ruiming case (#41) involved a potential marriage fraud by victim Ruan (a Vietnamese lady), who was killed by her husband, Ling. One netizen generalized the case to denigrate all Vietnamese women and said, "There are many Vietnamese women who commit marriage fraud." Interestingly, another netizen commented positively on the good looks of Vietnamese women and said, "Vietnamese ladies are pretty and [their skin color is] white, better than the Chinese. You wouldn't know it if you have not been there." In two cases involving sex offenders (Hu Cunbiao and Wang Yong, #29; Yang Xueqi, #62), India was mentioned and implied as a place suitable for sex offenders.

Sex and sexual orientation discrimination occasionally surfaced in six cases. As detailed in chapter 5, six females were death-sentenced in our sample, two of whom were convicted of homicide (Sun Zhifu, #17; Feng Xiujuan, #32). In Sun's case, Sun murdered victim Yang and tried to commit suicide but survived. Her diagnosed schizophrenia was ruled not severe enough to warrant a reduced sentence. One netizen tried to argue gendered punishment and said, "Men would be treated as normal even with mental problems. Women would be punished more leniently if they have some very minor mental issues. This is China's 'gendered law.'" Two netizens immediately countered: "Read carefully. This is a woman, death-sentenced!" and "This is a woman. The upstairs slapped his own face!" In Feng's case, Feng had an affair with her first love, and her request for a divorce was rejected by her husband. Feng murdered her three children and attempted suicide but was saved. A number of netizens left comments to generalize Feng's crime to evil women. One said, for example, "Femme fatale (红颜祸水). Such an evil woman should be shot to death for ten thousand times and more." Another cited a poem: "No wonder the old saying [says], 'Teeth of a green bamboo viper, a tail of a wasp, none is as poisonous as the heart of an evil woman (青竹蛇儿口, 黄蜂尾上针, 两者皆不毒, 最毒妇人心).' In the eyes of a woman crazily in love, even family love would be a hateful burden." A few others commented on the "virgin effect" with comments such as "Nothing is more poisonous than an evil woman's heart. Proven again: [one needs to] look for a virgin and first love, very important. Otherwise, [watch out for] being forced to wear a green hat [a Chinese idiom that means "to be a cuckold"] at the minimum or losing lives of family members at the worst" and "If your wife is not a virgin, safety measures should be heightened [implying a higher risk of an affair by one's wife]." One netizen further blamed feminists for their "bad influence," saying, "Those feminist bitches subvert worldviews (毁三观)."

Two other cases, those of Yang Dazhi (#21) and Yang Xueqi (#62), involved multiple sexual offenses against young women. A number of netizens left comments to show their admiration for defendants' "achievements." One claimed, for instance, in the Yang Xueqi case (#62), "All [victims] are virgins, marvelous! Big brother, worth it!" It was reported in this case that Yang's wife turned out to be a lesbian, and Yang could have committed his crimes to retaliate against the betrayal of his wife. Five netizens attacked homosexuals accordingly. One commented, "Lesbians are a worse group compared to gays. It is said that they are very selfish with dirty characters." Another encouraged actions against Yang's wife and her partner: "If you [Yang] are good, [you] should have laid [implying by force] both your former wife and her lover. That is a true man!" Four other netizens countered such remarks. One asked, "I'm speechless with regard to those who attacked the homosexuals. Did they rob you, burn down your house or kill someone? Is it a crime to be a homosexual? I can only heh-heh." Another challenged the reporting and said, "The story [was] quoted out of context. They got divorced many years ago, [a fact] not explained. This is to mislead people against the homosexuals. Don't you know how it affects the homosexuals?"

Compared to comments against villagers discussed above, the Lin Senhao incident (#1) presented a unique case of criminals with high intelligence. To some netizens, Lin's educational background (being a master's student at a well-known university) only aggravated his crime. One netizen pointed out, "To those who argued for a second chance on Lin's behalf because he is a highly educated student, what made you argue so? Do sentencing standards have something to do with one's education? People with high education and intelligence are more fearful, and their dangerousness is worse." Others echoed and generalized Lin's crime to crimes by people with high intelligence and made comments such as "Skunks with high education should be dealt with extreme punishment" and "Educated people (读书人) with such an [evil] character are too many. Kill, kill, kill. They study in order to set them apart (出人头地), by fair means or foul." In a rare exchange, the impact of one's major was a focus; one netizen commented, "Males who study science and engineering should read, read more, and read early books on humanities for self-improvement to avoid such tragedies." Another countered immediately, "Those who study humanities are worse."

In short, various forms of discrimination were evident in our sample. Besides unfoundedly generalizing a particular case to a whole class of people, such discriminatory remarks often included derogatory or insulting language to attack others, thus a strong indicator of irrationality.

Reason with Comparisons

One example of netizens' rational reasoning is their comparison of one crime and punishment with another. Such case comparisons explicitly occurred in 39 cases (61.9% of all cases) at different levels (table 4). First, netizens compared offenders in the same case and argued for disparate sentencing. In the Gao Yulun et al. case (#44), Gao, Li, and Wang carried out a prison break and killed a guard. Gao and Wang were death-sentenced, but Li was sentenced to life imprisonment. One netizen challenged Li's sentence and asked, "Why spared a skunk? This kind of felons and repeat offenders, all should be shot to death!" Similarly, in the Luo Xiaohua and Chen Rihong case (#57), Luo was sentenced to immediate death, but Chen received a suspended death sentence though both committed heinous crimes (rape and homicide). Again, netizens questioned Chen's suspended death sentence (e.g., "Why one with suspended death only? Both should be executed immediately").

Second, many netizens compared offenders in different cases who committed same or similar crimes but received different punishment. In the He Shenguo case (#42), He was death-sentenced for murdering two workers at a local household registration office after his request to register his fourth child was denied (see chapter 7). One netizen compared He's experience with others and commented, "The principal of Lanxiang gave over-quota births,[7] director Zhang gave over-quota births,[8] [but] nothing has happened; all laws and regulations are applied only to the poor people, which is evident to all!" Though the netizen's comment was not fully accurate (e.g., director Zhang reportedly paid millions in fines for his over-quota births), the logic of the argument is rational. For another example, the Huang Qinghen case (#2) involved cross-border child abduction and

---

7. Shandong Lanxiang Senior Technical School (山东蓝翔高级技工学校), founded in 1984, is a well-known private training school in China. The principal of Lanxiang, Rong Lanxiang (容兰祥), has six children and his over-quota births made the news in 2014.

8. Zhang Yimou (张艺谋) is a world-known Chinese movie director. Zhang has four children, and his over-quota births with his second wife (three children) made the news in 2013.

human trafficking (from Vietnam to China). As a principal offender, Huang was death-sentenced. One netizen compared this case to domestic trafficking cases and commented, "Domestic human traffickers appear not to be death-sentenced. [This case] involved Vietnamese comrades, ha-ha [mimicking laugh]. Bad luck."

Netizens were often baffled by different results from different courts for cases with similar natures. In their comparisons, they referenced some well-known cases. The most-referenced case in our sample was a traffic accident case that occurred in Nanjing (see note 1 in chapter 2). A BMW driver named Wang Jijin, who was driving at a high speed, crashed into another vehicle and killed two passengers in 2015. Wang was convicted of endangerment of public safety, sentenced to 11 years of imprisonment, and ordered to pay 1.7 million yuan to his victims' families for civil compensation. The most controversial issue of the case focused on Wang's psychiatric problem. After the accident, police investigation ruled out the possibility that Wang was under the influence of alcohol or drugs. Two separate psychiatric evaluations, one conducted in Nanjing and the other in Beijing, suggested that Wang suffered from an "acute and transient psychotic disorder" at the moment of the accident. Wang's psychiatric problem was reportedly accepted by all parties (e.g., the prosecutor, the defense, victim representatives) during Wang's trial and might have influenced the final sentencing of the court. The "Nanjing BMW case" generated heated discussions by the public, and many questioned Wang's lenient sentence. The case was mentioned in 11 cases in our sample, and netizens universally questioned it as a wrong decision. For instance, the Chen Yun case (#31) involved Chen's drunk driving, which killed six victims. Though Chen's family compensated all victims' families (with a total amount of over 130,000 yuan) and pleaded for another chance for Chen, he was death-sentenced. One netizen commented, "[Chen] deserved to die! This is much wiser than Nanjing's [decision], and did not make an excuse on a transient psychotic disorder." Another partially disagreed and said, "Sentencing [Chen] to death causes no arguments. But the characteristics of drunk driving are the same as that of 'a transient psychotic disorder': before the accident occurred, [the defendant] knew the existence of a potential danger; when it occurred, [the defendant] cannot control it. Nevertheless, the sentences are very different." In the Jin Fusheng case (#59), Jin committed his crime (endangerment of public security) by driving his vehicle into a crowd. Seeing Jin's death sentence, one netizen asked, "Why was the Nanjing BMW driver found with a psychiatric disorder?"

Similarly, one netizen in the Ou Changsheng case (#63) commented, "A correct death sentence [for Ou]! [But] the Nanjing BMW [driver] also killed two people. Why [was he] not death-sentenced? Are laws different in different places?"

Another popular case (referenced in five cases) was the Li Tianyi (李天一) rape case. In 2013 Li was involved in a gang rape in Beijing at the age of 17 and was convicted and sentenced to 10 years of imprisonment. Despite his age, many questioned Li's sentence and suspected that his father, Li Shuangjiang (李双江), a nationally known tenor, might have used his clout to influence the final sentence. For instance, in the Hu Cunbiao and Wang Yong case (#29), netizens compared the defendants' crime (rapes) and death sentences to Li's case. One asked, "Li Tian'x' [spelled as in the original] is about the same. Why was he kept alive?" Another concurred and asked, "It is all right to sentence ordinary people to death, but claim that it is too harsh to sentence those in Li Tianyi case to one or two years?" Note that this netizen's argument contains an inaccurate fact: none of the five defendants in the Li Tianyi case was sentenced to one or two years. Two were sentenced to three-year imprisonment but were put on probation, and others received sentences of longer terms. Nevertheless, the netizen meant to question the fairness and equity of court sentences via case comparisons. In the Yuan Junkai et al. case (#12), one netizen brought up Li's case again and mocked Li by saying, "I guarantee that Li Tianyi would be a true man again once released! 'The Little Caesar with Penis' (银枪小霸王) [an insulting nickname given to Li for his infamous reputation] has earned his reputation (并非浪得虚名)!"

As the case with the most comments in our sample, the Lin Senhao incident (#1) was referenced in six other cases. For example, several netizens mentioned Lin's situation in the Li "xx" case (#55). In this case, Li, a fugitive at large, stabbed victim Wang to death in public and was going after Wang's son before he was arrested. Li was charged with homicide and assault and received a suspended death sentence. Netizens compared Lin's immediate death sentence with Li's suspended death sentence and made comments such as "How to compare [Li's] with Lin Senhao's social harm? Or is it regional differences?" "Poisoning by a student, an immediate execution; a fugitive at large killing in public and resisting arrest, only suspended death; dog-fart court"; and "Putting together this case with Lin Senhao's would show ridiculousness of the Chinese judiciary." Similarly, netizens compared Lin's death sentence to Luo Xiaohua and Chen Rihong's crimes and sentences (#57) with comments such as "Compared to Lin Senhao, these two animals deserve to be shot to death a hundred times more. What are judges doing? Are they safeguarding justice? Took a bribe? How sad."

At the same time, netizens in the Lin Senhao case referenced many other cases. On the one hand, some cited other cases to argue that Lin's life should have been spared. For instance, some compared Lin's poisoning to the poisoning case of Gu Kailai (谷开来), the wife of Bo Xilai (薄熙来). Bo is a former Chinese politician and served as a member of the Central Politburo of the Communist Party before he was found guilty of corruption crimes and sentenced to life imprisonment in 2013. Gu was convicted of murdering a British businessman, Neil Heywood, in 2012 and received a suspended death sentence, which was commuted to life imprisonment in 2015. One netizen asked, "For those who support Lin's death sentence, do you have [a sense of] justice? Did Bo's wife [Gu] who poisoned [Heywood] receive a death sentence? Fake justice." Another commented on Gu's commutation and said, "Do you know, the wife of the Party Secretary [referring to Gu; Bo served as the Party Secretary of Chongqing before his fallout] who poisoned [Heywood], her sentence was commuted today. How come you [referring to Lin] did not get a sentence reduction? Do you know why?" Another netizen echoed that idea, saying, "Same crime: homicide; same conclusion: a death sentence; but the difference is: one is executed, the other commuted. Talking about their crime means: one poisoned drinking water, the other wine; about their status: one is a student, the other a lawyer; about their impact: one is domestic, the other international. Why? No meritorious behavior was mentioned in [Gu's] commutation." On the other hand, many netizens cited other cases to support Lin's death sentence. Some mentioned another campus poisoning case, which occurred at Tsinghua University. In 1994 and 1995, a female student named Zhu Ling (朱令) was poisoned and paralyzed. After numerous diagnoses, Zhu's symptoms were found to resemble that of thallium poisoning. Though the police conducted a series of investigations over the years, no official charges were filed against anyone. Zhu Ling's case was brought up in Lin's case. Netizens shared sympathy for Zhu but also worried that Lin would be able to get away without punishment (if the court were to find insufficient evidence to convict Lin). One mentioned specifically, "I suspect that it would end up with an outcome similar to that of the Tsinghua poisoning case. It would be decided by a 'top-down' order. The poisoner Sun [referring to Sun Wei 孙维, Zhu Ling's classmate and roommate, whom many believed was the true culprit] is still at large and receives no punishment." After Lin's execution, one netizen compared Lin with Sun Wei and said, "Do you remember the Tsinghua poisoning case? The suspect Sun Wei is still at large given her family connections. Without any connection, [Lin] only ended up with an execution. This is China."

Third, many netizens compared different crimes and argued that punishment with one crime is unreasonably harsher or lighter than the other. In the Lin "x"ping and Ye "x"tian case (#16), three drug offenders were executed. Netizens compared this case with many others. For instance, one commented, "Ruling the country by law? [One offender] stabbing the victim 66 times received only a suspended death sentence.[9] Ruling the nation by law is tough on ordinary people but lenient on officials." Another wrote, "Fucked. Is this [drug trafficking] more serious than children abduction and trafficking? Than murder and arson? Than a people's representative stabbing the victim scores of times [referring to the Xu Qingyi case cited in note 9]? Than compulsory acquisition of land which led to human death? If [people] with three kilograms [of drugs] and merely a few hundred grams of sales were [all] death-sentenced, China would have five times as many death row inmates!" Facing such comparisons, one netizen countered, "[Let's] judge the case as it stands (就事论事). Sometimes comparison is not necessary and cannot be done. It is evident that the suspect trafficked drugs and murdered people. It should be handled according to law. It is meaningless to make comparisons. If you have no power, don't challenge the bottom line of the law. There is no equality on the earth. Even taking the seemingly equal national college entrance exam, there are ghost exam takers (枪手). Not many equalities are waiting for you. Without diamond tools, don't take on porcelain work (没有金刚钻,别揽瓷器活)."

International Comparison

Besides domestic comparisons, netizens turned to practices in other nations for comparisons in 18 cases (28.6% of all cases; see table 4). First, netizens referred to other nations for comparisons of sentencing, punishment, and legal procedures. In the He Jian case (#50), one netizen turned to Singapore and suggested whipping, writing, "Criminals are

---

9. In 2014, due to a conflict of demolition and relocation, an official and local people's representative in the Inner Mongolia Autonomous Region, Xu Qingyi (徐庆屹), got into a fight with a villager and stabbed the victim 66 times with a knife, killing the victim. Xu was convicted of murder and received a suspended death sentence.

not afraid of imprisonment, nor death by shooting. They fear physical suffering. [We] should learn from Singapore and use whipping, which would remedy various kinds of criminals and improve public safety. Only physical suffering teaches [them] a mental lesson." In the Lin Senhao case (#1), several netizens brought up the O. J. Simpson case. One mentioned, "[We] should follow proper legal procedures and find one guilty with evidence. Like the O. J. Simpson case in the United States, everyone knew that he did it, but there was a problem with evidence from the prosecution, so that he cannot be found guilty." Another concurred: "I feel like that this case could end up like the Simpson case: everyone believed that Lin is guilty, but there is doubt on key evidence, which benefits the defendant who should be found not guilty. This shows the spirit of the contemporary legal system: presumption of innocence." Others pointed out fundamental differences between China and the United States and questioned the applicability of the Simpson case in China. One netizen wrote, "China's law enforcement aims for substantive justice, better to kill a thousand innocent people than let go one guilty person. The US aims for procedural justice, better to let go a guilty person than kill an innocent. The Simpson case is an example. The strategy of [Lin's] lawyers now fits the American system. Chinese judges would think [differently]: if he is not death-sentenced, (1) what would happen if the victim's family causes trouble? (2) What would happen if no one dares to live in a university dorm? (3) What would happen if another similar case occurs?" Another netizen added, "China follows presumption of guilt, [while] foreign nations follow presumption of innocence. In China, as long as one has no evidence to prove his innocence, he is guilty, likely to be found guilty. [We should] stick to laws. Everyone [should] be equal before the law. Don't be influenced by emotions."

Second, netizens also turned to foreign nations to compare other issues that were unique to the nature of a particular case. For instance, they turned to other nations' medical practices to compare them with China's health-care system in the Lian Enqing and Wang Gang cases (#14 and #13) and discussed how divorce cases are handled in the United States in the Feng Xiujuan case (#32). In the Liu Danao case (#47), via comparison to other nations, Liu's supporters not only argued that Liu's death sentence was too harsh (e.g., "I remember that a Norwegian guy bombed a market and killed 71 people. He received merely 21 years of imprisonment.[10] In

---

10. Anders Behring Breivik is a Norwegian far-right extremist. In 2011 he killed eight people via bombing and shot dead 69 other victims. In 2012 he was convicted of mass

contrast, Liu's death sentence is too harsh!!"), but also pointed out a lack of fundamental protection of private properties in China (e.g., "Proof by facts shows that the US is right: in the US, one's land belongs to individuals and no one can take it. In China, land belongs to the country. You only have the right to use it. Conflicts would easily generate when compensation is involved [in demolition and relocation]. Flaws of the system lead to hidden problems"). In the Yang Xueqi case (#62), when some netizens questioned police inefficiency in cracking the case, one netizen countered and wrote, "Speaking objectively, from the start of intensive investigation in September 2011 to the arrest [of Yang] in March 2012, the speed is not slow. Several serial killer cases in the US took over ten, sometimes twenty years to solve. There are still unsolved cold cases, not to mention serial rape cases. Cracking cases is not easy for the police. Of course [we] hope that the police can further improve their efficiency and believe that they will do better and better."

While netizens relied on the same logic (i.e., case comparison) in their arguments, they could have held very different positions and reached different conclusions. Take, for example, netizens' debate on deterrence and abolition in the Lin Senhao case (#1). As discussed in chapter 3, one netizen (ID "229488296") posted three questions in May 2015, one of which challenged supporters of deterrence to show statistical proof for their argument. Both supporters and opponents of deterrence turned to foreign nations to buttress their arguments. One netizen argued that "China cannot abolish capital punishment! Just look at the mess in South Africa after its abolition!" Another compared mainland China with Hong Kong and wrote, "Why is it that in Hong Kong, crime rates are declining without capital punishment and in China with capital punishment crime rates are increasing? If [you] don't understand society, don't make nonsense comments. People like you won't progress." Another argued that it is not fair to compare China with other nations: "Statistics need to be compared under the same conditions. What are the conditions of their economic levels and population competence in European nations and the US? What are the conditions in China? Don't brag nor denigrate [others]. In China, abolition would only lead to increased crime rates. According to your comparison, I may reference North Korea with very low crime rates, where they execute people with cannons." This was echoed by another netizen who left the following lengthy comment:

---

murder and sentenced to 21 years of imprisonment.

(1) Can you show statistics that abolition would lead to crime declines? (2) More nations in the world still use capital punishment;[11] (3) capital punishment is an effective means to deter crimes. It may not be the most effective means. But this is not a reason for abolition, because you cannot provide the best means. (4) Nations that abolished capital punishment are often small and [people] believe in Jesus. Therefore, religion is related to one's national conditions. Check the increasing crime rates in South Africa after its abolition in 1994, in South Korea after its abolition in 1997, and in the US after the Congress in 1977 annulled a moratorium of capital punishment.[12] Which one did not witness increased crime rates? Sri Lanka, India, etc., which one has not resumed its capital punishment after abolition? The US has capital punishment, [and] Japan too. Why England does not as a capitalist nation? The US has a huge population and its crime population is large, and thus has capital punishment. China as a big nation is different from small nations. Besides, the British society is very stable, people live a comfortable life, population competence is high and desires for crimes are few, thus very different.

In the meantime, there were others who rejected the utility of turning to other nations for comparisons. They made comments such as "Sharen changming, it is still the standard that China needs to stick to. Abolition of capital punishment by European nations and the US,[13] we cannot do it, at least not now"; "In China, don't take foreign nations for examples. It is because of cultural and value differences. When the most fundamental is misunderstood (书没读明白的), one likes to make 'international comparisons' and always believes that foreign practices are right. But it is contrary to Chinese culture, sharen changming and qianzhai huanqian";

---

11. This is factually wrong. As reported by the Death Penalty Information Center (https://deathpenaltyinfo.org/), by the end of 2017 the total number of nations that had abolished capital punishment in law or practice had reached 142, and only 56 nations retained the use of capital punishment.

12. This is inaccurate. It is the US Supreme Court decision in *Gregg v. Georgia* (1976) that revived the use of capital punishment in the United States after a brief period of no use due to the *Furman v. Georgia* (1972) decision.

13. Based on information from the Death Penalty Information Center, as of July 2020, 28 states in the US retain capital punishment while 22 states stopped using it. The comment by the netizen is thus partially inaccurate.

and "Who told you abolition is a progress? Is it true that shit by European and American people smells good?" Another netizen turned to an extreme example to reject abolition and wrote, "What a laughable theory. If one's evil deeds are not faced with harsh consequences, there would be more and more evil people. Abolition? The guy in Northern Europe who killed scores of people [likely referring to Anders Behring Breivik in Norway] and lives in a prison room with better conditions than economy inns still complains that his X-Box is outdated and wants more games. I don't see such a treatment humane, but ridiculous." Yet another criticized the alternative long-term incarceration in Western nations and said, "Though some Western nations have abolished capital punishment, [they may] mete out sentences with hundreds or thousands of years? How many years does a human life last? Are they going to bury one's ashes in a prison cell after one dies? This is more evil than capital punishment! Laughable."

In sum, case comparisons were frequently made by netizens in our sample. Though not perfect (e.g., sometimes with inaccurate or wrong facts), such comparisons often presented strong elements of logical reasoning (even with debatable logic) and advanced netizens' deliberation and exchange of argumentative claims, thus being rational in a Habermasian sense.

Making Suggestions

In 24 cases (38.1% of all cases) netizens made suggestions tailored to issues exposed in a particular case (table 4). In the Huang Qinghen case (#2), for example, one netizen supported another's suggestions to crack down on child abduction and said, "Nowadays, losing a child would bring a calamity to a family. A netizen proposed to revise the Criminal Law: criminals who abduct women and children for profit shall be subject to capital punishment. Upon household registration, children's fingerprints should be collected and saved so that kidnapped children won't be able to get registered [under a different name] and be found timely. . . . Please circulate in the name of [saving] children!!!" In the Peng Shu and Hu Haolong case (#3), a netizen proposed to fight against corruption and suggested that "only after establishing an effective supervision system, especially via participation by the public, can corruption be effectively stopped." In the Liu Danao case (#47), a few netizens made constructive suggestions to handle economic disputes in demolition and relocation cases, such as "In fact, there are better solutions after demolition and relocation. For example, [we] may use the total size of one's relocated household as shares of dividends for revenues garnered by the developer" and "Every day things like this happened. Why cannot the government put forward compensation standards for demolition and relocation? To group lands into several categories and compensate the owner based on the category of one's land. Illegally constructed houses get no compensation; otherwise [pay] full compensation. Once compensated, houses would be demolished. Those who demand an unreasonably high price won't work anymore, whose houses shall all be demolished."

Facing the same issue, netizens sometimes proposed different solutions, even some that were contrary to each other. For instance, mental illness presented an issue in several cases and netizens proposed different solutions. In the He Jian case (#50), one commented, "To facilitate development of a civilized society, our government needs to establish a full set of laws and regulations and institutions to deal with citizens with mental disorders. Remember the humanitarian principle: mental disorders are diseases not crimes." Nevertheless, more netizens (by the number of comments) proposed tougher laws against the mentally ill. In the Zhao Zihui case (#60), one netizen wrote, "For this criminal [Zhao], our nation should sentence him like this: even if he is mentally ill, he should be death-sentenced as a normal person. After the sentencing, put him in a psychiatric hospital to serve time if he still suffers from his mental disorder. Once his disorder is gone, he shall be immediately executed. If he is no longer ill after his sentencing, he shall be executed like a normal person. In this way, 'mental disorder' is no longer an excuse to escape legal punishment." Granted, such a "get-tough" approach can and should be subject to further scrutiny based on contemporary moral and legal standards, as outlined in the Habermasian model.

While constructive suggestions indicated strong rational reasoning, there were also questionable and problematic suggestions. In the Hu Cunbiao and Wang Yong case (#29), one netizen wrote, "I have said it before: male teachers of elementary and middle schools must be castrated before their employment, to prevent such sexual crimes in the future." Instead of being constructive, this comment was more like cursing to vent one's anger. In the Feng Xiujuan case (#32), a netizen made a similar cursing suggestion: "[Feng] should be paraded in public before her execution, to show it to those who have had an affair!" In the Liu Danao case (#47), one proposed a "smarter" crime and wrote, "The affairs of the world are constantly changing (世事无常). If someday this [forced relocation] happens to you, [you] must control (忍), control, and control [yourself]. Let them tear down your house. Remember their looks and find out their home address and family members. You should know: a fatal traffic accident without [the driver] fleeing the accident site would subject the driver to 7-year imprisonment at most! If [the driver] is found with an acute and transient psychotic disorder, even lighter punishment! Please remember: control yourself!" This suggestion sounded like crime coaching indeed. In the Yang Xueqi case (#62), to thwart sexual offenses and predators, one netizen made a bold call and said, "Strongly recommend establishment of red-light districts [to legalize prostitution]." Though prostitution is illegal in China, this legalization proposal might well be an outcome of rational deliberation given the actual rampancy of illegal prostitution.

Rationality in the Virtual Domain

In this chapter we have focused on the issue of rationality. Though netizens' explicit usage of the term fits into a general definition of rationality based on logical reasoning, we suggest that Habermas's concept of communicative rationality is more instructive and better suited within our context. When the standard is exclusively placed on logical reasoning, for instance, some examples of personal attacks can be argued as rational (e.g., serving instrumental purposes); cursing might well fulfill certain psychological needs of some netizens, particularly in the virtual domain. Nevertheless, neither of these examples would pass the Habermasian standards, as they target individuals instead of their arguments, stymie the process of open and public debate and deliberation, and defeat the ultimate goal of mutual understanding and consensus building.

Applying the Habermasian model, we identified both elements of rationality and irrationality in our sample. Major examples of irrationality include personal attacks, cursing, calling for legal punishment of innocent people and forgoing legal procedures, and various forms of discrimination. Collectively, these examples failed to meet the Habermasian standards, due to violations of the three validity dimensions (e.g., punishing innocent people and forgoing legal procedures would violate contemporary moral and legal norms; various types of discrimination are based on flawed reasoning not supported by scientific evidence), or carrying disruptive and damaging effect on the communication process or the consensus-building outcome (e.g., personal attacks, cursing, discrimination).

In contrast, though not perfect, the case comparisons and constructive suggestions by the Chinese netizens in our study presented good instances of rational arguments. It is through domestic case comparisons that netizens questioned fairness and equity in contemporary Chinese society; it is through international comparisons that they brought in different perspectives from other nations and yearned to learn from better (or worse) practices. Even for those who rejected international comparisons based on their understanding of "unique conditions" in China, their argumentative claims could be interpreted as conducive to enrichment of the discussion and their arguments are, of course, subject to further scrutiny per the Habermasian model. In contrast, rationality can be questioned in cases in which the usefulness of international comparisons was categorically rejected. In making suggestions, destructive ones aimed only to vent would fail the test of Habermas's rationality, but constructive ones aimed to stimulate netizens' communication and help them reach consensus would prevail.

As pointed out (Herold and Marolt, 2011), the Chinese internet is indeed filled with a cacophony of conflicting opinions (both rational and irrational) coupled with emotional outbursts, and it is not yet a Habermasian ideal public sphere (Habermas 1989). Short of other viable alternatives in reality, however, Chinese netizens' online comments and discussions have become a unique form of Chinese public opinion. In this rare opportunity to voice one's concerns, Chinese netizens still have much to learn, if the Habermasian model is desirable, a topic we return to in the concluding chapter.

CHAPTER 9

The Lin Senhao Case
A Live Debate of Life or Death

Among all of the cases in our study, the famous Lin Senhao poisoning case generated the most comments (n = 17,611). It was reported in four different months (January, May, August, and December) in 2015 with 30 reports. Table 5 lists the total numbers of netizens' comments and reply comments, along with the starting and ending time of each round of commenting; it also summarizes the content of the reports by month. In this chapter we first briefly review the Lin Senhao case and summarize the top themes of netizens' comments. Then we focus on four key issues of netizens' debate, including Lin's legal defense, whether he deserved forgiveness, netizens' assessment of Lin's and Huang's families, and how Lin's supporters and opponents tried to influence public opinion and court rulings.

Review of the Case

Lin Senhao and Huang Yang both entered the medical school of Fudan University in 2010 as master's students. They had shared the same dorm room since 2011, but they did not get along. On March 31, 2013, Lin poisoned the water in the drinking water dispenser of their room with N-Nitrosodimethylamine (NDMA). On April 1 Huang drank the poisoned water, became ill, and was hospitalized. On April 12 the police detained Lin as a primary suspect in the incident. On the sixteenth, Huang died in the hospital. The official forensic analysis indicated that the NDMA poison led to a liver malfunction, which, in turn, resulted in the failure of other organs and Huang's eventual death.

On April 19 the police officially arrested Lin for Huang's death. On February 18, 2014, the Shanghai second intermediate people's court (the court of first instance) convicted Lin of murder and sentenced him to death. The first instance court found that as a master's student Lin knew that NDMA was deadly, had studied the effect of the poison in animal research, and purposely poisoned the drinking water, which led to Huang's illness and eventual death. During Huang's hospitalization, Lin did not surrender to the police and disclose the source of poison.

After the trial, 177 Fudan University students sent a petition letter to the Shanghai High Court (the court of second instance) to plead for Lin's life. On January 8, 2015, the Shanghai High Court affirmed Lin's death sentence and sent the case to the Supreme People's Court (SPC) for its final review and approval. During the SPC's review, Lin's father tried to change Lin's two defense lawyers (Si Weijiang, 斯伟江, and Tang Zhijian, 唐志坚, hired for the appeals), but Lin rejected the new attorney (Xie Tongxiang, 谢通祥). An SPC judge panel in charge of Lin's case held hearings with Lin's defense attorneys and even met Lin's father (an unusual move) to listen to his opinion. On December 9, 2015, the SPC approved Lin's death sentence, and Lin was promptly executed on the eleventh.

Lin's case generated a number of academic studies in China, which can be grouped into four types. First, some studies focused on the legal issues involved in Lin's case, such as expert witness testimony in criminal trials (Z. Wu 2015) and the interaction and potential conflict between online minyi and judicial decision making (Chi and Ding 2016; H. Xu and Wan 2015). Second, a number of studies turned to Lin's mens rea and discussed psychological issues from either an individual or a social perspective (Z. Wang and Ni 2016; X. Zhao 2015). These studies argued that Lin's psychological defects (or lack of proper education) led to the tragedy and proposed measures to avoid similar mistakes. Third, some studies cited Lin's case as an example of problems with China's existing educational system and called for curriculum improvement (Y. Gao and Liu 2015; L. Huang 2015). Lastly, a few studies analyzed Lin's case from the perspective of criminology and paid particular attention to "crimes committed by people with high IQs" (高智商犯罪) (M. Li 2015; Z. Wang and Qian 2015). Merely citing Lin's case as an example, none of these studies examined the content and nature of netizens' opinions in detail.

Table 5. Summary Statistics of Netizens' Comments and Content of Reports

Month	# of comments; Date/time of the first and last comments	# of reply comments	Content of report(s)
January (one report)	300 1/8/2015; 15:33 1/8/2015; 22:09	128	• On January 8, the Shanghai High Court affirmed Lin's conviction and death sentence
May (three reports)	8,570 5/27/2015; 03:08 8/3/2015; 15:25	3,551	• On May 26, an SPC panel held a hearing with Lin's defense attorneys, who questioned (1) the lethal amount of the poison, (2) the likelihood that Huang died due to other reasons, (3) Lin's mens rea, and (4) procedural issues with regard to Lin's trial • Victim's father claimed that he never received financial compensation or apology from the Lins and insisted on Lin's death
August (four reports)	2,425 8/3/2015; 04:36 8/12/2015; 17:46	773	• On July 21, the media reported two letters from Lin's attorneys written by Lin, in one of which Lin admitted his poisoning • Lin's father insisted on changing Lin's defense attorneys • Lin's father shared that Lin's mother had not been told about Lin's death sentence • On July 28, an SPC judge met Lin's father to listen to his opinions, an unprecedented move • On July 31, Lin's father and attorneys submitted legal documents to SPC judges, which questioned evidentiary problems
December (22 reports)	6,316 12/10/2015; 07:55 1/9/2016; 13:35	1,231	• Lin was interviewed on December 7 and mentioned "death means payback to the victim's family" • Lin's father was notified on December 8 that Lin's death sentence was approved, and was told to go to Shanghai and meet Lin on December 11 • Lin's father and attorney arrived in Beijing on December 9 to lodge more petitions to both the SPC and the SPP (Supreme People's Procuratorate); their protest petition to the SPP was rejected, as they did not receive the SPC's official death sentence approval judgment (which did not arrive in time) • Lin's attorney tried to approach victim's family but failed on December 9

Table 5.—(continued)

Month	# of comments; Date/time of the first and last comments	# of reply comments	Content of report(s)
			• Lin was executed on December 11 • A 10-minute meeting with Lin's father was arranged before Lin's execution; Lin's father decided not to donate Lin's body, contrary to Lin's wishes • Victim's father mentioned that he would consult with his attorney on a potential civil compensation lawsuit • An SPC judge briefed the media on key issues, including fact findings of the case, reasons for Lin's death sentence approval, and reasons for rejections of defense arguments
Total	17,611	5,683	

Top Themes

In table 6 we rank the top ten themes (sometimes with ties) based on the counts of netizens' comments in each month.[1] A close examination of the top themes reveals a few patterns, though there is significant variation monthly. First, some themes were consistently ranked the highest in each month. For instance, netizen interactions and punishment justifications always ranked either first or second. Another theme, comments directed at Lin (either opposing or supporting him), was also consistently ranked high. Second, some themes apparently reflected the progress of the legal proceedings and the impact of news reporting in their ranking. For instance, the number of comments that either showed sympathy for Lin or explicitly rejected such sympathy, and comments that questioned the "delay and waste" in Lin's legal proceedings all had "ups and downs" at different phases of the case (see chapter 5).

Third, some themes were consistently ranked in the middle tier across all four months, including comments questioning Lin's verdict and death sentence and comments directed at both Lin's family and the victim and his

---

1. Note that with further combinations, some top themes in table 6 do not exactly match with those in table 1 in chapter 2.

Table 6. Top Themes by Months

Theme Rankings	January (counts)	May (counts)	August (counts)	December (counts)
1	Netizen interactions (57)	Netizen interactions (2,211)	Netizen interactions (530)	Punishment justifications (1,582) Netizen interactions (1,579)
2	Punishment justifications (55)	Punishment justifications (1,501)	Punishment justifications (400)	Support for death sentence (903)
3	Opposing/supporting Lin (30)	Opposing/supporting Lin (1,354)	On Lin's family (299)	Opposing/supporting Lin (651) Questioning verdict/death sentence (647)
4	Sympathy/no sympathy (21) On Lin's family (20)	Questioning/ supporting defense (918)	Opposing/supporting Lin (278)	Sympathy/no sympathy (636)
5	Support for death sentence (18)	Support for death sentence (891)	Support for death sentence (267)	On victim/victim's family (580)
6	Causes of crime (14) Leniency/no leniency (14)	Questioning verdict/death sentence (528)	Questioning/ supporting defense (214)	On Lin's family (528)
7	On victim/victim's family (12) Questioning verdict/death sentence (11)	Leniency/no leniency (406)	Questioning verdict/death sentence (208)	Lessons and wishes (436)
8	Lessons and wishes (7)	On victim/victim's family (376)	On victim/victim's family (185)	Causes of crime (421)
9	Analysis of netizens' comments (5)	On Lin's family (328)	Delay and waste (116)	Questioning/supporting defense (298)
10	Questioning/ supporting defense (4)	Delay and waste (211) Analysis of netizens' comments (210)	Causes of crime (104)	Delay and waste (252) Leniency/no leniency (252)

family. Despite their steady rankings, specific issues discussed under these themes varied at different phases of the legal proceedings. For instance, one issue that emerged in December involved potential civil compensation for the victim's family. As discussed in chapter 5, when Huang's father was pondering a civil compensation lawsuit after Lin's execution, netizens weighed in with 120 comments. Unlike the majority support for Lin's death sentence, the majority opposed the idea of civil compensation this time and argued that "Lin's family owed nothing to the Huangs" after Lin's payback and that greed by the Huangs "would offend the public's feelings." Despite the great diversity (breadth, depth, and variations), we focus on four issues below that intertwine many key themes and issues.

Debate on Lin's Legal Defense

Lin was found guilty of homicide and death-sentenced by the first instance court on November 28, 2014. During the first instance trial, Lin claimed that he had no criminal intent to murder Huang. Rather, he claimed that he poisoned Huang as a prank on April Fool's Day. Lin's defense argued that Lin's homicide was indirect and that after being detained by the police, Lin confessed, thus showing his remorse. Both arguments by Lin and his defense were rejected. Instead, the court found in its judgment that Lin "had criminal intent to hope for Huang's death;" Lin's poisoning was "cruel, its consequence severe with great social impact"; and Lin's confession did not justify lenient punishment. On January 8, 2015, Lin's death sentence was affirmed by the Shanghai High Court. During the second instance trial, Lin insisted that he had no homicide intent, and as a prank, he had diluted the water after he poured in the NDMA. Lin's defense introduced an expert witness, Hu Zhiqiang (胡志强), who questioned the evidence indicating that Huang's death was caused by the NDMA. Contrary to the forensic evaluation introduced by the prosecution, Lin's defense introduced a second evaluation conducted by a Beijing institute and argued that Huang's death was triggered by Huang's hepatitis B, which led to his liver malfunction and eventual death. Given the conflicting results, Lin's defense requested a third evaluation and demanded mass spectrograms (质谱图) of previous diagnoses from the first evaluation (which apparently had not been introduced as evidence). Further, Lin's defense argued that Lin had no criminal intent and thus did not commit homicide; they urged the High Court to find Lin's behavior as "intentional assault leading to human death" and to sentence him to a prison term of 10 to 15 years. The High Court again rejected arguments by Lin and his defense team. In particular, it found prosecutorial evidence sufficient, rejected the new forensic evaluation introduced by the defense, and denied the request for a third evaluation. Lin's lack of criminal intent argument was rejected due to a lack of corroborating evidence. Citing Lin's crime means "cruel" and "its severe consequence with great societal impact," the High Court affirmed Lin's death sentence. During the SPC's review and approval, Lin's defense essentially repeated its legal arguments put forth in the appellate review. In its verdict, the SPC judge panel reiterated facts found by two lower courts, rejected arguments by Lin and his defense team, and approved Lin's death sentence.

Supporters and opponents of Lin disagreed on the merits of his defense. On the issue of criminal intent, Lin's supporters believed his April Fool's Day prank story and argued that he had no intent to murder Huang (in 96 comments). For instance, one netizen said, "Yes, [Lin] should bear criminal liability, but not deserving a death sentence. His behavior was intentional but the outcome of Huang's death was unexpected. As a result, this case should be found negligent homicide (过失杀人)." Given the difficulty in proving Lin's criminal intent, one netizen suggested that "[the evidence of] this case is difficult to prove [as to] whether [Lin] meant to kill Huang or let Huang suffer greatly. A suspended death sentence should be applied." On the contrary, Lin's opponents rejected his prank story (in 132 comments) and argued that he did indeed have the intent to kill (164 comments). For example, as cited in chapter 4, when a netizen identifying himself as Baogong supported Lin and his prank, another netizen immediately countered and said, "Don't dog fart here. Why not use Oreo toothpaste, but lethal poison? Still finding excuses on behalf of Lin." Many netizens agreed with the courts that Lin's "no rescue effort" during Huang's hospitalization was equivalent to murderous intent (expressed in 354 comments). As one netizen pointed out, "Whether it is intentional assault or homicide depends upon whether he made a rescue effort when the victim was in danger. If [it was] only intentional assault without intent to kill, [Lin] should have thought about and taken necessary actions to save [Huang's] life. Unfortunately, he offered no help when he knew Huang's life was in danger, and the doctors cannot find a proper treatment, which led to Huang's death. Therefore, the murder intent was obvious and [it] is not an excuse of teaching Huang a lesson." To counter the "no rescue" argument, Lin's supporters argued for his fear and his hope to get away with his poisoning. One netizen wrote, "I believe the reason why

Lin did not confess then was his hope that Huang could have been treated successfully. If he confessed, even if Huang lived, he would have to face the punishment of law; if not confessed, he would be able to get away with legal punishment. He might *not* have actually hoped for Huang's death. But due to his selfishness and his 'dare not face the consequence' character, it led to the loss of Huang's life." Notice that Lin's supporters and opponents might have interpreted the same piece of evidence differently. For instance, court findings showed that Lin conducted animal (i.e., mice) experiments to test the effect of the NDMA. To Lin's opponents, this proved his premeditation; to Lin's supporters, it could have lent more credibility to his prank story, as he was trying to calculate the quantity that would not be lethal (though he failed unintentionally).

During the second instance trial, arguments by Lin's defense team (in particular on the sufficiency of the quantity of NDMA used and the possibility of Huang's death caused not by the NDMA but other factors, such as Huang's hepatitis B) again drew heated discussions among netizens. Lin's supporters viewed these arguments as valid and tied them to Lin's argument that he lacked criminal intent. One netizen said, "Now Lin's excuse was whether Huang's death was caused by the NDMA or triggered by the NDMA. A big difference between these two. Though both led to Huang's death, one would be able to rule out homicide intent, the other not." In contrast, Lin's opponents rejected and even mocked these arguments. On the issue of NDMA sufficiency, one netizen joked, "If a person did a prank by firing one shot at the abdomen of [Lin's] lawyer's mother, who died due to bleeding after more than an hour, would the lawyer argue that one single shot was not powerful enough and let go the shooter?" Another directly questioned the quantity standard and said, "I think that Lin should poison his lawyers to make them dumb. What do you mean 'not reaching a sufficient lethal quantity'? Have you tried it? Some people are physically weak and might die on a small quantity. Is there such a standard?" Lin's opponents also rejected the argument that Huang's death might have been caused by other factors even though it had been triggered by the poison. One netizen argued, "To follow your logic, there wouldn't be murderers anymore. Victims won't die immediately on site but only after bleeding. So the murderer only assaulted [the victim], but the victim died on his own because of bleeding. Is that right?" A rather popular proposal by Lin's opponents was "Give him the dose of his own medicine (以彼之道还施彼身). If he survives, then no death sentence will be given" (83 comments). Fortunately, that did not happen.

Angry with Lin's defense lawyers and expert witness Hu, Lin's opponents not only rejected their arguments but also questioned their morality (in 616 comments against lawyers and 76 comments against Hu). One netizen commented, "Lawyers like Si Weijiang and Tang Zhijian, they don't speak in legal language but talk nonsense. They dare question the verdict of the court merely based on suspicions. This is sorrow of our times and society! There are also the so-called expert witnesses such as Hu Zhiqiang, who talked a lot of nonsense (大放厥词). It is so laughable!" Many called for official sanctions against unethical lawyers and legal experts and worried that their arguments might have worked in favor of real criminals. One netizen commented, "I think lawyers these days have no ethical standards. The National People's Congress should come up with regulations on such matters, not to allow 'not guilty' defense. Besides, is it contrary to legal principles for family members to demand change of lawyers so many times?" Another said, "Public execution [of Lin] for deterrence. Sentence that lawyer to one year imprisonment and suspend his license for 10 years. If [Lin is] not executed, many would follow suit. You, lawyer, are the root cause of disasters!" Another targeted Hu and said, "Lin's father paid Hu Zhiqiang, a 'legal expert' for nothing. Hu Zhiqiang argued that Huang Yang did not die because of the NDMA but an acute hepatitis B. If this argument worked, many people would have died." At the same time, a small but not insignificant number of netizens supported defense rights by lawyers and legal experts (in 126 comments), though some of them may not agree with their arguments. For instance, one netizen countered the argument of sharen changming and defended one's legal defense right, writing, "Sharen changming is a moral standard, not a legal principle. Lawyers have their professional ethics, and their basic principle is the 'priority of laws' (规则至上). One's defense right is protected by the Constitution, and it is a 'must' for the laws. It was in slavery and feudal societies when [people] had no such right. Without such a right, you would not be alive." Another netizen countered the critique that lawyers took advantage of the law by "finding holes of the law" and said, "Although I support a death sentence too … law needs lawyers to split hairs. Lawyers defending their clients, what is there to be accused of?"

It should be noted that even among Lin's supporters, people held different views about what the proper defense strategy should be. Many argued that the "not guilty" defense strategy was wrong and actually caused Lin to lose his life. One netizen pointed out, for instance, that "in fact, I felt that Lin might have had a chance of saving his life before the first instance trial, that is, to show sincere remorse and bravely embrace any consequences, in order to gain a sense of sympathy and forgiveness from the victim's family and society. It is 'the April Fool's Day prank' defense that completely buried Lin! The immediate effect of such a defense after the first instance trial was that Huang's father made up his mind not to forgive Lin. You should know that the forgiveness of the victim's family is the only life-saving straw to clutch at!" Some directly blamed Lin's attorneys for choosing a strategy that was not in the best interests of Lin and his family but that of the attorneys (see chapter 6).

Another notable difference between Lin's supporters and opponents was their approach to legal principles such as the presumption of innocence and procedural justice. For Lin's supporters (some of them seemingly from a legal background), it is fundamental to uphold such important principles. As one netizen commented, "I believe that procedural justice is a fundamental part of judicial justice. Every citizen should enjoy rights accorded by law and follow proper legal procedures to express one's opinion when there are different opinions. This is judicial progress and our judiciary is moving toward justice and equity. 'I disapprove of what you say, but I will defend to the death your right to say it.'" One netizen criticized the verdict of the second instance trial based on the presumption of innocence and wrote, "The biggest problem of the verdict of the second instance trial is that the court did not answer questions raised by defense lawyers but rejected them as nonreliable. This is equivalent to placing the burden of proof on the defendant. In criminal cases, defense only needs to raise doubt and prosecution needs to explain the doubt. If not able to rule out the doubt, evidence should not be accepted. This is the basic principle of the presumption of innocence." As discussed in chapter 8, some cited the O. J. Simpson case and hoped that Lin's case could become the Chinese version of that case (that is, finding Lin not guilty when the evidence is insufficient). In contrast, Lin's opponents were more likely to downplay the importance of procedural justice and the presumption of innocence and to argue for substantive justice and emphasize the characteristics of the Chinese system. One netizen said, for instance, "But Chinese culture always regulates people with morality, not cold laws, and emphasizes on human feelings. For example, a car accident hits a person. Even if the person is 100% at fault, the driver needs to provide some compensation. Laws are more equitable but lack human feelings. How to treat the rule of law and rule of man, for most people, depends on which side can provide bloody buns and comfort one's dirty heart." Another netizen argued in favor of substantive justice and wrote:

> Between substantive justice and procedural justice, substantive justice is more important. Like eating, it is meant to eat in the mouth. If you emphasize on procedural justice, put up your chopsticks, take the food, not too much nor too little, but eventually do not send to mouth but to the trash bin, what's the point of such procedural justice? Without substantive justice, all [steps] of procedural justice are meaningless. It's like a factory that produces good products. With ten thousand steps, if [you] do not produce the final product, all previous steps are equal to zero!! Thus, procedural justice is the zeros of 10,000, and the substantive justice is the 1 in front. Without the 1, all zeros could end up with a zero.

Yet another openly questioned the presumption of innocence and said, "[This is] TMD [cursing words; see chapter 4] to puff up at one's own cost (打肿脸冲胖子) in a chaotic society! Nowadays, presumption of innocence is popular. Murderers colluded with corrupt officials all TMD [benefited from] presumption of innocence! The official Chen Hui (陈辉) in Yunnan who killed his mistress,[2] the master's student in Xiangtan who killed his rival in love,[3] both TMD [benefited from] presumption of innocence! Likely devil Lin would [benefit from] presumption of innocence too with more bribery! Watch out, everyone, [there would be] more and more murderers."

---

2. In March 2012 Chen reportedly murdered his girlfriend, Hu. Nevertheless, at trial Chen was found not guilty due to insufficient evidence. Chen was an official working at the Yunnan Navigation Management Bureau (云南省航务管理局).

3. In 2003 Zeng Aiyun (曾爱云), a master's student at Xiangtan (湘潭) University, was involved in a murder case. Reportedly, Zeng, a deceased male victim, and a female student were involved in a love triangle. Zeng was charged with homicide and sentenced to death three times by the Xiangtan intermediate people's court in 2004, 2005, and 2010, respectively. Nevertheless, his death sentence was rejected by the SPC and the Hunan High Court. Finally, in July 2015 Zeng was found not guilty by the Xiangtan intermediate people's court.

Forgiveness or No Forgiveness: Lin vs. Huang

The ultimate decision about Lin's life or death unavoidably separated netizens into two camps: those supporting his death and those opposing his death. When comparing netizens who explicitly supported Lin's death sentence (2,079 comments) to netizens who explicitly rejected or questioned his death sentence (1,394 comments), the former group outnumbered the latter by a roughly 3 to 2 ratio. Nevertheless, more netizens explicitly expressed sympathy for Lin (757 comments) than rejecting such sympathy (53 comments), and more netizens explicitly called for leniency than rejecting it (559 comments vs. 198 comments).

Lin's supporters called for leniency and forgiveness based on a number of reasons. First, they believed that Lin did not have murderous intent but made a bad mistake. Accordingly, Lin deserved a second chance and could use his knowledge and training to pay back the Huangs and society in general. One netizen commented, "If you give him a chance, he could serve society. Do you know there is a high demand for doctors in remote regions?" Some netizens knew that the forgiveness of the Huangs was the key and openly pleaded with them for leniency. One netizen commented, "Sincerely ask Huang's father: is it true that you won't be able to live peacefully unless Lin is dead? If so, I believe Lin deserves to die. If you won't be able to live peacefully even with Lin's death, please forgive him! Let him take care of you two [Huang's parents] down the road."

Second, Lin's supporters countered the argument that Lin caused great harm to society, and they did not see Lin as a person with an evil heart who would commit more crimes after his incarceration. One netizen commented, "People like Lin, whose crime harms only one aspect [of society] and its impact is small, could be spared." Many argued that Lin had a good personal character and got along with his classmates and teachers (this is why "over a hundred students petitioned for his life"). Moreover, Lin's status as a highly educated student at a nationally known university gained him sympathy from some netizens. Many argued, again, that Lin could be saved to serve society with his knowledge and training. After Lin's execution, many expressed their sympathy with comments such as "What a pity, two highly gifted students lost!"

Third, a small group of netizens questioned the sufficiency of evidence in Lin's conviction (in 88 comments), expressed concerns about a wrongful conviction (74 comments), and favored application of the "killing fewer and killing cautiously" policy in Lin's case (106 comments). For instance, one netizen turned to the presumption of innocence and said, "Presumption of innocence. Cannot judge subjectively. A death sentence should [be used] very cautiously." Another tried to reason in the shoes of the Huangs and suggested that "from Huang's father's perspective, [he] should demand a full investigation of the true cause of Huang's death and the true perpetrator when there is insufficient and conflicting evidence, not to kill a person to fill in the number based on a coincidence." Some worried that if Lin were not given a chance, future similarly situated criminals would have no incentive to abate their crimes. One netizen asked, "Could Lin's death sentence lead to a situation in the future where an offender would always go for a kill every time he is targeting a victim? [Because] there is little difference [in punishment] whether the offender leaves room (留余地) or not [in his offense]. Take another look: how many are willing to help old folks who fall on street?[4] [I'm] truly afraid that the Ma Jiajue case would occur again:[5] [once the offender knew] he would be killed anyway, he would kill everyone who offended him."

Last but not least, Lin's supporters called for leniency based on their strong belief that forgiveness and love, instead of punishment and resentment, would make society better and represent civilization and progress. Two real stories of forgiveness were shared by netizens in May. The first story involved a last-minute pardon by an Iranian mother. In this case, Balal Abdullah was sentenced to death for stabbing a 17-year-old victim, Hosseinzadeh, to death during a street fight in 2007 and was scheduled to be hanged in April 2014. As reported, moments before Abdullah's execution, the victim's mother approached Abdullah, asked for a chair to stand on, slapped him, but announced her forgiveness. Abdullah's mother ran up to Hosseinzadeh's mother and hugged her, and the two women wept in each other's arms. The second story occurred in China and involved the murder of the Pfrangs. In April 2000 four youngsters broke into the

---

4. The netizen referred to a case without naming it. In 2006 Peng Yu (彭宇) was involved in an accident with 64-year-old Xu Shoulan (徐寿兰) at a bus stop in Nanjing. Xu claimed that Peng ran into him, which caused his fall and physical injury. Peng denied his fault and claimed he was helping the fallen Xu get up. Eventually Peng and Xu settled in a lawsuit with an agreement not to disclose the "truth" to the public. Nevertheless, the Peng Yu case was widely portrayed as a case in which a good Samaritan was penalized by his good deed and thus stirred a big round of public debate.

5. Ma Jiajue (马加爵) was a college student at Yunnan University and murdered four students in 2004. Ma was convicted of homicide, death-sentenced, and executed in the same year.

house of the Pfrangs in Nanjing, Jiangsu province, for robbery but ended up murdering the family, including Jürgen (51 years old); his wife, Petra (40); daughter, Sandra (15); and son, Thorsten (13). Jürgen Pfrang was a German manager working for Daimler Chrysler. All four criminals were death-sentenced. After the killing, Pfrang's mother flew from Germany to Nanjing, learned about the case, and wrote to the court, petitioning to spare the lives of the four criminals. Seeing the impact of lack of education on these criminals (and their crimes), a group of volunteers subsequently founded the Pfrang Association (普方基金会, http://www.pfrangassociation.org/) in 2000, which is dedicated to helping underprivileged children in Jiangsu province to attain education. Both of these stories were shared to encourage netizens' forgiveness. Moreover, a small number of netizens openly advocated abolition (in 96 comments) and encouraged forgiveness as a step moving toward eventual abolition. For instance, one netizen commented, "In society today, sentencing Lin to death is correct. When the majority of online comments expressed leniency, it would be time to abolish capital punishment, which is progress of the society. As everyone embraces love, forgiveness, and kindness, is it still necessary to keep capital punishment in society?" Many netizens recommended an alternative sentence (e.g., life imprisonment) as a better option (99 comments). One netizen recommended long-term incarceration and said, "A life for a life is sometimes not a good medicine. Sentence [Lin] for life imprisonment without possibility of sentence reduction in 30–40 years (I don't know if the law has this option). This would maximize Lin's punishment and comfort Huang's father, and Lin's father won't be broken. To forgive others is to bless oneself." To counter the argument of Lin's opponents to "put oneself in the shoes of the victim's family" (e.g., "what if it were your son who was poisoned?"), one netizen argued, "Even with a death sentence, Huang won't come back to life. But it will destroy two families forever. Many asked 'what if the poisoned were your son'; I'd also like to ask: what if it were you who made a mistake? Wouldn't you like an opportunity for redemption?"

In contrast, Lin's opponents rejected forgiveness for several reasons. First, they questioned Lin's personal character (in 1,149 comments). Many condemned Lin's "April Fool's Day prank" story (132 comments) and believed that Lin showed no remorse (169 comments), thus not deserving a second chance. Moreover, court-found facts such as Lin's animal experiments to test the NDMA effect and his "no rescue effort" during Huang's hospitalization lent more support to opponents' belief in Lin's evil character. One netizen simply said, "His biggest mistake was to watch another life disappearing and wait for the outcome as a prank." Another elaborated and wrote, "Lin's heart is hard. [The fact that] Huang's life is in danger after being poisoned did not waken his heart. It is often said that a human heart has a soft nature, but his has not. Otherwise, he would not do nothing when Huang was in danger. Maybe he only had the satisfaction of retaliation. He is a cold person by nature (骨子里). This kind of person is very fearful, and if saved, they may commit another crime. Lin's behavior has challenged the bottom line of morality and is a serious crime, and [he] deserves to die." Granted, as discussed above, Lin's defense strategy (pleading not guilty throughout his trials and appeals with no apology and compensation to the Huangs) did not bode well with his opponents and did more damage to his character. Moreover, related to Lin's character, many netizens rejected the possibility of Lin's rehabilitation and argued that he would commit more crimes if his life were spared. One netizen commented, "People like him could do more damage to society if they are released back to society. Imagine allowing him to go back to society after scores of years of imprisonment: is he going to remorse for his crime and pay back to society? The answer is negative. He would only retaliate against society." Some cited the famous story of "the farmer and the viper" (农夫和蛇) from Aesop's Fables to warn about Lin's potential danger.[6]

Second, Lin's status as a highly educated student was viewed negatively only by his opponents. For instance, one netizen condemned Lin for abandoning his oath as a medical student and future doctor, writing, "As a medical student himself, I think [Lin] must die. He forgot the oath of medical students, 'to alleviate human sufferings and promote human health (除人类之病痛, 助健康之完美),'[7] and the Hippocratic Oath, to 'do no harm'! Because of some frictions, [he] forgot the original purpose of his medical study. How could he be a good doctor?" Many argued that Lin's high education level should not be a mitigating factor (in 106 comments). Instead, they expressed concerns about crimes committed by highly educated people with high IQs. One netizen wrote, "If no death sentence, China will face a collapse of morality. We are at the brink of such a collapse. Medical students should respect lives. Some lawyers only focus

---

6. In this story, a farmer picked up a viper that was half-dead from the cold. After the farmer had warmed the viper, the viper killed the farmer with a fatal bite. The lesson of the fable is not to show one's kindness to the evil.

7. For the full version of the oath of medical students in mainland China, see https://baike.baidu.com/item/医学生誓言

on the specifics of laws but ignore social impact. Yao Jiaxin [see chapter 3] killed people visibly (杀人有形), and Lin Senhao killed invisibly (杀人无形). If people like Lin are not sentenced to death, more highly educated people would follow suit. There would be a new phenomenon: students kill others with high technology but are not death-sentenced." Some also expressed concerns about differential treatment based on education levels. One commented, "What is controversial in this case is not whether Lin deserves to die, but his status as a master's student at a well-known university, because of which many called for leniency and not to kill. If he is just an ordinary migrant worker, they would definitely support his death sentence. If this is true, where is heavenly justice and law?" Another echoed, "For those who petitioned for another chance for Lin Senhao because he is a highly gifted student, what makes you think so? Are sentencing standards tied to one's education level? Crimes committed by people with high education and intelligence are more dreadful and their damaging impact is often greater."

Third, some netizens focused on Lin's crime and argued that poisoning is very dangerous and could have caused much more harm to society. For public safety purposes alone, no forgiveness should be allowed. One netizen asked, "What if more people drank the [poisoned] water then? A death sentence is correct." Another said, "No leniency shall be given to murderers with premeditation. Forgiveness to them is cruelty to ordinary people in society." Some tied public safety to deterrence. One netizen wrote, "Why no lenient sentence? Because poisoning as a behavior of endangerment of public security does great harm to society, especially for Lin, who is small-minded and vicious, worse than a viper or a scorpion. If [he is] sentenced more leniently, it would be a very bad precedent. Nowadays, campus violence often occurs and all retaliation means are horrible. For such a typical case of retaliation against one's roommate, if we disregard its serious nature and encourage forgiveness, do we still have collective safety on campus? Do we still have principles of society?"

Fourth, many netizens put themselves in the shoes of the victim's family and argued that Lin's death would be the only relief to the Huangs and that without a death sentence, it may encourage more retaliations by victims' families in similar cases in the future. For instance, one netizen rejected the argument of Lin's mistake and said, "Can he correct this mistake? Unless he can bring back the dead." Some specifically rejected Lin's supporters' proposition that Lin's life be spared so that he could take care of the Huangs. One netizen countered and wrote, "If intentional homicide can be forgiven because of this proposition, law is a joke. It is not an issue of who wants him dead. Rather, it is that he should bear criminal liabilities equivalent to his behavior. And you think that a couple who lost their only son would allow the murderer to take care of them? What a joke." Another agreed, saying, "Allow a murderer who killed their own son to support them? What a fart. It is already tragic to lose a son. You ask them to face the murderer every day? If so, here comes an opportunity to revenge for their son."

Lastly, some netizens pointed out that in case of no immediate death sentence for Lin, the alternative sentencing options (e.g., a suspended death sentence, life imprisonment) in China are not harsh enough and Lin might be released sooner than he deserved. One netizen commented, "Without real life imprisonment, [we] cannot forgive! Only if [our] nation changes the law that allows imprisonment of a murderer until his death can we talk about forgiveness!" With regard to Lin's supporters' argument that forgiveness is better than punishment, opponents cited a famous phrase from the Confucian *Analects* (论语) to counter the appropriateness of forgiveness in Lin's case: "To requite resentment with kindness, with what then will you requite kindness (以德报怨, 何以报德)?"[8]

Compared to Lin, the attention given to victim Huang was much less, and most comments were made within the context of their discussion of Lin. Judicial judgments at three levels (i.e., the first instance court, the second instance court, and the SPC) only vaguely described the case in words such as "Due to disagreement with Huang over trifling matters of everyday life, Lin decide to poison Huang" and "Huang and Lin never had major conflicts but only small issues over lifestyle and verbal communication due to long-term inhabitancy," but they did not provide much detail. Some of Lin's supporters argued that Huang was indeed at fault (in 212 comments) and that it was Huang's bullying that pushed Lin over the limit. One netizen commented, "Whoever is pitiful must have a cause to be despised. If [Huang] forced another to kill him, he went too much (够过分的). Both are highly gifted students. I believe too that there was more to be explained between them." Many blamed Huang's faulty character. One netizen wrote, "Huang Yang is not a good bird [insulting word in

---

8. The full version is as follows: Someone said, "To requite resentment with kindness, what do you think of that?" The Master said, "With what then will you requite kindness? Requite resentment with justice; requite kindness with kindness" (*The Analects*, chapter 14).

Chinese] either. [He] discriminates and mocks [others], stabs [others] in the back (背后捅刀), and is mean (心胸狭窄)." Another concurred and said, "Two tragedies. Huang's death cannot be all Lin's fault. Huang's self-approbation and arrogance and his character led to his death first." Yet another contrasted Huang with Lin and said, "Both teachers and students petitioned for Lin's life! It is proof that Lin's character is 1,000 times better than Huang's! Just check the appearance of both Huang's father and Huang! [They] are not someone who can be easily dealt with (不是省油的灯)! Harsh and cruel (桀骜不驯)! Often look down upon others! Arrogant!" Nevertheless, Huang's supporters left almost four times as many comments (811 to be exact) to support the victim and argued that nothing justified Lin's poisoning.

Lin's Family vs. Huang's Family

Netizens' debate in Lin's case spilled over to both his and Huang's families—in particular, their fathers, as both acted as the spokesperson of each family. Lin's father was in the spotlight in both August and December. In August it was reported that Lin's father tried to change Lin's defense lawyers and told the media that Lin's mother had not yet been told about his death sentence. Further, an SPC judge who handled Lin's case met his father to listen to his opinions, an unprecedented move, as it is not required by law. In December, after learning of the SPC's approval of Lin's death sentence, Lin's father, along with Lin's attorney, tried to lodge last-minute petitions to save Lin's life but failed. Lin's father managed to meet Lin one last time before his execution and, against Lin's wishes, decided not to donate his body after the execution. Huang's father was in the news both in May and December. In May, Huang's father claimed that he never received any financial compensation or apology from the Lins and insisted on Lin's death. In December, when he was interviewed after Lin's execution, Huang's father mentioned the possibility of a civil compensation lawsuit.

The total number of comments against the Lins (681) more than tripled the number of comments supporting them (209). Comments on the Lins again reflected different values held by netizens. For netizens who opposed Lin's father, many held the Lins responsible for their failed parental education, citing the famous phrase "failing to educate a child is the fault of the father (子不教父之过)." For instance, one netizen said, "[The

Lins] only gave their child intelligence, but not a healthy personality! Failure of the parents!" Another concurred: "His parents are responsible to a large degree. Therefore, they have to bear it when others blame them. This is their retribution. Chickens come home to roost (害人终害己)." Some directly blamed the Lins for their son's paranoid (偏执) character, which led to his crime. One netizen criticized Lin's father and said, "Do you know, it is the attitude of parents like you that always seek the best resources for their children but did not teach them how to be good people. As a result [it] produces so many selfish scums of society." The netizen went on and mentioned the famous fictional figure She Taijun (佘太君), who sacrificed several sons for the country during the Song dynasty, and shamed Lin's father for his selfish motivation. Countering the argument that a good father should try everything to save his son, some netizens made it clear that it was Lin's father's "not my fault and no apology" approach that triggered their resentment. One netizen wrote, "Saving [your] son's life is not wrong, but [you] cannot bark like a crazy dog. After the poisoning, [Lin's father] not only made no apology to the Huangs, but vilified the Huangs with vicious language like enemies every time. Now [he] claimed that his son did not poison at all, and Huang died of hepatitis. How dare you make such an irresponsible claim!" Some netizens believed that morally Lin's father was even worse than Lin. For instance, one mentioned that "[Lin] already admitted his poisoning, but this shameless father still insisted no fault. [It is] pitiful and despicable, deserving [netizens'] curses!" Another netizen focused on Lin's father's last-minute effort and his words after Lin's execution and wrote, "Look at his father, who insisted [Lin was] not guilty and tried to change lawyers to exonerate Lin. After the execution, [he] still said that his son is too foolish. [Having] such a son-of-a-bitch father, how could the son not face death? If [Lin] admitted his crime and showed remorse, he might have received life imprisonment. With good behavior, [he might] be out in 20 years and be able to bury his parents [after their death] (送终). Brother [referring to Lin], find good parents for reincarnation in the next life."

As discussed in chapter 8, a small number of netizens expressed their willingness to forgo proper legal procedures and called for punishment of the innocent. In Lin's case, a small number of netizens argued for "no appeals" (14 comments) and called for legal punishment against the Lins (84 comments). For example, one netizen commented, "If saved, this person [Lin] would be a big risk. As a vicious villain, the higher his education level is, the more risk he poses.... His parents still supported his appeals. Is this different from harboring criminals? So wrong." Angry with Lin's father, one netizen called for legal action and said, "Lin's father is obstructing justice. Petition the judicial system to detain [him]." Another concurred and demanded actions against both Lin's father and lawyers, saying, "Don't forget to hold Lin's father and lawyers criminally liable, to punish those scums who protect the evil!"

Contrary to opponents, supporters of Lin's father argued that he did everything a good father is supposed to do. One netizen said, "This is normal behavior of a father. Outsiders like you and me are not qualified to judge his father. If a child is in trouble, any parent would do the same. If his father did not take any action to defend, I would say that he should be subject to criticism then." Some argued that Lin's father's relentless rescue effort actually "earned their respect" and showed the "true love." One netizen brought back memories of the Chinese Cultural Revolution and condemned the behavior of people who voluntarily reported crimes of family members. Specifically, the netizen wrote, "A typical Cultural Revolution remnant! We Chinese, a couple would go apart when calamity is on its way; once a father was brought down, a son would immediately declare break-off of any relationship! Where is humanity? . . . Lin deserves to die without any sympathy. But his father tried everything to rescue. What's wrong with that? Should he sit at home, drink for celebration, and talk about punishing his own in the name of justice (大义灭亲) to reporters? If so, our society would be extremely devoid of humanity!" To many supporters, Lin's father was entitled to pursue any legal resort permitted by law. One netizen emphasized the importance of procedural justice and said, "I don't understand why so many people view it selfish and shameless for Lin's father to safeguard the legal interests of his son with proper legal means? Isn't it true that the Hu'ge case [see chapter 3] has taught us the importance of procedural justice?" Supporters of Lin's father disagreed that the Lins should be held responsible for Lin's crime either morally or legally. Rather, they believed that the Lins were victims of their son's crime as well, and many explicitly expressed sympathy for them (187 comments). One netizen argued, for instance, that "[Lin] is already a doctor student.[9] [You] still blame his parents for failure of education. Did his parents teach him how to poison [people]? For those who accuse Lin's father, use your brain." Another expressed sympathy and wrote, "Lin's father is the biggest victim of this case and has to bear the pain at his age. Looking at his hope-

---

9. This is a misstated fact. Lin was a master's student.

less expression in the first picture, it is really sad! Lin deserves to die and has received his punishment. But please do not go after his family. Those who accused Lin's father should not have done it. Humans are species with feelings, not to mention [the loss of] a person closest to oneself. Can anyone feel the pain of a father who has to witness his son's death! Everything started with Lin Senhao, and let's end it with Lin Senhao! Poor parents." Moreover, some netizens strongly condemned those who called for legal punishment against the Lins. One netizen said, "Why condemn them [the Lins]? Sharen changming. Law has already punished his son. Why target his father? Isn't it true that [we] are crying for more legalization daily? If [we do] as you suggested, we might go back to a feudal society and wipe out family members of nine generations."

Compared to Lin's family, the Huangs were under the spotlight much less frequently. As a result, the number of comments about the Huangs was much smaller: 65 comments were made against them, while 13 comments supported them; in addition, netizens explicitly expressed sympathy for the Huangs in 52 comments. The majority of negative comments (55 out of 65 comments) were made in December when news broke out during an interview with Huang's father after Lin's execution. Reportedly, Huang's father simply mentioned in a calm tone that "an execution is an execution (执行了就执行了吧)" and that he would consult his lawyers on a potential civil compensation lawsuit against the Lins. Some netizens found his cold reaction unsympathetic and disrespectful. One netizen commented, "The pain of losing his son, sympathy for Huang's father. But the little reaction (轻描淡写) of Huang's father after Lin's execution shows that he is a cold-blooded person too! [He] had no sympathetic words at all for the loss of Lin's young life due to his mistake. A person who only feels sympathy for one's own but disregards others does not deserve respect either!" On the potential civil lawsuit, as mentioned earlier, the majority of netizens indeed opposed the idea. They argued that Lin paid back with his own life and the Huangs were greedy to go after the Lins. One netizen wrote:

> Lin Senhao is already executed, a payback he deserved! The Huangs has readdressed the injustice on behalf of their son. It is weird (滑稽) for them to discuss the likelihood of a civil compensation suit with lawyers. A sugar cane won't be sweet on both ends (甘蔗不可能两头甜) [a Chinese proverb that implies that nothing is perfect and one cannot get everything]. When you chose Lin Sen-

hao's death, you gave up financial compensation. Their choice of readdressing the injustice let people see Huang's father's [saying] that 'once a person is gone, it is useless with more money.' But now comes a civil compensation claim? They won't get anything, but only earn themselves a reputation of being greedy.

Another netizen tied Huang's father's lack of empathy and demand for compensation to Huang Yang's death, implying bad influence of Huang's father over his son's character. Specifically, the netizen wrote, "How come I don't feel sympathetic to Huang Yang's death but to Lin Senhao's death? It is because Huang's father showed no sympathy to Lin's father's grave sorrow and desperation! Now, with Lin's death, Huang's father, who declared no wishes for compensation before, demands money. How obvious the wild ambition of a wolf cub (狼子野心昭然若揭)! No wonder his son was poisoned to death! Like father, like son!" In contrast, supporters of Huang's father pointed out that he deserved sympathy as the most innocent victim of the case and that his insistence on Lin's death served justice. One netizen commented, "He is the most innocent victim of the incident. He did not forgive the person who brought him harm. But he did not resent and even forgive Lin's father. He did everything humanely possible (仁至义尽)." Another said, "I'd like to salute to the Huangs! You resisted the pressure and did not let the murderer's father take advantage of you! [You] upheld justice for your son! Huang's soul in heaven would be proud of you! You revenged for him!"

As discussed in chapter 5, Chinese netizens often speculated on the socioeconomic background of defendants and believed that a defendant with a powerful connection would be able to influence the outcome of a case. Lin's case was no exception, as the background of both families was discussed (in 46, 41, and 84 comments in May, August, and December, respectively). In May and August, when the SPC was reviewing Lin's case and listening to opinions by Lin's lawyers and his father, many netizens speculated on how the Lins were able to use their financial power and connections to influence the case. One netizen commented, "It seems that the Lins have a lot of money. It's true that money talks (有钱能使鬼推磨). In China, [one] can buy a life with money and power." Another said, "The grandfather of the murderer [Lin] is the vice president of the Revolutionary Committee of the Chinese Kuomintang, very powerful in connections. It is said that the command of 'letting him off the hook (放一马)' is from the top level." Very likely this comment was based on a rumor or a pure fabrication, as others pointed out that the Lins were just an ordinary family. In December, after Lin was executed, netizens' comments seemingly turned around on the family's background. One commented briefly, "You died because you don't have a powerful (牛逼) father." Another echoed, "If the Lins had money and a powerful status, I believe the outcome would be very different. At most a suspended death sentence! For an honest (老实巴交) peasant [Lin's father], this is the outcome!" At the same time, some netizens speculated on the Huangs' influence. One netizen commented, "[The court] did not explain well the causal relationship between poisoning and [Huang's] death. The Huangs are rather powerful. The case has some minor problems (瑕疵)!" Another said, "I'm a lawyer. Not to discuss first whether Lin's case is a wrongful conviction. I only want to say that nowadays in China, cases like this one are rarely death-sentenced. The Huangs are powerful."

Minyi and Yulun

In the case that generated the most comments, Lin's supporters and opponents took advantage of the online platform to express their opinions and argued that the other camp tried to improperly influence public opinion (minyi or yulun 舆论) and the court rulings (in 226 comments). The dedication from both camps was strong, and there were aggressive netizens who left multiple messages to galvanize their camp. For instance, one user (ID "5786204880") in Nantong, Jiangsu province, left 20 messages to support Lin on December 13 between 9:12 p.m. and 10:36 p.m. Further, there were comments from both camps that contained "facts" that were not officially verified. For instance, in May one netizen claimed that though Lin dared not step forward to admit his poisoning during Huang's hospitalization, he did "send a text to disclose the poisoning source. Otherwise, the police won't be able to crack the case." Another claimed that once Huang felt sick after drinking the poisoned water, he asked Lin to help him with a B-scan ultrasonography. "Knowing the damage of the poisoning was to Huang's liver, Lin told Huang that his liver was fine." Both comments, one defending and the other blaming Lin, contained purported facts that were not found by the courts but could have influenced netizens' opinions. Though Lin's extended legal review allowed netizens' full discussion online, it raised concerns that fervent netizens might be able to improperly influence minyi and court decisions. As a result, one netizen commented,

"The ruling should have come sooner. Such a long time allows too much time for shuijun [see chapter 4] to influence netizens' opinions. Thus the Chinese law is not working well with such a long delay."

Immediately after the initiation of the SPC's review, many netizens already suspected that the SPC would eventually approve Lin's death sentence. One netizen wrote, "I believe that the odds for SPC approval are high, despite so many questions and doubts. The final sentencing of our nation is influenced by the media and yulun and considers minyi and stability. [It] will not sacrifice the present societal stability for Lin's case, and [we] cannot compare [our system] with that of Western nations because of their [high] collective quality and the low [quality] level of the majority of Chinese ordinary people living in inland. Lin is basically doomed!" Noticing that many people supported Lin's death sentence because of the social impact or indignation generated by the case (261 comments), some netizens explicitly pointed out that the social impact argument would doom Lin. One netizen said, "Heh-heh [sound mimicking a sneer], nothing can be done (没办法). Yao Jiaxin was executed like this. There is a principle called 'bad social impact' in domestic sentencing standards. To put it simply: when your goose is cooked (事情闹大了), the only option is to kill the chicken to scare the monkey. To prevent similar crimes, he has to die." Another concurred: "The pressure of yulun is too much. Assuming there is sufficient evidence [on sufficiency of the poison], the poisoner will be death-sentenced! No use to fight, as yulun cannot accept it if the poisoner is spared." Yet another rejected the social impact argument and wrote, "Chinese people have no belief and no sympathy and give no chance for redemption. Calling for kill every day (成天打打杀杀), [we] still hold on to the old belief of sharen changming and qianzha huanqian. When we make a decision, we always use one term, 'social impact,' and say that if we don't do this, it will have some social impact. I think that many of our decisions were influenced by the so-called social impact. You truly believe that if Lin is not executed, tens of thousands of cases of poisoning would occur?"

Seeing the majority support for Lin's death and some blatant calls for the court to expedite his execution, Lin's supporters expressed deep worries about public indignation (minfen) and how it might influence the SPC's review. One netizen put it bluntly: "Those penzi [see chapter 4] online ... [are] so emotional. Is this ruling the country by law? The SPC is not supposed to approve Lin's death sentence. Being verbally attacked by you like this, [Lin is] doomed." Another lamented the influence of minfen: "This case apparently generated minfen. It's impossible to save Lin's life. This is obviously wrong. We don't need indignant 'red guards' [referring to the Red Guards of the Cultural Revolution period]. We need law, pure law." Yet another worried about pressure faced by Lin's lawyers and said, "Please respect criminal lawyers as a profession. Fewer and fewer people are doing this profession, because they cannot take the pressure of yulun. Hope no more cursing as yulun, [which] would force lawyers to give up evidence they have." Another netizen contrasted the reaction of online yulun in Lin's case with that of the Lian Enqing case (#14) and wrote, "People should be treated equally before the law. Regardless of one's status, profession, education level, and skill set, [they] should be applied with the same legal principles. . . . Our online yulun is bizarre: the doctor killer in Wenling, Zhejiang province, [Lian] committed his crime with cruel means and caused grave consequences and was death-sentenced. However, he drew sympathy from many people online, and some even supported killing doctors. . . . In contrast, in the Lin Senhao case, because he is a master's student, the picture is completely different online, with the majority calling for a kill with a deafening voice." The netizen went on to call for a careful review by the SPC.

Some of Lin's supporters labeled his opponents' calls for killing "online violence" (79 comments) and rejected it as true minyi. One netizen commented, "Hope SPC review judges are not going to be misled or kidnapped by bloody comments from sociopaths! Online violence is never [representing] minyi!! Only those who are simple-minded, low competent, and lazy; received little education; and have nowhere to vent their anger would call for killing every day!" Another directly pointed fingers at netizens who called for a kill and said, "[I] read those comments. China is far from a system of the rule of law. A group of online mob. What made you have the right to order the SPC what to do? To demand the law to execute a person? [You] need to learn and respect the law." Others argued that the fact that netizens utilized minyi to press the court reflected the problem of the Chinese legal system. One netizen argued strongly, "I find that Chinese people enjoy talking about the rule of law, but [they] believe in the rule of man by nature." Another agreed, saying, "Netizens' comments reflect the backwardness of China's legal system. The public is hoping for the rule of law on the one hand and trampling the law on the other hand. From the very beginning, [they] called for kill of Lin and [his] lawyers. If you are so capable and don't turn to lawyers in your whole life, I would be truly impressed." One netizen lamented how yulun can influence law but not other social issues and said, "I don't think Lin will die, unless being pressured by yulun, like Yao [Jiaxin] case.... If yulun can kidnap law, how sad [it would be]! How come our yulun cannot kidnap corruption, housing price, and detestable moral standards?"

After Lin's execution in December, many netizens again shared their belief that the death decision was influenced by minyi and minfen. One netizen commented, "But for the vociferous exposure (大肆渲染) by the media, Lin would have received a suspended death sentence at most. Not being sympathetic to Lin, [I] only feel that Chinese law is sometimes kidnapped by the media. That's it. I don't want to see meek law without independence." Another netizen focused on the social impact: "The justice sword helped vent their [the Huangs'] grievance.... Based on present judicial principles, even criminals who killed people are rarely death-sentenced.... The fundamental reason is that this case has drawn national attention and had great social impact. If [the court] let him off the hook, it might lead to grave consequences. However, many criminals who are more heinous than Lin were sold (出卖) [probably implying 'being spared'] by judges because of the silence, low status, and lack of impact of the victim's family." Again, Lin's supporters blamed opponents who "called for kill online." One netizen wrote, "Sentencing Lin Senhao to death is done through formal legal procedure but also by a group of hypocritical virtual onlookers. Lin Senhao is wicked. But those who claimed justice by calling for the death of Lin Senhao and a life for a life are more fearful and dreadful. Without self-examination, [they] only hoped a person to die soon. The victim's family has the right to resent, but social yulun should be more rational. In this case, we see how justice-seeking netizens watched a person die and yulun cursed a cold person."

To counter Lin's supporters, Lin's opponents made a number of efforts. First, they emphasized the severe nature of Lin's poisoning and argued that leniency for Lin would generate a bad social impact. One netizen commented, for instance, "If Lin is not executed, cases against roommates in universities would increase a hundred times; no sharen changming anyway. Lin's case will produce grave consequences with a bad social impact, much worse than the Peng Yu case in Nanjin [see note 4]." Indeed, the concern about more campus crimes because of Lin's case made trendy the phrase "Thank my roommate for not killing me (谢室友不杀之恩)" (explicitly cited in 12 comments). Though it sounds like a joke, its increasing popularity offered support to the argument of social impact. As one netizen pointed out, "To save Lin, those elite [students] at Fudan University manipulated online media, which actually doomed Lin. The phrase 'Thank my roommate for not killing me' suddenly gained popularity among friends, which showed clearly the backlash of minyi. Who would dare defy the popular will of the people (冒天下之大不违)?"

Second, Lin's opponents counterargued that it was Lin's supporters and the media who tried to improperly influence yulun to save Lin's life. For instance, one netizen attacked public intellectuals and said, "A big group of public intellectuals jumped forward and called for leniency (刀下留人) and abolition of capital punishment, tried to take advantage of yulun to kidnap law and trials, and eventually argued for human conscience (人性良知). From the very beginning, it is those against capital punishment who caused trouble and petitioned for leniency. [I] don't see people petitioned for a death sentence." Another wrote, "Those with brain please notice the timing of the first instance trial. This case was death-sentenced by the first instance trial. Then came yulun that spoke [leniency] for Lin. Gladly, our judiciary was independent and not kidnapped by yulun. The second instance trial affirmed the original sentence. For those who claimed that yulun doomed Lin, you may wash and sleep. This time it is a failed attempt by yulun to save Lin's life." Many questioned media reporting and argued that the media did not pay enough attention to the victim's family but played the sympathy card on behalf of the Lins. One netizen said, "Yulun [has been] leaning toward the murderer. Is it meant to buy more time to produce more news reports? Why not report the victim's family?"

Third, not sure how the SPC would rule in its final review, especially with signs that looked potentially favorable to Lin (e.g., SPC judges' unprecedented meeting with Lin's father), Lin's opponents pressured the SPC to take quick action to appease public indignation. One netizen wrote, "The SPC should not have met the father of a death-sentenced criminal, very inappropriate. Is it because Lin has protection from the top (中央有人罩着)? For a case with clear facts that has generated great national social impact, a death sentence is absolutely correct. Any irresponsible excuse is useless! Only quick approval of the death sentence is the best comfort to the Lins [probably meaning 'the Huangs' here] and a correct answer to Chinese people! Strongly demand that the SPC end the case more swiftly and severely. Otherwise, Lin's case will trigger more cases, and it would be too late to regret!" Another concurred, writing, "The Lins, shameless. And the court? No action! What are you waiting for? Kill Lin Senhao and give Huang justice." Yet another netizen followed and suggested, "Since law generates no action, let netizens make the decision?"

Last but not least, Lin's opponents argued that the majority support for Lin's death sentence truly reflected minyi. One netizen said, "The one-sided yulun reflected the good conscience of the public, and it proves correct the decision by the courts of first and second instances and justice." Another wrote, "Some claimed that yulun influenced law. Is it so? What about 'the masses have discerning eyes (群众的眼光是雪亮的)'? It shows that judicial sentencing to a large extent agrees with the majority opinion! Why don't you influence the court with yulun not to death-sentence [Lin]? You cannot, because you sided with the minority, or you took the position of the murderer. Your voice is weak, [and you'd] better save it! Justice will prevail against evil!" Moreover, contrary to those who worried about improper influence of yulun, some of Lin's opponents openly supported the function and necessity of yulun. One netizen commented, "Without social yulun, law would lean more toward the powerful. Law is a mandatory force; yulun is a moral force. What is justice? In many times, popular support (民心) is justice. Take official corruption, for example. [A corrupt official] would be a true man again after expulsion from the Party. The only justice then is yulun by ordinary people." Another netizen compared mass yulun with lawyers' arguments and said, "Why [do you] call analyses by the masses influence of yulun? But the chicanery by lawyers is valid? Are analyses of the masses incorrect? We cannot do the brilliant defense (雄辩) of the lawyers who 'called a stag a horse' [see note 3 in chapter 6]."

Both Lin's supporters and opponents seemingly agreed on one thing—that is, the online comments section of news sites such as Sina.com.cn has become an important platform for public opinions. Everyone has the right to express one's opinion (as long as it is permitted by law) and differences should be expected. In May, when one netizen called for abolition of capital punishment and tried to shut down others' critique by ending his comment with the phrase "[This is an] individual opinion and no verbal attack if you dislike my comment (不喜勿喷)," a number of netizens countered. One netizen wrote, "You enjoyed it when expressing your own opinion but rejected others' counterarguments by announcing 'no verbal attack if you dislike my comment' and called others scums. [You] need to be responsible for your comments in social media. To reject any debate and critique with such a simple phrase, it is too naïve." Another added, "Others have freedom of speech too. Besides, no one personally attacked you or used foul language (爆粗口) but took the matter on its merits (就事论事). Is this verbal attack? Simply because they disagree with you, they become scums of human society? Why 'no verbal attack if you dislike my comment'? Facing counterarguments or misunderstanding is the price that a speaker (发声者) has to pay, don't you know?"

Lin's case officially ended with his execution on December 11, but netizens' active online debate continued. Whether the SPC's approval of Lin's death sentence was actually influenced by minyi online may never be known and is only subject to speculation. What is most striking about Lin's case is netizens' debate on almost every subject discussed by netizens, from support for and justification of Lin's death sentence, to sympathy and forgiveness for Lin, to views about Lin's and Huang's families, to views about Lin's legal defense, to reasons about Lin's crime, to issues about minyi and yulun and many others. Such debate fundamentally reflected different values held by netizens in contemporary China. Seeing their diverse opinions and heated debate, one netizen asked, "In this case, who represents public opinion? Which side represents justice?" To one particular netizen who commented on whether forgiveness should be granted to Lin, it was about individuals' choices. The netizen wrote specifically, "If he is not unpardonably evil (不是十恶不赦) and morally wicked, I would forgive him regardless of his criminal intent even if the crime occurred to me. If he can rehabilitate and become a useful person to society, I'll give him a second chance. It is your belief in human good or evil (人心善恶问题). Your choice."

With Lin's case coming to an end, many netizens expressed good wishes (in 134 comments, e.g., "Wish the two souls [of Lin and Huang] make peace in heaven and show love to the world") and drew personal lessons (in 370 comments, e.g., "Impulse is devil," "Learning to be a good person is a constant theme of education"). Many others reflected on the significance of the case. Some believed that its impact was positive. For instance, one netizen summarized: "After three years of back-and-forth and confrontations of both sides, the case came to a conclusion. It generated great social impact, drew significant attention, and consumed many judicial resources. But it has a positive effect—that is, it functioned as a lesson of live legal education to citizens nationwide and displayed the full legal process from litigation procedure to evidence collection and to criminal liabilities." Another concurred and said, "Three years. This case [was] fully transparent. [You] can watch the trial online and see defense arguments and responses by courts, which is not easy." Another added, "Through its twists and turns, the case exposed problems of investigation and adjudication, which helped the progress of China's legalization [of the legal system]. Its positivity merits pondering. Hope everyone can 'take it seriously (较真),' and hope every case would be handled properly and legally." Nevertheless, there were critics who demanded more. One netizen questioned the transparency of the case and wrote, "Heh-heh, 'being open' is good. But was it transparent? How come [the prosecution] did not produce the mass spectrograms [of the forensic evaluation], which would be critical to sentencing? And conflicting [forensic] evaluations? Why not have a new evaluation by a third party? How come Lin's father and Lin could not talk about the case when they met? As a father, he wanted to know why his son turned to poisoning. Why couldn't he ask? And how come they could not send the [SPC's] official death sentence approval judgment to Lin's lawyer and father in time, but waited until after Lin's execution? What were judges afraid of? Is this sentence fair and just? Is the public convinced?" Another netizen sharply pointed out the vulnerable status of law to Chinese netizens and said, "As a matter of fact, to all who called for kill or not, they have long lost in their hearts their trust and patience to the law. Be it *gong-jia-fa*, or the media, their ultimate social responsibility is to provide to the public undisputable facts and a fair and just sentence based on such facts! This is the foundation of law and where media's public trust comes from!"

Regardless of the content of netizens' comments and many concerns associated with them (e.g., about online violence, use of foul language, attempt to improperly influence minyi and court rulings), many netizens indeed positively praised the right to voice one's opinion online. One netizen commented, "To be able to discuss the case online is already a huge progress. It allows both sides of the case to learn more through debate, and it allows netizens to learn the consequences, very meaningful." Another said, "[I] very much enjoyed reading comments! There are experts indeed and [I] learned! Most comments are emotional, but the main theme (主旋律) carried positive energy!" Though not an average case, Lin's case (along with many other cases in our study) set a new platform for Chinese netizens to share their opinions and conduct debate publicly. In many ways, the capability of Chinese netizens to exercise such a right is more important than a legal decision in a particular case.

CHAPTER 10

Public Opinion in a Unique Form

In this final chapter we argue that short of other effective alternatives, Chinese netizens' online comments and discussions have become a unique form of public opinion. Though with many problems, the internet provides a platform that allows Chinese netizens to express their independent opinions and to exchange information and engage conversations with others. In the case of death sentences, it has become an important means for netizens to seek "justice and fairness" based on their own standards and judgments, condemn the evils (e.g., criminals, official corruption), and sometimes question criminal justice professionals and criticize the government, its officials, and unpopular policies. Looking forward in this chapter, we make some suggestions to media reporting, the government, and Chinese netizens. We conclude with some overall lessons that we have drawn from this empirical study.

Public Opinion Online

The development and use of the internet has fundamentally transformed people's lives in the world, and China is no exception. As of December 2018 the total number of Chinese netizens has reached 829 million, and 98.6% of them access the internet via their mobile phones (CNNIC 2019). From the very beginning of China's internet development, the Chinese government has been actively involved. In fact, as pointed out, the big internet boom in China was made possible through state-centric intervention strategies and state-driven projects (Hartford 2000; Harwit 2008). As a result, the government not only retains the ownership of and controls the main internet infrastructure, but it also keeps tight surveillance over internet use and enables various governmental regulations (e.g., Liang and Lu 2010).

There was high hope that China's internet development, free flow of information, and formation of civil cyber groups might bring democracy to China (Kluver 2005; Taubman 1998; G. Yang 2003), and many studies paid particular attention to the country's new online activism and debated over the viability of a Chinese form of civil society propelled by its internet use (Herold and Marolt 2011; Lagerkvist 2010; H. Sun 2010; Tai 2006; Yang 2009; Zheng 2008; Y. Zhou 2006). Nevertheless, democracy in China seems to be as far-reaching as it once was. In his study on technological empowerment, Zheng (2008) distinguishes political liberalization from political democratization. While the latter requires a structural change (e.g., from an authoritarian regime to a democratic government), the former can exist within an existing political framework without democratization. As Zheng points out, authoritarian rulers may tolerate or even promote liberalization at certain times to reach goals such as gaining public support and legitimizing its authority. Internet use and development in China has provided new opportunities for political liberalization and empowers both the state and the society in a complex interactive process.

This is what we witnessed in netizens' comments on death sentences in China. Short of an ideal civil discourse setting, netizens turned to online forums to express their opinions and conduct discussions, and to engage interactions with other netizens, without challenging the authoritarian Party-state. Liang's 2014 study of the impact of internet development on China's legal reform distinguished two types of internet users' participation and involvement: one being responsive to governmental initiatives and the other being proactive (e.g., self-initiated internet mass incidents). It is the latter that has dominated the stage of Chinese netizens' internet use in the past two decades and has most worried the Chinese government. Much of the governmental effort of regulation, censorship, and manipulation (e.g., data fabrication) thus aims to diffuse the tension of potential "social unrest" and silence collective expressions (King et al. 2013, 2017).

Let's return to Jürgen Habermas (1989) once more for his study of the public sphere. As a link between the private and public realms, Habermas envisioned the public sphere as a domain where individuals can freely discuss and identify societal problems with the potential to influence political actions. Tied to his concept of communicative rationality (1984/1987), Habermas's public sphere allows the public to engage in critical public debate, including discourses that are critical of the state authority. When the public sphere functions as a regulatory institution against the state authority, it conveys the idea of participatory democracy and projects how public opinion could shape political actions. Key conditions of Habermas's public sphere include equal access to participation, demarcation of the private sphere and of a public sphere (e.g., not directly interfered by the state authority), viability of public debate in an unrestricted fashion (e.g., guaranteed by one's basic rights such as freedom of speech, freedom of press, freedom of assembly and association, etc.), and formation of public opinion based on rational deliberation. To Habermas, lack of rational deliberation and critical public debate, even a modern-day voting system, does *not* amount to a public opinion. Instead, the outcome of such an election system could merely serve to legitimize political actions without real public participation. Indeed, in his study of the structural transformation of the public sphere (1989), Habermas expressed deep concerns about the decline of the public sphere due to various reasons such as the influence of mass media and changing nature of representative politics.

Compared to Habermas's idealized public sphere, Chinese netizens' online discussions as a unique form of public opinion suffer from a number of serious problems, despite impressive growth over the years. On the one hand, as detailed in chapter 8, Chinese netizens still have much to improve on when it comes to their rational deliberation of public issues. Compared to conventional media outlets, the Chinese netizens' online discussions in our study exhibited a number of characteristics, including but not limited to instant responses to news; free-style communication (in writing format and content); being playful (e.g., quick wit, use of jokes); high frequency of foul language, cursing, and personal attacks; aggressive posting (including spreading fake news); and a high degree of suspicion (e.g., about identities and motivations of others). These features, though not necessarily unique to Chinese netizens, are not what Habermas envisioned. On the other hand, strong intervention and regulation of internet use by the Chinese government also departs significantly from the Habermasian model. There is always serious concern about the overreaching of the government's power both online and offline to take away Chinese citizens' already limited rights of free speech. Such an uncertain but constant threat could lead to self-discipline and censorship by Chinese media and netizens themselves, especially in matters of a sensitive nature (Hassid 2008; Liang and Lu 2010). This is, of course, directly contrary to Habermas's ideals.

Despite these problems, we should not overlook nor underestimate the significance of netizens' online discussions as a platform in contemporary Chinese society. Scholars have debated if netizens' proactive participation

Public Opinion in a Unique Form 263

constitutes a special Chinese form of civil society, and some have hoped that China's internet politics can eventually help the transition of China's political culture, moving toward a more rational, objective, democratic, just, and transparent culture (e.g., G. Xiong 2012). Though short of being a Habermasian public sphere, online discussion does empower ordinary Chinese netizens in a unique way (Herold and Marolt 2011). It is evident in this study that Chinese netizens are not afraid of voicing their independent opinions on death sentences. As one netizen commented in the Lin Senhao case (#1), "It is already a huge progress to allow netizens to discuss the case online. It allows both sides to learn more about the case and keeps them informed about the consequence, very meaningful." Another netizen summarized the significance of the case and said, "Every major case being followed by the public becomes a propeller for the progress of the Chinese judiciary."

In several cases, netizens called for further public participation via jury trials. In the Liu Danao case (#47), for instance, one netizen commented, "Trial by the people. Any demolition and relocation action without permission by the owners and a final ruling by a court would be a forced relocation. This driver [Liu] should not be death-sentenced. Without a jury, a judge has the final say. Alas. If tried by the people, [he] would not be death-sentenced." In the Lian Enqing case (#14), one netizen wrote, "I believe that if this killing did not occur at a major hospital but at a private and small clinic, the defendant would be very unlikely to be sentenced to death! If the court turned to a jury for a final decision, I believe it would not have been a death sentence either!" Another netizen, however, immediately countered with "How naïve! You suggest that people are free to kill doctors from private and small clinics and they won't face capital punishment! Even with a jury, people are not all like you. I'm one of them and I believe that he should pay back his life for his killing!" In the Lin Senhao case (#1), two more netizens argued about the function of a jury system. One netizen pointed out the possibility that "[one's] background and connection, money and inflexibility of law could all affect the final ruling." The same person then turned to the subject of jury trials and said, "Jury trials seen in developed nations or Hong Kong and Singapore won't be practiced in the mainland! A real common law [system] is based on human nature! And not based on documents and decision by a powerful judge! If this is not changed, more wrongful convictions would occur!" Another was more pessimistic and wrote, "A jury system cannot guarantee that the ruling is fair and equitable. There are some classic cases in Hong Kong. The assumption that [the] law treats everyone equally is wrong itself. Law only treats most people fairly, in order to maintain functions of the society. Most people are law-abiding. [Law] is a tool of the governor, not a balance (秤)." Despite differences of netizens' opinions on functions of a jury trial, these examples showed that some netizens longed for more civil participation and believed that it could have made a difference in the outcomes. When the access to public debate and civil participation is limited offline, netizens turn to online forums for participation, including learning, sharing, and contributing ideas and suggestions.

"Seeking Justice" in the Eyes of Netizens

As death penalty cases inevitably involve confrontation between the good and the evil, with the help of online discussion forums, this study has demonstrated that Chinese netizens show their willingness and sometimes zeal to pursue justice. Though with a great degree of diversity, Chinese netizens' comments collectively reflect not only their fundamental notions of justice, such as their strong feelings against crimes and criminals, official corruption, social inequality, and bad governmental policies, but also their belief in "fairness and equity." As one netizen commented in the Lin Senhao case (#1), "[I] very much enjoyed reading comments! There are experts indeed and [I] learned! Most comments are emotional but the main theme carried positive energy!" The positive energy, we argue, primarily comes from netizens' notions and pursuit of justice.

We witnessed a number of features in their efforts of "seeking justice." First, netizens often rely on their common sense and intuitions in making judgments. As detailed in chapter 8, Chinese netizens frequently turned to case comparisons in judging the "correctness" of a ruling. To many netizens, case comparison presents a straightforward means for them to see justice in action and to compare the results of different cases. Even if a decision could be perfectly legal (that is, a rational decision based on application of correct laws), netizens can still challenge it if the result offends their fundamental notions of justice in comparison to other cases. This is likely true in many other nations and societies as well. Due to lack of proper legal knowledge and training, laypeople often rely on their commonsense notions of justice in making judgments. A side effect of this practice, particularly in China, is its potential impact on procedural justice. When what matters to ordinary people is the final outcome (as they demand the "correct" decision), it may weaken the role played by procedural justice and pose potential danger to the criminal justice system (e.g., the influence of yulun over judicial decision making, Belkin, 2017).

In addition to making comparisons to similar domestic cases, netizens turned to historical and international comparisons from time to time. Historically, netizens made comparisons to historical or fictional figures, many of whom, such as Baogong (see chapter 4) and Di Renjie (see chapter 6), have been established as model judges in China's history. To a great extent this reflects netizens' high expectations of righteous judges and officials who would be willing to defend justice on behalf of ordinary people, a fundamental notion of lay justice. Internationally, netizens cited foreign laws and practices as references for China's practice. For instance, in the Liu Danao case (#47), many netizens supported Liu's behavior to protect his own property (i.e., home). One netizen cited a famous quote from William Pitt (1st Earl of Chatham) to comment on the protection of private property and the "rule of law" in England, saying, "'The wind may blow through, the rain may enter, but the King cannot enter.'[1] That is the rule of law." Though this particular netizen, well educated and likely with a law background, may not represent a "typical" Chinese netizen, his call to protect private property was echoed by many others (in 92 comments).

Second, in making judgment, netizens were often able to relate to their own experience and knowledge. This is particularly true when a common problem was the focal point of discussion. In the Lian Enqing case (#14), netizens submitted 149 comments sharing their own negative experiences in dealing with doctors and hospitals (vs. 11 comments of positive experiences). Their firsthand personal knowledge constituted a major source of their discussions and judgment. Partially as a result, Lian's case generated the second most comments in our sample when netizens questioned and challenged China's health-care system (see chapter 7). As one netizen wrote in summary, "Lian's case is not about an individual. 'To explode in silence, or to die in silence (不在沉默中爆发, 就在沉默中死亡).'[2] Lian Enqing's anger and hatred is against the whole health-care system, not

---

1. Note that the quote used by the netizen is a popular abbreviated version. The original is as follows: "The poorest man may in his cottage bid defiance to all the forces of the Crown. It may be frail—its root may shake—the wind may blow through it—the storm may enter—the rain may enter—but the King of England cannot enter—all his force dares not cross the threshold of the ruined tenement!" Speech on the Excise Bill, House of Commons (March 1763).

2. This is a quote from Lu Xun's 1926 work *In Memory of Miss Liu Hezhen* (纪念刘和珍君). Lu Xun (鲁迅) is the pen name of Zhou Shuren (周作人, 1881–1936), a leading figure of modern Chinese literature.

against a single doctor, though it befalls on a doctor. Everyone has experience of visiting hospitals and knows that there is brightness and darkness. This is in fact a result of both providing treatment to patients and making profits at the same time. This conflict cannot be solved at the present stage, and doctors and patients should try to understand each other."

Third, Chinese netizens often demanded real actions by the government and supported strong leadership: for crimes and criminals, they demanded crackdown and punishment; for corrupt officials, they demanded more and harsher discipline and sanctions; for wrongful convictions and dirty cops, they demanded accountability; for incompetent judges and government officials, they longed for righteous model officials such as Baogong; for extended and delayed trials, they demanded sooner and expedited actions (and a small number of them even called for forgoing proper procedures). It is through such actions that people see the government and government officials at work and justice being served.

Fourth, Chinese netizens also displayed a high degree of suspicion and distrust due to many problems in reality such as declining morality, increasing social inequality, and worsening corruption. One specific example of their high degree of suspicion is their concern about shuijun and penzi online (see chapter 4). Often netizens speculated about the possibility of shuijun who attempted to mislead people. For example, in the Lin Senhao case (#1), one netizen called for actions against shuijun and said, "[Our] nation should enact laws to punish shuijun online who post comments on behalf of others for money and organizers of shuijun. These people [aim to] destroy social morality, subvert the government, and promote treason and must be severely punished." It is interesting to see that Chinese netizens demand more information and transparency with high degrees of distrust and suspicion, a feature of Chinese netizens in the age of the internet. Take penzi, for another example. Though netizens have seemingly reached an agreement on the harmfulness of penzi, the definition and scope of penzi is often undefined and confusing. In the Fan Jieming case (#23), one netizen commented on the lack of effective emergency management and wrote, "[Fan] killed six people in six hours. It shows that emergency management did not do well. [The crime was done] by a hunting gun. If it were a machine gun, it would have been 600 people! [The police] only know how to conduct crime scene investigation, but don't know how to take actions to hunt down the suspect. In my opinion, [the key issue] is not how to sentence this person but how to improve emergency management of public security!" Without providing any explanation, another netizen immediately claimed, "This is a classic penzi!" In the Wang Changping case (#19), one netizen criticized dirty cops: "These days, news about crimes by the police who knowingly violate the laws is frequent, which made ordinary people bitterly disappointed. There were shuijun who preached to give them the right to carry weapon earlier. Please imagine: if the police who manufacture and traffic drugs carry guns, should we send these shuijun with no knowledge, fear, and brain to arrest them? Who dares to arrest the police? Attack police? I'll shoot you to death on site!" Another countered and labeled this netizen penzi and said, "[This is] a typical trick (一贯伎俩) by penzi. As long as there is one bad person among public employees, the whole profession consists of scumbags! Please ask [yourself]: which profession does not have bad persons! Which nation and region do not have bad persons! What is the purpose of such reasoning, besides an ill intention (别有用心)?" It appears that the definition of penzi has been broadened to cover anyone who dared to criticize society in these examples, a likely result of netizens' high degree of suspicion and distrust.

Fifth, our data showed that Chinese netizens today are not afraid of voicing concerns based on their own notions of justice and fairness. From individual faults, such as wrong decisions by judges, corruption by government officials, and foul play by professionals (e.g., police, lawyers), to problems of governmental policies, such as that of China's health-care system and the demolition and relocation practice, Chinese netizens were not shy of critiques. It is interesting to notice that Chinese netizens both called for strong governmental actions and challenged bad policies and actions if they viewed them as problematic. Such open criticism illuminates some features of a Habermasian public sphere, but what is unknown is the extent to which netizens' online actions can make a real difference offline.

In sum, though the internet platform has many limitations and problems, Chinese netizens' active discussion on death sentences shows some potential to become a unique form of public opinion in China, short of other effective alternatives. Netizens' pursuit of justice was built on their own fundamental notions of "fairness and justice," which went beyond the state-sanctioned notion of justice (Sapio, Trevaskes, Biddulph, and Nesossi, 2017). The real myth and challenge lies in how the Party-state responds to such a unique form of public opinion.

Suggestions for Media Reporting

Based on netizens' comments, we suggest that the media may try to improve its reporting on capital cases in a number of areas. First, as netizens demand more facts and truth, the media should be more transparent in their reporting and aim to provide more comprehensive coverage with balanced information. As discussed in chapter 5, reporters in very few cases in our sample followed up on their stories. The majority of cases were reported rather formalistically or even formulaically (e.g., description of crimes, sentencing information) with little room or effort to expand on other aspects of the story. In only a few cases did reporters manage to interview key parties such as judges and defense lawyers; besides the Lin Senhao case (#1), reporters tried to cover victims and their families in only two cases. The insufficiency of creative coverage may have reflected lack of efforts by editors and reporters or might be related to limitations of the substance due to other reasons and concerns (e.g., information control and censorship). Whenever feasible, however, more comprehensive coverage with balanced reporting would be helpful to the potential audience.

Second, reporters should work on accurate reporting and fact-checking. In the Fan Jieming case (#23), one netizen criticized inaccurate reporting by the editor and said, "Little editor, be dedicated, all right? This is the trial of first instance, not a 'final' sentence. There will be the trial of second instance by the Shanghai High Court, and the review and approval by the Supreme People's Court [SPC]." Timely updates are of particular importance when confusing, wrong, or even manufactured "fake news" is circulated by netizens from all sources, including unreliable ones such as rumors. Timely and accurate reporting would help keep the public informed and clarify or correct inaccurate or wrong facts.

Third, specific to death penalty cases, it would be helpful for reporters and editors to explain relevant laws and provide a brief review of background information and necessary legal procedures. In a story on the Zhao Zhihong case (#4) that came out in May 2015, the reporter included an educational paragraph at the very end of the story, explaining that the decision by the Inner Mongolian High Court (the court of second instance) was a final decision based on China's two-tiered trial system, that Zhao's death sentence would be reviewed by the SPC next, and that Zhao would face execution once his death sentence was approved by the SPC. This educational information is very helpful to the reader and should be encouraged in other stories of capital cases. It appeared, however, only once among the 63 cases in our study.

Suggestions for the Government

Based on netizens' comments, some suggestions can be made to the Chinese government as well. First, the Chinese government should work hard to rebuild public trust. As shown in previous chapters, the decline of trust in contemporary Chinese society has been evident in several aspects, such as interpersonal relations (e.g., Hu "x," #7), doctor-patient relations (e.g., Lian Enqing, #14), citizen-government relations (e.g., corruption cases such as Peng Shu and Hu Haolong, #3), coworker relations (e.g., Zhang Weilan et al., #20; Fan Jieming, #23), student-teacher relations (e.g., Yang Dazhi, #21), familial relations (e.g., Li Lei, #28; Yuan Lijun, #30; Feng Xiujuan, #32; Zhao Xu, #38; Li "x," #58), and netizens' distrust of the criminal justice system and its professionals (e.g., wrongful convictions cases such as Zhao Zhihong, #4; cases involving dirty cops such as Wang Changping et al., #19). In the Lin Senhao case (#1), one netizen lamented the lack of trust by netizens and wrote, "As a matter of fact, to all who called for kill or not, they have long lost in their hearts their trust and patience to the law. Be it *gong-jia-fa* or the media, their ultimate social responsibility is to provide to the public undisputable facts and a fair and just sentence based on such facts! This is the foundation of law and where media's public trust comes from!" In the Lian Enqing case (#14), one netizen commented on lack of trust, writing, "Lack of trust: the root cause is that society lacks trust. Patients do not trust doctors, and doctors do not respect patients. By extension, the public does not trust government officials, and these bureaucrats (老爷们) rarely truly care for shitizens (屁民) [powerless citizens in the context of China]. As a result, it is easy to generate mistrials."

Second, the Chinese government should consider opening up proper channels for public discussion and participation. In our data, despite their differences, netizens demand more information and truth seeking. This demand reflected their desire to be informed and, to some extent, to be involved in civil dialogues and participations. When they have doubts and questions, they demand answers and actions from the government. In the Lin Senhao case (#1), one netizen praised the official clarifications by an SPC judge in charge of the case who gave an interview after the approval of Lin's death sentence. In the interview, the judge explained six key issues of Lin's case, including why Lin was found guilty of homicide and the rationale for the SPC's approval of his death sentence. The netizen welcomed this effort and wrote:

Thumbs up for the court, for its responses to questions about this case. It is not easy and it requires a new notion. When faced with questions from society, some of our workplaces and superiors would avoid them, hide [the truth], or be an ostrich and dare not face challenges directly, which leads them to a difficult position, a valuable lesson! In fact, for many things, it would be nothing if you take them easy. As a human being, who makes no mistakes? It is true to a workplace and even a nation. It is normal to have questions from the masses. Just answer them directly. To those who lack understanding, be patient and explain. Accept your fault if you make a mistake and correct it soon. Why [do you choose to do nothing and] be questioned continuously by others, bit by bit, until [you] are forced to tell the truth!

Opening up proper and effective channels that allow and address public questions in key sensitive cases would be very helpful in facilitating communications between the criminal justice system and the masses.

Third, related to the two suggestions above, governments at all levels should take responsibility and be more transparent in information sharing. On the one hand, regaining public trust requires prompt actions, as only when the masses see governmental actions (with good results) will they lend their support and build trust. On the other hand, the government should also take initiative to guide and educate the masses. For instance, facing challenges from some netizens who call for expedited legal processes or forgoing necessary legal procedures, judges and other relevant personnel should make efforts to explain to such people what the proper legal procedures are and why it is important to follow them. Surrendering oneself (e.g., judges and courts) to the demands of the masses due to high pressure without scrupulous examination might work out in the short run, but it would not benefit the long-term interests of China's judicial system (Belkin 2017).

Fourth, to regain people's trust also requires more structural adjustments, changes, and reforms at different levels. As seen in chapter 7, many cases in our sample exposed major issues of contemporary Chinese society such as social inequality, declining morality, corruption and abuse of power. To deal with these problems effectively would require structural adjustments and reforms. Two other examples, though found at the micro level, are tied to fundamental structural issues of China's criminal justice system: one is the prevalence of wrongful convictions, and the other is netizens' distrust of and challenges against criminal defense lawyers (and legal experts and public intellectuals). To effectively deal with both issues also requires systemic and structural changes to the criminal justice system (e.g., to improve the vulnerable status of criminal defense lawyers; to break the assembly-line work style by the *gong-jian-fa*).

Last but not least, citing C. W. Mills, Habermas (1989) contrasted the "public sphere" with the "mass" (249). Two key points that set the former apart from the latter require that the state authority *not* penetrate the public but protect the public's autonomy (and their rights of speech, press, assembly, and association) and maintain proper and effective channels that allow critical public debate. Such liberal and democratic ideas would likely present the most challenges to the Party-state in China and face the fiercest resistance in reality. One direct example of such government interference is data fabrication online by official shuijun, the "50-cent party members" (King et al. 2017). Needless to say, the notorious reputation of the "50-cent party members" attests to its lack of credibility and utility among netizens.

Suggestions for Netizens

There is plenty of room for Chinese netizens to improve in the future. To some extent, what Chinese netizens can do is affected by what is allowed by the Party-state. Evidence is abundant in this study that they will respond and participate once channels are opened up. Beyond the scope of this study, there is also evidence that Chinese netizens are proactively taking advantage of the internet for civil dialogue, participation, and action. For instance, in 2014 a group of lawyers and volunteers founded an online platform that aims to help with wrongful conviction cases (http://www.xiyuanwang.net/, 洗冤网). When opportunities present themselves, more and more such civil groups would likely emerge in contemporary Chinese society.

Focusing on netizens themselves, it seems that they can self-improve in several aspects based on our analysis of rationality (see chapter 8). First, netizens should learn to be more civilized discussants online. The high frequency of foul language is presently a dominant feature among their discussions. If complete elimination of foul language is not possible (e.g., due to psychological needs of human beings), netizens need to learn how to "vent" their strong emotions (e.g., anger, frustration, dissatisfaction) in ways that are less harmful to others. As revealed, personal attacks based on foul language and personal threats seemed to have only counterproductive effects in their online communication (which is probably true in their offline communication as well). If Habermas's communicative rationality is desirable, many Chinese netizens still have much to learn about how to conduct critical, even contentious public deliberation in a civil, non-insulting, and nonviolent manner.

Second, compared to the requirement of conducting public debate in a non-offensive and civil manner, potential substantive improvement on how to make rational validity claims would be more challenging for Chinese netizens. For instance, netizens should avoid making various discriminatory remarks and comments, which were still widely prevalent in our cases. Further, Chinese netizens can work on the three *validity dimensions* suggested by Habermas (1984/1987), including propositional truth, normative rightness, and subjective truthfulness/sincerity (see the summary in chapter 8). Two examples that violated these validity dimensions include netizens' citing or manipulating wrong facts and calling for violence. While passing along inaccurate facts inadvertently is one thing, deliberately fabricating fake facts is another. For instance, in the Lin Senhao case (#1), one netizen wrote in August (when Lin's case was reviewed by the SPC), "During his interrogation, Lin Senhao admitted his poisoning. Just when he was about to explain that he felt the poison quantity was too much and might be dangerous and thus he poured some water out, a police officer shook his head to stop Lin from speaking. Lin thought [the officer] did it for goodwill and then stopped talking. Is it true that during interrogation there is something you may say and something you may not?" It is very *unlikely* that this netizen had firsthand, personal knowledge about this scene of "police interference during Lin's interrogation." If the netizen simply made up this fact to appeal to others in an effort to save Lin's life, it would be irrational (fabricating facts), wrong (morally), and potentially illegal. For another example, in the Lian Enqing case (#14), one netizen supported Lian and commented, "Please be clear that it is because Lian cannot find a solution to his problem everywhere, then he killed the doctor! Doctors should take care of the illness of the patient once they agreed to treat the patient. It's all right if the illness was not fully cured. But it became worse with treatment (居然越治越狠), and they refused to provide compensation [to Lian]. Anyone in Lian's shoes would have got angry!" Again, the statement that Lian's illness became worse with treatment was not verified and could be due to imagination (or manipulation) of the netizen. The effect of such an inflammatory statement could have further provoked emotionally charged netizens.

As discussed in chapter 4, a very small number of netizens expressed deep worries about emotional and irrational behaviors of some netizens who openly called for killing and labeled such behaviors "online violence." In the Lin Senhao case (#1), one netizen challenged emotional netizens who pushed for the death sentence and wrote, "[I'd like to] ask netizens in heated discussion: how many of you came to the conclusion of a death sentence or not based on laws? Very few. All of you did it based on 'I believe, I think.' It is all self-will but not laws and application of laws—exactly because of your self-will, no matter how the court rules, some of you will curse and accuse the court's ruling unjust. Tell you, how the court rules depends on laws, not '[what] I believe' online. Netizens should realize that we should abide by the laws at any time, not '[what] I believe.'" Moreover, as discussed in chapter 8, some netizens openly called for legal punishment of the innocent, again an irrational behavior.

Granted, learning to be more rational is not easy. Data in our study suggest that Chinese netizens are not afraid of voicing their independent opinions and engaging in conversation and debate with others. Nevertheless, there is much room for improvement on learning from others, conducting critical self-reflection, and reaching compromises with others. All of these are necessary if a Habermasian open and public debate and deliberation is the long-term goal for the purpose of discussion enrichment, gaining mutual understanding, and building consensuses.

Overall Lessons

Our study was designed to examine the content and nature of China's public opinion on its use of death sentences. Lacking access to a national representative sample, we turned to Chinese netizens as a proxy of the general public. Granted, the netizen sample in our study is different from the overall population (see discussion in chapter 1); nevertheless, the rich data in our cases and the often repetitive patterns observed across cases (an indicator of reliability and data saturation) lent confidence in our discussion. Collectively, we may draw a number of overall lessons from netizens' comments in this study.

First, the most important message is the *great degree of diversity* among Chinese netizens' opinions on capital punishment and, in particular, the use of the death sentence. Though the majority of netizens supported the concept of capital punishment as shown in past survey studies, the oversimplified measure of people's support (e.g., based on the typical survey question "Do you support the use of capital punishment"?) fails to uncover the diversity and nuances of people's opinions on the subject (Ellsworth and Ross 1983; Jones 1994). In the case of China, netizens' comments displayed a significant amount of diversity. As seen (e.g., chapters 2 and 5), the diversity of Chinese netizens' opinions was reflected in three important aspects: on the broad range of topics covered by their opinions (the breadth), on diverse views covered in each topic (the depth), and on the variances of netizens' opinions given different circumstances of cases (variations).

Such a high degree of diversity reflects to some extent the changing contours of contemporary Chinese society, as traditional values and norms of Chinese society clash with that of other nations and societies in the process of globalization. In a major case such as that of Lin Senhao (chapter 9), it is interesting and somewhat striking to see that there was both support and opposition to almost every subject discussed by netizens, from support and justification of Lin's death sentence, to sympathy toward Lin, to views about Lin's and Huang's families, to Lin's legal defense, and to issues about judicial verdicts. As shown in chapter 3, even among supporters or opponents of the death penalty, their rationales for support or opposition varied tremendously. While most people supported traditional notions of justice (e.g., sharen changming), there were a small but not insignificant group of avant-garde netizens who called for leniency (not punishment) and abolition of China's death penalty, questioned the utility of capital punishment and the fairness of its use, and argued that it is barbarian and a violation of human rights.

When we further examine application of capital punishment in specific cases, we witness even more variations among netizens' opinions. Subject to influence of various factors such as crime type, information regarding defendant and victim, legal procedure, and media reporting (see chapter 5), netizens' opinions could vary significantly from one case to another. It is evident that Chinese netizens are not afraid of sharing their opinions online, sometimes with very bold and critical statements indeed. In cases involving unpopular governmental policies, for example, they explicitly expressed their rejection and even lent majority support to offenders in such cases, showing their willingness to downgrade the significance of offenders' crimes or even overlook them (see chapter 7). Such bold voices and opposition suggest that the government-claimed "overwhelming public support" is misleading and fails to uncover the nuances of netizens' true opinions.

Second, despite such a high degree of diversity, the *influence of Chinese culture* is apparent in the majority of netizens' opinions. Concepts such as sharen changming and "killing one to deter a hundred" heavily influenced netizens' support of death sentences (at least as a general concept). Such culture impact is intrinsic to netizens' fundamental notions of justice as discussed earlier. Though there are minority opinions that questioned the validity of sharen changming, deterrence, and minfen (see chapter 3), such voices are often too weak to compete against the dominant majority group. It is interesting to note that Habermas specifically categorized one's attitude toward the death penalty as "the lowest level of communication," because such an attitude is often culturally taken for granted but rarely rationally challenged (1989, 245). To put it differently, there is plenty of room to educate and challenge the masses on these traditional beliefs. Indeed, some Chinese legal scholars have already identified such a challenge in promoting further reforms on capital punishment (e.g., M. Zhang 2005b; B. Zhao 2015).

At the same time, it is worth noting how a traditional sense of justice and fairness could work differently at different stages of a case. For instance, in the Lin Senhao case (#1), the majority of netizens supported Lin's death sentence, viewing it as a fair and just punishment to Lin's crime. Nevertheless, the majority of netizens turned against victim Huang Yang's family when Huang's father was considering pursuing a civil compensation suit after Lin's execution. To these people, once Lin paid his debt with his own life, going after Lin's family for money was thought of as being greedy and would not live up to the standards of the traditional Chinese moral teachings such as virtue and kindness. It is likely that the influence of such traditional culture is what makes China "Chinese," and it may pose obstacles to further reforms of China's use of capital punishment (e.g., reduction or abolition). For example, the general public is well educated about China's history of drug problems, which is widely accepted as a legitimate justification for the country's war on drugs, including its use of capital punishment against drug offenders (chapter 5).

Several specific indicators of the cultural influence can be gleaned from our data, including but not limited to (1) netizens' preference for heavy penalties, (2) their preference for substantive justice (e.g., willingness to forgo procedural protections and favor the "correct" outcome), and (3) their indifference to and underestimation of the significance of criminal defense. Netizens' preference for heavy penalties is tied closely to their belief in retribution and deterrence (chapter 3), and it also affected how netizens evaluated the performance of criminal justice professionals (chapter 6). Such a preference, though it reflects netizens' fundamental notion of justice, may run afoul of other demands of modern criminal justice reforms, such as rehabilitation and, in particular, restriction and reduction of China's use of capital punishment. Netizens' preference for substantive justice over procedural justice has been identified as a problem in China for a long time (L. Wang 2001; W. Zuo and Zhuo 2000). In this study specifically, many netizens openly cast doubt on the prolonged but required judicial review process and referred to it as "delay and waste"; some even expressed their willingness to forgo required legal procedures. Further, netizens' distrust of criminal defense lawyers and their conscious or unconscious comments to undervalue the work of criminal lawyers are very concerning and nerve-racking. How to mitigate or change such negative influence of traditional Chinese culture and properly guide Chinese citizens in building a modern criminal justice system that provides fundamental due process protections to individuals who face criminal charges still presents a major challenge in the future. The challenge is likely the most severe in capital cases, as the stakes are high and the crimes in such cases are often the most severe.

Third, netizens' *comments and discussions are embedded in contemporary Chinese society* and reflect their opinions about the existing social problems and systems, from concerns about rising crime rates and public safety, to rampant corruption, to problems of the educational system, to problems of the health-care system, to declining morality and mammonism, to widening social inequality, to privileges enjoyed by governmental officials and the wealthy, and to fairness of the judicial system. For instance, official corruption is one of few examples in our sample that generated very little disagreement among netizens. Netizens worried about the rampancy of official corruption (and its effect in the judicial system), condemned corrupt officials, and demanded harsh(er) punishment. Such a universal voice may signal future difficulty in restricting the use of capital punishment in corruption crimes (Miao 2013; W. Zhang 2015a). Another interesting example is netizens' speculation on the power and connection of parties (e.g., defendant and victim), as they suspect that parties with power and connection may be able to use their clout to influence the outcome of specific cases. Often netizens' speculation and suspicion are *not* well founded; for example, in the Lin Senhao case (#1), netizens speculated that the Lins were using their connection to influence judges' rulings during the SPC's review of Lin's death sentence in May and August. Nevertheless, netizens switched their position in December after Lin's death sentence was approved and began to speculate that victim Huang's family was more powerful and resourceful and able to influence the final decision. The most dramatic examples of the embedment of netizens' opinions in existing social, systemic, and structural problems in China come from netizens' strong criticisms and challenges to unpopular governmental policies such as the one-child birth control policy (He Shenguo case, #42), China's health-care system and practice (Lian Enqing case, #14), and the country's demolition and relocation policy (Liu Danao case, #47). In these cases, netizen's dislike of governmental policies gained defendants' sympathy and landed netizens' support. One obvious lesson, mentioned earlier, is that to change people's opinions in such cases, additional structural changes to China's existing systems are necessary. However, whether improvement of existing systems would lead to changes to netizens' opinions on China's use of capital punishment is still subject to debate and remains to be seen.

The fact that public opinion of a nation reflects existing problems and systems of that nation is likely true universally. What is unique in China's case is features of the country's problems and systems in contemporary society. Particularly relevant to our examination, a number of systemic and structural issues of the Chinese judiciary that might have influenced death sentence decisions or the way netizens assessed such decisions include lack of judicial independence, the perceived impact of minfen by both netizens and the judiciary, and netizens' deliberate efforts to influence yunlun. Lack of judicial independence has been a long-acknowledged problem in China (e.g., Liang 2008), and top leaders of the Chinese government and judiciary often openly reject the notion of judicial independence and make it explicit that the law should be a tool to serve the interests of the Party. In 2015, for instance, the SPC president, Zhou Qiang (周强), explicitly rejected Western notions of judicial independence and separation of powers.[3] In the 2019 SPC Work Report delivered in March,

---

3. See "China's Top Court Rejects Judicial Independence as 'Erroneous Thought,'" *The Guardian*, February 26, 2015 (https://www.theguardian.com/world/2015/feb/26/chinas-top-court-rejects-judicial-independence-as-erroneous-thought) (accessed March 26, 2019).

Zhou listed "Deep learning of Xi Jinping thought on socialism with Chinese characteristics for a new era and insistence of the absolute leadership of the Chinese Communist Party [CCP]" as the number one highlight in 2018, above other routine work highlights (SPC 2019). It is no secret that China's criminal justice system is serving the interests of the CCP as a tool. Judicial independence still looks like an unreachable dream for China.

The masses know the game well. Given the priority of maintaining stability and building a harmonious society, netizens showed their willingness to play yunlun online to proactively influence the outcome of a case (e.g., see the Lin Senhao case in chapter 9). In such efforts, the distinction between one's right to express an individual opinion and one's effort to present a collective voice and deliberately pressure a court and influence the decision of a particular case is increasingly blurred and mixed. As Fu (2016) has argued, this peculiar form of Chinese penal populism often targets individual cases and tries to influence judicial sentencing instead of legislation or governmental policies. Facing pressure from netizens, Chinese courts are in a difficult position to uphold the law and answer minyi at the same time (Belkin 2017; Miao 2013). Chinese netizens sometimes were able to mount significant pressure and force a "correct" decision, but such short-term success may well carry a long-term negative impact on the Chinese judiciary.

Fourth, our study presented a unique opportunity to examine the *rationality* of Chinese netizens' discussions and deliberations online, a key component missing from past studies. Over four and a half decades ago, Justice Thurgood Marshall hoped that public education would be able to persuade the American public to give up capital punishment in his famous hypotheses (see chapter 1). Nevertheless, he did not specify under what conditions such public education should be carried out. In a rare effort, Sato (2014) explored how focus group discussions as a proxy of public deliberation may change Japanese people's support for capital punishment. Our study examined Chinese netizens' exchanges in a natural setting without any artificial intervention. The evidence is mixed. On the one hand, Chinese netizens are not afraid of sharing their opinions and engaging in conversation and debate with others. On the other hand, there was little evidence of their willingness to make compromises and adjustments, not to mention complete change of opinions by sometimes emotionally charged netizens whose minds were often previously determined. Though there are obvious limitations with this form of online exchange (e.g., ample confusing or conflicting information, little guidance), the results raise the question as to whether netizens' freedom of speech online can bring positive changes to their opinions on China's laws on capital punishment. As seen in chapter 8, netizens' comments contained examples of both irrationality and rationality, and there is still much for Chinese netizens to learn and improve. Given the nature of anonymity without face-to-face interaction, online discussions presented an open platform for netizens to express their opinions (almost unregulated) and vent their feelings (uncontrolled). Whether it is death sentences or other topics of public nature, how to guide Chinese netizens to better utilize this unique platform of public opinion continues to be a challenge, especially when other viable channels to participate in public discussion and debate are lacking in China.

Last but not least, though the focus of our study was on China and the lessons drawn above are China-specific, we argue that the results of this study have broad and general implications for other nations in the world as well, thus contributing to studies of public opinion in general and studies of public opinion on the death penalty in particular. As argued in chapter 1, our methodology has been innovative and unique and can be applied in other nations, especially when survey studies of public opinion based on a representative sample of the general population are not feasible in a nation given its condition. Moreover, when dealing with a sensitive topic such as public opinion on capital punishment, our approach taps into a great source—that is, netizen data—despite its limitations, and potentially minimizes problems of some methodological issues such as social desirability bias in survey studies. Our study reveals significant advantages of examining netizen data, as it could enhance both reliability and validity of traditional public opinion research. For example, the enhancement of validity is evident in the great depth of netizens' diverse opinions on capital punishment, as they actively participated in the online platform to voice their opinions—sometimes "extreme" opinions—anonymously, particularly when a viable alternative has not been available offline. In addition, as seen in China, netizen data has special strength in studying the influence of a nation's culture and social, economic, and legal conditions. What are expressed, questioned, debated, and demanded by netizens are often embedded within a specific context. Although we may reasonably expect some common lessons across nations (e.g., netizens "seek justice" based on their common sense and personal experiences; there is ample room for netizens to improve on conducting civilized and rational public debate; the media should continue working on accurate reporting and fact-checking), unique features of netizen data in a particular nation would reveal its cultural impact and existing societal conditions. In the case of China, we may glean meaningful lessons from netizens' demand for governmental interventions (e.g., to quash crimes) and strong leadership and their willingness (by the majority) to downplay the role of procedural justice and criminal defense rights. Both commonalities and particularities are key elements of comparative studies, and this study sheds significant light on our understanding of public opinion on capital punishment not only in China but also from a comparative perspective worldwide.

APPENDIX 1

List and Summary of All Cases

This appendix lists the 63 cases discussed, first displaying the case number and names of the defendants, followed by summaries of the facts of the case and the legal history and rulings.

Case # Defendant(s) and Date(s) reported
1 Lin Senhao (林森浩)
1/8/15; 5/27/15; 8/3/15; 8/12/15; 10/9/15; 12/9/15; 12/10/15; 12/11/15; 12/12/15; 12/16/15; 12/17/15

Facts of the Case: Lin (a 28-year-old), a Shantou native (in Guangdong province), entered Zhongshan University with a high exam score (780) for his bachelor degree and entered Fudan University as a master's student in medical school in 2010. Recommended by Zhongshan University, Lin was accepted without taking an examination.

Lin and Huang Yang (a 27-year-old) both joined Fudan University in Shanghai as medical graduate students and shared the same dorm. On 3/31/13, Lin allegedly poisoned water in the drinking water dispenser with N-Nitrosodimethylamine; on 4/1, Huang drank the water, became ill, and was sent to Zhongshan Hospital, and his condition worsened on 4/3. From 4/1 to 4/11, Lin did not disclose the truth to the police. Not until 4/12, when Lin was named the primary suspect and detained, did he confess. On 4/16, Huang died; Lin was formally arrested on 4/19.

Huang's father insisted on Lin's death sentence and claimed that Lin and his family never apologized nor compensated him for Huang's death. Lin's father was reportedly not satisfied with Lin's attorneys (Si Weijiang and Tang Zhijian) in the appeal process, and on 6/15/15, Xie Yongxiang became Lin's new lawyer.

Legal History and Rulings: Lin's trial of first instance started on 11/27/13; on 2/18/14 the No. 2 Intermediate People's Court in Shanghai convicted him of homicide and sentenced him to death. On 12/8/15, the trial of second instance started; on 1/8/15, the Shanghai High Court affirmed Lin's death sentence. On 5/26/15, in the process of its final review and approval, the Supreme People's Court (SPC) held a hearing in which Lin's attorneys argued that Lin's death sentence was excessive.

On 7/28/15, an SPC judge met Lin's father to listen to his complaints, a rare practice; on 7/31/15, Lin's attorney (Xie) and his father submitted their complaint and other relevant materials to the SPC. In December 2015, Lin's death sentence was approved by the SPC, and on 12/11/15, Lin was executed.

2   Huang Qinghen (黄清恒, female)
     1/26/15

Facts of the Case: 24 offenders (including 18 women and possibly nine Vietnamese nationalities) were involved in cross-border child abduction. From October 2010 to June 2011, 22 children were abducted from Vietnam and sold to Guangdong province in China for profit.

Legal History and Rulings: On 5/16/14, the intermediate people's court in Fangchenggang city sentenced Huang to death; on 1/26/15, the verdict and sentence were upheld by the Guangxi provincial High Court.

3   Peng Shu (彭曙) and Hu Haolong (胡浩龙)
     2/7/15

Facts of the Case: From 2002 to 2010, Peng and Hu were in charge of the highway system in Hunan province and received bribes of 188 and 170 million yuan, respectively. On 9/27/10, both were arrested.

Legal History and Rulings: On 2/3/15, the intermediate people's court in Loudi city convicted Peng and Hu of receiving bribes, corruption, and other crimes, and sentenced both of them to death.

4   Zhao Zhihong (赵志红)
     2/9/15; 4/30/15; 5/1/15

Facts of the Case: From 1996 to 2005, Zhao (born in 1972) raped and murdered multiple women, including a 12-year-old. Zhao was charged with homicide, rape, robbery, and theft in 22 offenses.

Legal History and Rulings: On 11/28/06, during Zhao's closed-door trial, Zhao admitted his guilt in a 1996 rape-murder case; the court suspended the trial as a result. Hu'ge (Huugjilt) was convicted and executed for this crime. Given Zhao's admission, the Inner Mongolia High Court started a retrial and exonerated Hu'ge posthumously on 12/15/14. On 2/9/15, the intermediate people's court in Huhe Haote city convicted Zhao and sentenced him to death, and on 4/30/15, the High Court affirmed Zhao's death sentence.

5   Liu Han (刘汉) et al.
     2/10/15

Facts of the Case: Offenders Liu Han, Liu Wei, Tang Xianbing, Zhang Donghua, and Tian Xianwei were convicted of organizing criminal gangs and committing numerous crimes, including homicide.

Legal History and Rulings: On 2/9/15, these offenders were executed. A family visit was arranged before their executions.

6 Tuo Heti (帕提古丽·托合提, female) et al.
   3/12/15

Facts of the Case: On 3/1/14, a group of eight terrorists attacked the railway station in Kunming, causing 31 deaths. Four offenders were killed on site, and others were arrested, including Tuo Heti.

Legal History and Rulings: On 10/28/13, three other terrorists killed three victims at Tiananmen Square in Beijing. All were convicted, sentenced, and executed. On 9/12/14, given her pregnancy at the time of her offense, a capital sentence was not applicable. Tuo Heti was sentenced to life imprisonment, and three other offenders were sentenced to death. The case was being reviewed by the SPC.

7 Hu "x" (胡某)
   3/17/15

Facts of the Case: Due to a business dispute, starting on 6/10/12, Hu illegally detained victim Zhang for over 80 days and then drowned and sank Zhang in an iron cage in a lake on 8/31/12.

Legal History and Rulings: The intermediate people's court in Hangzhou city held open trials four times from June 2014 to February 2015. The court convicted Hu of both illegal imprisonment and homicide and issued a suspended death sentence to Hu on 3/16/15.

8 Wang Yuefu (王月福)
   3/19/15

Facts of the Case: A group of seven offenders were charged with arson committed on 3/21/14. One victim was killed on site, and three others were seriously injured.

Legal History and Rulings: The case was tried twice by the intermediate people's court in Qingdao city. The principal offender, Wang, was sentenced to death.

9 Zhai "x"de (翟某德)
   4/20/15

Facts of the Case: On 7/24/14, Zhai (with a lengthy criminal record) tried to borrow 30 yuan from his neighbor Zhang. After being rejected, Zhai stabbed Zhang with a knife over 20 times and killed him. Zhai took 250 yuan and some other items (including a laptop computer) and was arrested on the second day.

Legal History and Rulings: On 4/19/15, Zhai was convicted of homicide and robbery and sentenced to death by the intermediate people's court in Zhuhai city.

10   Ruan Fangcheng (阮氏芳成, female) et al.
        4/29/15

Facts of the Case: Colluding with others (including codefendant Zhang Yuanzhen), Ruan (a Vietnamese citizen) smuggled illegal narcotics (about 5.2 kilograms) from Hanoi to Guangzhou and Dongxing city in Guangxi province in June 2012.

Legal History and Rulings: On 4/29/15, Ruan was convicted and sentenced to death. Zhang received a suspended death sentence.

11   Wu Qinyuan (武钦元)
        5/15/15

Facts of the Case: On 12/2/96, victim Han (female) was raped and died at home. On 12/22/96, Han's husband, Yu Yingsheng, was arrested for the crime. He was later convicted and sentenced to life imprisonment. On 5/31/13, the Anhui High Court initiated a reinvestigation and decided to open a retrial on 6/27/13. On 8/13/13, the High Court acquitted Yu after the retrial. On 11/27/13, defendant Wu was arrested and confessed his crime of 17 years earlier.

Legal History and Rulings: On 5/15/15, Wu was convicted of rape and sentenced to death by the intermediate people's court in Wuhu city (in Anhui province).

12   Yuan Junkai (袁俊凯) et al.
        5/23/15

Facts of the Case: Yuan (56 years old) had a lengthy criminal record and was sentenced to suspended death in 1989. He was paroled on 10/18/07 and completed his parole on 1/23/09. On 10/9/12, Yuan abducted victim Tang with a codefendant and raped and murdered her. Defendant Liu Yanming (24 years old) had served one year of probation for theft in 2011. On February 18 and 19, 2013, Liu abducted victims Ding and Zhao and raped and murdered both. On 12/12/12, Wei Lingyao (24 years old) raped victim Bai, who died during the crime.

Legal History and Rulings: Yuan was sentenced to death by the No. 2 intermediate people's court in Beijing. Liu was convicted of both rape and homicide and sentenced to death by the No. 2 intermediate people's court in Beijing. Wei was convicted of rape and sentenced to death by the No. 2 intermediate people's court in Beijing. The death sentences of all three were reviewed and approved by the SPC and all were executed.

13   Wang Gang (王刚)
        5/26/15

Facts of the Case: Wang was arrested three times for drug trafficking. He claimed that he had committed his crimes to raise money to cure his uremia.

Legal History and Rulings: The Inner Mongolia High Court reduced Wang's death sentence to a suspended death sentence.

14   Lian Enqing (连恩清)
        5/26/15

Facts of the Case: On 3/20/12, Lian received a nasal operation at the No. 1 People's Hospital in Wenling city (in Zhejiang province). Lian continuously complained about the result of the operation despite the fact he was informed that the operation had been successful. On 10/25/13, Lian went to the hospital and stabbed three doctors, one of whom (Wang Yunjie) died.

Legal History and Rulings: On 1/27/14, the intermediate people's court in Taizhou city convicted Lian of homicide and sentenced him to death. On 4/1/14, the Zhejiang High Court affirmed Lian's death sentence. On 5/25/15, Lian was executed. Before his execution Lian's parents and his younger sister visited him.

15   Zhang Xiangxi (张祥喜)
        6/3/15

Facts of the Case: Zhang (born on 9/11/65) was a Han person with a middle school education and unemployed; he was convicted of kidnapping in 1995 and child molestation in 2010. On 10/30/14, Zhang battered three elementary school students with an iron stick, killing two and seriously injuring one. He was detained on 11/5/14 and arrested on 11/13/14.

Legal History and Rulings: On 6/3/15, Zhang was convicted of homicide and sentenced to death by the intermediate people's court in Shangrao city (in Jiangxi province).

16   Lin "x"ping (林某平); Ye "x"tian (叶某田)
        6/8/15

Facts of the Case: Three offenders (including Lin and Ye) were convicted of drug trafficking and executed.

Legal History and Rulings: The Guangdong High Court affirmed the conviction and sentence of the defendants. Their death sentences were approved by the SPC.

17   Sun Zhifu (孙志富, female)
        6/11/15

Facts of the Case: Sun's husband is the half brother of five-year-old victim Yang's grandpa. Sun had a bad relationship with Yang's grandma. On 8/20/14, Sun murdered Yang when he was alone. When the police searched her home, Sun tried to commit suicide by poisoning but survived. Later Yang's father committed suicide due to Yang's death. Although Sun was diagnosed with schizophrenia, her disease was ruled not severe enough to warrant a reduced sentence.

Legal History and Rulings: On 6/10/15, the intermediate people's court in Hefei city (in Anhui province) sentenced Sun to death.

18   Liang Kaiwu (梁开武)
        6/12/15

Facts of the Case: On 8/23/02, Liang killed a security guard, Cao, and took a semiautomatic machine gun. On 12/1/02, Liang (with his cousin Shi) robbed victim Zeng, an accountant of a local company, took 410,000 yuan, and murdered Zeng. On 5/25/15, Liang was arrested.

Legal History and Rulings: On 1/24/15, Liang was sentenced to death by the intermediate people's court in Zhiyang city (in Shan'xi province). On 6/11/15, Liang was executed.

19   Wang Changping (王长平) et al.
        6/18/15

Facts of the Case: Wang (55 years old) was a former police officer and colluded with Han Xuedong (51 years old) and Sun Shiquan to manufacture narcotics (over 220 kilograms). On 5/22/14, all three were arrested.

Legal History and Rulings: On 4/17/15, Wang and Han were found as principals in the crime and sentenced to death by the intermediate people's court in Dandong city (in Liaoning province); Sun received a suspended death sentence.

20   Zhang Weilan (张伟兰) et al.
        7/4/15

Facts of the Case: From October 2011 to August 2012, Zhang colluded with a group of codefendants (a total of 21 offenders), murdered four miners (Jiang Fapin, Yuan Defu, Xie Shiyou, and Li Zihua), and claimed fraudulent financial compensation of 1.8 million yuan (as family members of the deceased miners).

Legal History and Rulings: On 8/7/2014, the intermediate people's court in Handan city (in Hebei province) convicted the offenders of homicide and sentenced Zhang, Zhao Jun, Zhang Chengyong, Xu Decheng, and Yan Zhuangyong to death; Yan Dengpeng to suspended death; and others to other punishment. On December 9 and 10, 2014, the High Court of Hebei held the trial of the second instance and on 7/3/15 upheld the sentences.

21   Yang Dazhi (杨大志)
        7/6/15

Facts of the Case: Yang (born in 1974) was the principal of the Xianjin elementary school in Tianba village (Qixingguan district). From 2010 to 2014, he molested and raped six students, from ages 8 to 13. Yang was detained on 5/24/14 and arrested on 6/4/14. Reportedly, Yang's family members (and the local government) tried to "settle" his crimes via financial compensations (50,000 to 100,000 yuan) and asked the victims to sign an agreement not to expose his crimes.

Legal History and Rulings: On 5/5/15, the intermediate people's court in Bijie city (in Guizhou province) convicted Yang of rape and child molestation and sentenced him to death.

22 Wang "x" (王某)
    7/18/15

Facts of the Case: Wang (46 years old) was a former employee of a restaurant (named Hotpot City) and was laid off two days before his crime. Due to resentment, on 6/3/14 Wang abducted and murdered a 10-month-old boy who was the son of the brother-in-law of Wang's boss. Wang was sentenced to a four-year imprisonment for arson in 2004.

Legal History and Rulings: On 7/16/15, the intermediate people's court in Jiaxing city (in Zhejiang province) convicted Wang of homicide and sentenced him to death.

23 Fan Jieming (范杰明)
    7/29/15

Facts of the Case: On 6/22/13, Fan (in his 60s) killed a coworker, Zhang, due to a financial dispute. On his run, Fan killed four more people with his hunting gun.

Legal History and Rulings: On 7/29/15, Fan was convicted of homicide and robbery by the No. 2 intermediate people's court in Shanghai city and sentenced to death.

24 Zheng Dalong (郑大龙) and Yang Shengjian (杨升键)
    7/29/15

Facts of the Case: On 2/7/13, Zheng and Yang coaxed and detained victims Fei and Liu (Fei's wife) and forced them to give up the security code of their bank card; Zheng and Yang covered their victims' mouths with duct tape and their hands, which caused the death of both victims. Zheng and Yang withdrew 1,500 yuan using the bank card. Both offenders had committed other crimes such as theft.

Legal History and Rulings: Zheng and Yang were arrested on 4/9/13. They were convicted of robbery and theft by the No. 2 intermediate people's court in Beijing on 6/20/14, and both were sentenced to death. On appeal, the Beijing High Court sent the case back for a retrial because of insufficient evidence. On retrial, both were convicted again and sentenced to death.

25 Wang Hua (王华) et al.
    8/10/15

Facts of the Case: Since the 1990s, Wang organized a criminal gang and committed crimes such as arson, assault, etc.

Legal History and Rulings: On 8/10/15, Wang and 18 others were convicted and sentenced by the intermediate people's court in Hebi city (in Henan province). Wang and codefendant Sun Peiguo were sentenced to death; another codefendant,

Sun Peichao, was sentenced to suspended death; others were sentenced to other punishment.

26 Gu Junshan (谷俊山)
   8/10/15

Facts of the Case: Gu was charged with his crimes on 3/31/14. Gu was born in 1956, of Han ethnicity. He was a military lieutenant general by rank and served as deputy minister of the general logistics department.

Legal History and Rulings: On 8/10/15, a military court convicted Gu of a number of crimes—including corruption, receiving bribes, embezzlement, bribery, and abuse of power—and sentenced Gu to suspended death.

27 Deng Fang (邓方)
   8/22/15

Facts of the Case: On 8/10/13, Deng murdered and raped victim Chen and took her 50 yuan. On 12/10/14, Deng raped and murdered Xie.

Legal History and Rulings: On 8/21/15, the intermediate people's court in Yueyang city (in Hunan province) convicted Deng of homicide, rape, robbery, and molestation of a corpse, and sentenced Deng to death.

28 Li Lei (李磊)
   8/28/15

Facts of the Case: Li (born in 1980) married Wang Meiling and had two sons. On 11/23/09, Li killed Wang, his two sons (one 6-year-old and one 2-year-old), his younger sister, and parents; he was arrested in December. Li was convicted of homicide and sentenced to death. After approval by the SPC, Li was executed on 9/16/11.

Legal History and Rulings: An inheritance lawsuit was filed by four surviving relatives. The people's court in Daxing district (in Beijing) ruled over this civil lawsuit, which was reported.

29 Hu Cunbiao (胡存彪) and Wang Yong (王勇)
   9/7/15; 9/8/15

Facts of the Case: From 2010 to 2012, Wang committed a series of rapes against 16 female students, including eight victims under 14 and eight others between 14 and 18. From 2004 to 2012, Hu committed a series of crimes, including rapes against 11 women (including seven victims under 14, and three others between 14 and 18), molestation against seven minors under 14 and another between 14 and 18, and eight robberies.

Legal History and Rulings: Wang was convicted and sentenced to death by the intermediate people's court in Wuhu city (in Anhui province); after SPC's approval, Wang was executed on 9/7/15. Hu was convicted and sentenced to death by the intermediate people's court in Zaozhuang city (in Shandong province). After the SPC's approval, Hu was executed.

30   Yuan Lijun (袁立军)
      9/9/15

Facts of the Case: On 1/28/12, Yuan had a fight with his wife, Wang, and Wang's son, Wang "x"xi. Yuan killed both, dismembered the bodies, and buried them. On 2/8/12, Yuan was arrested, and the victims' bodies were found based on Wang's confession.

Legal History and Rulings: On 9/8/15, Yuan was convicted and sentenced to death by the intermediate people's court in Zhuhai city (in Guangdong province).

31   Chen Yun (陈运)
      9/9/15

Facts of the Case: On 12/26/14, Chen got drunk after attending a party and consuming alcohol. He drove his vehicle at a 100 km/hour speed on a road with a 50 km/hour speed limit and killed six passengers. Chen called 120 for help and called his family as well after the accident. He took a taxi home to see his family but surrendered himself to the police around 11 o'clock that night. Chen's family compensated each victim's family with 23,000 yuan (over 130,000 yuan for six victims) and pled for leniency on Chen's behalf (and that of his two young sons).

Legal History and Rulings: On 9/8/15, Chen was convicted by the intermediate people's court in Bengbu city (in Anhui province) and sentenced to death.

32   Feng Xiujuan (冯秀娟, female)
      9/12/15

Facts of the Case: In July 2013, Feng started an affair with her first love, Liao. After Feng's husband learned about it, Feng asked for a divorce but was rejected. On 10/21/13, Feng purchased 10 bottles of rat poison and took her three children with her (one 8-year-old daughter, one 5-year-old daughter, and one 4-year-old son). On 10/22/13, she drowned the younger daughter and the son and strangled the older daughter to death. She drank the poison and cut her own wrist to commit suicide but survived.

Legal History and Rulings: Feng was convicted of homicide and sentenced to death by the intermediate people's court in Shaoguan city (in Guangdong province). On 12/9/14, the Guangdong High Court affirmed the trial court conviction and sentence, and the SPC approved the death sentence. On 9/11/15, the intermediate people's court in Shaoguan city executed Feng.

290　APPENDIX

33　　　Yang Chaoquan (杨朝全)
　　　　9/25/15

Facts of the Case: On 4/11/13, 37-year-old Yang burglarized a home and ran into the owner on his way out. Yang killed the 58-year-old owner and was arrested on 4/17.

Legal History and Rulings: Yang was convicted of robbery and burglary by the intermediate people's court in Yichang city (in Hubei province) and sentenced to death. His death sentence was approved by the SPC. On 9/18/15, Yang's parents and older brother visited him, and he apologized to his parents. At noon, Yang had his last meal with officer Yan (who was in charge) and bowed to Yan for his support over the last two years. Yang was executed afterward.

34　　　Lumei (禄眉氏, female), Huang Wenxie (黄文协) et al.
　　　　10/9/15

Facts of the Case: Led by Lumei and Huang Wenxie, a group of 15 criminals trafficked heroin (over 20 kilograms) from Vietnam to China from 2008 to 2013.

Legal History and Rulings: The provincial court in Liang Shan (Tinh Lang Son in Vietnamese) sentenced both Lumei and Huang to death.

35　　　Wang Jianghua (王江华) and Wang Jinpeng (王金朋)
　　　　10/15/15

Facts of the Case: Both Wangs were from Heilongjiang province and met in a laojiao facility in Zibo (in Shandong province) in July 2008; in 2009, both were released after serving their times. On 12/22/10, a couple who ran a jewelry store were robbed and injured. On 12/29/10, both Wangs robbed a jewelry store and caused the death of Li Wenyuan (31 years old). On 2/26/11, a female worker of a jewelry store was robbed and injured. Both Wangs were arrested on 3/6/11.

Legal History and Rulings: In December 2012, the intermediate people's court in Qingdao city (in Shandong province) convicted Wang Jianghua of homicide and Wang Jinpeng of robbery and sentenced both of them to death.

36　　　Huang "x" (黄某)
　　　　10/16/15

Facts of the Case: The 65-year-old Huang was a Hong Kong resident. On 8/18/13, he tried to smuggle 23.9 kilograms of cocaine from Brazil to Beijing and was detected.

Legal History and Rulings: On 10/16/15, Huang was convicted of drug trafficking and sentenced to death by the No. 3 intermediate people's court in Beijing.

37 Xiao "x" (肖某) et al.
    10/20/15

Facts of the Case: From November 2012 to December 2013, Xiao and his codefendants were trafficking illegal narcotics.

Legal History and Rulings: On 10/20/15, the intermediate people's court in Jingmen city (in Hubei province) sentenced Xiao "x" and Deng "x" to death; Chen "x", Zhang "x," and three others to suspended death; and 13 others to various punishment.

38 Zhao Xu (赵旭)
    10/23/15

Facts of the Case: The 42-year-old Zhao suspected that his wife, Hu, had an affair. On 11/5/13, he strangled his son to death and stabbed Hu to death.

Legal History and Rulings: Zhao was convicted of homicide and sentenced to death by the No. 2 intermediate people's court in Beijing. After the SPC's approval, Zhao was executed on 10/23/15.

39 Wang Zongren (王宗仁)
    10/27/15

Facts of the Case: Wang (69 years old) had dated victim Ying (70 years old) since 2009 and had an affair. In 2011, Wang divorced his wife. On 1/9/15, Wang got into a verbal fight with Ying and killed her. Wang dismembered her body and tried to flush it through the toilet and threw the rest into the sea. On 1/10/15, Wang was arrested.

Legal History and Rulings: Wang's trial started on 9/25/15. On 10/25/15, the intermediate people's court in Beihai city convicted Wang of homicide and sentenced him to death.

40 Deng "x" (邓某)
    11/4/15

Facts of the Case: Deng (46 years old) and victim Li (50 years old) were coworkers. Deng was invited to attend the wedding of Li's daughter in May 2014. Lacking gift money, Deng did not go. As a result, the two families got into in a verbal fight. Deng's wife, Xia, had a heart attack and was sent to hospital. Deng asked Li to reimburse him for the hospital bills but was rejected. On 8/3/14, Deng got into another verbal fight with Li, temporarily lost his sanity, and stabbed Li and his wife, Luo. Li died in the hospital.

Legal History and Rulings: The intermediate people's court in Guang'an city (in Sichuan province) sentenced Deng to death; Deng appealed.

41   Ling Ruiming (凌瑞明)
      11/6/15

Facts of the Case: In 2004, Ling married a Vietnamese lady, Ruan. Nevertheless, Ruan lived in other places, using the excuse of work. On 7/22/04, Ling went to Ruan's place, killed her and two other women, and injured two others. On 11/11/04, persuaded by family members, Ling surrendered to the police.

Legal History and Rulings: On 11/6/15, the intermediate people's court in Fangchenggang city convicted Ling and sentenced him to death. The court did not rule out the possibility that Ruan had committed marriage fraud.

42   He Shenguo (何深国)
      11/12/15

Facts of the Case: On 7/22/13, He tried to register his fourth child, but his request was denied. On 7/23/13, He came back with a knife and killed two workers at the registration office (Zhao "x" and Huang "x"han) and injured four others. He was arrested on site.

Legal History and Rulings: On 6/19/14, He was convicted of homicide and sentenced to death by the intermediate people's court in Fangchenggang city (in Guangxi province). On 11/16/14, the Guangxi High Court affirmed his death sentence. After his death sentence was approved, He was executed on 11/12/15.

43   Wang Yihuan (王逸环)
      11/12/15

Facts of the Case: On 8/6/2013, Wang stabbed victim Ye to death. Ye was a people's representative of Liunan district in Liuzhou city; Wang was a former member of the political consultation committee of the Liunan district. Wang argued that due to withdrawal of Ye's shares, Wang's wife's shares had suffered financial loss. Wang tried to talk to Ye several times but couldn't reach a solution. After killing Ye, Wang called 110 (emergency) and stayed on site for the police to arrest him.

Legal History and Rulings: On 8/26/14, the intermediate people's court of Liuzhou city (in Guangxi province) convicted Wang of homicide and sentenced him to death. The Guangxi High Court opened its trial of second instance on 12/24/14 and affirmed Wang's death sentence on 1/23/15. After the SPC's approval, Wang was executed on 11/12/15.

44   Gao Yulun (高玉伦) et al.
      11/13/15; 11/14/15

Facts of the Case: Gao and Li Haiwei and Wang Daming were imprisoned in the same cell due to previous convictions (homicide, homicide, and assault, respectively, in 2013 and 2014). They planned a prison break on 9/2/14 and killed a guard, Duan Baoren. Li, Wang, and Gao were rearrested on 9/3, 9/4, and 9/11, respectively.

Legal History and Rulings: All three were convicted of organizing a prison break (Gao and Wang as principals and Li as an accomplice), homicide, and assault. The intermediate people's court in Ha'erbing city (in Heilongjiang province) sentenced Gao and Wang to death and Li to life imprisonment on 11/13/15.

45   Liu "x" (刘某)
       11/17/15

Facts of the Case: Liu (20 years old) and his codefendant, Du (18 years old), abducted victim Liu (female, 34 years old) and robbed her of 22,000 yuan using her bank card on 6/3/14. On 6/4, they asked Liu's husband to pay 500,000 yuan as ransom. Liu "x" killed victim Liu to cover up his crime. On 12/8/2013, Liu and Du abducted 28-year-old Chang (female) and robbed her of 16,000 yuan via her bank card.

Legal History and Rulings: Liu was convicted of both kidnapping and robbery and was sentenced to death by the No. 2 intermediate people's court in Beijing on 11/17/15. Du, being a minor at the time of the crimes, self-surrendered and was sentenced to a 16-year imprisonment.

46   Song Yongtian (宋永田) et al.
       11/19/15

Facts of the Case: A group of five Taiwanese (led by 62-year-old Song, 44-year-old Wang Shangming, 53-year-old You Fulong, 42-year-old Ma Xinan, and 33-year-old Wang Mingshun) and two Cantonese (31-year-old Zhuo Chuyang and 39-year-old Cai Qijing) colluded in drug trafficking. On 8/22/12, they were arrested in Zhuhai and a total of 12 kilograms of narcotics were seized.

Legal History and Rulings: On 3/13/14, the intermediate people's court in Zhuhai city (in Guangdong province) sentenced Song to death, Wang, You, and Zhuo to suspended death, and the remaining offenders to other punishment. The trial court sentences were affirmed by the Guangdong High Court on 11/14/14. After the SPC's approval, Song was executed on 11/18/15.

47   Liu Danao (刘大孬)
       11/19/15; 11/20/15

Facts of the Case: On 6/1/2010, a demolition and relocation company planned to demolish some houses. Liu, in his white car, tried to stop the demolition and drove into the relocation team a few times. Liu fled from the crime scene but self-surrendered later. Four people were killed and many others injured. Reportedly, 302 of the 320 families of the village had signed a relocation agreement, including the Lius.

Legal History and Rulings: Liu was convicted and sentenced to death by the intermediate people's court in Zhengzhou city (in Henan province) on 11/23/10; the Henan High Court affirmed his death sentence. On 11/20/15, Liu was executed after the SPC approved his death sentence.

48	Yang "x"ping (杨某平) et al.
	11/21/15

Facts of the Case: In 2000, Yang, and his codefendants Yang "x"gui, Wang "x"rong, and Wang "x"hui broke into victim Gong's home for burglary and caused the death of Gong and his two daughters; Gong's wife survived. By June 2014, all four offenders were arrested.

Legal History and Rulings: The intermediate people's court in Yichang city (in Sichuan province) found Yang, Yang, and Wang "x"rong as principals of the crime and Wang "x"hui as an accomplice (due to his younger age and good attitude). All were convicted of robbery. The two Yangs and Wang "x"rong were sentenced to death; Wang "x"hui received a suspended death sentence.

49	Wu "x"hua (吴某华)
	11/22/15

Facts of the Case: On 6/15/15, Wu (52 years old) sneaked into Zheng's home and killed three people (Zheng "x"wei, 44; Zheng "x" [female], 73; and Zheng "xx" [the 8-year-old grandson of Zheng "x"]) and injured Zheng "x"you. Wu resisted police officers but was arrested after being injured by the police. Wu had a drug history of over 10 years and had been sentenced to three and a half years in 2003 for drug trafficking. He had served his time and was released in 2006.

Legal History and Rulings: On 11/20/15, Wu was tried by the intermediate people's court in Haikou city (in Hainan province); he expressed little remorse during his trial. On 12/10/15, Wu was convicted of homicide and sentenced to death.

50	He Jian (何剑)
	11/23/15; 11/24/15; 11/25/15

Facts of the Case: He had suicidal thoughts but decided to kill others. On 1/11/13, He killed a couple (male: 76, female: 70). On 3/7/14, He murdered another 28-year-old woman, Wu, and robbed her of 6,800 yuan using her bank card.

Legal History and Rulings: The intermediate people's court in Liuzhou city (in Guangxi province) started He's trial on 11/27/14 and ultimately convicted and sentenced He to death. After the SPC's approval, He was executed on 11/23/15.

51	Wang Baiyang (王佰阳)
	11/29/15

Facts of the Case: Born in 1976, Wang was a former police officer with a middle school education. To pay his gambling debts, Wang, along with codefendant Gao, abducted Yuan (27 years old) on 10/6/12 and asked for a ransom of two million yuan. Yuan's family raised 1.62 million. After receiving the ransom, Wang strangled Yuan to death. Wang was arrested on 11/13/12. During his detention, Wang planned an escape with three cellmates and promised each of them 50,000 yuan upon success. The escape failed on 1/25/13.

Legal History and Rulings: Wang was convicted of robbery, homicide, and organizing a prison escape. He was sentenced to death by the trial court, and the death sentence was affirmed by the Shan'xi High Court. On 9/11/15, the SPC interrogated Wang via long-distance technology. After the SPC's approval, Wang was executed on 11/27/15.

52	Wu Youxin (吴友新) et al.	
	12/2/15	

Facts of the Case: From 2009 to 2011, Wu and his codefendants (including Chen Xiaoxin, Liu Quanyou, and Liu Xianggang) murdered three miners (Liu "x," Zeng "x," and Pei "x") and fraudulently claimed compensation as family members of the deceased.

Legal History and Rulings: The intermediate people's court in Yangquan city (in Shan'xi province) convicted Wu, Chen, Liu, and Liu of homicide and sentenced them to death.

53	Yang Ruixi (杨瑞喜)	
	12/4/15	

Facts of the Case: On 8/17/12, Yang (49 years old) killed six people with his knife, including a 19-year-old girl, Xue; a 58-year-old, Liu; a 49-year-old, Zhang; and Zhang's father and wife.

Legal History and Rulings: In July 2013, the No. 2 intermediate people's court in Beijing sentenced Yang to death. After the SPC's approval, Yang was executed on 12/3/15.

54	Zhang "x"yi (张某一)	
	12/15/15	

Facts of the Case: On 1/28/15, victim Liu Yong (a 35-year-old police officer) witnessed a crime and tried to stop offender Zhang (who injured another with his knife). After being stabbed 16 times by Zhang, Liu died in a hospital. Zhang self-surrendered the next day. Liu was survived by his two sons (10 and 7 years old).

Legal History and Rulings: The intermediate people's court in Jingzhou city (in Hubei province) sentenced Zhang to death.

55	Li "xx" (李某某)	
	12/16/15	

Facts of the Case: Defendant Li was absconding after being pursued by the police for physically assaulting his ex-wife. Li run into victim Wang (the brother of his ex-wife) and Wang's son on the street. Wang called the police and tried to stop Li from taking off. Li stabbed Wang to death and was arrested by the police as he went after Wang's son.

Legal History and Rulings: Li was charged with homicide and assault. The intermediate people's court in Jinan city (in Shandong province) took into consideration marital and family disputes and sentenced Li to the death penalty with a two-year suspension. The People's Procuratorate decided to protest the ruling.

56   Pan Guohui (潘国辉) et al.
       12/16/15; 12/17/15;

Facts of the Case: A group of 19 drug traffickers were involved, including Pan Guohui, Pan Guoguang, Zhai Zhenfa, Pan Yunwei, Pan Yuefeng, Pan Yunwen, Zhong Rihua, Cheng Liuxiang, Lin Weifu, and others. From October 2013 to May 2014, they manufactured illegal narcotics (about 2,600 kilograms) five times.

Legal History and Rulings: On 12/16/15, the intermediate people's court in Huizhou city (in Guangdong province) sentenced Pan, Pan, Zhai, Pan, and Pan to death. Pan, Zhong, Cheng, and Lin received suspended death sentences.

57   Luo Xiaohua (罗小华) and Chen Rihong (陈日红)
       12/18/15

Facts of the Case: On 7/1/02, Luo and Chen met both victims (19 and 14, respectively) at a train station; they raped both girls and strangled them to death. On 6/6/13, it was determined that Luo's DNA matched the residuals at the crime scene. Luo and Chen were arrested on 6/8/13 and 7/4/13, respectively;

Legal History and Rulings: On 3/20/14, the intermediate people's court in Shaoguang city (in Hunan province) convicted both men of rape and homicide and sentenced Luo to death and Chen to suspended death. On 12/9/14, their death sentences were affirmed by the Hunan High Court. After the SPC's approval, the intermediate people's court in Shaoguang carried out Luo's execution on 12/17/15.

58   Li "x" (李某)
       12/22/15

Facts of the Case: On 6/10/14, Li asked for 50,000 yuan from his father and was rejected. Li had a verbal fight with his mother-in-law in the metro. Police on site took both to the police office and released both after two hours. Li's mother-in-law again used abusive language; Li lost control and stabbed her three times. She died in a hospital, and Li was later arrested. Li (36 years old) seemed to have gambling issues. His parents had divorced when Li was eight. Li's father gave him 10,000 yuan to pay for his debts. Li divorced his wife in 2013 and claimed that he was planning to use the 50,000 yuan he had requested to remarry his ex-wife.

Legal History and Rulings: On 12/21/15, Li was convicted of homicide and sentenced to death by the intermediate people's court in Nanjing. Li's father expressed his opinion that he would like to see Li being sentenced to death.

59 Jin Fusheng (金复生)
   12/24/15; 12/25/15;

Facts of the Case: Due to disputes with Beijing Sanlitun Economic Management Center, Jin drove a vehicle and crashed into an employed driver of the center and then into a crowd of 11 people, killing three. Jin attempted to attack Wang (another employee of the center) in July 2014 with his car but failed.

Legal History and Rulings: On 12/24/15, the No. 3 intermediate people's court in Beijing convicted Jin of endangering public security and attempted homicide and sentenced him to death. Jin's defense pointed out that when Jin was hospitalized in the No. 2 detention center, he tried to save a suicidal inmate on 1/25, which should be weighed as mitigation. This argument was accepted by the court but ruled insufficient to save Jin's life.

60 Zhao Zihui (赵子辉)
   12/25/15; 12/26/15; 12/27/15

Facts of the Case: On 3/27/14, Zhao (born in 1982; 32 years old) stabbed 18 people, causing six deaths (a 73-year-old male, a 67-year-old female, a 64-year-old female, a 59-year-old male, a 24-year-old male, and a 23-year-old female).

Legal History and Rulings: On 12/25/15, the No. 3 intermediate people's court in Beijing convicted Zhao of homicide and sentenced him to death. Zhao's defense claimed Zhao's psychiatric history as mitigation; the prosecution argued that Zhao should bear limited criminal responsibility. Zhao's defense argument about his self-surrender was rejected by the court.

61 Li "x" (李某) #2
   12/28/15

Facts of the Case: In 2007, Li's wife, Zhang, asked for a divorce. Out of anger, Li went to Zhang's mother's home and attacked Zhang and her mother with a knife. Zhang was injured and her mother died. Li was arrested on site.

Legal History and Rulings: Li was convicted of homicide and sentenced to death. Afterward, Zhang found out that Li owned a house. Zhang and her daughter sued Li's mother. Given the fact that there was no valid will, the people's court in Miyun (in Beijing) divided the property equally among three parties.

62 Yang Xueqi (杨学奇)
   12/29/15; 12/30/15

Facts of the Case: Born on 2/3/70, Yang was of Han ethnicity with an elementary school education. From 1998 to 2012, Yang committed eight rapes and 10 attempted rapes; he also committed three thefts with a total value of 4,200 yuan. Only two of his 14 victims reported the crimes. The average age of victims was 16, and two were minors. On 3/28/12, the police matched Yang's DNA with the residuals on the crime scenes. Yang was arrested on 5/9/12. From 1987, Yang was sentenced five times for theft, robbery, and escape, and served prison terms five times. Yang confessed that his wife was a lesbian, which made him angry, and he had decided to retaliate after his divorce.

Legal History and Rulings: On 5/7/13, Yang was convicted of rape and molestation and sentenced to death by the intermediate people's court in Xuchang city (in Henan province). The Henan High Court affirmed Yang's death sentence on 12/11/13, and his death sentence was approved by the SPC on 12/25/14.

63   Ou Changsheng (欧长生)
      12/30/15; 12/31/15

Facts of the Case: From June to July 2014, Ou prepared seven bomb devices. On 7/15/14, Ou boarded and bombed a bus (No. 301), killed two people, and injured many others. He was arrested on 7/16/2014.

Legal History and Rulings: On 12/30/15, the intermediate people's court in Guangzhou (in Guangdong province) convicted Ou of explosion and sentenced him to death.

APPENDIX 2

List of Officially Charged Crimes and Number of Offenders Being Charged

Crimes (number of multiple offenders)	Jan.	Feb.	Mar.	Apr.	May	June	July	Aug.	Sep.	Oct.	Nov.	Dec.	Total
Homicide	1	1	1 (2)	1	3	3	3 (8)	2	2	3	9 (10)	8 (12)	37 (48)
Kidnapping children	1												1
Criminal gang organization and involvement		1 (5)						1 (3)					2 (8)
Corruption-related offenses		1 (2)						1					2 (3)
Terrorism			1 (3)										1 (3)
Arson			1										1
Drug offenses				1 (2)	1	2 (6)				3 (10)	1 (4)	1 (9)	9 (32)
Sexual offenses		1			2 (4)		1	1	1 (2)			2 (3)	8 (12)
Bomb explosion												1	1
Robbery, kidnapping & theft							1 (2)		1	1 (2)	3 (6)		6 (11)
Endangerment of public safety									1		1	1	3
Total	2	4 (9)	3 (6)	2 (3)	6 (8)	5 (9)	5 (11)	5 (7)	5 (6)	7 (15)	14 (21)	13 (26)	71 (123)

Note: (1) Blank cells indicate a "zero count"; (2) some offenders were charged with multiple offenses (e.g., rape and homicide). As a result, the total number of crimes ($n = 71$) is more than the total number of cases ($n = 63$).

APPENDIX 3

Total Numbers of Netizens' Comments, Reply Comments, and Use of Foul Language

Cases	Comments (n)	Replies (n)	Comments with foul language (n)
Lin Senhao	17,611	5,683	4,902
Huang Qinghen	1,505	5	9
Peng Shu & Hu Haolong	123	26	3
Zhao Zhihong	104	12	11
Liu Han et al.	26	2	2
Tuo Heti et al.	35		11
Hu "x"	138	17	9
Wang Yuefu	6		
Zhai "x"de	58	16	11
Ruan Fangcheng et al.	8		1
Wu Qinyuan	70	18	2
Yuan Junkai et al.	535	86	84
Wang Gang	140	39	9
Lian Enqing	4,660	2,433	1,902
Zhang Xiangxi	58	16	8
Lin "x"ping and Ye "x"tian	1,981	928	656
Sun Zhifu	28	6	
Liang Kaiwu	18	2	5
Wang Changping et al.	281	76	164
Zhang Weilan et al.	739	169	121
Yang Dazhi	256	35	53
Wang "x"	18	4	
Fan Jieming	571	181	42
Zheng Dalong and Yang Shengjian	22	4	4
Wang Hua et al.	22	2	
Gu Junshan	12		
Deng Fang	89	22	8
Li Lei	248	98	73
Hu Cunbiao and Wang Yong	304	67	66
Yuan Lijun	5		

Appendix 3—(*continued*)

Cases	Comments (*n*)	Replies (*n*)	Comments with foul language (*n*)
Chen Yun	130	22	5
Feng Xiujuan	334	117	96
Yang Chaoquan	782	343	172
Lumei et al.	28	3	
Wang Jianghua and Wang Jinpeng	3		
Huang "x"	42	12	2
Xiao "x"	5		
Zhao Xu	41	12	7
Wang Zongren	3	1	
Deng "x"	28	4	2
Ling Ruiming	44	13	20
He Shenguo	730	309	200
Wang Yihuan	75	18	9
Gao Yulun et al.	219	72	39
Liu "x"	22	5	
Song Yongtian et al.	58	3	6
Liu Danao	3,221	221	312
Yang "x"ping et al.	18	3	1
Wu "x"hua	309	23	60
He Jian	72	4	14
Wang Baiyang	32	2	4
Wu Youxin et al.	113	9	23
Yang Ruixi	37	13	13
Zhang "x"yi	87	36	24
Li "xx"	239	13	33
Pan Guohui et al.	6		
Luo Xiaohua and Chen Rihong	242	22	39
Li "x"	3		
Jin Fusheng	178	16	35
Zhao Zihui	198	15	22
Li "x" (#2)	3		
Yang Xueqi	1,394	50	231
Ou Changsheng	145	10	39
Total	**38,512**	**11,318**	**9,564**

Note: Blank cells indicate a "zero count."

APPENDIX 4

Basic Reporting Statistics by Cases

Cases	Number of words	With video(s)?	Length of video	With picture(s)?	Other useful information
Lin Senhao	1,468*	21	3 min. 55 sec. (avg.)	38	
Huang Qinghen	989			2	
Peng Shu and Hu Haolong	1,704	1	1 min. 52 sec.	1	
Zhao Zhihong	1,128*	2	1 min. 23 sec. (avg.)	4	Educational paragraph in the May 1 story
Liu Han et al.	198	2	9 min. 27 sec. (avg.)	2	
Tuo Heti et al.	228				
Hu "x"	2,367	1	3 min.	4	
Wang Yuefu	460			1	
Zhai "x"de	457				
Ruan Fangcheng et al.	650				
Wu Qinyuan	1,602			1	Interview of the wrongfully convicted Yu Yingsheng
Yuan Junkai et al.	1,012				
Wang Gang	111				
Lian Enqing	334			6	
Zhang Xiangxi	853				
Lin "x"ping & Ye "x"tian	768			9	
Sun Zhifu	570				
Liang Kaiwu	2,249				
Wang Changping et al.	1,643				
Zhang Weilan et al.	1,055				
Yang Dazhi	948			2	
Wang "x"	621				

Appendix 4.—*(continued)*

Cases	Number of words	With video(s)?	Length of video	With picture(s)?	Other useful information
Fan Jieming	749	1	1 min. 46 sec.	2	
Zheng Dalong and Yang Shengjian	620				
Wang Hua et al.	729				
Gu Junshan	89				
Deng Fang	556				
Li Lei	1,084	1	2 min. 3 sec.		
Hu Cunbiao and Wang Yong	574*				Interview of a judge who was in charge of the case
Yuan Lijun	474				
Chen Yun	1,876			1	Description of the judgment day in courtroom; interview of a judge who commented on sentencing
Feng Xiujuan	707				
Yang Chaoquan	924*			6	
Lumei et al.	842			4	
Wang Jianghua and Wang Jinpeng	4,924				
Huang "x"	1,126*			1	
Xiao "x"	586				
Zhao Xu	362				
Wang Zongren	568*			2	
Deng "x"	2,183				
Ling Ruiming	885				
He Shenguo	794*			2	
Wang Yihuan	1,304			1	
Gao Yulun et al.	625*	2	2 min. 42 sec. (avg.)	18	Three responsible officials reportedly held accountable
Liu "x"	747				
Song Yongtian et al.	668*				
Liu Danao	667*			4	

Appendix 4.—(continued)

Cases	Number of words	With video(s)?	Length of video	With picture(s)?	Other useful information
Yang "x"ping et al.	493				
Wu "x"hua	2,924			2	Information on victim, conflicts between Wu and victim, and Wu's family relationship reported
He Jian	346*	1	3 min. 33 sec.		
Wang Baiyang	1,118				
Wu Youxin et al.	1,138			1	
Yang Ruixi	196*	1	3 min. 7 sec.		
Zhang "x"yi	1,496			1	Victim's family information reported
Li "xx"	1,266			2	
Pan Guohui et al.	1,579			2	
Luo Xiaohua and Chen Rihong	982				
Li "x"	593				
Jin Fusheng	581*	4	2 min. 50 sec.	2	Defense lawyer's opinion mentioned; and interviewed other lawyers
Zhao Zihui	862*				Follow-up report and follow-up interview with defense lawyer
Li "x" (#2)	1,541				
Yang Xueqi	2,603	1	55 sec.		Judicial judgment attached
Ou Changsheng	672				
Average	1,023				

Note: (1) Blank cells indicate a "zero count"; (2) the number of words with an asterisk "*" is the average word count of all reports in a case.

APPENDIX 5

Select List of Foul Words

屁 (fart)	有病 (holy crap)	贱 (contemptible)	畸形 (deformed)	屎 (shit)	粪 (shit)
狗 (dog)	变态 (maniac)	脑残 (brain damaged)	装逼 (being pretentious)	畜生 (animal)	垃圾 (trash)
辣鸡 (trash)	傻逼 (asshole)	Sb (asshole)	2b (stupid asshole)	渣滓 (dregs)	Tm (fuck)
老东西 (old fool)	人渣 (scumbag)	败类 (scumbag)	妈逼 (fuck)	Mb (fuck)	恶魔 (devil)
无赖 (rascal)	讼棍 (pettifogger)	他妈的 (fuck)	好东西 (evil)	恶魔 (devil)	妈的 (fuck)
麻痹 (fuck)	猪 (pig)	胡说 (nonsense)	不要脸 (shameless)	Tmd (fuck)	

References

Belkin, I. 2017. Justice in the PRC: How the Chinese Community Party has struggled with managing public opinion and the administration of criminal justice in the Internet age. In *Justice: The China experience*, ed. F. Sapio, S. Trevaskes, S. Biddulph, and E. Nesossi, 195–228. Cambridge: Cambridge University Press.

Biao, X. 2007. How far are the left-behind left behind? A preliminary study in rural China. *Population, Space, and Place* 13: 179–91.

Blumenthal, D., and W. Hsiao. 2015. Lessons from the East—China's rapidly evolving health care system. *New England Journal of Medicine* 372 (14): 1281–85.

Bohm, R. 1987. American death penalty attitudes: A critical examination of recent evidence. *Criminal Justice and Behavior* 14 (3): 380–96.

Bohm, R. 1992. Retribution and capital punishment: Toward a better understanding of death penalty opinion. *Journal of Criminal Justice* 20 (3): 227–36.

Bohm, R. 2017. *Deathquest: An introduction to the theory and practice of capital punishment in the United States* (5th ed.). London: Routledge.

Bohm, R., L. Clark, and A. Aveni. 1990. The influence of knowledge on reasons for death penalty opinions: An experimental test. *Justice Quarterly* 7 (1): 175–88.

Bohm, R., R. Vogel, and A. Maistro. 1993. Knowledge and death penalty opinions: A panel study. *Journal of Criminal Justice* 21 (1): 29–45.

Bowers, W., M. Vandiver, and P. Dugan. 1994. A new look at public opinion on capital punishment: What citizens and legislators prefer. *American Journal of Criminal Law* 22 (1): 77–150.

Boyazis, R. 1998. *Transforming qualitative information: Thematic analysis and code development*. Thousand Oaks, CA: Sage.

Brace, P., and B. Boyea. 2008. State public opinion, the death penalty, and the practice of electing judges. *American Journal of Political Science* 52 (2): 360–72.

Britt, C. 1998. Race, religion, and support for the death penalty: A research note. *Justice Quarterly* 15 (1): 175–91.

Burgason, K., and L. Pazzani 2014. The death penalty: A multi-level analysis of public opinion. *American Journal of Criminal Justice* 39 (4): 818–38.

Cao, L. 2007. Returning to normality: Anomie and crime in China. *International Journal of Offender Therapy and Comparative Criminology* 51 (1): 40–51.

Cao, L., and F. Cullen. 2001. Thinking about crime and control: A comparative study of Chinese and American ideology. *International Criminal Justice Review* 11: 58–81.

Cao, S. 2006. The empirical study on the school adaptation of the left-behind children. *Youth Studies* 3: 16–19.

Caron, E. 2013. Interactions between chengguan and street vendors in Beijing: How the unpopularity of an administration affects relations with the public. *China Perspectives* 1: 17–28.

Chen, J., and R. N. Lai. 2013. Pricing relocation-redevelopment projects for city expansion: The case in China. *Real Estate Economics* 41 (4): 925–57.

Chen, R. 2000. From streamline operation to centering on adjudication: A thought on the reform of criminal justice in China [in Chinese]. *Legal Studies* (法学) 3: 24–34.

Chen, X. 2017. Parental migration, caretaking arrangement, and children's delinquent behavior in rural China. *Asian Journal of Criminology* 12 (4): 281–302.

Chen, X., Q. Huang, S. Rozelle, Y. Shi, and L. Zhang. 2009. Effect of migration on children's educational performance in rural China. *Comparative Economic Studies* 51 (3): 323–43.

Chen, X., and X. Jiang. 2019. Are grandparents better caretakers? Parental migration, caretaking arrangements, children's self-control, and delinquency in rural China. *Crime and Delinquency* 65 (8): 1123–48.

Chen, X., N. Liang, and S. F. Ostertag. 2017. Victimization of children left behind in rural China. *Journal of Research in Crime and Delinquency* 54 (4): 515–43.

Cheong, T. S., and Y. Wu. 2015. Crime rates and inequality: A study of crime in contemporary China. *Journal of the Asia Pacific Economy* 20 (2): 202–23.

Chi, X., and L. Ding. 2016. On conflict and compromise between online public opinion and judicial trials: The Fudan poisoning case as an example [in Chinese]. *Journal on News Research* (新闻研究导刊) 7 (11): 47.

China Internet Network Information Center (CNNIC) 2017. The 39th China Statistical Report on Internet Development (available at http://www.cnnic.cn/).

China Internet Network Information Center (CNNIC) 2019. The 43rd China Statistical Report on Internet Development (available at http://www.cnnic.cn/).

China Population and Employment Statistics Yearbook. 2018. Beijing: China Statistics Press.

China's Top Court Rejects Judicial Independence as "Erroneous Thought": Blow for hopes of reform as country's most senior judge, Zhou Qiang, urges Community [*sic*, Communist] party to resist "mistaken viewpoints" including separation of powers. *The Guardian*, February 26, 2015 (https://www.theguardian.com/world/2015/feb/26/chinas-top-court-rejects-judicial-independence-as-erroneous-thought) (accessed March 26, 2019).

China Statistical Yearbook. 2018 (available at http://www.stats.gov.cn/tjsj/ndsj/2018/indexch.htm).

Cochran, J. K., and M. B. Chamlin. 2006. The enduring racial divide in death penalty support. *Journal of Criminal Justice* 34: 85–99.

Cullen, F. T., B. S. Fisher, and B. K. Applegate. 2000. Public opinion about punishment and corrections. *Crime and Justice* 27: 1–79.

Cummings, L. 2002. Why we need to avoid theorizing about rationality: A Putnamian criticism of Habermas's epistemology. *Social Epistemology* 16 (2): 117–31.

Dallmayr, F. 1988. Habermas and rationality. *Political Theory* 16 (4): 553–79.

Deng, X., and A. Cordilia. 1999. To get rich is glorious: Rising expectations, declining control, and escalating crime in contemporary China. *International Journal of Offender Therapy and Comparative Criminology* 43 (2): 211–29.

Deng, X., L. Zhang, and A. Leverentz. 2010. Official corruption during China's economic transition: Historical patterns, characteristics, and government reactions. *Journal of Contemporary Criminal Justice* 26 (1): 72–88.

Deng, Y. 2017. "Autonomous redevelopment": Moving the masses to remove nail households. *Modern China* 43 (5): 494–522.

Durham, A., P. Elrod, and P. Kinkade. 1996. Public support for the death penalty: Beyond Gallup. *Justice Quarterly* 13 (4): 705–736.

Ebenstein, A. 2010. The "missing girls" of China and the unintended consequences of the one child policy. *Journal of Human Resources* 45 (1): 87–115.

Ellsworth, P. C., and L. Ross. 1983. Public opinion and capital punishment: A close examination of the views of abolitionists and retentionists. *Crime and Delinquency* 29 (1): 116–69.

Falco, D., and T. Freiburger. 2011. Public opinion and the death penalty: A qualitative approach. *Qualitative Report* 16 (3): 830–47.

Fan, D. P., K. A. Keltner, and R. O. Wyatt. 2002. A matter of guilt or innocence: How news reports affect support for the death penalty in the United States. *International Journal of Public Opinion Research* 14 (4): 439–52.

Fan, F., L. Su, M. K. Gill, B. and Birmaher. 2010. Emotional and behavioral problems of Chinese left-behind children: A preliminary study. *Social Psychiatry and Psychiatric Epidemiology* 45 (6): 655–64.

Feng, Y. 2009. Urban housing demolition and relocation in China. *New Zealand Association of Comparative Law Yearbook* 15: 117–43.

Feteris, E. 2003. The rationality of legal discourse in Habermas's discourse theory. *Informal Logic* 23 (2): 139–59.

Fu, H. 2016. Between deference and defiance: courts and penal populism in Chinese capital cases. In Liang and Lu, *Death penalty in China*, 274–99.

Gao, X., and J. Long. 2015. On the petition system in China. *University of St. Thomas Law Journal* 12: 34–55.

Gao, Y., and Y. Liu. 2015. A survey of high school student life education: On life education related issues from the Lin Senhao poisoning case [in Chinese]. *Jichu Jiaoyu Yanjiu* (基础教育研究) 7: 22–24.

Goodkind, D. 2017. The astonishing population averted by China's birth restrictions: Estimates, nightmares, and reprogrammed ambitions. *Demography* 54: 1375–1400.

Gong, T. 1997. Forms and characteristics of China's corruption in the 1990s: Change with continuity. *Communist and Post-Communist Studies* 30 (3): 277–88.

Gong, T. 2002. Dangerous collusion: Corruption as a collective venture in contemporary China. *Communist and Post-Communist Studies* 35: 85–103.

Gong, T. 2003. More than mere words, less than hard law: A rhetorical analysis of China's anticorruption policy. *Public Administration Quarterly* 27: 159–87.

Gong, T. 2006. Corruption and local governance: The double identity of Chinese local governments in market reform. *Pacific Review* 19: 85–102.

Gunaratne, S. A. 2006. Public sphere and communicative rationality: Interrogating Habermas's eurocentrism. *Journalism and Communication Monographs* 8 (2): 93–156.

Guo, Y. 2008. Corruption in transitional China: An empirical analysis. *China Quarterly* 194: 349–64.

Habermas, J. 1984/1987. *The theory of communicative action* (Vols. 1 & 2). Boston: Beacon Press.

Habermas, J. 1989. *The structural transformation of the public sphere: An inquiry into a category of bourgeois society*. Cambridge: MIT Press.

Han, H., X. Shu, and X. Ye. 2018. Conflicts and regional culture: The general features and cultural background of illegitimate housing demolition in China. *Habitat International* 75: 67–77.

Hanser, A. 2016. Street politics: Street vendors and urban governance in China. *China Quarterly* 226: 363–82.

Harris, P. 1986. Over-simplification and error in public opinion surveys on capital punishment. *Justice Quarterly* 3 (4): 429–55.

Hartford, K. 2000. Cyberspace with Chinese characteristics. *Current History* 99 (638): 255–62.

Harwit, E. 2008. *China's telecommunications revolution*. Oxford: Oxford University Press.

Hassid, J. 2008. Controlling the Chinese media: An uncertain business. *Asian Survey* 48 (3): 414–30.

He, J. 2016. *Back from the dead: Wrongful convictions and criminal justice in China*. Honolulu: University of Hawai'i Press.

He, Z. 2000. Corruption and anti-corruption in reform China. *Communist and Post-Communist Studies* 33: 243–70.

He, Z. 2009. On choice of capital offenses and guidance of minyi in China's death penalty reform [in Chinese]. *Criminal Science* (中国刑事法杂志) 1: 111–17.

Herold, D. K., and P. Marolt, eds. 2011. *Online society in China: Creating, celebrating, and instrumentalising the online carnival*. London: Routledge.

Hood, R. 2018. Is public opinion a justifiable reason not to abolish the death penalty? A comparative analysis of surveys of eight countries. *Berkeley Journal of Criminal Law* 23 (3): 218–42.

Hsiao, W. 1995. The Chinese health care system: Lessons for other nations. *Social Science and Medicine* 41 (8): 1047–1055.

Hsieh, M., and F. D. Boateng. 2015. Perceptions of democracy and trust in the criminal justice system: A comparison between mainland China and Taiwan. *International Criminal Justice Review* 25 (2): 153–73.

Hu, H., S. Lu, and C. Huang. 2014. The psychological and behavioral outcomes of migrant and left-behind children in China. *Children and Youth Services Review* 46: 1–10.

Hu, M., and M. Dai. 2014. Confidence in the criminal justice system: Differences between citizens and criminal justice officials in China. *Criminology and Criminal Justice* 14 (4): 503–24.

Hu, M., B. Liang, and S. Huang. 2017. Sex offenses against minors in China: An empirical comparison. *International Journal of Offender Therapy and Comparative Criminology* 61 (10): 1099–1124.

Hu, S., S. Tang, Y. Liu, Y. Zhao, M. Escobar, and D. de Ferranti. 2008. Reform of how health care is paid for in China: Challenges and opportunities. *The Lancet* 372 (22): 1846–53.

Huang, L. 2015. Research on the personality education of teenagers: The Fudan University 4.1 case of poisoning [in Chinese]. Master's thesis. Northeast Normal University.

Huang, X., M. Dijst, and J. van Weesep. 2017. Social networks of rural–urban migrants after residential relocation: Evidence from Yangzhou, a medium-sized Chinese city. *Housing Studies* 32 (6): 816–40.

Jacobs, D., and S. Kent. 2007. The determinants of executions since 1951: How politics, protests, public opinion, and social divisions shape capital punishment. *Social Problems* 54 (3): 297–318.

Jia, J. 2016. On the basis of public opinion of the death penalty [in Chinese]. *Legality Vision* (法制博览) 3: 139–40.

Jiang, Q., S. Li, and M. W. Feldman. 2013. China's population policy at the crossroads: Social impacts and prospects. *Asian Journal of Social Science* 41 (2): 193–218.

Jiang, Q., and Y. Liu. 2016. Low fertility and concurrent birth control policy in China. *History of the Family* 21 (4): 551–77.

Jiang, Q., and J. J. Sánchez-Barricarte. 2013. Child trafficking in China. *China Report* 49 (3): 317–35.

Jiang, S. 2016. Public opinion and the death penalty. In Liang and Lu, *Death penalty in China*, 247–73.

Jiang, S., E. Lambert, and V. Nathan. 2009. Reasons for death penalty attitudes among Chinese citizens: Retributive or instrumental? *Journal of Criminal Justice* 37: 225–33.

Jiang, S., E. Lambert, and J. Wang. 2007. Capital punishment views in China and the United States: A preliminary study among college students. *International Journal of Offender Therapy and Comparative Criminology* 51 (1): 84–97.

Jiang, S., E. Lambert, J. Wang, T. Saito, and R. Pilot 2010. Death penalty views in China, Japan, and the U.S.: An empirical comparison. *Journal of Criminal Justice* 38 (5): 862–69.

Johnson, D. T., and M. Miao. 2016. Chinese capital punishment in comparative perspective. In Liang and Lu, *Death penalty in China*, 300–326.

Johnson, D. T., and F. E. Zimring. 2009. *The next frontier: National development, political change, and the death penalty in Asia.* Oxford: Oxford University Press.

Jones, P. 1994. It's not what you ask, it is the way that you ask it: Question form and public opinion on the death penalty. *Prison Journal* 73 (1): 32–50.

Kelley, J., and J. Braithwaite. 1990. Public opinion and the death penalty in Australia. *Justice Quarterly* 7 (3): 529–63.

King, G., J. Pan, and M. E. Roberts. 2013. How censorship in China allows government criticism but silences collective expression. *American Political Science Review* 107 (2): 326–43.

King, G., J. Pan, and M. E. Roberts. 2017. How the Chinese government fabricates social media posts for strategic distraction, not engaged argument. *American Political Science Review* 111 (3): 484–501.

Kluver, R. 2005. US and Chinese policy expectation of the Internet. *China Information* 19 (2): 299–324.

Ko, K., and C. Weng. 2012. Structural changes in Chinese corruption. *China Quarterly* 211: 718–40.

Kong, D. 2017. Public opinion of capital punishment and its retention and abolition [in Chinese]. *Modern Communication* (现代交际) 14: 78–80.

Kuang, L., Y. Zeng, K. Li, S. Liu, M. Chen, C. Dai, and X. Zhang. 2010. A survey on criminal justice professionals' attitudes toward the death penalty [in Chinese]. In *Opinion survey report on China's death penalty*, ed. D. Oberwittler, S. Qi, L. Kuang, Y. Zeng, K. Li, S. Liu, X. Chen, Y. Dai, and S. Zhang, 63–224. Taibei: Yuanzhao Press.

Lagerkvist, J. 2010. *After the Internet, before democracy: Competing norms in Chinese media and society.* Bern, Switzerland: Peter Lang.

Lambert, E., and A. Clarke. 2001. The impact of information on an individual's support of the death penalty: A partial test of the Marshall hypothesis among college students. *Criminal Justice Policy Review* 12 (3): 215–34.

Lao, D. 2015. A reconstruction of death penalty application standards [in Chinese]. *Chinese Journal of Law* (法学研究) 1: 170–90.

Lee, M. H. 2011. Migration and children's welfare in China: The schooling and health of children left behind. *Journal of Developing Areas* 44 (2): 165–82.

Li, B., and H. Zhang. 2017. Does population control lead to better child quality? Evidence from China's one-child policy enforcement. *Journal of Comparative Economics* 45: 246–60.

Li, E. 2016. The difficulties in China's death penalty systemic reform and solutions [in Chinese]. *Journal of Wuling* (武陵学刊) 41 (4): 53–61.

Li, J. 1995. China's one-child policy: How and how well has it worked? A case study of Hebei province, 1979–88. *Population and Development Review* 21 (3): 563–85.

Li, L. 2012. The production of corruption in China's courts: Judicial politics and decision making in a one-party state. *Law and Social Inquiry* 37 (4): 848–77.

Li, L., M. Liu, and K. J. O'Brien. 2012. Petitioning Beijing: The high tide of 2003–2006. *China Quarterly* 210: 313–34.

Li, M. 2015. A psychological analysis of crimes committed by people with high IQs: The Fudan poisoning case as an example [in Chinese]. *Journal of Chinese Youth Social Science* (中国青年社会科学) 34 (4): 1–10.

Li, W. 2007. An analysis of public opinion and the fate of the death penalty [in Chinese]. *Legal System and Society* (法制与社会) 1: 58–59.

Li, Y., Q. Wu, L. Xu, D. Legge, Y. Hao, L. Gao, N. Ning, and G. Wan 2012. Factors affecting catastrophic health expenditure and impoverishment from medical expenses in China: Policy implications of universal health insurance. *Bull World Health Organ* 90: 664–71.

Li, Z. 2012. Revival and development of the criminal reconciliation system in China. *Social Sciences in China* 33 (4): 168–78.

Liang, B. 2005. Severe strike campaign in transitional China. *Journal of Criminal Justice* 33 (4): 387–99.

Liang, B. 2008. *The changing Chinese legal system, 1978—Present: Centralization of power and rationalization of the legal system*. London: Routledge.

Liang, B. 2014. Internet development and its influences on legal reform in China. *China: An International Journal* 12 (3): 27–54.

Liang, B. 2016. China's death penalty practice: Working progress, struggle, and challenges within the global abolition movement. In Liang and Lu, *Death penalty in China*, 1–30.

Liang, B., J. Liu, and H. Lu. 2019. Variability of death penalty attitude in China: An empirical test of the Marshall hypotheses. *Crime, Law and Social Change* 72 (3): 269–302.

Liang, B., and H. Lu. 2010. Internet development, censorship, and cybercrimes in China. *Journal of Contemporary Criminal Justice* 26 (1): 103–120.

Liang, B., and H. Lu, eds. 2016. *The death penalty in China: Policy, practice, and reform*. New York: Columbia University Press.

Liang, B., H. Lu, T. D. Miethe, and L. Zhang. 2006. Sources of variation in pro-death penalty attitudes in China. *British Journal of Criminology* 46: 119–30.

Liang, B., and C. Wilson. 2008. A critical review of past studies on China's corrections and recidivism. *Crime, Law, and Social Change: An International Journal* 50 (3): 245–62.

Liebman, B. L. 2013. Malpractice mobs: Medical dispute resolution in China. *Columbia Law Review* 113: 181–264.

Liebman, B. L. 2015. Leniency in Chinese criminal law? Everyday justice in Henan. *Berkeley Journal of International Law* 33 (1): 153–222.

Liu, G., X. Yi, and Y. Zhang. 2013. The tradition of public opinion and the current basis of China's death penalty [in Chinese]. *Academic Exchange* (学术交流) 231 (6): 86–89.

Liu, J. 2005. Crime patterns during the market transition in China. *British Journal of Criminology* 45: 613–33.

Liu, J. 2006. Modernization and crime patterns in China. *Journal of Criminal Justice* 34: 119–30.

Liu, S., and T. C. Halliday. 2016. *Criminal defense in China: The politics of lawyers at work*. Cambridge: Cambridge University Press.

Liu, S., M. Xiong, and B. Liang. 2019. The death penalty for foreign drug offenders in China: Legal protection and equal treatment. *European Journal on Criminal Policy and Research* 25 (4): 427–48.

Liu, Y. 2004. Development of the rural health insurance system in China. *Health Policy and Planning* 19 (3): 159–65.

Liu, Y., W. C. Hsiao, and K. Eggleston. 1999. Equity in health and health care: The Chinese experience. *Social Science and Medicine* 49: 1349–56.

Lu, H., Y. Li, and C. Hu. 2016. Criminal justice system and the death penalty. In Liang and Lu, *Death penalty in China*, 31–61.

Lu, H., and T. D. Miethe. 2007. *China's death penalty: History, law, and contemporary practice*. London: Routledge.

Lu, H., T. Miethe, and B. Liang. 2009. *China's drug practices and policies: Regulating controlled substances in a global context*. Burlington, VT: Ashgate.

Lu, H., T. Trejbalova, and B. Liang. 2019. Proceduralism, political embeddedness, and death penalty lawyers in China. *China Quarterly* 238: 353–74.

Lu, J. 2004. The criminal policy significance of the suspended death penalty system and its expansion [in Chinese]. *The Jurist* (法学家) 5: 137–41.

Lu, J. 2005. On application of the death penalty and public opinion [in Chinese]. *Journal of Zhengzhou University (Philosophy and Social Science Edition)* (郑州大学学报哲学社会科学版) 38 (5): 107–109.

Lu, J. 2015a. Death penalty reform in China in light of human rights [in Chinese]. *Journal of Beijing Normal University (Social Science Edition)* (北京师范大学学报社会科学版) 3: 124–32.

Lu, J. 2015b. A historical reflection on the Huugjilt case [in Chinese]. *China Law Review* (中国法律评论) 3: 25–30.

Lu, J. 2015c. A scientific interpretation of death penalty policies [in Chinese]. *Peking University Law Journal* (中外法学) 3: 614–21.

Lu, J., and S. Li. 2006. The choice of route to abolish the death penalty in China [in Chinese]. *Journal of Gansu Institute of Political Science and Law* (甘肃政法学院学报) 7: 45–55.

Lu, J., and C. Liu. 2011. The rhetoric of death penalty policies and its impact on lawmaking [in Chinese]. *Journal of South-Central University for Nationalities (Humanities and Social Science)* (中南民族大学学报人文社会科学版) 31 (3): 91–97.

Lu, J., and C. Liu. 2014. An analysis of multiple paths to restrict capital punishment [in Chinese]. *People's Procuratorial* (人民检察) 21: 5–9.

Lu, X. 2000. *Cadre and corruption: The organizational involution of the Chinese Communist Party*. Stanford: Stanford University Press.

McGarrell, E. F., and M. Sandys. 1996. The misperception of public opinion toward capital punishment: Examining the spuriousness explanation of death penalty support. *American Behavioral Scientist* 39 (4): 500–513.

Meng, Q., H. Fang, X. Liu, B. Yuan, and J. Xu. 2015. Consolidating the social health insurance schemes in China: Towards an equitable and efficient health system. *The Lancet* 386: 1484–92.
Miao, M. 2013. Capital punishment in China: a populist instrument of social governance. *Theoretical Criminology* 17 (2): 233–50.
Mills, J., and E. Zamble. 1998. Public attitudes towards the death penalty. *Journal of Police and Criminal Psychology* 13 (2): 76–86.
Minzner, C. F. 2006. Xinfang: An alternative to formal Chinese legal institutions. *Stanford Journal of International Law* 42: 103–179.
Murray, G. 2003. Raising considerations: Public opinion and the fair application of the death penalty. *Social Science Quarterly* 84 (4): 753–70.
Ng, K. H., and X. He. 2017. The institutional and cultural logics of legal commensuration: Blood money and negotiated justice in China. *American Journal of Sociology* 122 (4): 1104–43.
Nie, J. 2011. Non-medical sex-selective abortion in China: Ethical and public policy issues in the context of 40 million missing females. *British Medical Bulletin* 98: 7–20.
Niven, D. 2002. Bolstering an illusory majority: The effects of the media's portrayal of death penalty support. *Social Science Quarterly* 83 (3): 671–89.
Oberwittler, D., and S. Qi. 2009. Public opinion on the death penalty in China. Results from a general population survey conducted in three provinces in 2007/08 (Forschung Aktuell/research in brief 41). Freiburg, Germany: Max Planck Institute for Foreign and International Criminal Law.
Oberwittler, D., S. Qi, L. Kuang, Y. Zeng, K. Li, S. Liu, X. Chen, Y. Dai, and S. Zhang. 2010. *Opinion survey report on China's death penalty* [in Chinese]. Taibei, Taiwan: Yuanzhao Press.
Paik, W. 2011. Economic development and mass political participation in contemporary China: Determinants of provincial petition (*Xinfang*) activism, 1994–2002. *International Political Science Review* 33 (1): 99–120.
Qi, S., and D. Oberwittler. 2009. On the road to the rule of law: Crime, crime control, and public opinion in China. *European Journal of Criminal Police and Research* 15: 137–57.
Qin J., and B. Albin. 2010. The mental health of children left behind in rural China by migrating parents: A literature review. *Journal of Public Mental Health* 9 (3): 4–16.
Qiu, X. 2001. International human rights and capital punishment [in Chinese]. *Modern Law Science* (现代法学) 23 (2): 63–72.
Qiu, X. 2002a. From belief to human rights: The origin of capital punishment abolition [in Chinese]. *Law Review* (法学评论) 5: 10–19.
Qiu, X. 2002b. The morality of capital punishment [in Chinese]. *Political Science and Law* (政治与法律) 2: 51–54.
Qiu, X. 2003. The utilities of capital punishment [in Chinese]. *The Jurist* (法学家) 2: 56–64.
Qiu, X. 2004a. On the due process of the death penalty [in Chinese]. Modern Law Science (现代法学) 26 (4): 39–45.

Qiu, X. 2004b. Some thoughts on capital punishment [in Chinese]. *Law Review* (法学评论) 5: 18–27.

Ren, J. 2008. Institutionalized corruption: Power overconcentration of the First-in-Command in China. *Crime, Law and Social Change* 49: 45–59.

Sapio, F., S. Trevaskes, S. Biddulph, and E. Nesossi, eds. 2017. *Justice: The China experience*. Cambridge: Cambridge University Press.

Sato, M. 2014. *The death penalty in Japan: Will the public tolerate abolition?* Berlin: Springer VS.

Sen, A. 2002. *Rationality and freedom*. Cambridge, MA: Belknap Press of Harvard University Press.

Shen, A., G. A. Antonopoulos, and G. Papanicolaou. 2013. China's stolen children: Internal child trafficking in the People's Republic of China. *Trends in Organized Crime* 16: 31–48.

Shih, M. 2010. Legal geographies—governing through law: Rights-based conflicts and property development in Shanghai. *Urban Geography* 31 (7): 973–87.

Strandberg, C. 2017. A puzzle about reasons and rationality. *Journal of Ethics* 21 (1): 63–88.

Sun, G. 2009. An analysis of the relationship between death penalty abolition and minyi [in Chinese]. *Journal of East China University of Political Science and Law* (华东政法大学学报) 2: 94–99.

Sun, H. 2010. *Internet policy in China: A field study of Internet cafés*. Lanham, MD: Lexington Books.

Sun, Y. 2004. *Corruption and market in contemporary China*. Ithaca: Cornell University Press.

Supreme People's Court (SPC). 2019. The 2019 Work Report of the Supreme People's Court. Delivered at the 2019 meeting of China's National People's Congress, available at https://www.live.chinacourt.org/article/detail/2019/03/id/3791943.shtml (accessed March 26, 2019).

Swider, S. 2015. Reshaping China's urban citizenship: Street vendors, *chengguan*, and struggles over the right to the city. *Critical Sociology* 41 (4–5): 701–716.

Tai, Z. 2006. *The Internet in China: Cyberspace and civil society*. London: Routledge.

Tang, Y. 2006. On the public opinion and death penalty practice [in Chinese]. *Journal of Liaoning University (Philosophy and Social Sciences Edition)* (辽宁大学学报哲学和社会科学版) 34 (2): 156–60.

Tang, Y., and M. Wang. 2007. On public opinion and judicial control of capital punishment [in Chinese]. In *Criminal law practical problems in a harmonious society*, ed. J. Li, 863–70. Beijing: People's Public Security University of China Press.

Tanner, H. M. 2010. *Strike hard! Anti-crime campaigns and Chinese criminal justice 1979–1989*. Ithaca: Cornell University Press.

Taubman, G. 1998. A not-so world wide web: The Internet, China, and the challenges to nondemocratic rule. *Political Communication* 15 (2): 255–72.

Tian, X., C. Ding, C. Shen, and H. Wang. 2017. Does parental migration have negative impact on the growth of left-behind children? New evidence from longitudinal data in rural China. *International Journal of Environmental Research and Public Health* 14 (10): 1256.

Trevaskes, S. 2002. Courts on the campaign path: Criminal court work in the Yanda 2001 anti-crime campaign. *Asian Survey* 42 (5): 673–93.

Trevaskes, S. 2003. Yanda 2001: Form and strategy in a Chinese anti-crime campaign. *Australian and New Zealand Journal of Criminology* 36 (3): 272–92.

Trevaskes, S. 2004. Propaganda work in Chinese courts: Public trials and sentencing rallies as sites of expressive punishment and public education in the Peoples Republic of China. *Punishment and Society* 6 (1): 5–21.

Trevaskes, S. 2010. *Policing serious crime in China: From strike hard to kill fewer*. London: Routledge.

Trevaskes, S. 2015. Lenient death sentencing and the "cash for clemency" debate. *China Journal* 73: 38–58.

Tyler, T., and R. Weber. 1982. Support for the death penalty: Instrumental response to crime, or symbolic attitude? *Law and Society Review* 17 (1): 21–46.

Wagstaff, A., W. Yip, M. Lindelow, and W. C. Hsiao. 2009. China's health system and its reform: A review of recent studies. *Health Economics* 18: S7-S23.

Wang, L. 2001. Research on judicial reform [in Chinese]. Beijing: Law Press China (法律出版社).

Wang, X., and J. Zhang. 2018. Beyond the quantity–quality tradeoff: Population control policy and human capital investment. *Journal of Development Economics* 135: 222–34.

Wang, Y. 2015. Beyond revenge: Public opinion, court, and judicial control of the death penalty [in Chinese]. *Jilin University Journal (Social Science)* (吉林大学社会科学学报) 55 (4): 66–77.

Wang, Y. 2016. China's death penalty in a "state-power" based society. In Liang and Lu, *Death penalty in China*, 97–122.

Wang, Z. 2017. An analysis of public opinion on death penalty abolition [in Chinese]. *Journal of Guangzhou Open University* (广州广播电视大学学报) 17 (1): 91–112.

Wang, Z., and T. Ni. 2016. The same root, but fratricidal? A psychological interpretation of Lin Senhao's malignant poisoning criminal behavior [in Chinese]. *Journal of Nanchang Normal University* (南昌师范学院学报) 37 (3): 72–78.

Wang, Z., and R. Qian. 2015. An analysis of college student crimes [in Chinese]. *Journal of Shanghai Political Science and Law* (上海政法学院学报) 30 (4): 131–39.

Warr, M., and M. Stafford. 1984. Public goals of punishment and support for the death penalty. *Journal of Research in Crime and Delinquency* 21 (2): 95–111.

Weatherley, R., and H. Pittam. 2015. Money for life: The legal debate in China about criminal reconciliation in death penalty cases. *Asian Perspective* 39: 277–99.

Weber, M. 1968. *Economy and society: An outline of interpretive sociology*. New York: Bedminster Press.

Wedeman, A. 2005. Anticorruption campaigns and the intensification of corruption in China. *Journal of Contemporary China* 14 (42): 93–116.

Wedeman, A. 2008. Win, lose, or draw? China's quarter-century war on corruption. *Crime, Law, and Social Change* 49: 7–26.

Wedeman, A. 2012. *Double paradox: Rapid growth and rising corruption in China*. Ithaca: Cornell University Press.

Wu, Y., I. Sun, and Z. Wu. 2011. Support for the death penalty: Chinese and American college students compared. *Punishment and Society* 13 (3): 354–76.

Wu, Z. 2015. Rethinking the concept, institution, and technique of the appraiser's appearing in court in criminal cases: On the appellate trial of the Fudan poisoning case [in Chinese]. *Chinese Journal of Forensic Sciences* (中国司法鉴定) 81 (4): 8–14.

Xiang, Y. 2013. Criminal mediation in mainland China: A leap from judicial endeavor to legal norm. *Asian Journal of Criminology* 8: 247–56.

Xiao, X. 2009. The interaction between public opinion and death penalty application in the context of China [in Chinese]. *Journal of Shandong University of Science and Technology (Social Science Edition)* (山东科技大学学报社会科学版) 11 (1): 41–46.

Xiong, G. Q. 2012. The rise of China's Internet politics and the change of political culture [in Chinese]. *East Asia Treatises*, No. 93. East Asian Institute, National University of Singapore.

Xiong, M. 2016. Death penalty after the restoration of centralized review: An empirical study on capital sentencing. In Liang and Lu, *Death penalty in China*, 214–46.

Xiong, M., S. Liu, and B. Liang. 2018. Criminal defense and judicial sentencing in China's death penalty cases. *Psychology, Crime, and Law* 24 (4): 414–32.

Xu, H., and S. Wan. 2015. Public opinion supervision should not become trials by public opinion [in Chinese]. *Society* (社会) 2: 39–41.

Xu, J., and A. Jiang. 2019. Police civilization and the production of underclass violence: The case of para-police chengguan and street vendors in Guangzhou, China. *British Journal of Criminology* 59: 64–84.

Yang, C. 2011. An Analysis of the relationship between minyi and death penalty abolition [in Chinese]. *Journal of Inner-Mongolia Agricultural University (Social Science Edition)* (内蒙古农业大学学报社会科学版) 13 (4): 18–20.

Yang, G. 2003. The Internet and civil society in China: A preliminary assessment. *Journal of Contemporary China* 12 (36): 453–75.

Yang, G. 2009. *The power of the Internet in China: Citizen activism online*. New York: Columbia University Press.

Yip, W., and W. C. Hsiao. 2008. The Chinese health system at a crossroads. *Health Affairs* 27 (2): 460–68.

Yip, W., and W. C. Hsiao. 2009. China's health care reform: A tentative assessment. *China Economic Review* 20: 613–19.

Yip, W., W. C. Hsiao, W. Chen, S. Hu, J. Ma, and A. Maynard. 2012. Early appraisal of China's huge and complex health-care reforms. *The Lancet* 379 (9818): 833–42.

Yu, T., G. Q. Shen, Q. Shi, X. Lai, C. Li, and K. Xu. 2017. Managing social risks at the housing demolition stage of urban redevelopment projects: A stakeholder-oriented study using social network analysis. *International Journal of Project Management* 35: 925–41.

Yuan, B. 2009a. An investigation and analysis of public opinion on the death penalty and its internal conflict [in Chinese]. *Law Science* (法学) 1: 99–112.

Yuan, B. 2009b. A systemic interpretation of guidance of death penalty public opinion [in Chinese]. *Criminal Science* (中国刑事法杂志) 11: 21–29.

Yuan, B., F. Wang, Q. Ye, J. Kang, C. Tang, Y. Zhou, X. Geng, and J. Li. 2015. A practical investigation on the public opinion on death penalty cases: Empirical analysis of 217 cases of death penalty [in Chinese]. *Criminal Law* (刑法论丛) 3: 1–31.

Zang, X., and M. Musheno. 2017. Exploring frontline work in China. *Public Administration* 95: 842–55.

Zang, X., and J. Pratt. 2019. Are street-level bureaucrats in China hardnosed cops or consultants? An institutional account of policing behavior in autocracy. *Journal of Contemporary China* 28 (116): 232–44.

Zeng, S. 2015. An analysis of public surveys on the death penalty in China, United States, Japan, and South Korea [in Chinese]. *Journal of Daqing Normal University* (大庆师范学院学报) 35 (1): 39–43.

Zeng, S. 2016. Concepts, systems, and technology: The death penalty legal system and technical factors influence public opinion [in Chinese]. *Journal of Harbin University of Commerce* (哈尔滨商业大学学报) 146 (1): 124–28.

Zeng, S. 2017. An empirical analysis of public opinion on retention or abolition of capital punishment among economic crimes [in Chinese]. *Corporate Culture* (企业文化) 567: 153, 160.

Zhang, H. 2007. From resisting to "embracing?" the one-child rule: Understanding new fertility trends in a central China village. *China Quarterly* 192: 855–75.

Zhang, H., and X. He. 2011. Survey report on the death penalty [in Chinese]. *Present-Day Law Science* (时代法学) 9 (4): 59–68.

Zhang, M. 2005a. The gap between legal scholars and judges on death penalty issues [in Chinese]. *Peking University Law Journal* (中外法学) 17 (5): 543–56.

Zhang, M. 2005b. How criminal scholars should contribute to diminishing death penalty [in Chinese]. *Contemporary Law Review* (当代法学) 19 (1): 3–13.

Zhang, M. 2013. Change the notion of harsh punishment and make sentencing reasonable [in Chinese]. *People's Court Daily* (人民法院报), January 30, 6.

Zhang, N. 2010. Public opinion and the death penalty debate in China. *China Perspectives* 1: 85–96.

Zhang, N. 2016. Crimes of counterrevolution and politicized use of the death penalty during the Mao's era. In Liang and Lu, *Death penalty in China*, 62–96.

Zhang, Q. 2012. The death penalty is not sufficient to deter corrupt officials [in Chinese]. *Legal Daily* (法制日报), January 31, 7.

Zhang, W. 2015a. A study of the uniqueness of corruption offenses in death penalty legislation reform [in Chinese]. *Criminal Science* (中国刑事法杂志) 2: 1–13.

Zhang, W. 2015b. The value of public opinion in the context of death penalty reform [in Chinese]. *Eastern Forum* (东方论坛) 6: 101–111.

Zhao, B. 2015. Discussion on the criminal law issue of the restriction on the death penalty in China [in Chinese]. *Criminal Law* (刑法论丛) 1: 1–58.

Zhao, B., and W. Zhang. 2013. A brief analysis of the guidance of death penalty public opinion: From the perspective of cautious use of capital punishment [in Chinese]. *Journal of National Prosecutors College* (国家检察官学院学报) 21 (4): 41-54.

Zhao, J. 2015. Public opinion on the abolition of the death penalty: Measurement of the idea about inculpation of the crime of organizing prostitution [in Chinese]. *Chinese Journal of Law* (法学研究) 2: 26-41.

Zhao, X. 2015. On the management of negative emotions: A psychological analysis of the Fudan poisoning case [in Chinese]. *Enterprise Management* (企业管理) 1: 43-45.

Zheng, Y. 2008. *Technological empowerment: The Internet, state, and society in China*. Stanford: Stanford University Press.

Zhou, M., R. Murphy, and R. Tao. 2014. Effects of parents' migration on the education of children left behind in rural China. *Population and Development Review* 40 (2): 273-92.

Zhou, Y. 2006. *Historicizing online politics: Telegraphy, the Internet, and political participation in China*. Stanford: Stanford University Press.

Zuo, J. 2009. The influence of public opinion on the application of the death penalty [in Chinese]. *Hebei Law Science* (河北法学) 26 (2): 35-37, 51.

Zuo, W., and C. Zhuo. 2000. *Changes and reforms: A study of the modernization of the court system* [in Chinese]. Beijing: Law Press China (法律出版社).

Index

A life for a life, 52, 58, 66, 78, 88, 119, 199, 243, 255. *See also* Retribution; Sharen changming
Abolition, 2, 6, 10, 23, 30–31, 40–41, 47, 58–65, 77, 85–87, 90, 96, 103, 106, 163, 165–67, 204, 206, 224–26, 243, 256–57, 274–75; against abolition, 87–90. *See also* Abolitionists
Abolitionists, 103, 204–5
Aggravating circumstance, 3
Anders Behring Breivik, 223, 226
Appeal, 44, 48, 80–81, 136, 143, 145, 207, 210, 231, 244, 249, 281, 287, 291; appeal procedure, 27; appeal process, 44, 143; appeal right, 49; call for 'no appeals,' 35, 46, 208–9, 210, 248
Appellate courts, 21, 133, 143
Appellate review, 19, 21, 134, 236
April Fool's Day prank, 159, 235–36, 239, 243
Assembly line, 20, 271
Assistance of legal counsel, 21

Bai Yansong, 103, 204
Balancing leniency and severity (policy), 19, 21
Baogong, 97–99, 101, 112, 236, 265–66
Basic people's court, 20. *See also* Court of first instance
Beijing, 3–4, 7, 13, 51, 55, 146, 211–12, 219–20, 232, 235, 283–84, 287–88, 290–91, 293, 295, 297

Blind Well (movie), 31, 34, 56, 95
Bo Xilai, 221
Brazil, 120, 290
Breadth (on diverse themes), 18, 22, 26, 40–41, 44, 56–57, 90, 139, 235, 274
Breaking Bad (TV series), 29, 56
Bribe, 50, 122–23, 142, 145, 165, 181, 203, 221, 282; bribe money, 47, 68, 96; bribe-taking, 20, 69, 166, 172; bribery, 178, 240
Burden of proof, 239

Cao Xueqin, 147
Call for kill, 4, 81, 253–55, 259, 269, 273
Calling a stag a horse, 150–51, 158, 257
Capital crime, 3, 7, 9, 11, 46, 123, 144, 154, 203. *See also* Capital offense
Capital offense, 3, 11, 18–20, 39, 67, 116–17, 127, 129, 154, 157. *See also* Capital crime
Capital punishment, 1–2, 4–7, 9–10, 14–15, 18–20, 23, 40, 43, 47, 58, 67, 72, 77–81, 84–90, 96, 99–100, 103, 106, 120–21, 142, 155, 163, 166–67, 173–74, 180, 202, 205–6, 224–26, 243, 256–57, 263, 273–80. *See also* Death penalty
Case comparison, 25, 27, 29–36, 40–41, 49, 208–9, 218–26, 229, 264; international comparison, 41, 120, 222–26, 229, 265
Cash for clemency, 144, 164, 167
Changge (city), 50–51, 154
Checks and balances (lack of), 20

323

324   INDEX

Chen Hui (case), 240
Chen Yun (case), 31, 43, 62, 93, 108, 119, 141, 143, 164, 176, 208, 219, 289, 302, 304
Child abduction, 38, 67, 72, 119, 124, 170, 218, 226, 282
Child molestation, 127, 285, 287
Children left behind, 129, 178
China Internet Network Information Center (CNNIC), 12–15, 114, 260
Chinese characteristics, 115, 172, 186, 278
Chinese Communist Party (CCP), 22, 175, 278
Chinese Culture, 9, 65, 67–68, 72, 90, 102, 117, 126, 131–32, 167, 225, 239, 275–76, 279
Chongqing (city), 221
Civil participation, 264
Civil society, 261, 263
Commercialization, 24, 45, 51, 169–70. *See also* Marketization
Communicative rationality, 24, 198, 200, 202, 228, 261, 272; theory of communicative rationality (TCR), 200–201
Commutation, 221
Concurring argument, 23, 36, 91–92; concurring comments, 107–9; concurrence, 37, 93–94, 107–9
Confession, 97, 101, 145, 235, 289; forced confession, 153
Consensus, 3, 5, 201, 229; consensus-building, 200–202, 228, 273
Conviction, 97, 126, 159–60, 200, 232, 241, 285, 289, 292
Correctional system, 24, 48, 140, 154–56
Corruption, 3, 7, 9, 16, 24, 27, 47–48, 50–51, 68–69, 83–84, 96, 106, 117, 122–24, 129, 144–47, 153–54, 163, 165–67, 169, 172–73, 175–77, 180, 190, 197, 221, 226, 255, 266–67, 269–70, 276, 282, 288, 299; anticorruption, 9, 30, 32, 50, 176; official corruption, 24–25, 36, 172, 257, 260, 264, 276
Counterargument, 23, 36–37, 91–92, 95–98, 100–101, 107, 115, 152, 170, 257–58

Court of first instance, 97, 133, 231, 235, 246
Court of second instance, 19–21, 97, 133, 231, 246, 257, 268
Crime type, 3, 24, 116–23, 137, 139, 274
Criminal defense, 21, 24, 45–46, 157, 161, 167–68, 276, 280; *See also* Defense rights
Criminal defense lawyer, 24, 140, 168, 271, 276. *See also* Defense lawyers
Criminal gang, 38, 72, 76, 117–18, 124, 146, 153, 162, 176, 178, 282, 287, 299
Criminal justice policy, 19
Criminal justice practice, 9
Criminal justice professionals, 3, 24, 47, 260, 269, 276; *see also chapter 6*
Criminal justice reform, 9, 276
Criminal justice system, 6, 9, 20, 22, 24, 47–50, 68, 133–34, 265, 269–71, 276, 278; *see also chapter 6*
Criminal law, 11, 18–20, 56, 69, 73, 84, 116–17, 119, 121, 174, 226; (2011) Eighth Amendment, 20, 117, 119; (2015) Ninth Amendment, 20, 117, 174, 180–81
Criminal law scholars, 3
Criminal lawyers, 160, 254, 276
Criminal procedural law, 18–22
Cross-examination, 21
Cultural Revolution, 18, 81, 249, 254
Cursing (example of irrationality), 24, 27, 29–31, 33–36, 54, 112–14, 123, 149, 199, 204–6, 227–28, 240, 254, 262

Death by a thousand cuts, 39, 69–70, 108, 141, 175, 205–6
Death penalty, 1–10, 13–15, 18–24, 38, 41, 47–48, 50, 52, 58, 65, 68, 73, 77, 79–81, 83, 85–89, 103, 106, 116–17, 123, 140, 143, 148, 166, 205, 264, 268, 274–75, 279, 296; exemption (minors; pregnant women; seniors), 20. *See also* Capital punishment
Death Penalty Information Center, 225
Death sentence, 1–3, 8, 10, 14, 19–23, 25–43, 46–49, 53, 58–68, 71–88, 90, 96–99,

102–8, 110–11, 114, 116–29, 131, 133–45, 147–49, 160–61, 164, 166–67, 173–75, 178, 181, 183, 186, 188, 190, 192–93, 198, 200, 202–3, 206–7, 210, 214, 216, 218–24, 227, 231–38, 240–47, 253–61, 263, 267–69, 273–75, 277, 279, 281–86, 289–90, 292–96, 298; suspended death sentence, 10, 28, 30, 32, 34, 39, 46–47, 49, 80, 96, 98, 103–4, 110, 122, 141–42, 144–45, 147–49, 155, 160, 163, 167, 185, 218, 220–22, 236, 246, 252, 255, 283–84, 286, 294, 296; with immediate execution, 20, 22, 39, 47, 83, 104, 110, 114, 128, 136, 142, 144–45, 149, 163, 185, 210, 218, 220, 246. *See also* Execution
Defense lawyer, 17, 21, 35, 45, 76, 110, 157–62, 167–68, 204, 231, 238–39, 247, 268, 271, 276, 305. *See also* Criminal defense lawyers
Defense rights, 45, 46, 161, 238, 280
Dehui (city), 153
Delay and waste, 29, 31, 48, 134, 143, 233, 234, 276
Democracy, 261; deliberative democracy, 201
Demolition and relocation (policy), 24, 40, 49, 51–52, 65, 84, 98, 113, 118, 125, 132, 139, 142, 169, 192–97, 222, 224, 226–27, 263, 267, 277, 293; forced relocation, 33, 66, 113, 194, 196, 205, 228, 263. *See also* Liu Danao (case)
Deng Fang (case), 30, 61, 93, 141, 152, 208, 211, 215, 288, 301, 304
Deng "x" (case), 32, 53, 63, 94, 131, 171, 209, 291, 302, 304
Depth (on diverse views), 12, 18, 22–23, 26, 37, 40–41, 44, 56–57, 90, 139, 235, 274, 279
Deterrence, 6–7, 23, 40–41, 58–65, 67–68, 70–71, 74, 76–80, 86–87, 90, 100, 106, 123, 166, 224, 238, 245, 275–76; general deterrence, 67, 70, 74, 79; specific deterrence, 70, 74, 79
Di Renjie, 165, 265
Discrimination, 24, 32, 55, 96, 208–9, 211–18, 228; discrimination against villagers, 55, 213–15; national discrimination, 203, 215–16; race, ethnicity discrimination, 27, 215; regional discrimination, 30, 32–34, 36, 55, 211–13; sex and sexual orientation discrimination, 55, 216–17
Diversity (of public opinions), 5, 18, 22–23, 26, 37, 57, 70, 116, 139, 235, 264, 273–75
Drug offenses, 3, 7, 20, 117, 119–22, 176–77, 299; drug trafficking, 11, 34, 38–39, 47, 49, 79, 98, 102, 105, 120–21, 123–24, 127, 185, 222, 284–85, 290, 293
Drunk driving, 43, 119, 164, 176, 219
Due process, 6, 276

Earth, 65–66, 101, 110, 112, 130, 160, 170, 193, 222
Endangerment of public security, 43, 118, 176, 219, 245, 299
Equity, 9, 47, 142–43, 175, 195, 222, 229, 239, 264. *See also* Fairness and equity
Evidence, 19, 21, 76–77, 81–82, 97–98, 100, 104, 112, 117, 131, 134, 144, 148, 158, 161, 167, 170, 210, 221, 223, 228, 235–37, 239–42, 253–54, 258, 271, 278, 287; circumstantial evidence, 112; DNA evidence, 146
Execution, 1–2, 20, 22, 29–31, 34–36, 38–39, 44, 67, 69–72, 75–76, 79–83, 85, 88, 99–100, 114, 116–17, 121, 133, 135–38, 143–45, 150, 153, 163, 178, 210, 222, 227, 233, 235, 241–42, 247–48, 250, 253, 255, 258–59, 268, 275, 283, 285–86; public execution, 39, 68, 70, 106, 207, 238. *See also* Death sentence

Fairness, 23, 29, 34, 40–41, 43, 49–50, 58, 67, 77, 83–84, 274, 276; fairness and equity, 9, 47, 142–43, 195, 220, 229, 264. *See also* Justice and fairness
Fan Jieming (case), 30, 61, 69, 93, 107, 139, 146, 152, 163, 165, 172, 177, 208, 210, 266, 268–69, 287, 301, 304

326 INDEX

Fangchenggang (city), 181, 282, 292
Fear, 89, 95, 166, 186, 212, 223, 236, 267; fear of crime, 7
Feng Xiujuan (case), 31, 44, 62, 85, 91, 93, 124, 128–29, 132, 146, 208, 211, 215–16, 223, 227, 269, 289, 302, 304
Feng Zhiming, 138, 145, 150
Feudal society, 69, 86, 238, 250
50-cent party members, 16, 111, 271
Final review and approval (SPC's), 18–21, 99, 210, 231, 256, 281
Foul language, x, 23–24, 37, 54, 100, 104–6, 109, 111, 113, 202–5, 257, 259, 262, 271–72, 301–2
Freedom of assembly and association, 262, 271
Freedom of press, 262, 271
Freedom of speech, 257, 262, 271, 279
Fujian (province), 211; Fujianese, 211
Fujin (city), 173

Gambling, 34, 121, 153, 179, 294, 296
Gao Yulun (case), 32, 48, 63, 79, 82, 94, 107, 126–27, 137, 141, 154, 156, 173, 209, 215, 218, 292, 302, 304
"Get-tough" (policy), 19–20, 167, 227
Globalization, 274
Gong-jian-fa, 20, 271
Government, 4, 261; Chinese government, 1–2, 5–6, 8, 16–17, 19, 22, 25, 29, 31, 50–51, 53, 69, 75, 81, 95, 101, 111, 116, 120, 122, 129, 139, 146–47, 164–65, 172, 174–75, 177–79, 182–97, 227, 260–61, 266, 269–71, 277, 286
Governmental officials, 9, 16, 34, 42, 46–47, 50–51, 66–67, 97, 112, 190, 266–67, 269, 276
Governmental policy, 16, 40, 50–51, 84, 142, 180, 182–97, 264, 267, 274, 277–78
Great Britain, 81
Gu Junshan (case), 12, 30, 50, 61, 75, 93, 122, 124, 208, 288, 301, 304
Gu Kailai (case), 221
Guangdong (province), 1, 4, 7, 13, 17, 38, 55, 67, 211–12, 281–82, 285, 289, 293, 296, 298
Guangxi (province), 181, 212, 282, 284, 292, 294
Guangzhou (city), 1, 17, 140, 284, 298
Guizhou (province), 46, 55, 101, 104, 211–12, 287

Habermas, Jürgen, 24, 198, 200–202, 226–29, 261–63, 267, 271–73, 275
Harmonious society, 8, 171, 197; building a harmonious society, 22, 278
He Jian (case), 33, 63, 94, 109, 177, 209, 212–22, 227, 294, 302, 305
He Shenguo (case), 40, 44, 51–52, 63, 84, 91, 94, 98, 125–26, 132, 142, 164, 180–84, 192, 207, 209, 214–15, 218, 277, 292, 302, 304
Health-care system, 24, 40–41, 51, 77, 79, 84, 98, 104, 125, 132, 169, 184–92, 197, 223, 265, 267, 276–77
Heaven, 65–66, 69, 72, 77, 122, 130, 146, 151, 170, 181, 193–94, 205, 251, 258; heavenly justice, 71, 76, 207, 245; heaven's law, 71–72, 151
Heilongjiang (province), 173, 290, 293
Henan (province), 13, 55, 142, 192, 212–13, 287, 293, 298; Henan opera, 147
High people's court (provincial high court), 19, 20, 206; Anhui High Court, 284; Beijing High Court, 287; Guangxi High Court, 181, 282, 292; Hebei High Court, 286; Henan High Court, 142, 192, 293, 298; Hunan High Court, 240, 296; Inner Mongolian High Court, 98, 185, 268, 282, 284; Guangdong High Court, 285, 289, 293; Shanghai High Court, 97, 133–35, 231–32, 235–36, 260, 281; Shan'xi High Court, 295; Zhejiang High Court, 186, 285
Homicide, 11, 51, 68, 70, 72, 76–77, 80, 83, 85, 103, 105, 108, 117, 119, 120, 123–24, 126, 142, 144–46, 148, 166, 181, 186, 207, 216, 218, 220–21, 235–37, 240, 242, 245, 269, 281, 282–97, 299. See also Murder

Homosexual, 55, 138, 209, 217
Hong Kong, 13, 120, 212, 224, 263, 290
Hooligan, 193
Hu Cunbiao and Wang Yong (case), 31, 62, 76, 93, 106, 114, 151, 155, 166, 178–79, 205, 216, 220, 227, 301, 304
Hu "x" (case), 27, 45, 51, 59, 93, 130, 143, 157–58, 160–61, 169, 208, 283, 301, 303
Huang Qinghen (case), 38, 43, 59, 67, 69, 70, 72, 75, 93, 108, 119, 124, 129, 137, 170, 208, 218, 226, 282, 301, 303
Huang "x" (case), 32, 62, 94, 120, 209, 212, 290, 292, 302, 304
Huang Yang, 42, 45, 98, 101, 230–32, 235–38, 241, 243–44, 246–48, 250–52, 256, 258, 275, 281
Hubei (province), 3–4, 7, 290–91, 295
Hu'ge (Huugjilt) (case), 80, 82, 100, 133, 138, 145, 150, 206, 210, 249, 282
Human Rights, 6, 40, 87, 89, 166–67, 274
Humanity, 38, 95, 170–71, 175, 249; humanitarianism, 68–69, 86, 89–90; humanization, 156, 163
Hunan (province), 50, 122, 212, 240, 282, 288, 296
Hu Zhiqiang, 235, 238

Incapacitation, 7
India, 55, 101, 203, 216, 235
Inequality, 88, 166; social inequality, 9, 107, 264, 266, 270, 276
Inner Mongolia Autonomous Region, 49, 222
Innocence, 145, 223. *See also* Presumption of innocence
Interaction (netizens'), 14, 17, 23, 26–37, 49, 53, 137, 200–203, 231, 233–34, 261, 279; *see also chapter 4*
Intermediate people's court, 20, 97; Beijing intermediate people's court, 284, 287, 290–91, 293, 295, 297; Bengbu intermediate people's court, 289; Beihai intermediate people's court, 291; Bijie intermediate people's court, 287; Dandong intermediate people's court, 286; Fangchenggang intermediate people's court, 181, 282, 292; Guang'an intermediate people's court, 291; Guangzhou intermediate people's court, 298; Ha'erbing intermediate people's court, 293; Haikou intermediate people's court, 294; Handan intermediate people's court, 286; Hangzhou Intermediate Court, 283; Hebi intermediate people's court, 287; Hefei intermediate people's court, 285; Huhe Haote Intermediate People's Court, 282; Huizhou intermediate people's court, 296; Jiaxing intermediate people's court, 287; Jinan intermediate people's court, 296; Jingmen intermediate people's court, 291; Jingzhou intermediate people's court, 295; Liuzhou intermediate people's court, 292, 294; Loudi intermediate people's court, 282; Nanjing intermediate people's court, 296; Qingdao intermediate people's court, 283, 290; Shanghai intermediate people's court, 97, 231, 281, 287; Shangrao intermediate people's court, 285; Shaoguan intermediate people's court, 289, 296; Taizhou intermediate people's court, 285; Tanzhou intermediate people's court, 186; Wuhu intermediate people's court, 284, 288; Xiangtan intermediate people's court, 240; Xucheng intermediate people's court, 298; Yangquan intermediate people's court, 295; Yichang intermediate people's court, 290, 294; Yueyang intermediate people's court, 288; Zhengzhou Intermediate people's Court, 142, 192, 293; Zhiyang intermediate people's court, 286; Zhuhai intermediate people's court, 283, 289, 293
International community, 40, 87, 116
Internet, 8, 12–18, 73, 114, 229, 260–63, 266–67, 271; age of the internet, 55, 139; internet censorship, 15–16; internet user, 1, 12, 14–15, 261
Interrogation, 272

Irrationality, 4, 9, 24, 46, 54–55, 80, 113–15, 198–99, 202–18, 228–29, 272–73, 279. *See also* Rationality

Japan, 216, 225; Japanese, 14, 55, 215–16, 278
Jiangsu (province), 13, 17, 169, 243, 252
Jilin (province), 153
Jin Fusheng (case), 35, 42, 64, 68, 70, 75, 94, 117–18, 128, 131, 146, 209, 219, 297, 302, 305
Jining (city), 151
Judge, 3, 6, 8, 21–22, 24, 31, 34, 38, 45, 48, 78, 80–82, 104, 110, 117, 134, 140–49, 155, 158, 161, 166, 194, 200, 204–5, 207, 212, 221–23, 231–33, 236, 242, 247, 249, 254–56, 259, 263, 265–70, 277, 281, 304
Judiciary, 8–9, 20, 43, 143, 145, 160, 194, 220, 239, 256, 263, 277–78; judicial independence, 21, 80, 149, 164, 277–78; judiciary decision, 22
Jurisdiction, 20, 178
Jury, 263–64
Just desert, 23, 41, 58–65, 70–73
Justice, 1, 23, 27, 41, 48, 58–65, 70–71, 74, 98, 100, 114, 144, 146–47, 158, 171, 174–75, 181, 221, 239, 246, 249, 250–51, 255–58, 264–67, 274–76, 279; injustice, 66, 250–51; justice and fairness, 25, 71, 260, 267, 275; justice requirement, 23, 41, 58–65, 70–71; procedural justice, 9, 168, 210, 223, 239–40, 249, 274, 276, 280; substantive justice, 9, 223, 239–40, 275–76; vigilante justice, 74–75, *See also* Heavenly justice

Karl Marx, 171
Kidnapping, 38, 108, 117, 127, 129, 146, 178, 285, 293, 299
Killing fewer and killing cautiously (policy), 163–64. *See also* Balancing leniency and severity
Killing one to deter a hundred, 67, 275
King of Hell, 102, 161
Kunming (city), 39, 118, 283
Kuomintang, 251

Law, 3, 8, 18–19, 21, 23, 27–28, 31–32, 35–36, 39, 41, 46–49, 58–73, 75, 77–78, 81–87, 104–5, 108, 117–18, 120–22, 127–28, 132, 134–36, 141–45, 148–51, 153–55, 158, 161–66, 171–72, 174, 177–83, 185, 189–90, 193–95, 197, 199–202, 206, 210, 216, 218, 220, 222–23, 225, 227, 237–40, 243, 245–46, 249–50, 253–57, 259, 263–69, 273, 277–79; equal treatment of law, 30; law enforcement, 21, 35, 40, 47–49, 84, 154, 163, 223. *See also* Criminal law, Criminal procedural law, Rule by law, Rule of law
Lawmaker, 3, 47, 84, 140, 162–63
Legal expert, 6, 24, 47, 83, 123, 140, 162, 165–66, 238, 271
Legal procedure, 24, 41, 46, 82, 116, 133–36, 139, 143, 147, 196, 222–23, 228, 239, 249, 255, 268, 270, 274; forgo legal procedure, 24, 46, 136, 143, 206, 210, 228, 248, 266, 270, 275–76
Lei Feng, 175
Leniency, 17, 27–29, 42–43, 67–77, 83, 100, 106, 206–7, 234, 241–43, 245, 255–56, 274, 289
Lethal injection, 68, 143
Letters and visits, 146–47
Li Gang (case), 125
Li Lei (case), 30, 51, 61, 93, 108, 129, 208, 211, 269, 288, 301, 304
Li Tianyi (case), 220
Li "x" (case), 11, 35, 64, 94, 209, 296, 302, 305
Li "x" (#2) (case), 11, 35, 64, 94, 209, 297, 302, 305
Li "xx" (case), 34, 47, 64, 66, 71, 94, 103, 141, 148, 152, 163–64, 209, 212, 220, 295, 302, 305
Lian Enqing (case), 28, 40–41, 51, 53, 60, 66, 77, 79, 82, 84, 91, 93, 98, 101, 108, 110, 125–26, 132, 146, 184–92, 199, 204, 208, 211, 213, 223, 254, 263, 265, 269, 272, 277, 285, 301, 303
Liang Kaiwu (case), 29, 60, 69, 93, 139, 151, 177, 208, 286, 301, 303
Lianzuo, 69

Index   329

Life imprisonment, 5, 33, 40, 67, 79–80, 84, 86–90, 118, 136, 141–43, 155, 163, 165, 178, 210, 218, 221, 243, 246, 248, 283–84, 293; without the possibility of parole, 5, 33; without possibility of sentence reduction, 243

Lin Senhao (case), 1, 12, 17, 25–26, 28, 30, 34, 38, 42, 44–46, 56, 59–61, 64, 66–67, 70–71, 73–74, 76–80, 91, 93, 97–99, 101, 106, 110–15, 125, 129, 133, 136–37, 141, 149, 157–59, 161–62, 166, 175, 199–200, 205, 207–8, 210, 217, 220–21, 223–24, 263–64, 266, 268–69, 272–75, 277–78, 281, 301, 303; *see also* chapter 9

Lin "x"ping and Ye "x"tian (case), 17, 29, 49, 52, 60, 69, 72, 81, 83–84, 86, 88, 91, 93, 96, 99, 106, 108, 112–13, 120, 137, 140, 162, 164, 172, 175, 208, 212, 222, 301, 301

Ling Ruiming (case), 45, 63, 77, 83, 94, 108, 130, 209, 216, 292, 302, 304

Liu Danao (case), 13, 16, 33, 40, 49, 51–52, 63, 65, 82, 84, 94, 98, 113, 117–18, 125, 132, 139, 142, 145, 147, 162, 164, 192–97, 205, 209, 212, 223, 226–27, 263, 265, 277, 293, 302, 304

Liu Han (case), 12, 27, 59, 72–73, 93, 124, 176, 208, 282, 301, 303

Liu "x" (case), 32, 63, 94, 108, 209, 214, 293, 302, 304

Liuzhou (city), 43, 124, 174, 212, 292, 294

Lu Xun, 265

Lumei (case), 32, 62, 93, 120, 124, 208, 290, 302, 304

Luo Xiaohua and Chen Rihong (case), 34, 64–65, 110, 131, 145, 147, 149, 151, 163–65, 204, 212, 218, 220, 302

Ma Jiajue (case), 242
Maintaining order, 196
Maintaining social stability, 22, 76, 278
Mammonism, 180, 191, 197, 276
Mao Zedong, 171
Marketization, 171, 188
Marshall hypotheses, 4–5, 14
Mass-line (policy), 153

Media, 8, 45, 81, 124, 134–35, 159, 167, 189, 232–33, 247, 253, 255–56, 259, 262, 268–69, 279; media reporting, 23–25, 55, 81, 99, 102, 106, 116, 134, 136–39, 260, 268, 274; media supervision, 189; social media, 18, 136, 257

Medical malpractice, 40, 77, 79, 84, 125, 132, 189

Mental disorder, 36, 42, 48, 159–61, 227

Methodology, 1, 7, 10–18, 22, 92, 279

Minfen, 74–77, 253–55, 275, 277; questioning minfen, 80–81. *See also* Public indignation

Ministry of Justice, 85

Ministry of Public Security, 85

Minors, 20, 67, 108, 114, 151, 174, 176, 288, 293, 298

Minyi, 6–12, 18, 22, 25, 231, 252–59, 278. *See also* Public opinion; Yulun

Mitigating circumstances, 3

Mount Liang, 75, 185

Murder, 5, 20, 38–39, 42, 46, 49, 51, 56, 66, 69–72, 74, 77–80, 95–97, 103, 107, 121, 124, 143, 152, 170, 177, 180, 207, 216, 218, 221–22, 224, 231, 235–36, 240, 242–43, 282, 284–88, 294–95; murderer, 75, 77, 86, 96, 106, 113–14, 143, 145, 152, 154, 161, 165, 170, 172, 181, 183, 186, 207, 237, 240, 245–46, 251, 256–57

Nail households, 195–96
Nanjing (city), 17, 43, 219–20, 242–43, 296
Nanjing BMW case, 43, 219–20
National People's Congress, 19, 180, 238
Nian Bin (case), 206
Ningxia (province), 13
Norman Bethune, 189
North Korea, 69, 224

Offender, 3, 9, 11, 18, 20, 38–40, 42, 45–46, 48, 52, 57, 67, 69–76, 79, 83–84, 87, 99, 101, 105, 107, 117–21, 123–25, 127–31, 137, 142–43, 148, 152, 154, 156–57, 167, 170–71, 203–4, 218–19, 222, 242, 274, 282–83, 285–87, 293–95, 299; capital

Offender (*continued*)
  offender, 22, 42, 46, 157, 161–62, 177, 197, 210; drug offender, 49, 120, 222, 275; repeat offender, 151, 155, 218; sex offender, 203, 216
O. J. Simpson (case), 223, 239
One-child birth control policy, 16, 24, 40, 44, 51, 84, 98, 119, 126, 132, 138, 142, 169, 180–84, 277. *See also* He Shenguo (case)
Online violence, 23, 92–94, 109, 113, 254, 259, 273
Opium Wars, 120
Ou Changsheng (case), 35, 42, 64, 94, 103, 108, 110, 114, 118, 120, 128, 176, 178, 204, 209, 213, 215, 220, 298, 302, 305
Outrage, 38–39, 46, 50, 69, 70, 194, 196, 205
Over-quota birth, 44, 182–84, 207, 214, 218
Overwhelming public support, 1–3, 5–6, 32, 139, 275. *See also* Public support

Pan Guohui (case), 34, 64, 94, 176, 209, 296, 302, 305
Payback, 23, 41, 58–65, 70–71, 73, 135, 181, 232, 235, 250
Penal populism, 8, 278
Peng Shu and Hu Haolong (case), 27, 47, 50–51, 59, 68, 73, 84, 108, 122, 124, 173, 175–76, 203, 206, 226, 269, 303
Peng Yu (case), 242, 255
Penzi, 100, 111–13, 115, 120, 199–200, 253, 266–67
People's Republic of China (PRC), 2, 18, 85, 120–21
Personal attack, 23–24, 36–37, 45, 91–94, 100–107, 115, 160, 202–6, 228, 262, 272
Personal threat, 23–24, 37, 100, 104, 106–7, 202, 205, 272
Pettifogger, 101, 158, 161, 307
Pfrangs (case), 242–43
Poisoning, 25, 42, 56, 67, 79, 97, 124, 135, 206, 220–22, 230, 232, 235–36, 245, 247–48, 252–53, 255, 259, 272, 285

Police, 3, 20, 24, 29–30, 33, 35, 37, 42, 47–48, 51, 53, 56, 71, 75, 79, 83, 99, 103–7, 113, 119–20, 124, 126, 128, 130–31, 138, 140, 143, 145, 156, 160, 163, 173, 177, 179, 190, 193–94, 196, 204, 219, 221, 224, 230–31, 235, 252, 266–67, 272, 281, 285–86, 289, 292, 294–96, 298; challenges to the police, 149–54; internet police, 16; police department, 125, 152–53
Popular support, 257; popular will, 256
Presumption of innocence, 97, 223, 239–40, 242
Private property (protection), 34, 84, 194, 265
Privilege, 9, 14, 47, 49, 66–67, 82, 90, 163–64, 174, 243, 276
Procuratorate, 20–21, 85, 103–4, 141–42, 147, 154, 160, 204, 232, 296; procuratorate protest, 35, 104, 141–42, 147, 296
Prostitution, 107, 121, 152, 174, 179, 228; engagement in prostitution with a minor, 174; organizing prostitution, 3
Public debate, 200–202, 228, 242, 261–62, 264, 271–73, 279
Public indignation, 10, 22, 41, 74, 75, 123, 253, 256. *See also* Minfen
Public intellectuals, 24, 47, 103, 140, 162, 165–66, 256, 271
Public opinion, 1–6, 10, 22, 25, 57, 80, 114, 229–30, 252, 257–58, 260, 262, 267, 273, 277, 279–80. *See also* Minyi; Yulun
Public order, 23, 41, 58–65, 76; public safety, 43, 67–68, 75–76, 84, 90, 98, 219, 223, 245, 276, 299
Public participation, 262–63
Public sphere, 201, 229, 261–63, 267, 271
Public support, 2, 5, 8, 261. *See also* Overwhelming public support
Public trust, 8–9, 145, 167, 172, 193, 259, 269–70

Qin dynasty, 150
Qinghai (province), 13
Quota, 182. *See also* Over-quota birth

Rape, 46–47, 50, 69, 88, 101, 103, 106–7, 110, 118–19, 128, 130, 138, 145, 151–52, 161, 166, 173–74, 178–79, 203–4, 218, 220, 224, 282, 284, 286–88, 296–99; gang rape, 173, 220
Rational choice theory, 198–99
Rational deliberation, 14, 25, 41, 54, 91, 112, 115, 198, 201–2, 228, 262
Rationale, 5, 10, 23, 38, 41, 269, 274; *see also chapter 3*
Rationality, 4–5, 14, 24, 76, 91, 136, 261, 271, 278–79 (*see also chapter 8*); call for rationality, 113, 115. *See also* Communicative rationality; Irrationality
Recidivism, 29, 39, 48, 96, 127, 148, 154–55, 160, 167, 180, 203; recidivist, 127, 155
Red guards, 81, 254
Reeducation through labor, 207
Reform, 6, 9–10, 18–19, 86, 102, 126, 144, 148, 155–56, 161, 167, 171, 176, 180, 184–86, 188–89, 191, 197, 204, 261, 270, 275–76; economic reforms, 184
Rehabilitation, 103, 155, 167, 244, 276
Respect for lives, 41, 58–65, 76
Retention of the death penalty, 2, 88, 120, 225
Retribution, 6–7, 23, 41, 58–67, 72, 98, 153, 181, 248, 276. *See also* Sharen changming
Right to remain silent, 21
Robbery, 20, 83, 108, 117, 154, 161, 173, 178, 214, 243, 282–83, 287–88, 290, 293–95, 298–99
Ruan Fangcheng (case), 27, 38, 43, 59, 93, 120, 124, 208, 215, 284, 301, 303
Rule by law, 27
Rule of law, 68, 114–15, 164, 191, 193–94, 200, 205, 240, 254, 265
Rule of man, 206, 240, 254
Rule of the 2F, 109, 204

Safeguard, 19, 76, 115, 158, 221, 249
Sample, 8, 10–17, 25, 37–38, 40, 43, 45, 48, 54–55, 71–72, 81–83, 91, 103, 113, 115, 117, 119–20, 122, 124, 129, 133, 136, 152, 154, 157, 169, 176, 184, 186, 192, 199, 205, 211, 215–17, 219–20, 226, 228, 265, 268, 270, 273, 276; random sample, 7, 12–13; representative sample, 3, 273, 279; student sample, 5, 7
Sb (cursing term), 102, 104–6, 109, 149, 204–5, 307
Separation of powers, 277
Severity, 7, 80; severity of crime, 7; severity of punishment, 80
Sexual offense, 11, 117, 129–30, 151, 176, 178–79, 203, 217, 228, 299
Shandong (province), 13, 17, 75, 83, 146, 151, 212, 218, 289–90, 296
Sharen changming, 52, 58, 65–67, 70–71, 73–74, 77, 89–90, 129, 136, 166, 172, 175, 199, 204, 225, 238, 250, 253, 255, 274–75; question sharen changming, 78. *See also* A life for a life; Retribution
Sick man of Asia, 120
Shanghai, 13, 55, 73, 97, 133–35, 189, 212, 231–32, 235, 268, 281, 287
Shuijun, 16–17, 111–13, 199, 206, 253, 266–67, 271
Si Weijiang, 231, 238, 281
Sina.com.cn, 2–3, 10–11, 91, 257
Singapore, 80, 222–23, 263
Social desirability bias, 14, 17, 279
Social impact, 23, 41, 58–65, 74, 235, 245, 253, 255–56, 258. *See also* Public indignation
Social maintenance fees, 33, 182–84
Social unrest, 24, 51, 76, 169, 176–80, 197, 261
Song dynasty, 75, 97, 248
Song Yongtian (case), 33, 39, 56, 63, 94, 108, 120, 177, 209, 293, 302, 304
South Africa, 224–25
South Korea, 225
Sri Lanka, 225
State secret, 2, 20, 117
"Strike hard" campaign, 19–20, 76, 176–77

Suggestions (by netizens), 6, 25, 27–28, 30, 32–33, 35, 50, 54, 96, 103, 113, 131, 147, 155, 161, 208–9, 226–28, 229, 260, 264
Sun Zhifu (case), 29, 42, 60, 66, 93, 108, 124, 208, 216, 285, 301
Supreme People's Court (SPC), 18–22, 85, 88, 99, 134–36, 143–45, 181, 186, 192, 200, 210, 231–33, 236, 240, 246–47, 251, 253–54, 256, 258–59, 268–69, 272, 277–78, 281–85, 288–96, 298
Supreme People's Procuratorate (SPP), 85, 232
Survey, 2–7, 10, 12–15, 17, 23, 26, 57, 85, 115, 274, 279
Suspicion, 45, 55, 83, 138–39, 143, 145, 167, 238, 262, 266–67, 277

Taiwan, 13; Taiwanese, 34, 39, 56–57, 120, 293
Tang dynasty, 2
Tang Zhijian, 231, 238, 281
Tanzhou (city), 186
Tengzhou (city), 151
Terrorism, 117–18, 124, 176, 299; terrorists, 39, 118, 178, 283; terrorist attack, 76, 118; terrorist organization, 89
Theft, 214, 282, 284, 287, 297–99
Think in others' shoes, 23, 29, 92–94, 109–11, 187, 243, 245
Tibet, 13
Torture, 17, 69, 88, 153
Transparency, 55, 114, 139, 195, 259, 266; lack of transparency, 9
Trial of first instance, 20–21, 239, 256, 268, 281
Trial of second instance, 19–21, 159, 235, 237, 239, 256, 268, 281, 286, 292
Tuo Heti (case), 27, 39, 51, 59, 76, 93, 118, 124, 136, 140, 176, 178, 208, 283, 301, 303

United States, 4–5, 8, 14, 80, 167, 223, 225

Validity claim, 200–201, 272

Variation (of netizens' opinions), 3, 6, 9–10, 18, 133–35, 139, 233, 235, 274
Victim, 3, 8, 24, 27, 29, 31–35, 43–46, 49–50, 52–53, 56, 66–70, 72, 74–75, 77, 82, 87, 100–101, 103, 106, 110–11, 114, 116, 119, 124–25, 128–33, 135, 137–39, 141–44, 148, 151–53, 159, 164, 167, 169–71, 174, 179, 181, 183, 188, 194–95, 197, 205, 207, 210, 215–17, 219–20, 222–23, 233–37, 239–40, 242, 246–47, 249, 251, 268, 274–77, 283–89, 291–97, 305; victim's family, 25, 27, 29, 31, 35, 43, 45, 74–75, 119, 134, 219, 223, 232–35, 239, 242–43, 245, 255–56, 289, 305; victim's fault, 33, 138
Victimization, 7, 130
Vietnam, 38, 55, 67, 219, 290; Vietnamese, 45, 77, 83, 120, 124, 130, 216, 282, 284, 290, 292
Vignette, 4, 6, 12, 17
Violent crimes, 20, 24, 117–19

Wang Baiyang (case), 33, 63, 94, 153, 209, 294, 302, 305
Wang Changping (case), 29, 37, 53, 56, 60, 93, 105, 113, 120, 124, 128, 136, 138, 149, 152–53, 176–77, 199, 208, 210, 267, 269, 286, 301, 303
Wang Feng, 126
Wang Gang (case), 28, 41, 51, 60, 93, 98, 102, 108, 110, 122–23, 184–85, 208, 223, 284, 301, 303
Wang Hua (case), 30, 38, 51, 61, 93, 124, 176, 208, 287, 301, 304
Wang Jianghua and Wang Jinpeng (case), 12, 32, 62, 93, 208, 290, 302, 304
Wang "x" (case), 30, 61, 93, 208, 287, 289, 301, 303
Wang Yihuan (case), 43, 53, 63, 94, 124, 141, 174, 209, 292, 302, 304
Wang Yuefu (case), 27, 59, 93, 142, 208, 283, 301, 303
Wang Zongren (case), 32, 62, 94, 209, 291, 302, 304
Weber, Max, 198

Wenling (city), 77, 185, 254, 285
Wrongful conviction, 23, 27–29, 40–41, 46, 49, 58–65, 77, 81–82, 100, 119, 133, 138, 145–46, 150, 206, 210, 241, 252, 263, 266, 269, 270–71
Wu Qinyuan (case), 46, 49, 60, 81, 93, 118, 146, 149–50, 208, 284, 301, 303
Wu "x"hua (case), 33, 63, 73, 79, 85, 94, 110, 114, 121, 127, 138, 160, 163, 177, 209, 215, 294, 302, 305
Wu Youxin (case), 34, 39, 46, 56, 64, 72, 94, 161, 171, 209, 295, 302, 305

Xi Jinping, 122, 278
Xiao "x" (case), 32, 47, 62, 94, 209, 291, 302, 304
Xu Qingyi (case), 49, 222

Yang Chaoquan (case), 31, 52, 62, 65, 67, 71, 73, 81, 87–88, 91, 93, 99, 103, 108, 127, 137–38, 144, 174, 180, 208, 290. 302, 304
Yang Dazhi (case), 30, 46, 61, 70, 93, 101, 110, 128–29, 136, 141, 143, 166, 176, 178, 203, 208, 211, 217, 269, 286, 301, 303
Yang Ruixi (case), 34, 64, 94, 126, 143, 209, 295, 302, 305
Yang "x"ping (case), 33, 63, 94, 209, 294, 302, 305
Yang Xueqi (case), 13, 35, 46, 50, 64, 94, 107–8, 119, 127, 130, 138, 148–49, 151, 154–55, 174, 179, 209, 212–13, 216–17, 224, 228, 297, 303, 305
Yao Jiaxin (case), 80, 114, 245, 253
Yin Xiangjie, 177
Yu Yingsheng, 150, 284, 303

Yuan Junkai (case), 17, 28, 39, 46, 60, 68, 76, 80, 93, 96, 103, 127, 144, 148, 154–56, 163–66, 173, 175–76, 179, 203–4, 208, 211, 220, 284, 301, 303
Yuan Lijun (case), 31, 62, 93, 208, 269, 289, 301, 304
Yulun, 6, 25, 252–58, 265. *See also* Minyi; Public opinion

Zaozhuang (city), 151, 289
Zhai "x"de (case), 27, 38, 52, 59, 93, 105, 108, 121, 127, 138, 149, 203, 208, 283, 301, 303
Zhang Weilan (case), 30, 38, 56, 61, 69, 93, 95, 136, 149, 169, 171–72, 175, 208, 210–11, 214, 269, 286, 301, 303
Zhang Xiangxi (case), 29, 60, 93, 127–28, 154, 163, 208, 285, 301, 303
Zhang "x"yi (case), 34, 64, 94, 122, 138, 152, 160–61, 209, 295, 302, 305
Zhao Xu (case), 32, 62, 83, 94, 123, 129, 166, 209, 269, 291, 302, 304
Zhao Zhihong (case), 26–27, 43, 46, 49, 59–60, 75, 81–82, 93, 108, 118, 133, 138, 143, 145, 150, 208, 268–69, 282, 301, 303
Zhao Zihui (case), 35, 48, 64, 66, 85, 94, 110, 127, 141, 157–58, 160–62, 205, 207, 209, 227, 297, 302, 305
Zhejiang (province), 13, 77, 154, 185–86, 285, 287
Zheng Dalong and Yang Shengjian (case), 30, 61, 208, 301, 304
Zhengzhou (city), 142, 192, 195, 293
Zhou Qiang, 277
Zhu Ling (case), 221
Zibo (city), 146, 290